Verse by Verse Commentary on

THE MINOR PROPHETS

Hosea, Joel, Amos, Obadiah, Jonah, Micah, Nahum, Habakkuk, Zephaniah, Haggai, Zechariah, and Malachi

*Enduring Word Commentary Series
By David Guzik*

*The grass withers, the flower fades,
but the word of our God stands forever.*
Isaiah 40:8

Commentary on The Minor Prophets
Copyright ©2024 by David Guzik

Printed in the United States of America or in the United Kingdom

Print Edition ISBN: 978-1-939466-80-8

Enduring Word

5662 Calle Real #184

Goleta, CA 93117

Electronic Mail: ewm@enduringword.com

Internet Home Page: www.enduringword.com

All rights reserved. No portion of this book may be reproduced in any form (except for quotations in reviews) without the written permission of the publisher.

Scripture references, unless noted, are from the New King James Version of the Bible, copyright ©1979, 1980, 1982, Thomas Nelson, Inc., Publisher.

Contents

Hosea 1 - The Prophet and the Prostitute 9
Hosea 2 - Sin, Judgment, and Restoration 17
Hosea 3 - The Restoration of an Adulterous Wife 25
Hosea 4 - Israel's Sin and God's Remedy 28
Hosea 5 - The Folly of Trusting in Man's Deliverance 37
Hosea 6 - "Come, Let Us Return to the Lord" 41
Hosea 7 - The Oven, the Bread, and the Dove 47
Hosea 8 - Sow the Wind, Reap the Whirlwind 52
Hosea 9 - Exiled and Dried Up 57
Hosea 10 - Israel Has No King 62
Hosea 11 - Drawn with Gentle Cords 67
Hosea 12 - Ancient Jacob and Modern Israel 72
Hosea 13 - "I Will Be Your King" 76
Hosea 14 - Real Wisdom Turns Israel Back to the Lord 80

Joel 1 – The Day of the Lord Brings Judah Low 85
Joel 2 – The Day of the Lord and the Restoration of the Lord 91
Joel 3 – Judgment in the Valley of Decision 105

Amos 1 – Judgment on the Nations 113
Amos 2 – Judgment on God's People 119
Amos 3 – The Logic of God's Judgment 125
Amos 4 – "Yet You Have Not Returned to Me" 130
Amos 5 – The Offerings God Hates 137
Amos 6 – Woe to the Pride of Jacob 144
Amos 7 – Visions of Judgment and the Power of the Prophet's Prayer 149
Amos 8 – Like a Basket of Ripe Fruit 154
Amos 9 – Raising Up the Ruins 159

Obadiah – Judgment Against Israel's Brother 166

Jonah 1 – Jonah Runs from God 175
Jonah 2 – In the Belly of the Fish 184
Jonah 3 – Jonah Preaches Repentance in Nineveh, the City Repents 190
Jonah 4 – God Deals with a Prophet's Heart 195

Micah 1 – Coming Judgment on Israel and Judah 201
Micah 2 – God's Sinful People 207
Micah 3 – Against Princes and Prophets 212
Micah 4 – The Lord Reigns over Restored Zion 217
Micah 5 – A Ruler from Bethlehem 222
Micah 6 – In the Court of the Lord 227
Micah 7 – Israel's Confession and Comfort 233

Nahum 1 – Coming Judgment on Nineveh...240
Nahum 2 – Nineveh Conquered 248
Nahum 3 – Nineveh, the Wicked City..252

Habakkuk 1 – The Prophet's Problem 258
Habakkuk 2 – God Justifies His Judgment..265
Habakkuk 3 – The Prophet's Prayer..273

Zephaniah 1 – Coming Judgment and the Reasons for It 279
Zephaniah 2 – Judgment Against the Nations 285
Zephaniah 3 – The Lord Rejoices Over the Restoration of His People......290

Haggai 1 – Getting Priorities Straight...296
Haggai 2 – The Glory of the Second Temple 305

Zechariah 1 – The First Two Visions...314
Zechariah 2 – A City Without Walls 322
Zechariah 3 – The Cleansing of Joshua the High Priest 326
Zechariah 4 – By My Spirit, Says the Lord 332
Zechariah 5 – Two Visions Regarding the Cleansing of God's People 339
Zechariah 6 – A King and Priest..342
Zechariah 7 – Obedience Is Better than Ritual 347
Zechariah 8 – Jerusalem Restored..352
Zechariah 9 – A Humble King Conquers 359
Zechariah 10 – A Promise to Gather Israel 367
Zechariah 11 – Thirty Pieces of Silver..371
Zechariah 12 – Mourning for the Pierced One......................................377
Zechariah 13 – The Nation Purified 382
Zechariah 14 – Holiness to the Lord 388

Malachi 1 – "I Have Loved You" 394
Malachi 2 – Unfaithful Priests and Broken Marriages.........................403
Malachi 3 – The Messenger of the Covenant 412
Malachi 4 – The Sun of Righteousness 422

Bibliography..427
Author's Remarks 413

Hosea 1 - The Prophet and the Prostitute

A. The life and times of the Prophet Hosea.

1. (1a) Hosea the man.

The word of the LORD that came to Hosea the son of Beeri,

> a. **The word of the LORD**: Plainly said, Hosea was a *prophet*. He spoke forth the **word of the LORD**, and applied that word to his life, and to the people and circumstances around him. Hosea was a man, but he was a man God used to speak through.
>
> b. **Hosea the son of Beeri**: The name **Hosea** means "salvation." It comes from the same Hebrew root (*hoshea*) as the names *Joshua* and *Jesus*. Throughout the book, Hosea will show us that salvation is found in turning to the LORD and away from our sin.
>
> c. **Son of Beeri**: This tells us the name of Hosea's father. We also know that he had a wife named *Gomer* (Hosea 1:3), and two sons and a daughter (Hosea 1:4, 1:6, 1:9). Nowhere else in the Bible is Hosea mentioned.

2. (1b) The times Hosea lived in.

In the days of Uzziah, Jotham, Ahaz, *and* Hezekiah, kings of Judah, and in the days of Jeroboam the son of Joash, king of Israel.

> a. **Kings of Judah...king of Israel**: Hosea's ministry spanned the years 760 to 720 B.C. during the days of the *divided monarchy*. This was after days of David and Solomon, when the people of God divided in a civil war, creating two nations: Israel in the north, and Judah in the south. This is some 250 years after the time of King David, and some 650 years after Israel came into the Promised Land.
>
> b. **Uzziah, Jotham, Ahaz, and Hezekiah, kings of Judah**: Hosea's ministry was in the *northern* kingdom of Israel. We know this because in Hosea 7:5 he calls the king of Israel *our king*, and because his ministry is focused towards the northern kingdom of Israel and its capital city Samaria. But for

the benefit of his readers in the southern kingdom of Judah, Hosea gives them a reference point for the days of his ministry according to the **kings of Judah**.

c. **Jeroboam…king of Israel**: Hosea began his ministry in the days of Jeroboam II. From a political and economic standpoint Jeroboam II was a successful and good king (2 Kings 14:23-29). Israel prospered politically and materially under his reign, but it was a time of significant spiritual and moral decay. The terrible result of this decay wouldn't become evident until the days of Jeroboam II were finished.

i. A dramatic example of this is seen in the lives of the six kings that followed Jeroboam II during the time of Hosea's ministry. Of those six kings, four were violently overthrown and one died as a conquered exile in Assyria.

Kings of Israel during the Ministry of Hosea, 760 to 720 B.C.

Dynasty of Jehu		
Jeroboam II	793-752 B.C.	Gave throne to his son
Zechariah	753-752 B.C.	Assassinated
Dynasty of Shallum		
Shallum	752 B.C. (one month)	Assassinated
Dynasty of Menahem		
Menahem	752-742 B.C.	Gave throne to his son
Pekahiah	742-740 B.C.	Overthrown in coup d'etat
Dynasty of Pekah		
Pekah	752-732 B.C.	Assassinated
Dynasty of Hoshea		
Hoshea	732-722 B.C.	Died in exile

ii. Hosea began his ministry at a time when things were so politically successful and economically prosperous that people just didn't look to the Lord the way that they should. The seeds of idolatry, spiritual failure, and moral corruption sown in days of Jeroboam II produced a tragic harvest in the following years.

iii. Significantly, Jeroboam I was the first king of a divided Israel, leading a popular revolt against the high taxation of Rehoboam, son of Solomon (1 Kings 12). Jeroboam II followed in the wicked footsteps of Jeroboam I.

B. Israel's unfaithfulness and a promise of restoration.

1. (2) The command to take a prostitute as a wife.

When **the Lord began to speak by Hosea, the Lord said to Hosea:**

"Go, take yourself a wife of harlotry
And children of harlotry,
For the land has committed great harlotry
By departing **from the Lord."**

a. **The Lord said to Hosea**: God's first word to Hosea was something for his own life. This is how God almost always works. Hosea probably would have preferred it if God gave him a word for someone else. But before the prophet can speak to the nation, he first has to hear from God for himself.

b. **Go take yourself a wife of harlotry**: The word God had for Hosea wasn't easy. Hosea was told to take a prostitute for a wife. Why? Because **the land has committed great harlotry by departing from the Lord**.

i. Through His command to Hosea, God brings to life a consistent picture used throughout the Old Testament. In this picture, the Lord is the husband of Israel, and their passionate, chronic attraction for idols was like the lust of an adulterer. His people were as unfaithful as a prostitute was.

ii. In this vivid picture, we see how our idolatry and rejection of the Lord feels to God. When we put anything in front of the Lord, it hurts Him like unfaithfulness hurts the victim of an adulterous marriage. By commanding Hosea to **take…a wife of harlotry**, God will put Hosea in the place where he feels what God feels – and it won't feel good.

iii. "We cannot say that God grieves exactly as we grieve, if only because He controls all things and always works them out in accordance with His own good pleasure. Nevertheless, there is a parallel between God's feelings and ours." (Boice)

iv. Many commentators press the idea that Gomer was not a prostitute when Hosea first met and married her, she only *became* that later and Hosea knew from the Lord that she would become that. This may be the case, but we don't know this from the text. It could go either way.

2. (3-5) Hosea's marriage to Gomer and their first son.

So he went and took Gomer the daughter of Diblaim, and she conceived and bore him a son. Then the LORD said to him:

**"Call his name Jezreel,
For in a little *while* I will avenge the bloodshed of Jezreel on the house of Jehu,
And bring an end to the kingdom of the house of Israel.
It shall come to pass in that day
That I will break the bow of Israel in the Valley of Jezreel."**

a. **So he went and took Gomer**: We can assume that Hosea would never marry a prostitute except by the commandment of the LORD. It showed a lot of obedience for him to actually carry out this difficult command.

i. As will be made clear, when Hosea married Gomer, she did not give up her career as a prostitute. It wasn't that Hosea found a fallen woman and through love and kindness restored her to virtue. He married a prostitute – no doubt hoping she would give up her sin and be devoted only to him – and she stayed a prostitute.

ii. No doubt, this happened after the pattern of human nature. When Hosea and Gomer first married, she probably promised eternal love and devotion. She probably showed every sign of being committed to Hosea. But after a while, and in difficult circumstances, she fell back into prostitution. Perhaps it was out of boredom. Perhaps it was out of a feeling of neglect. Perhaps it was out of a sense of need. Sadly, we share the same inexcusable reasons for our idolatry, when we prefer another god to the LORD God.

iii. Some commentators believe this never really happened, and that Hosea is only telling a vivid story. They think it could never have happened because God would never have a prophet marry a prostitute. But Boice rightly observes, "If Hosea's story cannot be real (because 'God could not ask a man to marry an unfaithful woman'), then neither is the story of salvation real, because that is precisely what Christ has done for us."

b. **Call his name Jezreel**: The first son born to Hosea and Gomer was "**Jezreel**" and the name spoke of two things. First, **Jezreel** means "Scattered," and Israel would soon be scattered in exile by a conquering Assyrian army. Second, **Jezreel** refers to the Valley of Jezreel, where Jehu - the founder of the dynasty that put Jeroboam II on the throne - massacred all the descendants of Ahab, thus establishing his throne (2 Kings 10:11).

God directed Hosea to name his son **Jezreel** to confirm His promise to **avenge the bloodshed of Jezreel** by judging the **house of Jehu**.

i. Obviously, this was not good news to Jeroboam II. It said that his dynasty, the dynasty of Jehu, was coming to an end. In fact, after the death of Jeroboam II in 752 B.C. his son Zechariah barely reigned only six months before being assassinated (2 Kings 15:8-10), and that was the end of the **house of Jehu**.

c. **And bring an end to the kingdom of the house of Israel**: Just as the house of Jehu would fall, so would the whole **kingdom** of Israel. Before the prophetic ministry of Hosea was finished, Israel was defeated, destroyed, and taken captive by the mighty Assyrian Empire (2 Kings 17:20-23).

i. **Break the bow of Israel**: "The bow was a symbol of power in a day when it was the principle instrument of warfare. Thus a broken bow symbolized the loss of power." (Hubbard)

3. (6-7) A daughter born to Hosea and Gomer.

And she conceived again and bore a daughter. Then *God* **said to him:**
"Call her name Lo-Ruhamah,
For I will no longer have mercy on the house of Israel,
But I will utterly take them away.
Yet I will have mercy on the house of Judah,
Will save them by the LORD their God,
And will not save them by bow,
Nor by sword or battle,
By horses or horsemen."

a. **Call her name Lo-Ruhamah**: The name **Lo-Ruhamah** means "No Mercy." Every call to this child with the unfortunate name would remind Hosea and everyone else of coming judgment and exile.

b. **Yet I will have mercy on the house of Judah**: The army of Assyria that destroyed Israel also attacked Judah, but they did not conquer them. Instead, God miraculously fought on behalf of Judah against Assyria when the angel of the LORD killed 185,000 soldiers in the camp of Assyria in one night (2 Kings 19:35).

i. The fact that God had *no mercy* to Israel and *had mercy* towards Judah shows two things.

- First, it is true that Judah and her kings were more faithful unto the Lord during these years, as exemplified by King Hezekiah (2 Kings 18:1-8).

- Second, it does not really matter if Judah was more worthy of mercy than Israel was, because by its very nature mercy is mercy. If one *deserves* leniency, then leniency is a matter of justice, not mercy. Mercy is only shown to the *guilty*. Therefore it is within the wise and loving heart of God to show mercy to whom He will show mercy (Romans 9:15). But no one is ever *unfair* for *not* showing mercy.

4. (8-9) A second son born to Hosea and Gomer.

Now when she had weaned Lo-Ruhamah, she conceived and bore a son. Then *God* said:

**"Call his name Lo-Ammi,
For you *are* not My people,
And I will not be your *God*.**

a. **Call his name Lo-Ammi**: The name **Lo-Ammi** means "Not My People." Every call to this unfortunately named child reminded Hosea and everyone else that the people of Israel had pushed away the Lord God, and should no longer be considered His **people**.

i. Since Gomer did not give up her prostitution, there may have been a cruel irony in the name **Lo-Ammi**. Perhaps this son really was not the son of Hosea, but of another man. Perhaps the appearance of the child made this evident. The message God had to deliver to Israel through Hosea was hard enough, but God also made Hosea have to *live* it.

b. **For you are not My people, and I will not be your God**: This was not so much of a *sentence* or a *penalty*, as it was a *simple stating of fact*. It wasn't as if the people really wanted to be the people of God, yet God would not have them. Instead, the people of Israel rejected God, and here the Lord simply recognized that fact. He would not play "let's pretend": "You pretend to be My people and I will pretend to be your God." The time for those games was over.

5. (1:10-2:1) A promise of future restoration.

**"Yet the number of the children of Israel
Shall be as the sand of the sea,
Which cannot be measured or numbered.
And it shall come to pass
In the place where it was said to them,
'You *are* not My people,'
There it shall be said to them,
'*You are* sons of the living God.'
Then the children of Judah and the children of Israel**

Shall be gathered together,
And appoint for themselves one head;
And they shall come up out of the land,
or great *will be* the day of Jezreel!
Say to your brethren, 'My people,' and to your sisters, 'Mercy *is shown.*'

a. **Yet the number of the children of Israel**: Though God has promised judgment, the days of judgment won't last forever. After judgment, there will come a day of prosperity, increase, and blessing.

b. **Not My people…You are sons of the living God**: God would fulfill the promise of *Lo-Ammi* (Hosea 1:9), but the judgment would not last forever. One day Israel will return to the LORD, and once again be called **sons of the living God**.

c. **Then the children of Judah and the children of Israel shall be gathered together**: God promised a restoration so complete that the division caused by the civil war of Rehoboam and Jeroboam I – a division that stood for 170 years – would one day be erased.

i. We can say that one way this promise is fulfilled is in the church, where God brings together Israel, Judah – and even Gentiles – into one body (Ephesians 2:14-16).

d. **For great will be the day of Jezreel**: The first child of Hosea and Gomer was named *Jezreel* as a sign of judgment. But God promised a restoration so complete that **Jezreel** would once again be a name of greatness, not judgment.

e. **Say to your brethren, "My people," and to your sisters, "Mercy is shown"**: This shows that the redemption would be complete. The child named **Jezreel** had his name redeemed, and then the next two children (*Lo-Ruhamah*, "No Mercy" and *Lo-Ammi*, "Not My People") had their name redeemed as Israel would once again regarded as **"My People"** unto the LORD and **"Mercy is shown"** unto them. What was a sign of judgment would become evidence of redemption.

Hosea 2 - Sin, Judgment, and Restoration

A. Israel's sin.

1. (2-3) Charges against Israel.

"Bring charges against your mother, bring charges;
For she *is* not My wife, nor *am* I her Husband!
Let her put away her harlotries from her sight,
And her adulteries from between her breasts;
Lest I strip her naked
And expose her, as in the day she was born,
And make her like a wilderness,
And set her like a dry land,
And slay her with thirst.

> a. **For she is not My wife**: God paints Israel as an adulterous wife, who is no longer worthy to be compared to a wife. This shows that *relationship* was dramatically broken.
>
>> i. Israel lewdly offered herself to other gods, in the way that a woman lewdly offers herself to lovers. This is communicated by the phrase **her adulteries from between her breasts**. "The reference to her 'breasts' may imply that she had laid bare her bosom to entice her lovers.... If she did not change, she would be stripped naked" (Hubbard).
>
> b. **Lest I strip her naked and expose her...and make her like a wilderness**: God warns Israel that if she would not put away her harlot-like ways, she would be judged. Though *relationship* was broken, *blessing* continued – but would be taken away if Israel did not turn.

2. (4-5) Israel tries to justify her harlotry.

"I will not have mercy on her children,
For they *are* the children of harlotry.
For their mother has played the harlot;
She who conceived them has behaved shamefully.

For she said, 'I will go after my lovers,
Who give *me* my bread and my water,
My wool and my linen, my oil and my drink.'

>   a. **I will not have mercy on her children**: If Israel as a whole is represented as an unfaithful wife, then her children represent the individual people of Israel. If they do not turn back to the LORD, they will personally experience His judgment.
>
>   b. **I will go after my lovers, who give me my bread and my water, my wool and my linen**: Israel justified her harlotry because she received things from her "**lovers**." She looked at all the good she seemed to get from her sin, and it seemed like a good deal. Israel didn't understand the *passing pleasures of sin* (Hebrews 11:25).

B. God's judgment.

1. (6-8) How God will draw Israel back.

"Therefore, behold,
I will hedge up your way with thorns,
And wall her in,
So that she cannot find her paths.
She will chase her lovers,
But not overtake them;
Yes, she will seek them, but not find *them*.
Then she will say,
'I will go and return to my first husband,
For then *it was* better for me than now.'
For she did not know
That I gave her grain, new wine, and oil,
And multiplied her silver and gold–
Which they prepared for Baal.

>   a. **I will hedge up your way with thorns**: To bring Israel to repentance, God promised to set a hedge of thorns on the sides of her path, so that it would hurt whenever Israel went off the correct path, and so the wrong paths would be hard to find.
>
>   i. When God hedges our **way with thorns**, we usually don't like it. We sometimes think God is against us when the thorns hurt, and we can't find the wrong paths. But it is really one of the sweetest expressions of God's love to **hedge up your way with thorns** and to **wall us in**.
>
>   b. **I will go and return to my first husband**: When the passing pleasures of sin are finished, we often then see how good it was to follow the LORD.

In a marriage sometimes the grass can seem greener even with the best spouse; in our walk with the LORD our idols seem attractive until God exposes them. Then we are ready to **return to** our **first husband**, the LORD.

c. **For she did not know that I gave her grain**: Even when Israel went after other gods, the Lord still provided for her. This showed His great, unselfish love to Israel. Even though Israel took what God provided and **prepared** it **for Baal**, He still loved them.

> i. When Hosea provided for Gomer, she spent it on her adulterous lovers. It's as if Hosea went to the house of Gomer's lover, where she lived apart from her husband and in adultery. He knew that this scoundrel of a man couldn't provide for Gomer, and that she lived in poverty and rags. Hosea knocked at the door. He spoke to the man who answered, "Are you the man living with Gomer?" The man wondered what business it was of Hosea's; then he revealed: "I'm Hosea, her husband. I've brought these groceries and money so she can be provided for." When Hosea left, Gomer and her lover must have thought he was a fool. What a great dinner they had together with the food Hosea brought! But this is how the LORD loves us, lavishing blessing on us even when we are worshipping idols, providing us with blessings we waste on other gods.

c. **Which they prepared for Baal**: This principle shows how offensive idolatry really is to God. Whatever we give to an idol, we have received from God.

> i. God gives to man the trees of the forest and the iron in the ground. He gives man the brains to make an axe and nails from the iron, and the energy to cut down the tree, the skill to fashion the wood into beams. God gives man the cleverness to make a handle from the wood, and head from the iron, and combine it into an effective hammer. Then man takes the beams, the nails, and the hammer and he nails God to the cross – where God *willingly stretched out His arms*, dying on the cross to take the guilt and penalty man's sin deserved - and to make a new, restored relationship between God and man possible.

2. (9-13) How God will punish Israel.

"Therefore I will return and take away
My grain in its time
And My new wine in its season,
And will take back My wool and My linen,
***Given* to cover her nakedness.**
Now I will uncover her lewdness in the sight of her lovers,
And no one shall deliver her from My hand.

**I will also cause all her mirth to cease,
Her feast days,
Her New Moons,
Her Sabbaths–
All her appointed feasts.**

**"And I will destroy her vines and her fig trees,
Of which she has said,
'These *are* my wages that my lovers have given me.'
So I will make them a forest,
And the beasts of the field shall eat them.
I will punish her
For the days of the Baals to which she burned incense.
She decked herself with her earrings and jewelry,
And went after her lovers;
But Me she forgot," says the LORD.**

a. **I will return and take away My grain**: God gave grain to Israel, and she gave what He provided in sacrifices to Baal. So God would take away this provision, and as Israel felt her need and deprivation – perhaps she would then turn back to the LORD.

b. **But Me she forgot**: Israel enjoyed great prosperity during the time of Jeroboam II. But she used her prosperity for idolatry and the pursuit of ungodly pleasures, so God would take away her prosperity.

C. The restoration of Israel.

1. (14-15) Abundance and joy restored.

**"Therefore, behold, I will allure her,
Will bring her into the wilderness,
And speak comfort to her.
I will give her her vineyards from there,
And the Valley of Achor as a door of hope;
She shall sing there,
As in the days of her youth,
As in the day when she came up from the land of Egypt.**

a. **I will allure her…speak comfort to her**: Once Israel has felt the discomfort of her deprivation, then she will listen to the voice of God once again, and He will **allure** her back to Himself.

i. Spurgeon on **I will allure her**: "This is a singular kind of power: 'I will allure her;' not, 'I will drive her' not even, 'I will draw her,' or, 'I will drag her;' or, 'I will force her.' No, 'I will allure her.' It is a very remarkable word, and it teaches us that *the allurement of love surpasses* *in power all other forces.* That is how the devil ruins us; he tempts us with honeyed words, sweet utterances, with the baits of pleasure and the like; and the Lord in mercy determines that, in all truthfulness, he will outbid the devil, and he will win us to himself by fascinations, enticements, and allurements which shall be stronger than any force of resistance we may offer. This is a wonderfully precious word: 'I will *allure* her.'"

b. **The Valley of Achor as a door of hope**: **Achor** means, "trouble" so the **Valley of Achor** is the "Valley of Trouble." It was a place of trouble, where Achan's sin was discovered and judged (Joshua 7:26). God's restoration is so great that He will transform the "Valley of Trouble" into **a door of hope**.

c. **She shall sing there, as in the days of her youth**: When Israel is restored, she will be restored to joy. The passing pleasures of sin are forgotten and the true pleasures of God are restored.

2. (16-20) Relationship restored.

"And it shall be, in that day,"
Says the LORD,
"*That* you will call Me 'My Husband,'
And no longer call Me 'My Master,'
For I will take from her mouth the names of the Baals,
And they shall be remembered by their name no more.
In that day I will make a covenant for them
With the beasts of the field,
With the birds of the air,
And *with* the creeping things of the ground.
Bow and sword of battle I will shatter from the earth,
To make them lie down safely.
I will betroth you to Me forever;
Yes, I will betroth you to Me
In righteousness and justice,
In lovingkindness and mercy;
I will betroth you to Me in faithfulness,
And you shall know the LORD.

a. **You will call Me "My Husband"**: With great anticipation, God looked forward to the day when relationship would be genuinely restored with His people. *He wanted* an intimate love-relationship with His people, and longed for the day when His people would have a marriage-like love and commitment to their God.

b. **And not longer call Me "My Master"**: God was not satisfied with a fear-based, obedience-focused relationship with His people where they thought of Him primarily as **Master**. He wanted a relationship where they thought of Him primarily as **Husband**.

c. **I will take from her mouth the names of the Baals**: In Hebrew, the name "Baal" comes from the word "**Master**" and the two words sound alike. It was the **Baals**, the idols of the nations, which wanted this "master-slave" relationship with man. But not the LORD God; He wants a love-based, commitment-based relationship with His people.

d. **Bow and sword of battle I will shatter from the earth**: Ultimately, this blessing of restored relationship will result in a transformed earth, changed both ecologically (**beasts of the field…birds of the air**) and politically. This blessing will be fulfilled in the millennial earth, but we can come to know the transforming power of a restored relationship right now.

e. **I will betroth you to Me forever**: When relationship with the LORD is ultimately restored, it will never be broken again. Relationship will be restored on a solid foundation (**In righteousness and justice, in lovingkindness and mercy**), and will result in deeper and deeper relationship (**you shall know the LORD**).

3. (21-23) Blessing restored.

"It shall come to pass in that day
That I will answer," says the LORD;
"I will answer the heavens,
And they shall answer the earth.
The earth shall answer
With grain,
With new wine,
Wnd with oil;
They shall answer Jezreel.
Then I will sow her for Myself in the earth,
And I will have mercy on *her who had* not obtained mercy;
Then I will say to *those who were* not My people,
'You *are* My people!'
And they shall say, '*You are* my God!' "

a. **I will answer**: This is great blessing of real, vibrant relationship with God. Our hearts beat in rhythm to His, and so we want what He wants. So when we ask God to do things, we already ask what He wants to do – so He **will answer**.

i. This is the same principle Jesus taught: *If you abide in Me, and My words abide in you, you will ask what you desire, and it shall be done for you* (John 15:7).

b. **The earth shall answer with grain, with new wine, and with oil**: When relationship is where it is supposed to be, God abundantly provides. This is the same principle Jesus taught in Matthew 6:33: *But seek first the kingdom of God and His righteousness, and all these things shall be added to you.*

c. **They shall answer Jezreel**: The name "**Jezreel**" means "Scattered," and could be used in a negative sense (as in Hosea 1:4-5). But it was also the word used to describe the good scattering of seed, "Sowing." Here, the LORD promised a glorious redemption of the name **Jezreel**, which was first given as a sober reminder of scattering in judgment. It would become a prophecy of the promise, "**I will sow her for Myself in the earth**." God would restore His people to abundance and blessing. Scattering would be transformed into sowing.

d. **And I will have mercy on her who had not obtained mercy**: Hosea's second child, a daughter, was named *Lo-Ruhamah*, meaning "No Mercy" (Hosea 1:6). That name, originally given as a marker of judgment would be transformed into a mark of restoration.

e. **Then I will say to those who were not My people, "You are My people!"** Hosea's third child, a son, was named *Lo-Ammi*, meaning "Not My People" (Hosea 1:9). That name, originally given as a marker of judgment, is now transformed into a mark of restoration.

f. **And they shall say, "You are my God!"** With this, the restoration would be complete. The LORD would relate to His people as their God, and His people would relate to Him as His people. This is *relationship*, full of warmth and love, and what God longs for.

> i. Think about it: Which one of the pagan gods of the nations ever wanted the *love* of their followers? Which of them ever asked, "Do you love me?" False gods don't want our *love*, they want our fear, our obedience, our slave-like sacrifice and devotion. But the true God, the living God, isn't satisfied with just our fear, our obedience, or even with our slave-like sacrifice and devotion. *He wants our love, freely given and enjoyed in relationship with Him.* If we miss this, we miss the heart of God's work in us and for us.
>
> ii. We see *complete* restoration. All three of Hosea's children, named as marks of judgment, now have their names restored and made into marks of mercy, grace, and restoration. God is that good!

Hosea 3 - The Restoration of an Adulterous Wife

A. The restoration of Gomer.

1. (1) God commands Hosea to love Gomer again.

Then the LORD said to me, "Go again, love a woman *who is* loved by a lover and is committing adultery, just like the love of the LORD for the children of Israel, who look to other gods and love *the* raisin cakes *of the pagans."*

> a. **Go again, love a woman who is loved by a lover and is committing adultery**: God directed Hosea to go back to his wife, even though she was **committing adultery**. It wasn't in the past; it was in the present; yet he was commanded to go back to her and to **love** her.
>
>> i. This shows us that though Deuteronomy 24:1 and Matthew 19:7-8 *permit* divorce when adultery breaks the marriage union, it by no means *commands* divorce. If God *commanded* divorce in the case of adultery, then He would go against His own command here.
>>
>> ii. This also shows us an important principle about love: Hosea is *directed to love, even when it must have been hard to love.* We are filled with many romantic illusions about love, and one of these illusions is that love has very little to do with our *will* – we are just "captured" by love and follow whatever course it leads. But in principle, the Scriptures show us another way: That love is largely a matter of the *will*, and when we direct ourselves to love someone God tells us we must love, it can and will happen. This is why "We're not in love anymore" isn't valid grounds for a bad relationship or divorce. It assumes that love is something beyond or outside of our will.
>
> b. **Just like the love of the LORD for the children of Israel**: Why did God command Hosea to go back to his still-unfaithful wife? Not only for the sake of Hosea and his wife Gomer, but also so that they would become a

living lesson of the LORD's relationship with His people. They were still steeped in spiritual adultery, yet the LORD still loved them.

> i. When we think of the greatness of God's love and compassion towards us, it should make us much more loving, compassionate, and forgiving towards others.

2. (2-3) Hosea demonstrates his love to Gomer and restores her through purchase.

So I bought her for myself for fifteen *shekels* of silver, and one and one-half homers of barley. And I said to her, "You shall stay with me many days; you shall not play the harlot, nor shall you have a man—so, too, *will* I *be* toward you."

a. **So I bought her for myself**: Hosea didn't really need to "buy" his own wife, to hire her as a prostitute. She was his wife! But as a display of love and commitment, he went the "extra mile," beyond what was expected or even reasonable.

> i. In providing this way for his own wife, Hosea also showed her: "I can give you what the others can. You don't need them. Let me show you how I can provide for your needs."
>
> ii. Boice takes **bought her for myself** to mean that Gomer was sold as a slave and Hosea bought her out of her slavery. This is possible, but not necessary. It seems more natural to regard the payment as "buying her out of prostitution."

b. **You shall stay with me many days**: The point of paying Gomer wasn't just to get her to give up her trade as a prostitute. It was to bring her into relationship with Hosea, her husband. Relationship and living together was the goal.

B. The restoration of Israel.

1. (4) The fallen state of Israel.

For the children of Israel shall abide many days without king or prince, without sacrifice or sacred pillar, without ephod or teraphim.

a. **Without king or prince**: In her fallen state, Israel will not have the national or political leadership she needs.

b. **Without sacrifice or sacred pillar**: In her fallen state, Israel will not have the spiritual service she needs.

c. **Without ephod or teraphim**: In her fallen state, Israel will not have the supernatural guidance and direction she needs.

2. (5) The restored state of Israel.

Afterward the children of Israel shall return and seek the Lord their God and David their king. They shall fear the Lord and His goodness in the latter days.

> a. **The children of Israel shall return and seek the Lord their God**: In this time of political and spiritual ruin, Israel will **return and seek the Lord** again. This will mark their restoration – and there will be no restoration until they turn back to the Lord.
>
> b. **And David their king.... in the latter days**: This shows that this prophecy will be *ultimately* fulfilled in the millennial kingdom, where David will reign over Israel (Isaiah 55:3-5, Jeremiah 30:9, Ezekiel 34:23-25). But any individual *right now* can enjoy this blessing of restored relationship if they will turn back to the Lord.

Hosea 4 - Israel's Sin and God's Remedy

A. The charge against Israel.

1. (1-3) A statement of the charge: Israel's sin and God's remedy.

Hear the word of the LORD,
You children of Israel,
For the LORD *brings* **a charge against the inhabitants of the land:**
"There is no truth or mercy
Or knowledge of God in the land.
By **swearing and lying,**
Killing and stealing and committing adultery,
They break all restraint,
With bloodshed upon bloodshed.
Therefore the land will mourn;
And everyone who dwells there will waste away
With the beasts of the field
And the birds of the air;
Even the fish of the sea will be taken away.

> a. **The LORD brings a charge against the inhabitants of the land**: As if Yahweh brought Israel into a court of law, God here described the charges against disobedient Israel.
>
>> i. Adam Clarke on **brings a charge**: "What we should call a *lawsuit*, in which God is *plaintiff*, and the Israelites *defendants*. It is Jehovah *versus* Israel and Judah."
>
> b. **There is no truth or mercy or knowledge of God in the land**: Each of these three points is connected. When people forsake the **knowledge of God**, soon **truth** and **mercy** are both gone. **Truth** must be rooted in something more than personal opinion, and **mercy** means going beyond self-interest.

i. True wisdom and understanding always begin with the knowledge of God. Proverbs 9:10 says, *The fear of the* LORD *is the beginning of wisdom, and the knowledge of the Holy One is understanding.*

ii. **Or knowledge of God in the land**: Alexander Pope, a famous writer, once wrote: "Know then thyself, presume not God to scan; the proper study of mankind is man." But an even more famous writer, Charles Spurgeon, responded to Pope's statement: "It has been said by someone that 'the proper study of mankind is man.' I will not oppose the idea, but I believe it is equally true that the proper study of God's elect is God; the proper study of a Christian is the Godhead. The highest science, the loftiest speculation, the mightiest philosophy which can ever engage the attention of a child of God, is the name, the nature, the person, the work, the doings, and the existence of the great God whom he calls his Father."

c. **They break all restraint**: It all connects back to leaving **the knowledge of God**. Soon, **truth** and **mercy** are things of the past, and people no longer practice **restraint**. When man will not or cannot restrain himself, **bloodshed** and destruction follow.

i. Our modern age is completely set against the idea of **restraint**. You see it in advertising slogans of decades past:

- "To know no boundaries."
- "No rules, just right."
- "Just do it."
- "Break all the rules."
- "Peel off inhibitions. Find your own road."
- "Living without boundaries."

ii. The message is the same: You make your own rules. You answer to no one. You are the one that matters. Your universe revolves around you. You should only restrain yourself if you want to.

iii. The ultimate result is **bloodshed after bloodshed**. In the ancient Hebrew, this is literally "bloody deed touches bloody deed." "Apparently violent crimes had become so common that one seemed immediately to follow another, as if touching it." (Wood)

d. **Everyone who dwells there will waste away**: This is the tragic fruit of forsaking the knowledge of God, truth, mercy, and restraint. Satan sings sweetly to us, making us think or hope that casting these things away is a doorway to freedom – but it is only a path to destruction.

i. "Paul probably had Hosea's chapter in mind as he penned his own indictment of the gentile nations (cf. Hosea 4:6 with Romans 1:24, 26, 28; Hosea 4:7 with Romans 1:23; Hosea 4:11 with Romans 1:21, 22)." (Boice)

2. (4-8) The corrupt and ineffective leadership of the priests.

"Now let no man contend, or rebuke another;
For your people *are* like those who contend with the priest.
Therefore you shall stumble in the day;
The prophet also shall stumble with you in the night;
And I will destroy your mother.
My people are destroyed for lack of knowledge.
Because you have rejected knowledge,
I also will reject you from being priest for Me;
Because you have forgotten the law of your God,
I also will forget your children.

"The more they increased,
The more they sinned against Me;
I will change their glory into shame.
They eat up the sin of My people;
They set their heart on their iniquity.

a. **Your people are like those who contend with the priest**: In passages like Deuteronomy 17:9-12, God clearly commanded His people to listen to and submit to the priests, who would lead and help the people with the Word of God. But because the people cast off the knowledge of God, truth, mercy, and restraint, they wouldn't listen to the priests, and they contended with them instead.

i. This helps to explain the opening of the verse: **Now let no man contend, or rebuke another**. The idea is "They won't listen to the priest, but they **contend** with him instead. So, don't waste your time trying to **contend** or **rebuke** them yourself."

b. **Therefore you shall stumble in the day**: It's bad enough to stumble in the night, but at least we can understand it. But when God's people cast off the knowledge of God, restraint, and guidance from leaders then they shall **stumble** even **in the day**.

c. **The prophet also shall stumble with you in the night**: God paints a picture so bleak that even the **prophet** is dragged down to the level of the people and stumbles. Perhaps the prophet thought he was safe or immune because of his spiritual standing or reputation, but he is not. **The prophet also shall stumble with you.**

d. **My people are destroyed for lack of knowledge**: When God's people are **destroyed** and waste away, it isn't because God has lost either His love or strength. It's because His people **lack...knowledge**.

i. It isn't that God says His people are completely ignorant. They have *some* **knowledge**, but not enough. They may have just enough to make them think they know it all.

ii. What kind of **knowledge** did they **lack**? In the context, the first answer must be they lack *the knowledge of God* (Hosea 4:1). They know God some – perhaps a little – but not *enough*. Perhaps they felt they knew God well enough already.

iii. The second kind of **knowledge** they **lack** is the knowledge of God's Word (**you have forgotten the law of your God**). They know the Word of God some - perhaps a little - but not *enough*. Perhaps they felt they knew God's Word well enough already.

iv. It should not surprise us that there is a connection between knowing God and knowing His Word. Some people think that Bible knowledge is boring and brainy and not necessary for a real walk with God. But God and His Word are vitally connected. Psalm 138:2 says, *You have magnified Your word above all Your name*. When God sought for a term to express His nature, He calls Himself "The Word" (John 1:1).

v. When we know God for who He really is, it affects our conduct. "Where there is *no knowledge of God*, no conviction of his *omnipresence* and *omniscience*, private offences, such as stealing, adulteries, and so forth, will prevail." (Clarke)

e. **Because you have rejected knowledge, I also will reject you from being priest for Me**: Here we see who is responsible for the **lack of knowledge** among the people of God – the priests who **rejected knowledge**, the knowledge of God and His Word.

i. Teaching was an important duty of the priests (Deuteronomy 33:10, Ezekiel 44:23, Malachi 2:7). Their neglect of this demonstrates what an important place the minister, the pastor, the preacher has in presenting God and His Word to the people. If he neglects his duty to *preach the word* (2 Timothy 4:2), then he can't lead the people into the true knowledge of God, and will lead them into destruction.

ii. **I will also forget your children**: God will hold the unfaithful minister, pastor, or preacher accountable. They have much to answer for before God.

iii. **Priest for Me** reminds us that the priest didn't only serve on behalf of the people, but also on behalf of the LORD. The priest represented the people to God, but also represented – through the preaching of the word – God to the people.

f. The more they increased, the more they sinned against Me; I will change their glory into shame: God blessed the priests with *increase*, but they took God's blessing for granted and only **sinned against** God all the more. Blessing is a two-edged gift; it is obviously wonderful to be blessed, but it also brings more accountability and more opportunity for sin.

i. **They eat up the sin of My people**: "They did this by enjoying the benefits of the people's sins, such as taking bribes and eating the sin offerings. So the priests actually relished Israel's wickedness" (Wood).

3. (9-10) Judgment is promised.

And it shall be: like people, like priest.
So I will punish them for their ways,
And reward them for their deeds.
For they shall eat, but not have enough;
They shall commit harlotry, but not increase;
Because they have ceased obeying the LORD.

a. **Like people, like priest**: The priests may have thought they would be immune from the judgment coming upon Israel. After all, they were priests! But God promises that when it comes to judgment, **like people, like priest**.

i. There is no doubt that the priesthood of Israel was corrupt. "Jeroboam I had made priests 'from all sorts of people' (1 Kings 12:31; 13:33). Therefore, large numbers of true priests - and doubtless true prophets, also - had left the northern kingdom (2 Chronicles 11:13-16)" (Wood).

ii. There is also another way to understand the phrase "**like people, like priest**." It also means that *as the people go*, so go the priests. Sometimes people expect their religious leaders to be holy *for them* or *instead of them*. But since the "priests" come from the people, if the people are backslidden then many backslidden men will seek to be "priests."

b. **They shall eat, but not have enough**: One aspect of the judgment God promises is that Israel will not be blessed with increase. They will have, but it will never seem to be **enough**, and they will never be satisfied.

4. (11-14) The adultery of idolatry.

"Harlotry, wine, and new wine enslave the heart.
My people ask counsel from their wooden *idols*,
And their staff informs them

For the spirit of harlotry has caused *them* to stray,
And they have played the harlot against their God.

They offer sacrifices on the mountaintops,
And burn incense on the hills,
Under oaks, poplars, and terebinths,
Because their shade *is* good.
Therefore your daughters commit harlotry,
And your brides commit adultery.

I will not punish your daughters when they commit harlotry,
Nor your brides when they commit adultery;
For *the men* themselves go apart with harlots,
And offer sacrifices with a ritual harlot.
Therefore people *who* do not understand will be trampled.

a. **The spirit of harlotry has caused them to stray**: Israel's idolatry was like adultery against the Lord. Every sacrifice made to a pagan god was like an act of adultery.

i. The picture is striking when we consider *what a faithful and good husband the Lord is to His people*. Adultery is never excusable, but is even more heinous against a good, faithful, loving spouse.

ii. The picture is striking when we consider *how Israel wanted to add pagan gods to their worship of the Lord*. It isn't as if Israel officially said, "We want to leave the Lord, and now serve only pagan gods." Instead, Israel wanted to *add* the worship of pagan gods to their worship of the Lord. God received this the same way a husband would if his wife said, "I want you to still be my husband, I just want to take on a few more lovers also."

b. **For the men themselves go apart with harlots, and offer sacrifices with a ritual harlot**: Describing idolatry as spiritual adultery is especially appropriate when we understand that many pagan gods were "worshipped" by the hiring of a **ritual harlot**. This was far more enticing than just praying to a statue.

i. **I will not punish your daughters**: Because the men of Israel sinned this way, God would not single the women of Israel out for judgment when it came to this sin. God doesn't have a double standard for sexual conduct between men and women.

c. **Therefore people who do not understand will be trampled**: The idea of Hosea 4:6 is repeated (*My people are destroyed for lack of knowledge*). Without understanding God and His word, God's people are destined for destruction.

B. A warning to Judah.

1. (15) Judah is warned not to follow Israel's sinful ways.

"Though you, Israel, play the harlot,
Let not Judah offend.
Do not come up to Gilgal,
Nor go up to Beth Aven,
Nor swear an oath, *saying,* **'As the LORD lives'–**

> a. **Let not Judah offend**: At this time, God's people were divided into two nations - Israel to the north, and Judah to the south. Israel's apostasy was far more ingrained, so Judah is cautioned that they must not follow her neighbor's sinful ways.

> b. **Do not come up to Gilgal**: The cities of **Gilgal** and **Beth Aven** were centers of idolatry in Israel. For a citizen of Judah to travel there meant they shared in Israel's idolatry. When we get too close to sinful practices, they often rub off on us: *Do not be deceived: "Evil company corrupts good habits."* (1 Corinthians 15:33)

>> i. At one time, **Gilgal** was a place where prophets were trained under Elijah and Elisha (2 Kings 2:1; 4:38). But in Hosea's day it had become a center of false worship (Hosea 9:15; 12:11; Amos 4:4; 5:5).

>> ii. There was no city actually named **Beth Aven**. Hosea twisted the name of the city of *Bethel* - meaning "House of God" – into the more fitting name **Beth Aven**, meaning "House of Deceit." Bethel was the southern center of calf worship established by Jeroboam I (1 Kings 12:28-29).

2. (16-19) A summary of the charge: Israel's sin and God's remedy.

"For Israel is stubborn
Like a stubborn calf;
Now the LORD will let them forage
Like a lamb in open country.

"Ephraim *is* **joined to idols,**
Let him alone.
Their drink is rebellion,
They commit harlotry continually.
Her rulers dearly love dishonor.
The wind has wrapped her up in its wings,
And they shall be ashamed because of their sacrifices.

> a. **Israel is stubborn like a stubborn calf**: Cattle can safely feed out on the open range, because they are not easy prey for predators. But **a lamb**

in open country has strayed from the shepherd and is vulnerable. Hosea's point is plain: if you act like a stubborn cow, don't expect to be protected like an obedient sheep.

b. **Ephraim is joined to idols**: The tribe of "**Ephraim**" was the largest tribe in Israel. Therefore, the prophets often refered to Israel as "**Ephraim**."

c. **Ephraim is joined to idols, let him alone**: This is one way to express the judgment that is coming against Israel. God will simply leave Ephraim **alone**. When the mighty Assyrian army comes against them, they may fight for themselves - God will **let him alone**.

> i. We don't want God to leave us **alone** because we need Him to protect us against our spiritual enemies. Satan wanted to sift Peter like wheat, but Jesus did not leave Peter alone to face the attack. Jesus prayed for Peter, and he emerged victorious (Luke 22:31-32).

Hosea 5 - The Folly of Trusting in Man's Deliverance

A. Israel's sinful idolatry.

1. (1-3) Israel's leaders are rebuked for the sinful state of the nation.

"Hear this, O priests!
Take heed, O house of Israel!
Give ear, O house of the king!
For yours *is* the judgment,
Because you have been a snare to Mizpah
And a net spread on Tabor.
The revolters are deeply involved in slaughter,
Though I rebuke them all.
I know Ephraim,
And Israel is not hidden from Me;
For now, O Ephraim, you commit harlotry;
Israel is defiled."

a. **Hear this, O priests**: When God saw the sinful state of the nation of Israel, He saw that it was because the leaders did not lead in a godly way. It would be tempting for the priests to blame the people, but it was really the fault of the spiritual leadership (**priests**) and political leadership (**house of Israel**) of the nation.

b. **The revolters are deeply involved in slaughter, though rebuke I them all**: The real tragedy of Israel's sin wasn't so much that they stumbled. It was more so that they did not respond to God's **rebuke** when they did stumble. If a man knows how to humbly respond to God's correction, God can always work with him.

2. (4-9) Israel's double desolation.

"They do not direct their deeds
Toward turning to their God,

For the spirit of harlotry is in their midst,
And they do not know the LORD.
The pride of Israel testifies to his face;
Therefore Israel and Ephraim stumble in their iniquity;
Judah also stumbles with them.

"With their flocks and herds
They shall go to seek the LORD,
But they will not find *Him;*
He has withdrawn Himself from them.
They have dealt treacherously with the LORD,
For they have begotten pagan children.
Now a New Moon shall devour them and their heritage.

"Blow the ram's horn in Gibeah,
The trumpet in Ramah!
Cry aloud *at* Beth Aven,
'Look behind you, O Benjamin!'
Ephraim shall be desolate in the day of rebuke;
Among the tribes of Israel I make known what is sure.

a. **The pride of Israel testifies to his face**: Like all rebellion, Israel's rebellion was centered on *pride*. They arrogantly thought that what God said didn't really matter compared to their own opinions and desires.

b. **They shall go to seek the LORD, but they will not find Him**: When God promised to leave rebellious Israel alone (Hosea 4:17), it means that when they make superficial gestures of repentance, **they will not find Him**. Their repentance was superficial because **they do not direct their deeds toward turning to their God**.

i. In many ways today, people *think* they are seeking God when they really aren't. It's just a superficial investigation. For example, a man might say, "I grew up in the Baptist church and couldn't find God there. So, I went to the Methodist church and couldn't find God there. Then I went to the Pentecostal church but couldn't find God there. Now I'm at the Presbyterian church and can't find God." You may imagine you have searched hard after God, but that is an illusion. The truth is that you are running away from God. When He started to get close to you at the Baptist church, you left it and became a Methodist. When He started to get close to you at the Methodist church, you became a Pentecostal. You've followed the same pattern – a superficial search for God that backs away when you really start getting close to God.

ii. **He has withdrawn Himself from them**: It can happen. We can be so set in our sin and rebellion that God just leaves us to ourselves. Usually we don't even notice at first, but when we call upon the LORD and do **not find Him**, then we start to see the result of pushing God away.

c. **Ephraim shall be desolate in the day of rebuke**: Because God **has withdrawn Himself from them**, they will find no help or refuge when the Assyrian army attacks. They will be made **desolate**.

B. Israel's sinful trust in man for deliverance.

1. (10-13) Israel and Judah looked to man's wisdom.

"The princes of Judah are like those who remove a landmark;
I will pour out my wrath on them like water.
Ephraim is oppressed *and* broken in judgment,
Because he willingly walked by *human* precept.
Therefore I *will be* to Ephraim like a moth,
And to the house of Judah like rottenness.

"When Ephraim saw his sickness,
And Judah *saw* his wound,
Then Ephraim went to Assyria
And sent to King Jareb;
Yet he cannot cure you,
Nor heal you of your wound.

a. **The princes of Judah are like those who remove a landmark**: This means that the political leaders of Judah were corrupt and cheaters. They were the kind of men who would change property boundaries to their advantage if they thought they could get away with it. This reminds us that while Judah may have been better than Israel, they still had to repent.

i. "Judah's leaders, however, were not shifting physical property lines but spiritual lines established by God, changing the boundary between right and wrong, between true and false religion, between the true God and the idols." (Wood)

ii. We can imagine a citizen of Judah reading Hosea's prophecy and being a bit smug that their neighbor to the north was so roundly rebuked. God reminds Judah that she has her own sin to deal with.

b. **He willingly walked by human precept**: Ephraim's sinned by living by man's standards and opinions instead of God's. We can't walk **by human precept** unless we first reject God's precepts, and that was exactly what Israel did.

i. **Ephraim went to Assyria**: Israel was foolish enough to trust in man – her eventual conqueror – instead of trusting in God. Choosing a **King Jareb** instead of the LORD is always foolish and ends in ruin.

ii. "'Jareb' is not a known Assyrian's name but means 'warrior'." (Wood)

c. **Like a moth…like rottenness**: God will be the one who eats away and corrodes what Israel and Judah have. They will not be blessed, and they will not increase.

2. (14-15) God's judgment and the goal behind it.

"For I *will be* like a lion to Ephraim,
And like a young lion to the house of Judah.
I, *even* I, will tear *them* and go away;
I will take *them* away, and no one shall rescue.
I will return again to My place
Till they acknowledge their offense.
Then they will seek My face;
In their affliction they will earnestly seek Me."

a. **I will be like a lion**: God's judgment would come against Israel and Judah in subtle ways (*like a moth…like rottenness*). But it would also come in obvious, unmistakable ways. Both a moth and **a lion** bring destruction, just in different ways.

b. **In their affliction they will earnestly seek Me**: This was the goal of God's judgment against Israel. The goal was not destruction, but restoration. Sadly, it is often only in our **affliction** that we **earnestly seek** the LORD. Why not seek the LORD now, before **affliction** forces you to?

Hosea 6 - *"Come, Let Us Return to the LORD"*

A. A call to return to the LORD.

1. (1-2) Israel should trust in the God who chastened her.

Come, and let us return to the LORD;
For He has torn, but He will heal us;
He has stricken, but He will bind us up.
After two days He will revive us;
On the third day He will raise us up,
That we may live in His sight.

> a. **He has torn, but He will heal us**: Hosea prays with the right heart in response to the chastening hand of God. Instead of arguing with God, or resenting His correction, Hosea leads Israel in humble prayer.
>
>> i. This is a prayer that trusts the love of God and sees His loving hand even in correction. Often, a rebellious child will complain that their parents do not love them. Of course, the parents do love the child, but in their rebellion and lack of submission, they can't receive or respond to that love. Hosea prays with a different heart.
>
> b. **After two days He will revive us; on the third day He will raise us up**: Hosea prayed this full of confidence in God's love and power to restore. In the prayer, there is a shadowy prophecy of Jesus' resurrection on the **third day**. The context supports this wonderfully; on the cross Jesus was **torn** and **stricken** for our sake, yet He was also gloriously raised up **on the third day**.

2. (3) Walking in confidence.

Let us know,
Let us pursue the knowledge of the LORD.
His going forth is established as the morning;
He will come to us like the rain,
Like the latter *and* former rain to the earth.

a. **Let us pursue the knowledge of the LORD**: Israel's problem was described back in Hosea 4:6 (*My people are destroyed for lack of knowledge*). Hosea leads the nation in a repentant correction of this problem.

   i. We should also know that when we **pursue the knowledge of the Lord**, He blesses it. It must be more than superficial; it must be a pursuit. But when we endeavor to know the Lord, especially through His word, He reveals Himself to us. *He who comes to God must believe that He is, and that He is a rewarder of those who diligently seek Him.* (Hebrews 11:6)

b. **He will come to us like the rain, like the latter and former rain**: In Israel, the only way crops were watered was by **rain**. So, the farmer waited for the rain with great anticipation. When we anticipate and wait for God with this kind of earnest expectation, He answers and **will come to us**.

   i. Clarke on **the latter and former rain to the earth**: "The first, to prepare the earth for seed; this fell in *autumn*: the second, to prepare the full ear for the harvest; this fell *in spring*."

   ii. "Notice, again, it is a repeated gift. He shall give the former rain and the latter rain. If you have had grace once the Lord has more for you. Did you have happy times when old Dr. So-and-so was your pastor? Well, the doctor is dead, but God is not. Were you very much delighted when you used to sit in such-and-such a church, in years gone by, and have you moved into the country now? Yes, but God has not moved. He is in the country as well as in the town. You tell me you had such happy times when you were young. Yes, but God is neither younger nor older. Go to him, for he is the same yesterday, to-day, and for ever. Do you suppose that, because he gave you the former rain, he has emptied the bottles of heaven?" (Spurgeon)

c. **He will come to us like the rain, like the latter and former rain to the earth**: This passage along with others (Deuteronomy 11:14, Joel 2:23) were taken to give the name of the "Latter Rain Movement" starting in 1948.

   i. In 1948, a Oneness Pentecostal minister named William Branham held meetings at an orphanage and school founded by a Foursquare Church in North Battleford, Saskatchewan. Those attending the meeting were so impressed by the supernatural works - healing, prophecy, word of knowledge, and strange phenomenon - that they considered it a beginning of a new work of God on earth. In their newsletter, this is how they described it:

"All the great outpourings of the past have had their outstanding truths. Luther's truth was Justification by Faith. Wesley's was Sanctification. The Baptists taught the premillennial coming of Christ. The Missionary Alliance taught Divine Healing. The Pentecostal outpouring has restored the Baptism of the Holy Ghost to its rightful place. But the next great outpouring is going to be marked by all these other truths plus such a demonstration of the nine gifts of the Spirit as the world, not even the Apostolic world, has ever witnessed before. This revival will be short and will be the last before the Rapture of the Church."

ii. They felt that the Pentecostal denominations of their day were "dead" and "dry," and needed the blessing of the "Latter Rain," which would especially be marked by miraculous signs and supernatural works. The Pentecostal denominations – notably the Assemblies of God and the Foursquare Church denounced the Branham and the Latter Rain movement for both their teaching and practices.

iii. William Branham continued, drawing large crowds to his prophecy and healing crusades. He and a young evangelist named Oral Roberts led the Latter Rain Movement for several years. Branham's doctrine became more and more aberrant. Branham believed that the word of God was given in three forms: the Zodiac, the Egyptian pyramids, and the written scriptures. He also taught the "serpent seed" doctrine, which was based on his interpretation of Genesis 3:13, saying that Eve had sexual relations with the serpent in the Garden of Eden.

iv. The Latter Rain Movement, as led by William Branham and Oral Roberts eventually faded from prominence. Branham himself died in a traffic collision with a drunk driver in 1965. He died on Christmas Eve, and his faithful followers believed that he would rise from the dead, so they delayed his burial for several days. But the influence of the Latter Rain movement lived on. The Latter Rain popularized many attitudes and doctrines popular in revival movements today:

- The "five-fold ministry" and "restoration of apostle and prophets."
- The "foundational truths" of Hebrews 6:1-2.
- An emphasis on signs and wonders as marks of true revival.
- A strong emphasis on unity.
- Replacement theology, replacing Israel with the church.
- Dominion theology, saying the church will conquer and rule the world.

- An elitist attitude, promoting the idea of a group of "superchristians."

v. Many researchers – and many within these modern groups today – believe that many modern "revival" movements are really just a continuation of the Latter Rain movement. Movements such as "Joel's Army," the Manifest Sons of God, the Dominion Movement, the Kansas City Prophets, the Toronto Blessing, the Pensacola Revival are connected in some way to the Latter Rain movement. For example, Paul Cain – later to re-emerge as head of the Kansas City Prophets in 1989 - traveled with William Branham and called him "the greatest prophet that ever lived."

vi. The modern Latter Rain movement believes: "The Latter Rain is God's great end-time ministry. This concept as revealed in the Bible, comprises the restitution of the church to it's rightful place, the enormous last day revival and the harvest of souls before the great and terrible Day of the Lord. It is the outpouring of the Holy Spirit upon all flesh promised to us in the last days and the restoration of apostolic and prophetic gifts." (From latter-rain.com)

B. The sin of Israel and Judah.

1. (4-6) How God's people missed God's heart.

"O Ephraim, what shall I do to you?
O Judah, what shall I do to you?
For your faithfulness is like a morning cloud,
And like the early dew it goes away.
Therefore I have hewn *them* by the prophets,
I have slain them by the words of My mouth;
And your judgments *are like* light *that* goes forth.
For I desire mercy and not sacrifice,
And the knowledge of God more than burnt offerings.

a. **Your faithfulness is like a morning cloud**: It wasn't that there was *no* **faithfulness** among the people of God. It's just that whatever **faithfulness** there was quickly dissipated **like the early dew**.

b. **For I desire mercy and not sacrifice**: At this time, God's people were still good at bringing sacrifice (Hosea 5:6). But they had forsaken **mercy**, and they abandoned **mercy** because they gave up the knowledge of God and truth (Hosea 4:1). God would rather have right hearts, full of truth and mercy than sacrifice.

i. Jesus twice quoted this passage of Hosea to the religious leaders of His day (Matthew 9:13 and 12:7). They also missed the heart of God, focusing on the wrong and superficial things.

c. **And the knowledge of God more than burnt offerings**: Israel brought animals for sacrifice, but they never brought themselves as a living sacrifice (Romans 12:1). They missed what God really wants: a deep, close relationship with Him.

2. (7-11) The transgression of idolatry.

"But like men they transgressed the covenant;
There they dealt treacherously with Me.
Gilead *is* a city of evildoers,
***And* defiled with blood.**
As bands of robbers lie in wait for a man,
***So* the company of priests murder on the way to Shechem;**
Surely they commit lewdness.
I have seen a horrible thing in the house of Israel:
There *is* the harlotry of Ephraim;
Israel is defiled.
Also, O Judah, a harvest is appointed for you,
When I return the captives of My people.

a. **As bands of robbers lie in wait for a man, so the company of priests murder**: When the priests went to places of pagan sacrifice, it was a thieving, killing sin.

b. **Judah, a harvest is appointed for you, when I return the captives**: When the people of God came back into the land after the Babylonian exile, they mainly settled in the area of Judah. The **harvest** of returned exiles was mainly for Judah, not for Israel.

Hosea 7 - The Oven, the Bread, and the Dove

A. A heart like an oven.

1. (1-3) The sinful ignorance and willful blindness of Israel.

"When I would have healed Israel,
Then the iniquity of Ephraim was uncovered,
And the wickedness of Samaria.
For they have committed fraud;
A thief comes in;
A band of robbers takes spoil outside.
They do not consider in their hearts
***That* I remember all their wickedness;**
Now their own deeds have surrounded them;
They are before My face.
They make a king glad with their wickedness,
And princes with their lies.

> a. **They do not consider in their hearts that I remember all their wickedness**: The problem among the people and leaders of Israel was they forgot – willfully – that the LORD saw and remembered their sin. We often deliberately forget that the LORD sees and remembers when we sin. It may be secret before men, but not before God – He says, "**they are before My face.**"
>
>> i. The believer today should ask themselves: Have you forgotten? Do you think God doesn't see? Do you think God is blind to your adultery or pre-marital sex? Do you think your pornography habit goes unnoticed? Do you think God's eyes are closed when you get drunk or take drugs? There are many church-going people today who think that God forgets or never sees such things, because they do them and then they come to church and make a profession of godliness, pretending that those things are never part of their life.

ii. There is a precious promise for those who come to God under the New Covenant: *For I will forgive their iniquity, and their sin I will remember no more* (Jeremiah 31:34). We often wish that time would make God forget our sin, but it doesn't. Only the atoning substitute of Jesus, crucified in our place under the New Covenant makes God forget our sin.

b. **When I would have healed Israel**: God was willing to heal Israel from their sin and its effects, but not as long as they acted as if God did not see their sin. They had to treat God as He really is, a God who sees and remembers unrepentant, uncovered sin.

c. **They make a king glad with their wickedness**: This phrase, together with *princes have made him sick* (Hosea 7:5) and *all their kings have fallen* (Hosea 7:7) probably all refer to one of the successful assassination plots against the throne of Israel during the ministry of Hosea. Since there were four kings violently overthrown during his ministry, it's hard to exactly know which one he means.

2. (4-7) Israel's heart is inflamed after idols.

"They *are* all adulterers.
Like an oven heated by a baker–
He ceases stirring *the fire* after kneading the dough,
Until it is leavened.
In the day of our king
Princes have made *him* sick, inflamed with wine;
He stretched out his hand with scoffers.
They prepare their heart like an oven,
While they lie in wait;
Their baker sleeps all night;
In the morning it burns like a flaming fire.
They are all hot, like an oven,
And have devoured their judges;
All their kings have fallen.
None among them calls upon Me.

a. **Like an oven heated by a baker**: Israel was inflamed with desire and passion after idols like the coals of a freshly stoked fire, ready to bake bread.

i. Paul used the same image of "burning lust" in 1 Corinthians 7:9: *but if they cannot exercise self-control, let them marry. For it is better to marry than to burn with passion.*

b. **None among them calls upon Me**: Israel could not be **hot, like an oven** after idols and also call upon the LORD. They did in fact continue to sacrifice to the LORD (Hosea 5:6) but it was empty ceremony, not a true calling upon their covenant God.

3. (8-10) The pride and stubbornness of Israel.

"Ephraim has mixed himself among the peoples;
Ephraim is a cake unturned.
Aliens have devoured his strength,
But he does not know *it;*
Yes, gray hairs are here and there on him,
Yet he does not know *it.*
And the pride of Israel testifies to his face,
But they do not return to the LORD their God,
Nor seek Him for all this.

a. **Ephraim is a cake unturned**: The idea is of a "half-baked" cake. In that day, bread was often prepared as a cake that was cooked on both sides, something like a pancake. In thinking they can serve both the Lord and idols, Israel is like an **unturned** pancake – burned on one side, uncooked on the other.

b. **Aliens have devoured his strength, but he does not know it**: This makes the tragedy of Israel's ruin worse. The nation is being ravaged by sin but **does not know it**. They should know it, because even **the pride of Israel testifies to his face** – yet in their blind ignorance **they do not return to the LORD their God**.

i. Man has an amazing ability to deceive himself when he is in sin. Well did Jeremiah say, *The heart is deceitful above all things, and desperately wicked; who can know it?* (Jeremiah 17:9). Considering how easily we deceive our self, and how our sin can be apparent to everyone but us, Israel's condition isn't unusual:

- Burned and ruined – but he does not know it.
- Strength devoured – but he does not know it.
- Aging and weakening – but he does not know it.
- Pride testifies against him – but he does not know it.

ii. It was said of Samson after Deliliah cut his hair: *But he did not know that the LORD had departed from him* (Judges 16:20). This is where the people of Israel – and some followers of God today – were. They are far from God and already suffering the effects, but they can't see it.

c. **Yes, gray hairs are here and there on him, yet he does not know it**: Israel is as foolish as an old man who thinks and acts like he is still young.

i. "He began but to decline and decay, as a man doth when he grows toward 50." (John Trapp, 1654)

B. Silly like a dove.

1. (11-12) Like a dove, Israel flies about to the nations.

"**Ephraim also is like a silly dove, without sense—
They call to Egypt,
They go to Assyria.
Wherever they go, I will spread My net on them;
I will bring them down like birds of the air;
I will chastise them
According to what their congregation has heard.**

> a. **Ephraim also is like a silly dove, without sense**: Hosea piles image upon image. Now Israel is like a bird fluttering about, confused and without direction. They think they can escape God by running to other nations, but the Lord says, "**I will spread My net on them**."

> b. **I will chastise them according to what their congregation has heard**: Israel's guilt is increased **according to what** they have **heard**. Greater knowledge means great accountability. As Jesus said, *for everyone to whom much is given, from him much will be required; and to whom much has been committed, of him they will ask the more* (Luke 12:48).

2. (13-16) In running to the nations, Israel has run *away* from God.

"**Woe to them, for they have fled from Me!
Destruction to them,
Because they have transgressed against Me!
Though I redeemed them,
Yet they have spoken lies against Me.
They did not cry out to Me with their heart
When they wailed upon their beds.**

"**They assemble together for grain and new wine,
They rebel against Me;
Though I disciplined *and* strengthened their arms,
Yet they devise evil against Me;
They return, *but* not to the Most High;
They are like a treacherous bow.
Their princes shall fall by the sword
For the cursings of their tongue.
This *shall be* their derision in the land of Egypt.**

a. **They return, but not the Most High**: Israel saw their *problem*, but not their *sin*. When God's hand is against man, he easily sees he has a problem but often does not see it as *sin against the Lord*. So when Israel had problems, they **wailed upon their beds**, but not to the Lord. They sought remedies, but not from **the Most High**.

b. **They are like a treacherous bow**: Hosea adds another image, of a faulty bow that won't shoot an arrow straight. Everything that comes from Israel misses the mark, because **they are like a treacherous bow**. They are like a useless and dangerous weapon.

Hosea 8 - Sow the Wind, Reap the Whirlwind

A. Sowing idolatry, reaping exile.

1. (1-6) Casting off God and embracing idols.

"Set the trumpet to your mouth!
He shall come **like an eagle against the house of the** LORD,
Because they have transgressed My covenant
And rebelled against My law.
Israel will cry to Me,
'My God, we know You!'
Israel has rejected the good;
The enemy will pursue him.

They set up kings, but not by Me;
They made princes, but I did not acknowledge *them.*
From their silver and gold
They made idols for themselves—
That they might be cut off.
Your calf is rejected, O Samaria!
My anger is aroused against them;
How long until they attain to innocence?
For from Israel *is* **even this:**
A workman made it, and it *is* **not God;**
But the calf of Samaria shall be broken to pieces.

> a. **Set the trumpet to your mouth**: Trumpets were used to assemble God's people and to call troops to battle. Here, God commands the **trumpet** to sound to gather the mighty Assyrians against Israel for judgment, **because they have transgressed My covenant**.
>
> b. **Israel will cry to Me, "My God, we know You!"**: But their cry is not sincere, because **Israel has rejected the good**. They set up rulers and princes against the Lord, and were steeped in idolatry.

i. They said, **"My God, we know You!"** But they didn't really know God. It will be the same way for many church-goers today. Jesus said, *"Many will say to Me in that day, 'Lord, Lord, have we not prophesied in Your name, cast out demons in Your name, and done many wonders in Your name?' And then I will declare to them, 'I never knew you; depart from Me, you who practice lawlessness!'"* (Matthew 7:22-23).

ii. **They set up kings, but not by Me**: "To choose leaders without the direction of God is not only sinful, it is foolish. Those who follow their own wisdom in the choice of leaders inevitably get what they deserve" (Boice).

c. **The calf of Samaria shall be broken to pieces**: Israel made beautiful idols out of silver and gold, but they will not stand. In judgment, God will break them **to pieces**.

i. **Your calf is rejected** "is literally 'your calf stinks.'" (Wood) That's what God thought of their idols!

2. (7-10) Israel judged and regathered.

"They sow the wind,
And reap the whirlwind.
The stalk has no bud;
It shall never produce meal.
If it should produce,
Aliens would swallow it up.
Israel is swallowed up;
Now they are among the Gentiles
Like a vessel in which *is* no pleasure.
For they have gone up to Assyria,
Like a wild donkey alone by itself;
Ephraim has hired lovers.
Yes, though they have hired among the nations,
Now I will gather them;
And they shall sorrow a little,
Because of the burden of the king of princes.

a. **They sow the wind, and reap the whirlwind**: It will seem to Israel that the judgment they receive is worse than the sin they committed. This isn't true in the sense of God being worse to us than our sin deserves, but it is true in how judgment feels. This is usually because our sin is *sown* over a long period of time, but often *reaped* in a contracted period of judgment.

b. **Now they are among the Gentiles…now I will gather them**: God promised that Israel would face the conquering Assyrians and exile, but also that He would one day **gather them** again. This note of mercy is sprinkled through the song warning of judgment.

B. Why God will not accept their offerings.

1. (11-13) Israel considers God's word a **strange thing**.

"Because Ephraim has made many altars for sin,
They have become for him altars for sinning.
I have written for him the great things of My law,
But they were considered a strange thing.
For the sacrifices of My offerings they sacrifice flesh and eat *it*,
But the LORD does not accept them.
Now He will remember their iniquity and punish their sins.
They shall return to Egypt.

a. **They have become for him altars for sinning**: Israel foolishly built **many altars for sin**. So it is no surprise that those altars became **altars for sinning**. When we give ourselves opportunity and occasion for sin, it is never surprising when we end up **sinning**.

b. **I have written for him the great things of My law, but they were considered a strange thing**: In their sin and idolatry, Israel also rejected the Word of God. God had **great things** for Israel, but they seemed like a **strange thing** because their hearts were far from God.

c. **I have written for him**: This tells us the *author* of the Bible – God Himself. Spurgeon said it well: "This volume is the writing of the living God: each letter was penned with an Almighty finger; each word in it dropped from the everlasting lips, each sentence was dictated by the Holy Spirit."

i. "If this be the Word of God, what will become of some of you who have not read it for the last month? Most people treat the Bible very politely… When they get home, they lay it up in a drawer till next Sunday morning; then it comes out again for a little bit of a treat and goes to chapel; that is all the poor Bible gets in the way of an airing. That is your style of entertaining this heavenly messenger. There is dust enough on some of your Bibles to write "damnation" with your fingers." (Spurgeon)

d. **The great things of My law**: This tells us the *content* of the Bible - **great things**. The Bible speaks of the greatest and most important things of both life and eternity.

i. "The Bible treats of great things, and of great things only. There is nothing in this Bible which is unimportant. Every verse in it has a solemn meaning, and if we have not found it out yet, we hope yet to do it." (Spurgeon)

e. **But they were considered a strange thing**: This tells us the way the Bible is received by the *natural man*. Paul expressed the same idea in 1 Corinthians 2:14: *But the natural man does not receive the things of the Spirit of God, for they are foolishness to him; nor can he know them, because they are spiritually discerned.* The Word of God and the things of the spirit are **great things**, but seem like a **strange thing** when man is in sin and idolatry.

i. Sometimes people reject the Bible because they think "science" is superior. "But the science of Jesus Christ is the most excellent of sciences. Let no one turn away from the Bible, because it is not a book of learning and wisdom. It is. Would ye know astronomy? It is here: it tells you of the Sun of Righteousness and the Star of Bethlehem. Would you know botany? It is here: it tells you of the plant of renown-the Lily of the Valley and the Rose of Sharon. Would you know geology and mineralogy? You shall learn it here: for you may read of the Rock of Ages, and the White Stone with a name graven thereon, which no man knoweth, saving he that receiveth it. Would ye study history? Here is the most ancient of all the records of the history of the human race. Whatever your science is, come and bend o'er this book; your science is here" (Spurgeon).

f. **But the LORD does not accept them**: Sure, they still brought sacrifices to the LORD. But it was all just an outward ceremony because they were still steeped in sin and idolatry. Therefore, their sin remained uncovered, and God will **remember their iniquity and punish their sins**.

2. (14) When God's people forget their Maker, there is no refuge.

"For Israel has forgotten his Maker,
And has built temples;
Judah also has multiplied fortified cities;
But I will send fire upon his cities,
And it shall devour his palaces."

a. **For Israel has forgotten his Maker**: Israel **built temples**, but not unto the LORD who made them. Therefore, the judgment described in this chapter is coming upon them.

b. **Judah also has multiplied fortified cities**: While Israel practiced outright idolatry, Judah was guilty of a more subtle sin. They trusted in the **fortified cities** they built against the Assyrians. Those **cities** would be of no help (**I will send fire upon his cities**), and the only the LORD would preserve Judah from total destruction (Isaiah 37:33-36).

i. Perhaps we can capture some of the ungodly heart of Israel and Judah by examining our own attraction to grandness and nice facilities. What could be wrong with success and nice buildings? They can easily become idols if our hearts turn away from God. If God brings size and great buildings, it is wonderful – as long as we don't turn our eyes off Him, making those things idols.

Hosea 9 - Exiled and Dried Up

A. Israel exiled in judgment.

1. (1-4) The end of the good life in Israel.

Do not rejoice, O Israel, with joy like *other* peoples,
For you have played the harlot against your God.
You have made love *for* hire on every threshing floor.
The threshing floor and the winepress
Shall not feed them,
And the new wine shall fail in her.

They shall not dwell in the Lord's land,
But Ephraim shall return to Egypt,
And shall eat unclean *things* in Assyria.
They shall not offer wine *offerings* to the Lord,
Nor shall their sacrifices be pleasing to Him.
***It shall be* like bread of mourners to them;**
All who eat it shall be defiled.
For their bread *shall be* for their *own* life;
It shall not come into the house of the Lord.

> a. **Do not rejoice, O Israel, with joy like other peoples**: At the time Hosea brought this prophecy, things perhaps were not so bad in Israel. Maybe there were plenty of fun and good times among the people. But they shouldn't rejoice **like other peoples**, because judgment was on the way.
>
>> i. "It was probably the case, though we do not know this for sure, that Hosea delivered the opening part of this oracle as a sermon on the occasion of a harvest festival…characterized by feasting, mirth, and dancing." (Boice)
>
> b. **You have made love for hire on every threshing floor**: Israel practiced idolatry on the **threshing floor**, a place where grain was processed. They

worshipped idols here because they believed that it helped the harvest. Because of their idolatry, the LORD would curse their harvest, and **the threshing floor and the winepress shall not feed them.**

c. **They shall not dwell in the Lord's land**: Not only would God curse their grain and grape harvest, but He would also cast them out of the land in exile to both Egypt and Assyria. In the lands of exile there would be no bread or food for sacrifice to the LORD, only for survival (**their bread shall be for their own life**).

2. (5-9) The days of Israel's punishment in Egypt.

What will you do in the appointed day,
And in the day of the feast of the LORD?
For indeed they are gone because of destruction.
Egypt shall gather them up;
Memphis shall bury them.
Nettles shall possess their valuables of silver;
Thorns *shall be* **in their tents.**

The days of punishment have come;
The days of recompense have come.
Israel knows!
The prophet *is* **a fool,**
The spiritual man *is* **insane,**
Because of the greatness of your iniquity and great enmity.
The watchman of Ephraim *is* **with my God;**
But the prophet *is* **a fowler's snare in all his ways–**
Enmity in the house of his God.
They are deeply corrupted,
As in the days of Gibeah.
He will remember their iniquity;
He will punish their sins.

a. **They are gone because of destruction**: Israel did not honor the LORD in their **appointed** feast days, so the LORD will take them away. In their lands of exile, they will not be able to honor the feasts of the LORD.

b. **The prophet is a fool, the spiritual man is insane**: This is what the people of Israel said about Hosea. When things prospered and everyone was happy, Hosea announced coming judgment and called for repentance. They thought he was a fool and crazy.

i. "They said in effect, 'Who in his right mind would prophesy a judgment like this when we are in the midst of such a bountiful harvest, in itself a proof of God's blessing?'" (Boice)

c. **As in the days of Gibeah**: Judges 19 describes horrific crimes of perversion and violence in Israel in the days of the Judges. Hosea says that in his day it is just as bad in Israel.

B. Israel barren and dried up in judgment.

1. (10-14) God sends barrenness and bereavement.

"I found Israel
Like grapes in the wilderness;
I saw your fathers
As the firstfruits on the fig tree in its first season.
But they went to Baal Peor,
And separated themselves *to that* shame;
They became an abomination like the thing they loved.
As for Ephraim, their glory shall fly away like a bird–
No birth, no pregnancy, and no conception!
Though they bring up their children,
Yet I will bereave them to the last man.
Yes, woe to them when I depart from them!
Just as I saw Ephraim like Tyre, planted in a pleasant place,
So Ephraim will bring out his children to the murderer."

Give them, O LORD–
What will You give?
Give them a miscarrying womb
And dry breasts!

    a. **Like grapes in the wilderness…as the firstfruits on the fig tree**: God fondly remembered the days when Israel was faithful and fruitful unto Him. **Grapes in the wilderness** and the **firstfruits on the fig tree** are unexpected blessings. There was a time when Israel was something special to God, as if one found luscious **grapes in the wilderness**.

        i. "While they were faithful, they were as *acceptable* to me as *ripe grapes* would be to a *thirsty traveler* in the desert." (Clarke)

    b. **But they went to Baal Peor**: Israel's sin and idolatry in the days of Hosea was like their sin at **Baal Peor** in Numbers 25, associated with sexual immorality and idolatry.

    c. **They became an abomination like the thing they loved**: Israel loved their disgraceful idols, and they had become like them. We will become like the god we love and serve, whether it is the LORD or like an **abomination**.

d. **No birth, no pregnancy, and no conception**: In contrast to their past fruitfulness, now Israel will experience barrenness and bereavement (**I will bereave them to the last man**), given to them by the God they rejected.

e. **Give them, O LORD–What will You give?** The idea is that Hosea began an angry prayer against the people ("**Give them, O LORD**"), then he stopped because he checked his heart and didn't know what to pray ("**What will you give?**"). In the end, he asked for **a miscarrying womb and dry breasts**. Really, Hosea prayed for mercy. Knowing the coming judgment, he prayed "LORD, give them few children so those children will not have to face the horrors of Your coming judgment."

> i. Sometimes those who see themselves – perhaps accurately – as more spiritual and closer to God than others in a church or group get angry and frustrated with those who don't seem to have hearts burning for the LORD. Their frustration is understandable but the pause in Hosea's prayer should give them pause. It is a good thing to long for revival and spiritual passion among God's people, but if that makes us proud, angry, or bitter against others then Satan has won a great victory.

2. (15-17) God sends dryness and wandering upon Israel.

**"All their wickedness *is* in Gilgal,
For there I hated them.
Because of the evil of their deeds
I will drive them from My house;
I will love them no more.
All their princes *are* rebellious.
Ephraim is stricken,
Their root is dried up;
They shall bear no fruit.
Yes, were they to bear children,
I would kill the darlings of their womb."
My God will cast them away,
Because they did not obey Him;
And they shall be wanderers among the nations.**

> a. **All their wickedness is in Gilgal, for there I hated them**: As mentioned before in Hosea 4:15, God despised the city of **Gilgal** as a center of idolatry in Israel. At one time, **Gilgal** was a place where prophets were trained under Elijah and Elisha (2 Kings 2:1; 4:38). But in Hosea's day it had become a center of false worship (Hosea 4:15, 12:11; Amos 4:4, 5:5).

b. **I will drive them from My house**: In this sense, exile was the perfect punishment for Israel. They had disgraced God's **house**, His land, so He would "evict" them from His **house**.

c. **They shall bear no fruit…. I would kill the beloved fruit of their womb**: One of the major reasons Israel went after idols like Baal and Ashtoreth was because those gods were thought to bring fertility and fruitfulness. God reminds Israel that He is really the LORD over the womb, and that He will turn their fruitfulness into barrenness.

d. **My God will cast them away, because they did not obey Him**: This is exactly what the LORD promised under the terms of the Old Covenant (Deuteronomy 30:14-18). Thankfully, we can come to God by faith in a new and better covenant, where He promises to remember our sins no more (Hebrews 8:12, 10:16-17).

Hosea 10 - Israel Has No King

A. The analysis of Israel's sinful state.

1. (1-2) Israel's empty vine.

Israel empties *his* vine;
He brings forth fruit for himself.
According to the multitude of his fruit
He has increased the altars;
According to the bounty of his land
They have embellished *his* sacred pillars.
Their heart is divided;
Now they are held guilty.
He will break down their altars;
He will ruin their sacred pillars.

a. **He brings forth fruit for himself**: God blessed Israel with material abundance, but they spent it on themselves and their own idolatrous desires (**he has increased the altars**). Israel enjoyed the blessing of God, but used those blessings in ungodly ways.

i. Paul warns against the same sin in Galatians 5:13: *For you, brethren, have been called to liberty; only do not use liberty as an opportunity for the flesh*. Sometimes as Christians we take the liberty and blessing God gives and use them in ungodly ways.

b. **Their heart is divided; now they are held guilty**: Because Israel had received blessing, they were more responsible than ever to use it wisely. Because they used God's bounty in wicked ways, God would **break down their altars** to pagan gods and **ruin their sacred pillars** made unto idols.

i. **Their heart is divided**: The word **divided** is *halaq*, which has the ideas of "**divided**" (Genesis 14:15, 49:7), of "smooth" (Genesis 27:11, Psalm 55:21) or of "flattering" (Psalm 5:9, 36:2). So, it may be accurate to translate this phrase as **their heart is divided**, but it may also be that God meant to say that Ephraim has a "smooth, flattering," insincere heart.

ii. The idea of Israel's "smooth" or "insincere" heart is reflected by the adulteries of Hosea's wife Gomer earlier in the book. In the same way that an unfaithful spouse will *say* they love their partner, all the while living a lie, is the same way Israel's heart was towards God.

iii. Israel had this divided, insincere heart and expressed it on the altars of idolatry. Now, **He will break down their altars**. "Now God will do in *judgment* what *they* should have done in *contrition*, 'break down their altars, and spoil their images'" (Clarke).

2. (3-8) Israel's empty throne.

For now they say,
"We have no king,
Because we did not fear the Lord.
And as for a king, what would he do for us?"
They have spoken words,
Swearing falsely in making a covenant.
Thus judgment springs up like hemlock in the furrows of the field.

The inhabitants of Samaria fear
Because of the calf of Beth Aven.
For its people mourn for it,
And its priests shriek for it–
Because its glory has departed from it.
***The idol* also shall be carried to Assyria**
***As* a present for King Jareb.**
Ephraim shall receive shame,
And Israel shall be ashamed of his own counsel.

***As for* Samaria, her king is cut off**
Like a twig on the water.
Also the high places of Aven, the sin of Israel,
Shall be destroyed.
The thorn and thistle shall grow on their altars;
They shall say to the mountains, "Cover us!"
And to the hills, "Fall on us!"

a. **We have no king**: Under the judgment of the Lord, foreign powers dominated Israel so they no longer had their own king. Even the idols they honored and trusted so much will be taken to foreign lands as treasure for foreign kings.

b. **The thorn and thistle shall grow on their altars**: After the desolation of exile, the once-busy pagan altars of Israel were now overgrown with thorns and thistles. This was the result of Israel's rejection of the LORD and their embrace of pagan gods.

B. God's counsel to sinful Israel.

1. (9-11) God tells Israel to see their sin and to submit to His chastening.

"O Israel, you have sinned from the days of Gibeah;
There they stood.
The battle in Gibeah against the children of iniquity
Did not overtake them.
When *it is* **My desire, I will chasten them.**
Peoples shall be gathered against them
When I bind them for their two transgressions.
Ephraim *is* **a trained heifer**
That loves to thresh *grain;*
***B*ut I harnessed her fair neck,**
I will make Ephraim pull *a plow.*
Judah shall plow;
Jacob shall break his clods."

a. **You have sinned from the days of Gibeah**: Gibeah was already mentioned in Hosea 9:9, recalling the horrific sin described in Judges 19. Even though there was a **battle in Gibeah against the children of iniquity**, there was still iniquity in Israel. Here, God wanted a willfully blind Israel to see their sin and repent of it.

b. **When it is My desire, I will chasten them**: Like unruly farm animals, God would control and guide Israel and Jacob, even if they kicked against Him.

2. (12) God tells Israel to break up the hard ground of their heart.

Sow for yourselves righteousness;
Reap in mercy;
Break up your fallow ground,
For *it is* **time to seek the LORD,**
Till He comes and rains righteousness on you.

a. **Sow for yourselves righteousness; reap in mercy**: Israel had sown the seed of sin, and they would soon reap judgment from God. Even now, if they would sow **righteousness**, they would **reap in mercy** at the next harvest.

i. We all sow into our life but do we **sow** seeds of **righteousness**? What "crop" will grow up from the seeds planted today, or this past week, or this past month?

b. **Break up your fallow ground**: God builds on the picture of sowing and reaping by telling Israel to **break up your fallow ground** – ground that hasn't been plowed for more than a year. It is ground that is hard and stubborn, resistant to the seed. It does little good to sow seed on **fallow ground**; it must be broken up first.

i. Sometimes when the word of God goes forth and seems to have little effect, it is because it falls on **fallow ground** – the hard ground that will not allow the seed of the word to penetrate and become fruitful.

ii. Since **fallow ground** is hard, it probably doesn't "want" to be broken up. It is hard and compact, and the blade of the plow hurts as it cuts through. If the **fallow ground** could talk, it would probably cry out when it is plowed. Yet it is useless as ground as long as it is **fallow**.

iii. **For it is time to seek the Lord** reminds us of *how* we break up the fallow ground. We do it by seeking the Lord, not our self or idols.

iv. **For it is time** shows that the time to break up the fallow ground is *now*. "This should be immediately done: the season is passing; and if you do not get the seed in the ground, the early rain will be past, and your fields will be unfruitful" (Clarke).

c. **Till He comes and rains righteousness on you**: This tells us how long we should break up the fallow ground and sow the seed of righteousness. We do it until the harvest comes.

i. God's use of the figures of sowing and reaping remind us that harvest is sometimes a season away. Sometimes people expect to sow sin for years, but to immediately **reap in mercy** after sowing **righteousness** for one day. Stick with sowing in righteousness, you will **reap in mercy** in due time.

3. (13-15) God tells Israel the terrible result of resisting Him.

You have plowed wickedness;
You have reaped iniquity.
You have eaten the fruit of lies,
Because you trusted in your own way,
In the multitude of your mighty men.
Therefore tumult shall arise among your people,
And all your fortresses shall be plundered
As Shalman plundered Beth Arbel in the day of battle–
A mother dashed in pieces upon *her* children.

**Thus it shall be done to you, O Bethel,
Because of your great wickedness.
At dawn the king of Israel
Shall be cut off utterly.**

> a. **Because you trusted in your own way**: This is the essence of all sin. We trust in our **own way** instead of in God's way. Ruin always comes when we trust in our **own way** instead of God's way, and that ruin was about to come upon Israel.

Hosea 11 - Drawn with Gentle Cords

A. God's tender love for Israel.

1. (1-2) Israel: Called by God and called by the Baals.

"When Israel *was* a child, I loved him,
And out of Egypt I called My son.
As they called them,
So they went from them;
They sacrificed to the Baals,
And burned incense to carved images.

> a. **I loved him, and out of Egypt I called My son**: God remembered His tender love for Israel, when more than 500 years before the time of Hosea He brought them out of **Egypt**.
>
>> i. This is an "unexpected" prophecy fulfilled in the life of Jesus. Matthew 2:15 shows how the words **out of Egypt I called My son** were fulfilled when the child Jesus return from Egypt after escaping there on the eve of Herod's massacre of the innocents.
>
> b. **As they called them, so they went from them**: God called Israel out of Egypt, but the idolatry of the Baals called to Israel, and they forsook the LORD and followed the Baals (the local deities of Canaan).

2. (3-4) God's tender love for an unseeing Israel.

"I taught Ephraim to walk,
Taking them by their arms;
But they did not know that I healed them.
I drew them with gentle cords,
With bands of love,
And I was to them as those who take the yoke from their neck.
I stooped *and* fed them.

> a. **I taught Ephraim to walk... but they did not know that I healed them**: God does so much for His people that they are unaware of. Often,

we attribute some blessing directly from the hand of God to some other source.

> i. **Taking them by their arms**: The picture is of a parent teaching a child how to walk by holding the child's arms and supporting the child as they make their awkward steps.

b. **I drew them with gentle cords, with bands of love**: Even when God draws His people, it is with **gentle cords** of **love**, not with harsh manipulation or coercion. God wants to win us over, but not with brute force.

> i. Clarke on **gentle cords**: "This is a reference to *leading strings*, one end of which is held by the child, the other by the nurse, by which the little one, feeling some support, and gaining confidence, endeavours to walk. God, their heavenly Father, made use of every means and method to teach them to walk in the right and only safe path."

> ii. In the ancient world, the empires of Persia and Greece fought bitter wars. There was said to be a great difference between their soldiers. In the Persian army, soldiers were like slaves and driven into battle with whips and threats. In the Greek army, soldiers were free men and patriots, and fought for Sparta and Greece out of love for country and a sense of duty. The smaller armies of Greece usually beat the larger armies of Persia. God calls us as an army of free men, grateful patriots of the kingdom of God.

> iii. "Understand, then, it is true that no man comes to God except he is drawn; but it is equally true that God draweth no man contrary to the constitution of man, but his methods of drawing are in strict accordance with ordinary mental operations. He finds the human mind what it is, and he acts upon it, not as upon matter, but as upon mind. The compulsions, the constraints, the cords that he uses, are 'cords of a man.' The bands he employs are 'bands of love.'" (Spurgeon)

c. **As those who take the yoke from their neck** refers to relaxing and loosening the yoke-collar of a plowing animal, giving the animal rest and the freedom to breathe.

d. **I stooped and fed them**: God humbled Himself to minister to His needy people. One might almost think it is beneath the dignity and honor of God to stoop so for His people, but He never thinks so. This is the heart reflected in the servant nature of Jesus (Philippians 2).

B. God's strict hand towards Israel.

1. (5-7) Empty profession brings the chastening of God.

"He shall not return to the land of Egypt;
But the Assyrian shall be his king,
Because they refused to repent.
And the sword shall slash in his cities,
Devour his districts,
And consume *them*,
Because of their own counsels.
My people are bent on backsliding from Me.
Though they call to the Most High,
None at all exalt *Him*.

> a. **Because they refused to repent**: In this sense, it wasn't so much the sin of Israel that got them into trouble. It was their stubborn refusal **to repent** after their sin. For that, God would make sure that destruction and exile waited for them.
>
> b. **My people are bent on backsliding from Me. Though they call to the Most High, none at all exalt Him**: **Backsliding** means that at one time, Israel had a closer and more real walk with God. Now that is in the past, and their profession is simply empty. They **call to the Most High** in a formal sort of way, but they did not **exalt Him** with their lives.

2. (8-9) God's sympathy in the midst of chastening.

"How can I give you up, Ephraim?
How can I hand you over, Israel?
How can I make you like Admah?
How can I set you like Zeboiim?
My heart churns within Me;
My sympathy is stirred.
I will not execute the fierceness of My anger;
I will not again destroy Ephraim.
For I *am* God, and not man,
The Holy One in your midst;
And I will not come with terror.

> a. **How can I give you up, Ephraim?** Though the dark clouds of judgment are on the horizon, God takes no pleasure in the chastening about to come upon Israel. Instead He says, "**My sympathy is stirred**."
>
>> i. We are in sin, and guilty before God. Yet He says, **How can I give you up?** Justice demands that He do this, yet in His heart He must find a way of salvation. In this, God sends Jesus Christ, and on the cross Jesus was "given up" in our place.

b. **Admah.... Zeboiim**: These were two cities near Sodom and Gomorrah that were also destroyed (Deuteronomy 29:23). God says, "I can't bear to allow My people to be caught up in the destruction that will come upon all the nations, as **Admah** and **Zeboiim** were caught up on the destruction that came upon Sodom and Gomorrah."

c. **I will not again destroy Ephraim**: Though their sin deserves it, God will not wipe out Israel. He will leave a remnant and will restore the nation.

d. **For I am God, and not man**: The longsuffering, forgiveness, and compassion of the Lord toward His people seems unbelievable until we recognize that He is **not man**, but God. His love and forgiveness are of a different order. Charles Spurgeon observed that there are many differences between God and man in the matter of forgiveness.

- Man cannot hold back his anger very long.
- Man cannot bear with others when he is tired, stressed, or annoyed.
- Man will not reconcile if the person who offended him is a person of bad character.
- Man is often only willing to be reconciled if the offending party craves forgiveness and makes the first move.
- Man is often only willing to be reconciled if the offending party will never again do the wrong.
- Man, when he does reconcile, does not lift the former offender to place of high status and partnership.
- Man, when he is wronged, does not bear all the penalty for the wrong done.
- Man, when he attempts reconciliation, will not continue if he is rejected.
- Man will not restore an offender without a period of probation
- Man will not love, adopt, honor, and associate with one who has wronged him.
- Man will not trust someone who has formerly wronged them.

    i. What passes for forgiveness among men is nothing like the amazing forgiveness of God. "Suppose that someone had grievously offended any one of you, and that he asked your forgiveness, do you not think that you would probably say to him, 'Well, yes, I forgive you; but I – I – I – cannot forget it'? Ah! dear friends, that is a sort of forgiveness with one leg chopped off, it is a lame forgiveness, and is not worth much" (Spurgeon).

3. (10-12) The roar of God calls Israel back.

"They shall walk after the LORD**.**
He will roar like a lion.
When He roars,
Then *His* **sons shall come trembling from the west;**
They shall come trembling like a bird from Egypt,
Like a dove from the land of Assyria.
nd I will let them dwell in their houses,"
Says the LORD**.**

"Ephraim has encircled Me with lies,
And the house of Israel with deceit;
But Judah still walks with God,
Even with the Holy One *who is* **faithful.**

> a. **When He roars, then His sons shall come trembling from the west**: God spoke of the ultimate restoration of Israel, an expression of His mercy to Ephraim.
>
> b. **Ephraim has encircled Me with lies**: God made these promises knowing the present state of Israel. Though Judah was in a better place than Israel, God still made the promises with full knowledge of their present state.

Hosea 12 - Ancient Jacob and Modern Israel

A. The deeply rooted deceit of Israel.

1. (1) Israel trusts in deals and alliances with surrounding nations.

"Ephraim feeds on the wind,
And pursues the east wind;
He daily increases lies and desolation.
Also they make a covenant with the Assyrians,
And oil is carried to Egypt.

> a. **Ephraim feeds on the wind**: The idols and foreign alliances Israel trusts in are useless. They are like trying to feed **on the wind**.
>
>> i. Clarke on the **east wind**: "They are not only empty, but *dangerous* and *destructive*. The *east wind* was, and still is, in all countries, a *parching, wasting, injurious* wind."
>
> b. **Also they make a covenant with the Assyrians, and oil carried to Egypt**: Instead of trusting in the LORD, Israel trusted in deals and payoffs to the surrounding superpowers. It was foolish for them to think that Assyria or Egypt was more powerful or dependable than the LORD was.

2. (2-6) Ancient Jacob is an example of Israel's present deceit.

"The LORD also *brings* a charge against Judah,
And will punish Jacob according to his ways;
According to his deeds He will recompense him.
He took his brother by the heel in the womb,
And in his strength he struggled with God.
Yes, he struggled with the Angel and prevailed;
He wept, and sought favor from Him.
He found Him *in* Bethel,
And there He spoke to us–
That is, the LORD God of hosts.
The LORD *is* His memorable name.

So you, by *the help of* your God, return;
Observe mercy and justice,
And wait on your God continually.

> a. **He took his brother by the heel in the womb**: Here, God looked back at the patriarch Jacob and how Israel in Hosea's day was just like their forefather Jacob in the days of Genesis. In ancient Israel, a "heel-catcher" was a double-dealer, someone who achieved their goals through crafty and dishonest means. Through Hosea, God said, "That was Jacob then and it is Israel now."
>
> > i. "'To grasp the heel' also meant to go behind one's back in order to deceive or trick him, and this became the dominant characteristic of the man." (Boice)
>
> b. **In his strength he struggled with God**: The prophet recalls the struggle between Jacob and the Man of Genesis 32:24-30. Jacob refused to submit to God, so God demanded submission from him in a literal wrestling match.
>
> > i. **He struggled with God** reinforces a point already made clear in Genesis 32:24-30: Jacob wrestled with the Lord God, who appeared in human form as a Man. Since this was a unique messenger from heaven, He is also appropriately described as an **Angel** of the Lord.
>
> c. **He struggled with the Angel and prevailed; he wept, and sought favor from Him**: Inspired by the Holy Spirit, Hosea emphasized two more details from the Genesis 32:24-30 account. First, he told us that Jacob **prevailed** in the wrestling match. Second, he told us that Jacob **wept** in the struggle.
>
> > i. It could be said that Jacob **prevailed** in the only way anyone can when they struggle against God. We prevail when we lose and know it, surrendering to God.
> >
> > ii. It is important to know that Jacob **wept** because it helps us understand how desperate and broken he was as he hung on the Lord, now pleading only for a blessing.
>
> d. **So you, by the help of your God, return**: Jacob came to the place where he knew God had beaten him, and all he could do was hang on to God and plead for a blessing. **So you** speaks to Israel, saying they should return to God the same way.
>
> > i. **By the help of your God, return** reminds us that we can never even return to the Lord without His help. This shows how weak we are and how much we really depend on Him.

B. Judgment promised against a confident Israel.

1. (7-11) Though Israel is confident in its wealth, God will bring them low.

"A cunning Canaanite!
Deceitful scales *are* in his hand;
He loves to oppress.
And Ephraim said,
'Surely I have become rich,
I have found wealth for myself;
In all my labors
They shall find in me no iniquity that *is* sin.'

"But I *am* the LORD your God,
Ever since the land of Egypt;
I will again make you dwell in tents,
As in the days of the appointed feast.
I have also spoken by the prophets,
And have multiplied visions;
I have given symbols through the witness of the prophets."

Though Gilead *has* idols–
Surely they are vanity–
Though they sacrifice bulls in Gilgal,
Indeed their altars *shall be* heaps in the furrows of the field.

> a. **Surely I have become rich**: Hosea prophesied during a time of great prosperity, but spiritual and moral decadence in Israel. When things are good financially, it's hard for people to believe that their society is in trouble (**in all my labors they shall find in me no iniquity that is sin**).
>
>> i. **Canaanite** in this context probably means "merchant" because the Canaanites at this time were well-known merchants and traders. Clarke says, "Ephraim is as corrupt as those heathenish traffickers were."
>
> b. **I will again make you dwell in tents**: Though Israel enjoyed financial prosperity and fine homes, God's judgment would bring them into exile and humble **tents** again. This judgment is certain because God has **spoken by the prophets**, yet they did not listen.
>
> c. **Their altars shall be heaps in the furrows of the field**: Pagan altars were built high and stately to add dignity to the pagan god. When God's judgment comes, all those altars will be brought low, so the only altars will be the hills made by the **furrows of the field**.

2. (12-14) Reproach will return upon Ephraim.

Jacob fled to the country of Syria;
Israel served for a spouse,
And for a wife he tended *sheep*.
By a prophet the LORD brought Israel out of Egypt,
And by a prophet he was preserved.
Ephraim provoked *Him* to anger most bitterly;
Therefore his Lord will leave the guilt of his bloodshed upon him,
And return his reproach upon him.

> a. **Jacob fled to the country of Syria**: The previous passage brought up the impending exile of Israel, and now Hosea made a connection between the coming exile of Israel and Jacob's own exile when he fled from Esau to his uncle Laban in Syria.

> b. **By a prophet he was preserved…. Therefore his Lord will leave the guilt of his bloodshed upon him**: Though God sent prophets to Israel, they still rejected His word. They **provoked Him to anger most bitterly**, so God would leave them in their guilt, and **return** the **reproach** of Egypt's slavery upon them.

Hosea 13 - "I Will Be Your King"

A. Two pictures of judgment.

1. (1-3) Sinful Israel will be scattered like the morning clouds.

When Ephraim spoke, trembling,
He exalted *himself* in Israel;
But when he offended through Baal *worship*, he died.
Now they sin more and more,
And have made for themselves molded images,
Idols of their silver, according to their skill;
All of it *is* the work of craftsmen.
They say of them,
"Let the men who sacrifice kiss the calves!"
Therefore they shall be like the morning cloud
And like the early dew that passes away,
Like chaff blown off from a threshing floor
And like smoke from a chimney.

> a. **Now they sin more and more**: God never blessed Israel when they worshipped Baal, but that didn't stop them. They kept after their idolatry **more and more**.

> b. **The men who sacrifice**: This may instead have the idea of *engaging in human sacrifice*, and could be translated "the sacrificers of men." In ancient Israel human sacrifice was almost always child-sacrifice. Hosea already spoken of this horrible practice in Hosea 9:13 and perhaps in Hosea 5:2.

>> i. "Viewed together, the sin is a total perversion of values. A craftsman's work is elevated to divine status; human beings sacrifice their offspring to a metal object from whose lifeless form they also beg help; persons embrace with adulation the images of the very animals that they use for ploughing, threshing and hauling." (Hubbard)

c. **Therefore they shall be like the morning cloud and like the early dew that passes**: Because Israel trusted in themselves and in idols, they could not *stand*. They would pass like the **early dew**.

2. (4-8) Sinful Israel will be torn apart as if by a lion.

"Yet I *am* the Lord your God
Ever since the land of Egypt,
And you shall know no God but Me;
For *there is* no Savior besides Me.
I knew you in the wilderness,
In the land of great drought.
When they had pasture, they were filled;
They were filled and their heart was exalted;
Therefore they forgot Me.

"So I will be to them like a lion;
Like a leopard by the road I will lurk;
I will meet them like a bear deprived *of her cubs;*
I will tear open their rib cage,
And there I will devour them like a lion.
The wild beast shall tear them.

> a. **Yet I am the Lord your God ever since the land of Egypt**: Israel changed, but the Lord God did not. He was still the only God and the only Savior, and His people would be left desolate when they left Him.
>
> b. **They were filled and their heart was exalted; therefore they forgot Me**: It is a strange and terrible aspect of human nature that when times are good, we often forget the God who blessed us. When times are bad we are often more likely to turn our hearts back to God.
>
>> i. At the end of the 20th Century, Americans were in a season of unprecedented prosperity. Yet statistics show that in the 1990s churchgoers gave a smallest percentage of their income in contributions since the Great Depression. Sadly, often when we are **filled**, then we find our hearts **exalted**, and soon we forget God.
>
> c. **So I will be to them like a lion**: When we neglect and affront God as He blesses, we then will often face the chastening hand of God. It isn't because God hates us, but because we have demonstrated that we will only turn to Him when times are bad.
>
>> i. "The three mentioned – lion, leopard, and bear – were all native to Palestine and known for their relentless manner of killing prey." (Wood)

B. God, the only hope of Israel.

1. (9-11) The rejected King and the imposed king.

"O Israel, you are destroyed,
But your help *is* from Me.
I will be your King;
Where *is any other*,
That he may save you in all your cities?
And your judges to whom you said,
'Give me a king and princes'?
I gave you a king in My anger,
And took *him* away in My wrath.

> a. **You are destroyed, but your help is from Me**: Even when Israel felt the sting of God's chastening hand, they could still find **help** from the LORD, if they would only turn to Him.

> b. **I will be your King.... I gave you a king in My anger, and took him away in My wrath**: God wanted to be recognized as the King of Israel, no matter which man sat on the royal throne. When they rejected the LORD as King, He gave them the kind of kings their hearts wanted and deserved, and then even took those kings as further judgment.

2. (12-16) The sorrowful judgment of Ephraim and her children.

"The iniquity of Ephraim *is* bound up;
His sin *is* stored up.
The sorrows of a woman in childbirth shall come upon him.
He *is* an unwise son,
For he should not stay long where children are born.

I will ransom them from the power of the grave;
I will redeem them from death.
O Death, I will be your plagues!
O Grave, I will be your destruction!
Pity is hidden from My eyes."

Though he is fruitful among *his* brethren,
An east wind shall come;
The wind of the LORD shall come up from the wilderness.
Then his spring shall become dry,
And his fountain shall be dried up.
He shall plunder the treasury of every desirable prize.
Samaria is held guilty,
For she has rebelled against her God.
They shall fall by the sword,

Their infants shall be dashed in pieces,
And their women with child ripped open.

> a. **The sorrows of a woman in childbirth shall come upon him**: Labor pains often come unexpectedly, are intense, and increase in their pain and duration. In the same way, judgment would come upon Israel.
>
> b. **I will ransom them from the power of the grave; I will redeem them from death**: The sin and judgment of Israel were both great, but not greater than God's ability and power to redeem. He can even **redeem... from death**, so that **death** and the **grave** are mocked as defeated foes.
>
>> i. Paul quoted the Septuagint translation of Hosea 13:14 in describing our triumph over death in our sharing in the resurrection of Jesus: *O Death, where is your sting? O Hades, where is your victory?* (1 Corinthians 15:55)
>
> c. **Samaria is held guilty, for she has rebelled against her God**: In the long term, Israel will see the glory of God's redemption and His power over sin and death. In the near term, Israel will be chastened for their rebellion against God.

Hosea 14 - Real Wisdom Turns Israel Back to the L ORD

"This is a wonderful chapter to be at the end of such a book. I had never expected from such a prickly shrub to gather so fair a flower, so sweet a fruit; but so it is: where sin abounded, grace doth much more abound. No chapter in the Bible can be more rich in mercy than this last of Hosea; and yet no chapter in the Bible might, in the natural order of things, have been more terrible in judgment. Where we looked for the blackness of darkness, behold a noontide of light!" (Charles Spurgeon)

A. Israel's repentance and God's response.

1. (1-3) What Israel should say in their repentance.

O Israel, return to the L ORD your God,
For you have stumbled because of your iniquity;
Take words with you,
And return to the L ORD.
Say to Him,
"Take away all iniquity;
Receive *us* graciously,
For we will offer the sacrifices of our lips.
Assyria shall not save us,
We will not ride on horses,
Nor will we say anymore to the work of our hands, '*You are* our gods.'
For in You the fatherless finds mercy."

>   a. **Take words with you, and return to the L ORD**: In returning to the L ORD, Israel must come on God's terms, not their own. God says, "When you return to Me, **take words with you**. I want you to return to Me not with a silent feeling in your heart, but with proper words of repentance and trust in Me."

>>   i. When we come before the L ORD, it is essential to **take words with you**. There is a place for sharing the inarticulate feelings of the heart

with God, but that is not the essence of fellowship and prayer with Him. The worship of God is intelligent, and God made us able to communicate ideas and feelings with words. It isn't enough to sit before the LORD and feel love towards Him. Instead, **take words with you** – *tell God that you love Him*. It isn't enough to feel repentance before the LORD. Instead, **take words with you** and *tell God you repent before Him*.

ii. This is the same idea that Paul expressed in Romans 10:8-10: *But what does it say? "The word is near you, in your mouth and in your heart" (that is, the word of faith which we preach): that if you confess with your mouth the Lord Jesus and believe in your heart that God has raised Him from the dead, you will be saved. For with the heart one believes unto righteousness, and with the mouth confession is made unto salvation.* God commands us to communicate with Him in **words**, not only ideas or feelings.

iii. What words do we take with us? The best words are the words God gives us in His Word. When we communicate to God in the words and ideas of Scripture, we find an articulate and effective voice before God.

b. **Take away all iniquity; receive us graciously**: When we return to the LORD, taking words with us, we must first come humbly. We recognize our sin and our total dependence on the grace of God.

c. **For we will offer the sacrifices of our lips**: Literally, Hosea 14:2 says *for we will offer the calves of our lips*. Since bull calves were often brought for sacrifice, the translators felt justified in putting it **for we will offer the sacrifices of our lips**. However, the more literal rendering shows just how plainly our words of praise, worship, confession, petition, or intercession can be a sacrifice before God.

d. **Assyria shall not save us, we will not ride on horses, nor will we say anymore to the work of our hands, "You are our gods"**: When we return to the LORD, taking words with us, we come renouncing our dependence on all other things. We recognize that the LORD and the LORD alone can make the difference in our life.

e. **For in You the fatherless finds mercy**: When we return to the LORD, taking words with us, we come declaring His greatness. We tell of what a great and merciful God we have.

2. (4-7) God promises to restore a repentant Israel.

"I will heal their backsliding,
I will love them freely,
For My anger has turned away from him.

I will be like the dew to Israel;
He shall grow like the lily,
And lengthen his roots like Lebanon.
His branches shall spread;
His beauty shall be like an olive tree,
And his fragrance like Lebanon.
Those who dwell under his shadow shall return;
They shall be revived *like* **grain,**
And grow like a vine.
Their scent *shall be* **like the wine of Lebanon.**

a. **I will heal their backsliding**: God saw that Israel was bent on backsliding from Him (Hosea 11:7), but He promised to heal the backsliding of a repentant Israel. He did it not because Israel would deserve it, but because it is in His nature to **love them freely**.

i. The word is *compassionate*: **I will heal their backsliding**. This shows God looks on our **backsliding** more like a *disease* than a *crime*. He does not say, "I will pardon their backsliding." It is "as though he said, 'My poor people, I do remember that they are but dust; they are liable to a thousand temptations through the fall, and they soon go astray; but I will not treat them as though they were rebels, I will look upon them as patients, and they shall look upon me as a physician." (Spurgeon).

ii. The word is certain: **I will heal their backsliding**. Not "I might heal" or "I could heal" or "I can try to heal," but **I will heal their backsliding**. Come to God for healing of your backsliding, and He **will** do it! God is too great a physician to allow any patient to leave His office without being healed.

iii. The word is *personal*: **I will heal their backsliding**. He speaks to His people, and addresses them personally. We have to come to the Great Physician and say, "Heal *my* backsliding. I want to be the '**their**.'" To get the healing, you have to count yourself among the backsliders.

iv. Are you backsliding? The signs may not be so obvious to others. When you see a tree broken over in a windstorm, it's easy to think that it was the wind. If you look closer, you will often see that insects have been at work a long time on the tree, making it weaker and weaker. It really wasn't the wind that did it – other trees around it withstood the wind. It was the slow decline of strength, as insects nibbled away month after month.

b. This passage shows us what is restored when we return to the LORD.

- Growth is restored (**He shall grow**).

- Beauty is restored (**He shall grow like the lily**).
- Strength is restored (**lengthen his roots like Lebanon**).
- Value is restored (**His beauty shall be like an olive tree**).
- Delight is restored (**His fragrance like Lebanon**).
- Abundance is restored (**revived like grain... grow like the vine... scent shall be like the wine of Lebanon**).

c. **His branches will spread**: When God restores Israel, His people will be a blessing to others, not blessed only unto himself.

B. A new Israel.

1. (8) Renewed Israel is free from idols.

**"Ephraim *shall say*,
'What have I to do anymore with idols?'
I have heard and observed him.
I *am* like a green cypress tree;
Your fruit is found in Me."**

a. **What have I to do anymore with idols?** When God's people are healed from backsliding, they focus on the LORD Himself and not on any kind of idol.

b. **Your fruit is found in Me**: At one time, Israel thought they might find fruit in themselves or in the idols of the nations. Now, healed of their backsliding, they find their fruit only in God.

i. **Your fruit is found in Me** can have two ideas, equally true. First, we find the fruit to nourish our soul in God, and God alone. Second, we find the fruit that we are to bear unto the world in God, and God alone.

2. (9) Renewed Israel walks in wisdom.

**Who *is* wise?
Let him understand these things.
Who is prudent?
Let him know them.
For the ways of the LORD *are* right;
The righteous walk in them,
But transgressors stumble in them.**

a. **Who is wise?** The wise man will see the message throughout the Book of Hosea. He will understand that in His mercy, God offers a wonderful opportunity for repentance and restoration, and it is dangerous and foolish to neglect that invitation.

b. **The ways of the LORD are right**: Even in the midst of promised judgment, the wise and understanding man sees that **the ways of the LORD are right**, and that ever announcement of judgment is an invitation to repentance.

i. "In beauty of expression these final words of Hosea rank with the memorable chapters of the OT. Like the rainbow after a storm, they promise Israel's final restoration. Here is the full flowering of God's unfailing love for his faithless people, the triumph of his grace, the assurance of his healing - all described in imagery that reveals the loving heart of God." (Wood)

Joel 1 – The Day of the LORD *Brings Judah Low*

A. Locusts devastate the land of Judah.

1. (1-4) The remarkable plague of locusts upon Judah.

The word of the LORD that came to Joel the son of Pethuel.

Hear this, you elders,
And give ear, all you inhabitants of the land!
Has *anything like* this happened in your days,
Or even in the days of your fathers?
Tell your children about it,
***Let* your children *tell* their children,**
And their children another generation.

What the chewing locust left,
The swarming locust has eaten;
What the swarming locust left, the crawling locust has eaten;
And what the crawling locust left, the consuming locust has eaten.

> a. **The word of the LORD that came to Joel**: The prophet Joel spoke to the southern kingdom of Judah without making reference to the northern kingdom of Israel. It's hard to know when he prophesied because Joel doesn't mention any other kings or prophets. Many scholars date the book of Joel to 835 B.C.
>
> i. This makes Joel a *pre-exilic* prophet, who served before the fall of the northern kingdom of Israel (721 B.C.) and the southern kingdom of Judah (586 B.C.). Other pre-exilic prophets include Obadiah, Jonah, Hosea, Amos, Isaiah, and Micah. Joel is one of the earliest prophets – only Obadiah prophesied before his time (845 B.C.).
>
> ii. 835 B.C. was a time of turmoil and transition in Judah, at the end of the reign of the Queen Mother Athaliah and the beginning of the reign of King Joash. Athaliah seized power at the sudden death in battle of her son Ahaziah, who only reigned for one year (2 Kings

8:26, 2 Chronicles 22:2). Athaliah killed all her son's heirs, except for one who was hidden in the temple and escaped – one-year-old Joash (2 Kings 11:3). Athaliah's six-year reign of terror ended in 835 B.C. when the high priest Jehoiada overthrew her and set the seven-year-old Joash on the throne (2 Kings 11:4-21).

iii. During her six years as queen over Judah, Athaliah reigned wickedly. She was the granddaughter of the ungodly King Omri of Israel – making her daughter or niece to Ahab, one of Israel's worst kings (2 Kings 8:26). Athaliah raised her son Ahaziah to reign in the wicked pattern of Ahab, and even brought in Ahab's counselors to advise him (2 Chronicles 22:2-4). When Ahaziah was killed in battle Athaliah seized power and set her other sons to do evil, even desecrating the temple and its sacred things (2 Chronicles 24:7).

iv. If we are accurate in thinking that Joel prophesied in 835 B.C. then the judgment he described came toward the end of the six-year reign of ungodliness under Queen Athaliah. No wonder God brought a heavy hand on Judah!

v. "The name Joel means 'Jehovah is God' and therefore constitutes a short confession of faith, somewhat like the primary New Testament confession, 'Jesus is Lord.'" (Boice)

b. **What the chewing locust left, the swarming locust has eaten**: Joel was not announcing a coming judgment of the LORD. He describes their *present state* – devastated by successive swarms of locusts, first **chewing**, then **swarming**, then **crawling**, and finally **consuming**. Judah will experience a time of famine and financial ruin because of these locusts.

i. This plague was so unusual that Joel says, "**tell your children about it**." The times were so remarkably difficult that parents would tell their children, "I lived through the plagues of locusts."

ii. Boice writes that in 1915 a devastating plague of locusts covered what is modern-day Israel and Syria. The first swarms came in March, in clouds so thick they blocked out the sun. The female locusts immediately began to lay eggs, 100 at a time. Witnesses said that in one square yard, there were as many as 65,000 to 75,000 eggs. In a few weeks they hatched, and the young locusts resembled large ants. They couldn't yet fly and moved by hopping. They marched 400 to 600 feet a day (122 to 183 meters), devouring every speck of vegetation along the way. After two more stages of molting they became adults which could fly – and the devastation continued.

2. (5-7) An army of locusts against Judah.

Awake, you drunkards, and weep;
And wail, all you drinkers of wine,
Because of the new wine,
For it has been cut off from your mouth.
For a nation has come up against My land,
Strong, and without number;
His teeth *are* **the teeth of a lion,**
And he has the fangs of a fierce lion.
He has laid waste My vine,
And ruined My fig tree;
He has stripped it bare and thrown *it* **away;**
Its branches are made white.

>a. **Awake, you drunkards**: Joel tells the **drunkards** to wake up and see the devastation that the locusts had caused. They came like a mighty **nation**, a fierce army against Judah.

>b. **My vine…My fig tree**: God looks at the vines and fig trees of Judah and says they belong to Him, even in judgment.

3. (8-12) Judah mourns because of the destruction.

Lament like a virgin girded with sackcloth
For the husband of her youth.
The grain offering and the drink offering
Have been cut off from the house of the LORD**;**
The priests mourn, who minister to the LORD**.**
The field is wasted,
The land mourns;
For the grain is ruined,
The new wine is dried up,
The oil fails.

Be ashamed, you farmers,
Wail, you vinedressers,
For the wheat and the barley;
Because the harvest of the field has perished.
The vine has dried up,
And the fig tree has withered;
The pomegranate tree,
The palm tree also,
And the apple tree–
All the trees of the field are withered;
Surely joy has withered away from the sons of men.

a. **Lament like a virgin girded with sackcloth**: Joel told Judah that they should look at their condition and mourn, with all the emotion and passion of a young widow. They should not receive this plague of locusts stoically, with false bravado.

> i. In this, Joel didn't minimize the suffering at all. He wasn't like the dentist who says, "This may cause a bit of discomfort" when he really means "This is going to hurt and I am going to make you suffer." He deals with the suffering in a real way and says, "Let's turn back to the LORD."

b. **The priests mourn.... the land mourns.... Be ashamed, you farmers, wail, you vinedressers.... surely joy has withered away**: In vivid and poetic images, Joel shows how the whole nation mourns this great destruction brought by locusts.

> i. **The grain offering and the drink offering have been cut off**: It's remarkable to see that these sacrifices to the LORD at the temple only stopped when there was no more grain or wine to give to God. Queen Athaliah's reign was wicked, but she allowed the temple ceremonies to continue. This shows us that the devil doesn't mind ceremonies in themselves, and that the devil is more interested in *corrupting* true religion than *eliminating* it.

B. Drought devastates the land of Judah.

1. (13-14) A call to repentance.

Gird yourselves and lament, you priests;
Wail, you who minister before the altar;
Come, lie all night in sackcloth,
You who minister to my God;
For the grain offering and the drink offering
Are withheld from the house of your God.
Consecrate a fast,
Call a sacred assembly;
Gather the elders
***And* all the inhabitants of the land**
***Into* the house of the LORD your God,**
And cry out to the LORD.

a. **Gird yourselves and lament, you priests**: Joel called the religious leaders to lead the nation in repentance. He told the priests to **gird yourselves** for repentance, the idea being "prepare to do the work of repentance."

> i. Joel also told them *how* to do the work of repentance.

- **Consecrate a fast**: Make getting right with God so important that even eating isn't significant.
- **Call a sacred assembly**: Call for God's people to come together and repent.
- **Gather the elders**: Bring the elders together to lead in this act of repentance.
- **Into the house of the LORD your God**: Come to the place where you *should* meet together with God.
- **And cry out to the LORD**: Finally, simply cry out to God and trust that He will respond in mercy.

b. **For the grain offering and the drink offering are withheld from the house of your God**: When there was grain and wine to bring the people of Judah still brought offerings to the temple, either out of tradition or godly obedience. Now that there is no produce, there is no offering for **the house of your God**.

2. (15-20) The day of the LORD against Judah.

Alas for the day!
For the day of the LORD *is* at hand;
It shall come as destruction from the Almighty.
Is not the food cut off before our eyes,
Joy and gladness from the house of our God?
The seed shrivels under the clods,
Storehouses are in shambles;
Barns are broken down,
For the grain has withered.
How the animals groan!
The herds of cattle are restless,
Because they have no pasture;
Even the flocks of sheep suffer punishment.

O LORD, to You I cry out;
For fire has devoured the open pastures,
And a flame has burned all the trees of the field.
The beasts of the field also cry out to You,
For the water brooks are dried up,
And fire has devoured the open pastures.

a. **For the day of the LORD is at hand**: The idea behind the phrase **the day of the LORD** is that this is *God's* time. Man has his "day," and the LORD has His **day**. In the ultimate sense, **the day of the LORD** is fulfilled when Jesus judges the earth and returns in glory. In a lesser sense, a time of judgment as Judah experienced with the locusts and drought is also an example of **the day of the LORD**.

b. **The seed shrivels…. they have no pasture…the flocks of sheep suffer punishment…. fire has devoured the open pastures…. the water brooks are dried up**: Joel vividly described a devastating drought. It affected everything in Judah, and wildfires ravaged the dry land.

c. **O LORD, to You I cry out**: In this time of drought, all Judah could do was **cry out** to God. They were powerless to solve the problem of the drought. God sent them to a place where only heaven could help them, so they would look in no other place.

> i. In Luke 13:1-5 Jesus was confronted with the problem of a disaster that killed 18 people. Instead of acting as if it were just an accident of blind fate, Jesus used it as a wake-up call for repentance. Jesus showed that "Why did this disaster happen to them?" is the wrong question. The right question is "Am I ready to face such a disaster in this fallen world?"

Joel 2 – The Day of the LORD *and the Restoration of the* LORD

A. A mighty army to invade Judah.

1. (1-5) What the mighty army looks like.

Blow the trumpet in Zion,
And sound an alarm in My holy mountain!
Let all the inhabitants of the land tremble;
For the day of the LORD is coming,
For it is at hand:
A day of darkness and gloominess,
A day of clouds and thick darkness,
Like the morning *clouds* **spread over the mountains.**
A people *come,* **great and strong,**
The like of whom has never been;
Nor will there ever be any *such* **after them,**
Even for many successive generations.

A fire devours before them,
And behind them a flame burns;
The land *is* **like the Garden of Eden before them,**
And behind them a desolate wilderness;
Surely nothing shall escape them.
Their appearance is like the appearance of horses;
And like swift steeds, so they run.
With a noise like chariots
Over mountaintops they leap,
Like the noise of a flaming fire that devours the stubble,
Like a strong people set in battle array.

> a. **Let all the inhabitants of the land tremble; for the day of the LORD is coming, for it is at hand**: In Joel 1, the prophet spoke of the judgment

that *had arrived* in Judah (a plague of locusts and drought). In Joel 2, he begins by describing the judgment that *will come* – a mighty army set against Judah. Since this is all part of "God's day" not "man's day," it is described as **the day of the LORD**.

> i. When we are right with God, we *want* **the day of the LORD**. We long for Him to show His strength because we know that we abide in Him. When we are not right with God, we *dread* **the day of the LORD**, because when God shows Himself strong, His strength may work *against* us. In Joel's day Judah was not right with God; so **the day of the LORD** would be nothing but **darkness and gloominess** to them.

b. **A people come, great and strong**: It's hard to know what invasion Joel predicted here. Probably Joel warned of an invasion that never happened because Judah responded to the invitation to repent and God held back this army. The 40-year godly reign of King Joash in Judah began soon after the time of Joel's prophecy.

> i. There are some commentators who believe that Joel refers back to the army of locusts and describes them poetically. This is possible, but it seems best on balance to say that he wrote of a literal human army ready to come against an unrepentant Judah. Like an army of locusts, if they came, they would be massive, destructive, and unstoppable.

c. **A fire devours before them, and behind them a flame burns**: The urgent nature of this prophecy probably prompted Jehoiada to depose the wicked Queen Athaliah and set Joash on the throne, even though he was only seven years old (2 Kings 11:4-21). Perhaps Jehoiada would have waited until Joash was older, but Joel's prophecy showed him that it had to be done immediately.

2. (6-11) What the mighty army will do.

Before them the people writhe in pain;
All faces are drained of color.
They run like mighty men,
They climb the wall like men of war;
Every one marches in formation,
And they do not break ranks.
They do not push one another;
Every one marches in his own column.
Though they lunge between the weapons,
They are not cut down.
They run to and fro in the city,
They run on the wall;

They climb into the houses,
They enter at the windows like a thief.

The earth quakes before them,
The heavens tremble;
The sun and moon grow dark,
And the stars diminish their brightness.
The LORD gives voice before His army,
For His camp is very great;
For strong *is the One* who executes His word.
For the day of the LORD *is* great and very terrible;
Who can endure it?

    a. **They do not break ranks.... every one marches in his own column**: With a chilling poetic flair, Joel describes the discipline and effectiveness of this army. Because they keep ranks and work with energy (**they run to and fro in the city**) they bring a devastating attack on Judah.

        i. If we consider the people of God to be like an army – perhaps based on the military images Paul sprinkled through his letters – then this passage shows us two things that can make God's people more effective. First, they must *keep order*, with every soldier keeping ranks. Second, they must *work hard*, with every soldier serving with energy.

    b. **The LORD gives voice before His army**: As impressive as this army is, Joel does not want Judah to forget that its real power lies in the fact that God has sent them. They will be His tool of judgment against Judah – unless they repent.

        i. When the plague of locusts and the drought devastated Judah, you might have thought that Joel would encourage the people. He might have said, "Hang in there! Things are bad, but they will get better. Tough times don't last, but tough people do." Instead, Joel said, "You think that was bad? Worse is to come if we don't repent."

B. A promise of help to a repentant Judah.

1. (12-17) The prophet calls God's people to repent.

"Now, therefore," says the LORD,
"Turn to Me with all your heart,
With fasting, with weeping, and with mourning."
So rend your heart, and not your garments;
Return to the LORD your God,
For He *is* gracious and merciful,
Slow to anger, and of great kindness;
And He relents from doing harm.

Who knows *if* He will turn and relent,
And leave a blessing behind Him—
A grain offering and a drink offering
For the LORD your God?

Blow the trumpet in Zion,
Consecrate a fast, call a sacred assembly;
Gather the people,
Sanctify the congregation,
Assemble the elders,
Gather the children and nursing babes;
Let the bridegroom go out from his chamber,
And the bride from her dressing room.
Let the priests, who minister to the LORD,
Weep between the porch and the altar;
Let them say, "Spare Your people, O LORD,
And do not give Your heritage to reproach,
That the nations should rule over them.
Why should they say among the peoples,
'Where *is* their God?'"

> a. **Now, therefore…turn to Me with all your heart, with fasting, with weeping, and with mourning**: *Because* they heard the warning of judgment, God's people should repent. It doesn't make their repentance less valid because they had to be scared into it. The important thing is that they turn back to the LORD in *sincerity*, and God tells them how.
>
>> i. Sincere repentance is to **turn to** God, and therefore *away from* our sin.
>>
>> ii. Sincere repentance is done **with all your heart**, giving everything you can in surrender to God.
>>
>> iii. Sincere repentance is marked by *action* (**with fasting**) and *emotion* (**with weeping…mourning**). Not every act of repentance will include **fasting** and **weeping**, but if *action* and *emotion* are absent, it isn't real repentance.
>
> b. **Rend your heart, and not your garments**: One expression of mourning in Jewish culture was, and is, the tearing of the clothes. It was a way to say, "I am so overcome with grief that I don't care if my clothes are ruined and I look bad." Joel knew that someone could tear their **garments** without tearing their **heart**, and he described the kind of heart-repentance that really pleases God.

i. Spurgeon tells the story of a woman who came seeming to be in great sorrow, saying what a great sinner she was, but Spurgeon suspected her repentance wasn't sincere. He said, "Well, if you are a sinner of course you have broken God's laws. Let's read the Ten Commandments and see which ones you have broken." They started at the first: "You shall have no other gods before Me," and Spurgeon asked her if she ever broke that commandment. "Oh no," she said, "not that I know of." "'You shall not make any graven image' – did you ever break that one?" "Never, sir," she answered. As you might suppose, Spurgeon went through all Ten Commandments and she could not find a single one that she had broken, and what he suspected was true. She didn't really consider herself a sinner, and she was making a show of repentance because she thought it was expected of her.

c. **Return to the LORD your God, for He *is* gracious and merciful, slow to anger, and of great kindness; and He relents from doing harm**: Knowing the goodness and mercy of God is another motive for true repentance. We come to Him confident that He will heal and forgive, and that He may relent from the judgment He announced.

i. We don't repent with the idea "God is so mean that if I don't return to Him, He will destroy me." Instead, the idea is "God is so **gracious and merciful, slow to anger, and of great kindness** that He will spare me from what I deserve if I turn back to Him." Ultimately, it is His goodness that leads us to repentance (Romans 2:4).

d. **Let the bridegroom go out from his chamber, and the bride from her dressing room**: In addition to the same pattern of repentance he presented in Joel 1:14, Joel adds the ideas relevant to the **bridegroom** and the **bride**. The idea with these images is that in a time of repentance God's people cannot carry on "as usual." Usually, the **bridegroom** belongs in **his chamber** and the **bride** belongs in **her dressing room**, but not now – it was time to repent. True repentance does not carry on with business as usual.

e. **Let the priests, who minister to the LORD, weep between the porch and the altar**: Leaders among God's people must especially lead in repentance. They can't come with the attitude that "the people" must repent. They must regard themselves as the people and the people as themselves and lead in repentance.

f. **Spare Your people, O LORD, and do not give Your heritage to reproach**: Joel puts a rich prayer of repentance into the mouths of God's priests. It's as if the priests should pray with the thought, "How can we persuade God to have mercy on us?"

i. **Spare**: This implies that God's people deserve judgment, but they plead for mercy.

ii. **Your people**: This reminds God that they belong to Him and provides another motivation for mercy.

iii. **Do not give Your heritage to reproach**: This tells God that mercy to His people will bring Him glory among the nations and that judgment may bring His name into discredit.

2. (18-20) God promises to defend His repentant people against the mighty army.

Then the Lord will be zealous for His land,
And pity His people.
The Lord will answer and say to His people,
"Behold, I will send you grain and new wine and oil,
And you will be satisfied by them;
I will no longer make you a reproach among the nations.

"But I will remove far from you the northern *army,*
And will drive him away into a barren and desolate land,
With his face toward the eastern sea
And his back toward the western sea;
His stench will come up,
And his foul odor will rise,
Because he has done monstrous things."

a. **Then the Lord will be zealous for His land, and pity His people**: Judah could know that when God's people sincerely repent, He notices from heaven. His zeal and pity are then turned *to* His people.

b. **I will send you grain and new wine and oil… I will remove far from you the northern army**: God promised to restore material prosperity to a repentant Judah and to defeat the mighty army from the north. Because this mighty army had **done monstrous things**, God would turn the attention of His judgment away from His people and against this mighty army.

3. (21-27) Confidence in God's promise of restoration.

Fear not, O land;
Be glad and rejoice,
For the Lord has done marvelous things!
Do not be afraid, you beasts of the field;
For the open pastures are springing up,
And the tree bears its fruit;
The fig tree and the vine yield their strength.
Be glad then, you children of Zion,

And rejoice in the LORD your God;
For He has given you the former rain faithfully,
And He will cause the rain to come down for you—
The former rain,
And the latter rain in the first month.
The threshing floors shall be full of wheat,
And the vats shall overflow with new wine and oil.

"So I will restore to you the years that the swarming locust has eaten,
The crawling locust,
The consuming locust,
And the chewing locust,
My great army which I sent among you.
You shall eat in plenty and be satisfied,
And praise the name of the LORD your God,
Who has dealt wondrously with you;
And My people shall never be put to shame.
Then you shall know that I am in the midst of Israel:
I am the LORD your God
And there is no other.
My people shall never be put to shame.

a. **Be glad and rejoice, for the LORD has done marvelous things!** Joel looked forward to the restoration that God promised, and he told Judah to look forward in faith, and to praise God for the restoration He promised – even before they saw it with their own eyes.

b. **The open pastures are springing up, and the tree bears its fruit**: With the eye of faith, Joel could already see it happening. All around him were the lush, fruitful pastures and trees that God had restored after the destruction of the locusts.

c. **He has given you the former rain faithfully…and the latter rain in the first month**: At the end of Joel 1, the prophet saw the destruction drought brought. Now with the eye of faith, he sees God restoring both the **former** and the **latter** rain to Israel.

i. Ancient Israel had no irrigation system and relied on rain to water their crops. In a time of drought, nothing grew. God promises to restore both the **former rain** (falling in autumn) and the **latter rain** (falling in spring). When God restores these rains, Judah will have full threshing floors and wine vats.

ii. This passage along with others (Deuteronomy 11:14, Hosea 6:3) were taken to give the name of the Latter Rain movement started in 1948 by William Branham. Branham influenced a generation of

Pentecostal preachers, including a young protégé named Oral Roberts. Marked by strange and aberrant doctrine and practices, the movement eventually faded from prominence and Branham himself died in a traffic collision with a drunk driver in 1965. He died on Christmas Eve, and his faithful followers believed that he would rise from the dead, so they delayed his burial for several days. But the influence of the Latter Rain movement lived on. The Latter Rain popularized many attitudes and doctrines prominent in some revival movements today:

- The "five-fold ministry" and "restoration of apostle and prophets."
- The "foundational truths" of Hebrews 6:1-2.
- An emphasis on signs and wonders as marks of true revival.
- A strong emphasis on unity.
- Replacement theology, replacing Israel with the church.
- Dominion theology, saying the church will conquer and rule the world.
- An elitist attitude, promoting the idea of a group of "super-christians."

iii. Some researchers – and many within these modern groups today – believe that a number of modern "revival" movements are really just a continuation of the Latter Rain movement. Movements such as Joel's Army, the Manifest Sons of God, the Dominion Movement, the Kansas City Prophets, the Toronto Blessing, and the Pensacola Revival are connected in some way to the Latter Rain movement. For example, Paul Cain – later to re-emerge as head of the Kansas City Prophets in 1989 – traveled with William Branham and called him "the greatest prophet that ever lived."

d. **I will restore to you the years that the swarming locust has eaten**: God promised to **restore** what was taken away in chastisement. When the locusts did their work, it looked complete and final, but God promised that He could even restore **the years that the swarming locust has eaten**.

i. "It will strike you at once that the locusts did not eat the years: the locusts ate the fruits of the years' labour, the harvests of the fields; so that the meaning of the restoration of the years must be the restoration of those fruits and of those harvests which the locusts consumed. You cannot have back your time; but there is a strange and wonderful way in which God can give back to you the wasted blessings, the unripened fruits of years over which you mourned. The fruits of wasted years may yet be yours." (Spurgeon)

4. (28-32) The ultimate restoration and the ultimate day of the LORD.

"And it shall come to pass afterward
That I will pour out My Spirit on all flesh;
Your sons and your daughters shall prophesy,
Your old men shall dream dreams,
Your young men shall see visions.
And also on My menservants and on My maidservants
I will pour out My Spirit in those days.

"And I will show wonders in the heavens and in the earth:
Blood and fire and pillars of smoke.
The sun shall be turned into darkness,
And the moon into blood,
Before the coming of the great and awesome day of the LORD.
And it shall come to pass that whoever calls on the name of the LORD
Shall be saved.
For in Mount Zion and in Jerusalem there shall be deliverance,
As the LORD has said,
Among the remnant whom the LORD calls.

a. **It shall come to pass afterward**: After the restoration Joel spoke of previously in the chapter, there will come a time of ultimate restoration and blessing. This latter time will be marked by an outpouring of God's **Spirit on all flesh** – not only selected men at selected times for selected duties.

i. The Old Testament has a rich record of the work of the Spirit, but He was not poured out **on all flesh** under the old covenant. Instead, certain men were filled with the Spirit at certain times and only for certain duties. It was rather selective:

- Joseph was filled with the Spirit of God (Genesis 41:38).
- The craftsmen who built the tabernacle were filled with the Spirit of God (Exodus 31:3).
- Joshua was filled with the Spirit of God (Numbers 27:18).
- Othniel was filled with the Spirit of God (Judges 3:10).
- Gideon was filled with the Spirit of God (Judges 6:34).
- Jephthah was filled with the Spirit of God (Judges 11:29).

- Samson was filled with the Spirit of God (Judges 13:25, 14:6, 14:19, 15:14).
- Saul was filled with the Spirit of God (1 Samuel 10:9-10).
- David was filled with the Spirit of God (1 Samuel 16:13).

ii. Here, Joel looked forward to the glorious new covenant, when the Spirit of God would be poured out **on all flesh**. Why, even ***your* sons and daughters**, ***your* old men**, and ***your* young men** would be filled with the Spirit of God.

iii. This was fulfilled on the day of Pentecost when the disciples gathered in the upper room, waiting in Jerusalem for the outpouring of the Holy Spirit that Jesus promised would come (Acts 1:4-5). When the outpouring of the Spirit came, the 120 followers of Jesus were all filled with the Spirit and began to praise God in other tongues. Jerusalem was crowded at that time, because of the feast of Pentecost – so a crowd quickly gathered because of the commotion. Those who heard the disciples praise God in these miraculous languages began to mock them, claiming they were drunk. Peter stood up and boldly set the record straight: the disciples were not drunk at all, but this was a fulfillment of Joel's great prophecy of the outpouring of the Spirit.

iv. At first, any Jew would scoff at the idea of 120 followers of a crucified man being filled with the Holy Spirit. Based on their understanding of the Old Testament they would think, "These 120 people are not kings or prophets or priests; God only pours out His Spirit on special people for special duties. These are common folk, and God doesn't pour out His Spirit on them." Peter uses the prophecy of Joel to show them that things are different now, just as God said they would be. Now, the Holy Spirit is poured out upon all who believe and receive, even the common folk. Now God offered a new covenant relationship, and part of the new covenant was the outpouring of the Spirit for all who receive in faith.

v. Peter's sermon of the day of Pentecost also shows us that there is *never* any disparity between the work of the Spirit and the work of the word. When Peter was filled with the Spirit of God in the midst of miraculous signs and wonders as he had never experienced before, what did he do? He said, "Let's open up our Bibles to the book of Joel." He had a Bible study, one that both *taught the 120 disciples* (they better understood their experience according to the Scriptures) and *called the lost* to salvation.

vi. We also notice that Peter's application was exactly the same as the application made by the prophet Joel: *repent*. Joel said, *"Now, therefore," says the* LORD, *"Turn to Me with all your heart, with fasting, with weeping, and with mourning." So rend your heart, and not your garments; return to the* LORD *your God* (Joel 2:12-13) Peter said, *Repent, and let every one of you be baptized in the name of Jesus Christ for the remission of sins; and you shall receive the gift of the Holy Spirit.* (Acts 2:38)

b. **And also on My menservants and on My maidservants**: In this latter time, all the servants of the LORD will be filled with His Spirit in this unique and powerful way. Under the new covenant, every believer can receive the full measure of the Spirit and be used in a special and wonderful way.

i. Sometimes the common churchgoer simply wants a building to worship in, a nice service that isn't too offensive, and a good sermon – after that he thinks, *leave me alone*. That isn't new covenant Christianity, which sees the work of the ministry as belonging to the people, not the "clergy."

ii. Some people have taken this idea and run too far with it saying, "Therefore we don't need ministers or clergy. We believe in the priesthood of all believers, so there is no room for offices of any kind in the church." This ignores the clear teaching of Scripture, which says that the work of the ministry belongs to all the people of God, but the work of equipping the saints belongs to God-appointed offices and ministries (Ephesians 4:7-16). It is *because* the ministry belongs to all Christians that God has appointed offices and ministries to equip every saint to fulfill their role. Acts 2:42-47 describes a wonderful fulfillment of this ideal.

c. **I will show wonders in the heavens and in the earth**: This time of great outpouring of the Spirit of God will culminate with cataclysmic signs in the heavens and **the great and awesome day of the** LORD.

i. On the day of Pentecost, the prophecy of Joel was fulfilled, but not consummated. Peter rightly saw that this was a remarkable outpouring of the Spirit of God, given freely upon all who believe and receive, as was promised in the new covenant (Ezekiel 11:19, 36:24-28). The prophecy of Joel was also especially appropriate because the day of Pentecost ushered in the last days, with the beginning of the church as understood by the New Testament. Since that time, the church has not been rushing towards a distant edge that represents the consummation of all things. Instead, on Pentecost the church came to the edge – and has run parallel to the brink for some 2,000 years.

d. **Whoever calls on the name of the LORD shall be saved**: This is another glorious promise associated with the time Joel said **shall come to pass afterward**. In this time of the poured-out Spirit of God, salvation will no longer be a matter of association with national Israel. Instead, **whoever calls on the name of the LORD shall be saved** – no matter what nation they come from.

   i. This is a broad call – *whoever* **calls on the name of the LORD shall be saved**. "'Ah!' you say, 'I wish my name was written down in the Bible.' Would it comfort you at all? If it were written in the Scripture, 'Charles Haddon Spurgeon shall be saved,' I am afraid I should not get much comfort out of the promise, for I should go home, and fetch out the London Directory, and see if there was not another person of that name, or very like it. How much worse would it be for the Smiths and the Browns! No, my brethren, do not ask to see your name in the inspired volume; but be content with what you do see, namely, your character! When the Scripture says, 'Whosoever,' you cannot shut yourself out of that." (Spurgeon)

   ii. This is a call to prayer – **whoever *calls* on the name of the LORD shall be saved**. "You cannot perish praying; no one has ever done so. If you could perish praying, you would be a new wonder in the universe. A praying soul in hell is an utter impossibility. A man calling on God and rejected of God! – the supposition is not to be endured. 'Whosoever shall call on the name of the Lord shall be saved.' God himself must lie, he must quit his nature, forfeit his claim to mercy, destroy his character of love, if he were to let a poor sinner call upon his name, and yet refuse to hear him." (Spurgeon)

   iii. This is a call to come to the true God – **whoever calls on the name of the *LORD* shall be saved**. Coming to a false god, a god of your own imagination will do you no good. The god of your opinion does not exist and cannot save you. You must come to the God of the Bible. "The pity of it is that the most of people in these days worship a god of their own invention. They do not make an image of clay, or of gold, but they construct a deity in their minds according to their own thoughts. They proudly judge as to what God ought to be, and they will not receive God as he really is. What is this but a god-making as gross as that which is performed by the heathen? What can be more wicked than to attempt to imagine a better god than the one true and living God? As the deity of your fancy has no existence, I would not recommend you to trust in him." (Spurgeon)

iv. This is a call to come to God intelligently – **whoever calls on *the name* of the L**ORD **shall be saved**. "Now, by the word 'name' we understand the person, the character of the Lord. The more, then, you know about the Lord, and the better you know his name, the more intelligently will you call upon that name. If you know his power, you will call upon that power to help you. If you know his mercy, you will call upon him in his grace to save you. If you know his wisdom, you feel that he knows your difficulties, and can help you through them." (Spurgeon)

v. This is a certain promise – **whoever calls on the name of the L**ORD ***shall be saved***. It is a profound mystery why all do not receive this great invitation, but the text itself tells us that only a remnant receives it (**among the remnant whom the L**ORD **calls**). Yet all who do come are certainly saved. "Suppose we, who trust alone in Jesus, should perish, what then? Why, it would be to the everlasting dishonour of the Lord in whom we trusted. We should lose our souls certainly, but he would lose his honour. Think of one of us being able to say in hell, 'I trusted in the boasted Saviour's aid, and rested myself on God, and yet I am lost.' Sirs, heaven itself would be darkened, and the crown jewels of God would lose their lustre, if that could once be the case! But it cannot be. If you trust in the Lord God Almighty, he will save you as surely as he is God." (Spurgeon)

Joel 3 – Judgment in the Valley of Decision

A. A warning to the nations.

1. (1-3) A promise to bring back scattered and mistreated Israel.

**"For behold, in those days and at that time,
When I bring back the captives of Judah and Jerusalem,
I will also gather all nations,
And bring them down to the Valley of Jehoshaphat;
And I will enter into judgment with them there
On account of My people, My heritage Israel,
Whom they have scattered among the nations;
They have also divided up My land.
They have cast lots for My people,
Have given a boy as payment for a harlot,
And sold a girl for wine, that they may drink.**

> a. **In those days and at that time**: Joel's prophecy still concerns the time period connected with *it shall come to pass afterward* mentioned in Joel 2:28. This is the broad period of the last days, initiated by the Ascension of Jesus and the birth of the church on the day of Pentecost.
>
>> i. Many have the wrong idea of the "last days," thinking only in terms of the final years or months immediately before the return of Jesus in glory to this earth, or the rapture of the church. Scripturally, we can think of the last days as an *era*, one that began with the birth of the church on the day of Pentecost. Since that time, the church has not been rushing towards a distant edge that represents the consummation of all things. Instead, on Pentecost the church came to the edge – and has run parallel to the brink for some 2,000 years.
>
> b. **When I bring back the captives of Judah and Jerusalem**: In a lesser and immediate sense this was fulfilled in the return from the Babylonian exile. In the greater and ultimate sense it will be fulfilled in the end-times regathering of Israel, to the point where an expectant Israel welcomes Jesus

saying, "Blessed is He who comes in the name of the Lord" (Matthew 23:39) and salvation comes to Israel as a whole (Romans 11:26-27).

c. I will also gather all nations, and bring them down to the Valley of Jehoshaphat: Joel here describes the final gathering of the nations in rebellion against God at the battle of Armageddon (Revelation 16:12-16). There is no place in Israel known as the **Valley of Jehoshaphat** but the name **Jehoshaphat** means, "The LORD Judges." It describes God's place of judgment.

> i. "There is no such valley in the land of Judea; and hence the name must be *symbolical*. It signifies the *judgment of God*, or *Jehovah judgeth*." (Clarke)

> ii. This is a judgment of **all nations**. Joel was written at a time when a terrible plague of locusts brought the judgment of God upon the people of God. At a time like that, it is easy to think "God, You are dealing harshly with us, but what about the ungodly nations? We may be bad, but they are worse. Don't you care about them?" God used Joel 3 to assure His people that the **nations** will be dealt with.

d. I will enter into judgment with them there on account of My people: God's complaint against the nations is that they have mistreated His **people**. Primarily, this has in view the way the nations treat Israel, but also extends to how the nations treat the church. When God's people are mistreated, God takes it personally and will avenge it.

> i. In the judgment of the nations that Jesus described in Matthew 25:31-46, the criteria is not faith in Jesus Christ but how the nations have treated the people of Israel – the *brethren* of Jesus. Held on the earth after His return in glory, this judgment determines who is allowed to enter into the Millennial Earth, and who goes straight to judgment.

> ii. **They have cast lots for My people**: It is bad enough for man to regard any human life as cheap; it is worse to regard the **people** of God as cheap. God remembers and will repay.

2. (4-8) God warns the nations that He will retaliate against those who have mistreated His people.

**"Indeed, what have you to do with Me,
O Tyre and Sidon, and all the coasts of Philistia?
Will you retaliate against Me?
But if you retaliate against Me,
Swiftly and speedily I will return your retaliation upon your own head;
Because you have taken My silver and My gold,
And have carried into your temples My prized possessions.**

Also the people of Judah and the people of Jerusalem
You have sold to the Greeks,
That you may remove them far from their borders.

"Behold, I will raise them
Out of the place to which you have sold them,
And will return your retaliation upon your own head.
I will sell your sons and your daughters
Into the hand of the people of Judah,
And they will sell them to the Sabeans,
To a people far off;
For the LORD has spoken."

> a. **Will you retaliate against Me?** God virtually challenges the nations to come against Him or His people. He vows to **return your retaliation upon your own head** to those who come against Him or His people.
>
>> i. Judgment is about the only aspect of God's plan of the ages that is plainly logical. The grace and mercy of God are not plainly logical. Salvation by grace through faith is not plainly logical. The high standing and destiny of the believer in Jesus are not plainly logical. Judgment – God simply giving those who reject Him what they deserve – *is plainly logical.* It is as if God says to the wicked, "You rejected the mercy and grace of heaven, so I will give you the plain logic of earth: you will receive what you deserve before the holy court of My justice."
>
> b. **I will sell your sons and your daughters into the hand of the people of Judah**: The nations treated God's people with contempt and had no sense of their worth. Therefore, God will repay them with the contempt they put upon His people, vowing to **return your retaliation upon your own head**.
>
>> i. Trapp details the horrors that befell the ten Emperors of the Roman Empire that persecuted Christians:
>>
>> - Nero lost 30,000 of his subjects by pestilence, had his armies utterly defeated in Britain, suffered a revolution in Armenia, and was so hated by the senators of Rome that they forced him to kill himself.
>> - Domitian was butchered by his own soldiers.
>> - Trajan died of a foul disease.
>> - Severus died miserably on a military campaign in Britain.
>> - Maximus was cut in pieces, together with his son.
>> - Decius died as an exile in a far country.

- Valerian was whipped to death as a captive of the king of Persia.
- Aurelian was killed by his own soldiers.
- Diocletian poisoned himself.
- Maximum hanged himself.

ii. "Ye cannot tread upon the least toe in Christ's mystical body, but the head cries out from heaven, Why hurtest thou me?" (Trapp) Paul found this out on the road to Damascus, when Jesus asked him *Saul, Saul, why are you persecuting Me?* (Acts 9:4)

B. A proclamation to the nations.

1. (9-13) Gathering the nations for a war of judgment.

Proclaim this among the nations:
"Prepare for war!
Wake up the mighty men,
Let all the men of war draw near,
Let them come up.
Beat your plowshares into swords
And your pruning hooks into spears;
Let the weak say, 'I am strong.'"
Assemble and come, all you nations,
And gather together all around.
Cause Your mighty ones to go down there, O LORD.

"Let the nations be wakened, and come up to the Valley of Jehoshaphat;
For there I will sit to judge all the surrounding nations.
Put in the sickle, for the harvest is ripe.
Come, go down;
For the winepress is full,
The vats overflow–
For their wickedness is great."

a. **Prepare for war**: God challenged the nations to **prepare for war** against Him. They will one day do this exact thing (Revelation 16:12-16), but God will simply laugh at the puny and futile preparations by the nations (Psalm 2).

i. **Beat your plowshares into swords**: If you are going to go into battle against God, you should have every weapon available. You should also practice your best positive thinking: **let the weak say, "I am strong."** Nevertheless, the most positive attitude can't work when man sets himself against his Maker. There was a Broadway play titled "Your

Arms Too Short to Box with God." This is what the nations don't know but will learn the hard way.

b. **I will sit to judge all the surrounding nations**: Though the nations will come against God and His Messiah with every weapon and the most positive frame of mind, it is all for nothing. They will be plucked like a ripe harvest and crushed in judgment.

i. Psalm 2 beautifully expresses the folly of the nations and the triumph of the LORD: *Why do the nations rage, and the people plot a vain thing? The kings of the earth set themselves, and the rulers take counsel together, against the LORD and against His Anointed, saying, "Let us break their bonds in pieces and cast away their cords from us." He who sits in the heavens shall laugh; the LORD shall hold them in derision. Then He shall speak to them in His wrath, and distress them in His deep displeasure: "Yet I have set My King on My holy hill of Zion"* (Psalm 2:1-6).

c. **Put in the sickle, for the harvest is ripe. Come, go down; for the winepress is full**: Revelation 14:17-20 also uses this image of the winepress of the wrath of God to describe Jesus' judgment on the nations at Armageddon.

2. (14-17) The Day of the LORD in the valley of decision.

Multitudes, multitudes in the valley of decision!
For the day of the LORD is near in the valley of decision.
The sun and moon will grow dark,
And the stars will diminish their brightness.
The LORD also will roar from Zion,
And utter His voice from Jerusalem;
The heavens and earth will shake;
But the LORD will be a shelter for His people,
And the strength of the children of Israel.

"So you shall know that I am the LORD your God,
Dwelling in Zion My holy mountain.
Then Jerusalem shall be holy,
And no aliens shall ever pass through her again."

a. **Multitudes, multitudes in the valley of decision**: Joel looked out upon the Valley of Jehoshaphat at the battle of Armageddon, and saw **multitudes** facing their eternal fate – truly, it was a **valley of decision**, and those who fought against the LORD and His Messiah were in the wrong place in the **valley of decision**, ultimately fulfilled at the battle of Armageddon.

i. The idea of the "valley of decision" has been used in countless evangelistic meetings to show people that *they* stand in the valley of decision, and must decide for or against Jesus. Joel's context is exactly the opposite. Man does indeed stand in the **valley of decision**, but it is God who does the deciding, not man. It is a valley of judgment – and we should decide for Jesus right now so that we never stand in this **valley of decision**.

b. **The heavens and earth will shake**: Joel goes back to the descriptions of the cosmic cataclysm that were mentioned in Joel 2:30-31. In the midst of it all, **the LORD will be a shelter for His people, and the strength of the children of Israel**, and He will restore both His people and His city to glory.

3. (18-21) Blessing on God's people; desolation for the nations.

And it will come to pass in that day
That the mountains shall drip with new wine,
The hills shall flow with milk,
And all the brooks of Judah shall be flooded with water;
A fountain shall flow from the house of the LORD
And water the Valley of Acacias.

"Egypt shall be a desolation,
And Edom a desolate wilderness,
Because of violence against the people of Judah,
For they have shed innocent blood in their land.
But Judah shall abide forever,
And Jerusalem from generation to generation.
For I will acquit them of the guilt of bloodshed, whom I had not acquitted;
For the LORD dwells in Zion."

a. **The mountains shall drip with new wine…all the brooks of Judah shall be flooded with water**: After God's final victory, there is lasting abundance, and the days of drought are just a distant memory. Instead, **Egypt shall be a desolation**, along with the other enemies of the LORD and His people.

i. **A fountain shall flow from the house of the LORD**: Ezekiel 47 describes waters flowing **from the house of the LORD** in the time after Jesus' triumphant return, in the millennium. Zechariah 14:8 also speaks of a great flow of water from Jerusalem, emptying both into the Dead Sea and the Mediterranean Sea.

ii. The **Valley of Acacias** (Valley of Shittim) was a place associated with both failure and victory. It is located on the eastern side of the Jordan River, to the north of the Dead Sea. It was where the king of Moab sent his young women to the men of Israel to seduce them into idolatry and sexual immorality (Numbers 25:1-3). It was also the launching place for the armies of Israel when they set out against Jericho and Canaan in the days of Joshua (Joshua 2:1 and 3:1). When water **from the house of the L**ORD flows down to **the Valley of Acacias**, then God's grace and provision cover the past – every sin, every victory is covered over by Him.

b. But Judah shall abide forever…. for the LORD **dwells in Zion**: God will show mercy to His people and grant them forgiveness. This prophecy of Joel, which began with the desperate plague of locusts, ends with a promise of restoration and redemption.

i. "This is the last promise, but not the least. It referreth, saith Danaeus, to Christ taking our flesh, by which he dwelt among us being God manifest in the flesh…. since he dwelleth with his Church for ever, as it is in the precedent verse, and maketh her a true Jehovah Shammah, as she is called Ezekiel 48:35." (Trapp)

ii. "This prophet, who has many things similar to Ezekiel, ends his prophecy in nearly the same way: *Ezekiel* says of the glory of the Church, *Yehovah shammah*, THE LORD IS THERE. *Joel* says, *Yehovah shochen betsiyon*, THE LORD DWELLETH IN ZION. Both point out the continued indwelling of Christ among his people." (Clarke)

Amos 1 – Judgment on the Nations

A. The man and his message.

1. (1) Amos the man.

The words of Amos, who was among the sheepbreeders of Tekoa, which he saw concerning Israel in the days of Uzziah king of Judah, and in the days of Jeroboam the son of Joash, king of Israel, two years before the earthquake.

a. **The words of Amos**: This book of the prophet Amos is the only mention we have of this man in the Old Testament. The books of 1 and 2 Kings and 1 and 2 Chronicles do not mention this prophet, and he should not be confused with *Amoz*, the father of Isaiah the prophet (Isaiah 1:1).

i. The name **Amos** means *burden* or *burden bearer*. Since most of the prophecies of Amos concern coming judgment on either the nations surrounding Israel or judgment on Israel itself, he was a man with a *burden*.

b. **Who was among the sheepbreeders of Tekoa**: It seems that Amos had no formal theological or prophetic training, though there was a school of the prophets known as the *sons of the prophets* at that time (1 Kings 20:35, 2 Kings 2:3-15, 2 Kings 4:1, 2 Kings 4:38). Amos was a simple man, a farmer, who had been uniquely called to ministry.

i. Amos spoke of his background and calling in Amos 7:14-15: *I was no prophet, nor was I a son of a prophet, but I was a sheepbreeder and a tender of sycamore fruit. Then the* LORD *took me as I followed the flock, and the* LORD *said to me, 'Go, prophesy to My people Israel.'*

ii. Amos used an unusual word to describe his occupation. Instead of calling himself a *shepherd*, the literal ancient Hebrew described Amos as a *sheep raiser*. Amos probably chose this title to emphasize the fact that he really was a shepherd, and that he did not mean "shepherd" in a symbolic, spiritual sense. The way God used Amos reminds us of the way He used the twelve disciples of Jesus – common, workingmen used to do great things for God.

iii. Amos was from Tekoa, a city about ten miles from Jerusalem. It seems that he delivered his prophetic message at Bethel (Amos 7:13), one of the southernmost cities of Israel – not very far from Tekoa.

c. **Which he saw concerning Israel**: Amos was primarily a prophet to **Israel**, though he also spoke to many nations. He served in the days of the divided monarchy (in **the days of Uzziah king of Judah, and in the days of Jeroboam the son of Joash**). Most researchers date the ministry of Amos somewhere between 760 B.C. and 750 B.C.

i. When Amos served as a prophet, the people of God had been divided into two nations for more than 150 years. The southern nation was known as **Judah**, and the northern nation was still known as **Israel**. During the period of the divided monarchy the southern kingdom of Judah saw a succession of kings, some godly and some ungodly (**Uzziah** was one of the better kings of Judah). The northern kingdom of **Israel** saw nothing but a series of wicked kings. **Jeroboam the son of Joash** was one of the better kings among these wicked men – especially in a political and military sense – but he was still an ungodly man (2 Kings 14:23-29).

ii. For most of its history, the northern kingdom of Israel struggled against Syria – her neighbor to the north. But around the year 800 B.C., the mighty Assyrian Empire defeated Syria and neutralized this power that hindered Israel's expansion and prosperity. With Syria in check, Israel enjoyed great prosperity during the reign of Jeroboam II.

iii. **Two years before the earthquake**: "We have no independent record of this earthquake, so *that* phrase is no help to us in dating." (Boice)

2. (2) The message of Amos.

And he said:
"The LORD roars from Zion,
And utters His voice from Jerusalem;
The pastures of the shepherds mourn,
And the top of Carmel withers."

a. **The LORD roars from Zion**: Amos brought a message of judgment. The first two chapters of Amos describe the judgment of the LORD, first against Gentile nations then against Judah and Israel.

b. **And utters His voice from Jerusalem**: Israel – in direct disobedience to God – established rival centers of worship in Dan, Bethel, and Gilgal.

When Amos said that the LORD speaks from Jerusalem, he reminded all of Israel where the center of true worship was.

c. **The pastures of the shepherds mourn**: Since Amos was a shepherd himself (Amos 7:14) he knew how the judgment of God could affect the land. If God withheld rain, sent plagues, or allowed conquering armies to come upon the land, it made **the pastures of the shepherds mourn**.

d. **The top of Carmel withers**: Mount **Carmel** was prominent in the north of Israel, the site of Elijah's dramatic confrontation with the prophets of Baal (1 Kings 18:19-40). Since Elijah served before the time of Amos, it may be that Amos was reminding Israel of this victory of the Lord GOD over idolatry.

B. Judgment on the nations.

1. (3-5) Judgment on Damascus, the capital of Syria.

Thus says the LORD:

"For three transgressions of Damascus, and for four,
I will not turn away its *punishment*,
Because they have threshed Gilead with implements of iron.
But I will send a fire into the house of Hazael,
Which shall devour the palaces of Ben-Hadad.
I will also break the *gate* bar of Damascus,
And cut off the inhabitant from the Valley of Aven,
And the one who holds the scepter from Beth Eden.
The people of Syria shall go captive to Kir,"
Says the LORD.

a. **For three transgressions of Damascus, and for four, I will not turn away its punishment**: This phrase will introduce God's announcement of judgment against each nation. It didn't mean that **Damascus** only committed three sins, and then God thought of a fourth sin; it simply has the idea of "sin upon sin upon sin."

b. **Because they have threshed Gilead with implements of iron**: The region of **Gilead** belonged to Israel, and God promised to judge Damascus and the Syrians for coming against the land of God's people, and inflicting such complete destruction that it would be as if a deep plow had been run through the land.

i. "*Threshing sledges* with iron prongs or teeth are probably a figure of speech implying extreme cruelty and utter thoroughness in the treatment of those who opposed." (Hubbard)

c. **The people of Syria shall go captive to Kir**: This was fulfilled in 2 Kings 16:9, which describes when the Assyrians attacked Syria because King Ahaz of Judah paid them to. *So the king of Assyria heeded him; for the king of Assyria went up against Damascus and took it, carried its people captive to Kir, and killed Rezin* (2 Kings 16:9).

2. (6-8) Judgment on Gaza, a city of the Philistines.

Thus says the LORD:

"For three transgressions of Gaza, and for four,
I will not turn away its *punishment*,
Because they took captive the whole captivity
To deliver *them* up to Edom.
But I will send a fire upon the wall of Gaza,
Which shall devour its palaces.
I will cut off the inhabitant from Ashdod,
And the one who holds the scepter from Ashkelon;
I will turn My hand against Ekron,
And the remnant of the Philistines shall perish,"
Says the Lord GOD.

a. **Because they took captive the whole captivity to deliver them up to Edom**: **Gaza** was a city of the Philistines, on the coast to the west of Israel and Judah. Because they came against God's people to **deliver them up to Edom**, God promised to bring judgment against **Gaza** and the other cities of the Philistines (**Ashdod**, **Ashkelon**, and **Ekron**).

i. **The whole captivity**: "The condemnation here is not against slavery in and of itself, just as the previous oracle was not against war in and of itself. The crime is not that soldiers were enslaved after being taken in battle, which was the standard practice, but that the Philistines used their temporary supremacy to enslave whole populations – soldiers and civilians, men and women, adults and children, young and old – for commercial profit. Gaza did not even need the slaves. She merely sold them to Edom for more money." (Boice)

3. (9-10) Judgment on Tyre, a city of Lebanon.

Thus says the LORD:

"For three transgressions of Tyre, and for four,
I will not turn away its *punishment*,
Because they delivered up the whole captivity to Edom,
And did not remember the covenant of brotherhood.
But I will send a fire upon the wall of Tyre,
Which shall devour its palaces."

    a. **Because they delivered up the whole captivity to Edom**: Since the city of **Tyre** (of Lebanon, to the north of Israel) sinned against God's people as the Philistines did (Amos 1:6-8), they would receive a similar judgment (**fire upon the wall of Tyre**).

    b. **A fire upon the wall of Tyre**: The walls of a city were her defense and strength. If the walls were burnt, the city would be defeated.

4. (11-12) Judgment on Edom.

Thus says the Lord:

"For three transgressions of Edom, and for four,
I will not turn away its *punishment,*
Because he pursued his brother with the sword,
And cast off all pity;
His anger tore perpetually,
And he kept his wrath forever.
But I will send a fire upon Teman,
Which shall devour the palaces of Bozrah."

    a. **Because he pursued his brother with the sword**: The people of **Edom** descended from Esau, the brother of Jacob (later named *Israel*). In this way, the Lord could speak of the people of **Edom** as **brother** to the people of God, in that they shared common ancestors in Abraham and Isaac. God promised judgment against **Edom** because they attacked Judah (Numbers 20:14-21).

    b. **And cast off all pity; his anger tore perpetually, and he kept his wrath forever**: Edom held on to **anger** and **wrath** when they should have long before put it away. For this, the judgment of God would come against them. We need to learn to give our **anger** and **wrath** to God and let Him be our avenger.

5. (13-15) Judgment on Ammon.

Thus says the Lord:

"For three transgressions of the people of Ammon, and for four,
I will not turn away its *punishment,*
Because they ripped open the women with child in Gilead,
That they might enlarge their territory.
But I will kindle a fire in the wall of Rabbah,
And it shall devour its palaces,
Amid shouting in the day of battle,
And a tempest in the day of the whirlwind.
Their king shall go into captivity,

He and his princes together,"
Says the LORD.

> a. **Because they ripped open the women with child in Gilead**: The area of **Gilead** belonged to Israel and suffered attacks not only from Syria (Amos 1:3), but also from their neighbor to the west, **Ammon**. We could say that Ammon sinned against the *future* by killing babies in the womb.
>
> b. **Their king shall go into captivity, he and his princes together**: Because of their attacks against Israel God promised judgment against Ammon.

Amos 2 – Judgment on God's People

A. Judgment on Moab and Judah.

1. (1-3) The word of the LORD against Moab.

Thus says the LORD:

"For three transgressions of Moab, and for four,
I will not turn away its *punishment*,
Because he burned the bones of the king of Edom to lime.
But I will send a fire upon Moab,
And it shall devour the palaces of Kerioth;
Moab shall die with tumult,
With shouting *and* trumpet sound.
And I will cut off the judge from its midst,
And slay all its princes with him,"
Says the LORD.

> a. **Because he burned the bones of the king of Edom to lime**: Moab was a southern neighbor to Judah and this is the last of the six judgments Amos proclaimed against the Gentile nations in this section. God promised judgment against Moab because of their cruelty to Edom and her king.
>
>> i. We could say that Moab sinned against the *past* by desecrating the remains of an Edomite hero.

2. (4-5) The word of the LORD against Judah.

Thus says the LORD:

"For three transgressions of Judah, and for four,
I will not turn away its *punishment*,
Because they have despised the law of the LORD,
And have not kept His commandments.
Their lies lead them astray,
Lies which their fathers followed.

> But I will send a fire upon Judah,
> And it shall devour the palaces of Jerusalem."

a. **For three transgressions of Judah, and for four, I will not turn away its punishment**: It is remarkable to see the same judgment formula applied against Judah – the people of God – as was applied against the previous six Gentile nations. It shows that Judah piled sin upon sin upon sin in the same manner as the other nations.

> i. We find it easy – and comfortable – to expose and rebuke the sins of those who aren't the followers of God. That is what Amos did with the first six pronouncements of judgment, but just as Amos went on to look at sin among God's people, we should do the same.

b. **Because they have despised the law of the Lord**: Judah's sin was that they **despised** and disobeyed **the law of the Lord**. This was a higher accountability than God required of any of the six Gentile nations previously mentioned in Amos. God blessed His people with His **law** and **commandments**, but He expected them to honor and obey His word.

c. **Their lies lead them astray**: Since the word of God brings us *truth*, when we despise and disobey God's word we naturally embrace and follow **lies**. You can't reject the truth without grabbing hold of a lie.

d. **I will send a fire upon Judah, and it shall devour the palaces of Jerusalem**: Because Judah sinned like the other nations, they would be judged like the other nations, with **fire** against them and their **palaces** (Amos 1:4, 1:7, 1:10, 1:12, 1:14, 2:2).

> i. The repeated use of **fire** to express judgment is continued in the New Testament. Without doubt, Amos meant material fire coming against material walls and palaces, but the Bible also uses **fire** in a spiritual way, to describe the purifying work of God in the believer. The Bible says that God will test the works of each believer with fire, to burn away what is unworthy (1 Corinthians 3:13-15). The Bible says believers will be tested by fire (1 Peter 1:6-7).

> ii. When we think of God's purifying fire, we should think in the way Peter expressed in 1 Peter 4:17: *For the time has come for judgment to begin at the house of God*. We should invite God to burn down whatever "walls" or "palaces" we build against Him, so His work can continue in us and through us without hindrance.

B. Judgment on Israel.

1. (6-8) The sins of Israel.

Thus says the Lord:

"For three transgressions of Israel, and for four,
I will not turn away its *punishment*,
Because they sell the righteous for silver,
And the poor for a pair of sandals.
They pant after the dust of the earth *which is* on the head of the poor,
And pervert the way of the humble.
A man and his father go in to the *same* girl,
To defile My holy name.
They lie down by every altar on clothes taken in pledge,
And drink the wine of the condemned *in* the house of their god.

a. **For three transgressions of Israel, and for four, I will not turn away its punishment**: The pattern continued. The northern tribes of Israel had piled sin upon sin upon sin, just as the previous Gentile nations had.

b. **Because they sell the righteous for silver, and the poor for a pair of sandals**: Amos saw the injustice of the rich against the poor, and how the rich took cruel advantage of the poor. More importantly, God saw this injustice and promised judgment.

c. **A man and his father go in to the same girl**: Amos saw the sexual immorality and perversion of his day, and how standards that were once accepted were then disregarded.

i. This probably speaks of father and son using the same ritual, idolatrous prostitute. "They were licentious to the uttermost abomination; for in their idol feasts, where young women prostituted themselves publicly in honour of *Astarte*, the father and son entered into impure connections with the same female." (Clarke)

d. **They lie down by every altar on clothes taken in pledge**: Amos saw the idolatry of his day, and how people worshipped idols even as they cruelly oppressed the poor. Exodus 22:26-27 commanded, *If you ever take your neighbor's garment as a pledge, you shall return it to him before the sun goes down. For that is his only covering, it is his garment for his skin. What will he sleep in? And it will be that when he cries to Me, I will hear, for I am gracious.* The prophecy of Amos showed that God heard the cry of the oppressed in Israel and would bring judgment against them.

i. In combination, the whole picture is almost overwhelming. Amos pictured a man committing sexual immorality with a temple prostitute – the same girl his son visited the day before – and keeping warm with a garment extorted from the poor, toasting his success with wine bought with money dishonestly gained.

2. (9-12) The goodness of God to Israel and how they despised it.

"Yet *it was* I *who* destroyed the Amorite before them,
Whose height *was* like the height of the cedars,
And he *was as* strong as the oaks;
Yet I destroyed his fruit above
And his roots beneath.
Also *it was* I *who* brought you up from the land of Egypt,
And led you forty years through the wilderness,
To possess the land of the Amorite.
I raised up some of your sons as prophets,
And some of your young men as Nazirites.
Is it not so, O you children of Israel?"
Says the LORD.
"But you gave the Nazirites wine to drink,
And commanded the prophets saying,
'Do not prophesy!'

> a. **It was I who destroyed the Amorite before them**: God reminded Israel of His power and faithfulness to them in the past. When they first came into the Promised Land, they were afraid of the mighty nations like the Amorites. Yet God conquered them. How could they reject and despise a God who had done so much for them?
>
>> i. This principle – a walk with God based on gratitude for what He has done for us – is important for the Christian and shows why the believer must continually hear the message of the cross. We must live our lives in proper gratitude for what the LORD has done for us.
>
> b. **I raised up some of your sons as prophets**: God reminded Israel of the great privilege they had in working together with God. Gratitude for this great honor should have kept them humble and obedient before the LORD, but they rejected and despised Him (**commanded the prophets saying, "Do not prophesy!"**).
>
> c. **And some of your young men as Nazirites**: The vow of a Nazirite was a special vow of dedication to the LORD, and God gave the gift of this opportunity for a deeper walk with Him to Israel. Instead of receiving this honor with gratitude and humility, they rejected and despised the LORD (**you gave the Nazirites wine to drink**).
>
>> i. The vow of the Nazirite is described in Numbers 6 and was used to express a special desire to draw close to God and to separate from the comforts and pleasures of this world. Under the Nazirite vow a man would eat or drink nothing from the grapevine, would not cut his hair, and would not go near any dead carcass.

3. (13-16) Judgment to come upon Israel.

"Behold, I am weighed down by you,
As a cart full of sheaves is weighed down.
Therefore flight shall perish from the swift,
The strong shall not strengthen his power,
Nor shall the mighty deliver himself;
He shall not stand who handles the bow,
The swift of foot shall not escape,
Nor shall he who rides a horse deliver himself.
The most courageous men of might
Shall flee naked in that day,"
Says the Lord.

a. **I am weighed down by you**: God regarded the people of Israel as a weary burden, not as a joy. It is the difference between the pleasure a parent feels in dealing with an obedient child and the drudgery a parent feels in dealing with a stubborn, rebellious child.

i. Whenever justice is perverted – any time the rich receive preferential treatment, or the poor are oppressed – it burdens the God who sees from heaven and He promises to set it right.

ii. Whenever people cheat and manipulate and make money from others in questionable ways – even if it is legal – it burdens the God who sees from heaven and He promises to set it right.

iii. Whenever people unfairly profit at the expense of the unfortunate, it burdens the God who sees from heaven and He promises to set it right.

iv. "Now, it is to be understood, dear friends, before we proceed farther, that our text is but a figure, since God is not to be oppressed by man; all the sin that man can commit can never disturb the serenity of his perfections, nor cause so much as a wave upon the sea of his everlasting calm. He doth but speak to us after the manner of man.... so the Lord says that under the load of human guilt he is pressed down, until he crieth out, because he can bear no longer the iniquity of those that offend against him." (Spurgeon)

b. **Flight shall perish from the swift, the strong shall not strengthen his power**: One way the judgment of God would express itself against Israel was that they would find themselves unable to succeed in ways that they previously thought they were strong. Without the blessing of God, **the swift** isn't fast enough, **the strong** isn't strong enough, and **the mighty** isn't mighty enough to succeed. Israel was far too confident in their own ability, but God would bring them low.

i. We can escape this judgment by realizing *now* that even our strength is nothing without the Lord. Paul communicated this idea in 1 Corinthians 10:12: *Therefore let him who thinks he stands take heed lest he fall.* We can be more vulnerable in our perceived *strengths* than in our acknowledged *weaknesses*.

Amos 3 – The Logic of God's Judgment

A. The logic of God's judgment.

1. (1-2) God's love and care for Israel make their judgment unavoidable.

Hear this word that the LORD has spoken against you, O children of Israel, against the whole family which I brought up from the land of Egypt, saying:
"You only have I known of all the families of the earth;
Therefore I will punish you for all your iniquities."

> a. **Against the whole family which I brought up from the land of Egypt**: Israel's rejection and disregard of God were all the more inexcusable in light of God's great deliverance. When He brought Israel **up from the land of Egypt**, God proved His love and care for Israel; for God to speak **against** them shows He must have been sorely provoked.
>
> > i. The central act of redemption in the Old Testament was Israel's exodus from Egypt. All through the Old Testament, God called Israel to look back and remember Him as the one who freed them from Egypt. The central act of redemption in the New Testament – and in God's whole plan of redemption – is the work of Jesus on the cross. In the same way, we are called to constantly look back and remember what Jesus did on the cross and to live in light of that great fact.
>
> b. **You only have I known of all the families of the earth; therefore I will punish you for all your iniquities**: God made a clear connection between the great *privilege* of Israel (**you only have I known**) and the great *responsibility* this privilege brings (**therefore I will punish you**). If Israel thought that their standing as a specially chosen nation made them *less* responsible before God, they were tragically mistaken.
>
> > i. "The false deduction which is too often made is that if we are the privileged people of God, *therefore* we may look for His mercy, He will not punish us. That is not so. The measure of our privilege, in the

Divine economy, is the measure of our responsibility. Therefore if we fail to fulfill that responsibility He will not pass over our sins, but rather will visit upon us all our iniquities. It is well that those nations who boast of the Divine favour, should lay this lesson to heart." (Morgan)

2. (3-6) The inescapable logic of God's judgment.

Can two walk together, unless they are agreed?
Will a lion roar in the forest, when he has no prey?
Will a young lion cry out of his den, if he has caught nothing?
Will a bird fall into a snare on the earth, where there is no trap for it?
Will a snare spring up from the earth, if it has caught nothing at all?
If a trumpet is blown in a city, will not the people be afraid?
If there is calamity in a city, will not the LORD have done *it*?

a. **Can two walk together, unless they are agreed?** In this section, Amos connected six statements that were obviously true. The six statements of the obvious lead into a seventh statement, each one reinforcing this final point.

b. **If there is calamity in a city, will not the LORD have done it?** When judgment comes against the cities of Israel, everyone should know that it was the **LORD** who has **done it**. It won't be an accident, fate, or bad luck. It will be the hand of the LORD.

3. (7-8) The inevitable message of the prophet.

Surely the Lord GOD does nothing,
Unless He reveals His secret to His servants the prophets.
A lion has roared!
Who will not fear?
The Lord GOD has spoken!
Who can but prophesy?

a. **Surely the Lord GOD does nothing, unless He reveals His secret**: In context, Amos spoke of the coming judgment upon Israel. God revealed this **secret** to His prophets, and it was prophesied for years and years before it happened so Israel would have every opportunity to repent.

i. God especially reveals the secrets of His coming judgment, so that men will have time to repent and no reason to be surprised. "Such *secrets* of God are revealed to them, that they may inform the people; that, by repentance and conversion, they may avoid the evil, and, by walking closely with God, secure the continuance of his favour." (Clarke)

ii. We must remember the context of the book of Amos and understand that this *does not* mean that God does nothing without revealing it to a prophet first. In Ephesians 3:5 Paul described how God deliberately hid the nature of the church (being a new body, not Israel and not Gentile) from Old Testament prophets. This is one example of something that God didn't announce or explain until it happened, without giving a prior revelation to a prophet.

> b. **A lion has roared! Who will not fear? The Lord God has spoken! Who can but prophesy?** Amos is saying, "Don't blame me. I'm only the messenger." As natural as it is for a man to **fear** when a lion roars, that is how natural it is for the prophet to **prophesy** when the **Lord God has spoken**.

4. (9-10) The message of judgment against Israel goes to the surrounding nations.

"Proclaim in the palaces at Ashdod,
And in the palaces in the land of Egypt, and say:
'Assemble on the mountains of Samaria;
See great tumults in her midst,
And the oppressed within her.
For they do not know to do right,'
Says the Lord,
'Who store up violence and robbery in their palaces.'"

> a. **Proclaim in the palaces at Ashdod, and in the palaces in the land of Egypt**: The city of **Ashdod** was a leading city of the Philistines. God invited the nations – represented here by Philistia and Egypt – to come to **Samaria** (the capital city of the northern kingdom of Israel) and to see their sin (**great tumults in her midst, and the oppressed within her**).
>
>> i. Hubbard on the choice of the Egyptians and Philistines as witnesses: "Their reputations for injustice and brutality would be resented by the Israelites, who would consider themselves in every way morally superior to those whom God had summoned as witnesses." It would also "show that covenant law is not the only criterion for testing Israel's behaviour but that by any standards of international decency they have become culprits."
>
> b. **Who store up violence and robbery in their palaces**: The rich and powerful of Israel used their wealth and power to oppress and steal from others. God invited the nations to see the sin of Israel, so they could understand the judgment He would bring upon them.

B. The destruction God's judgment brings.

1. (11-12) Israel will be conquered and exiled.

Therefore thus says the Lord GOD:

"An adversary *shall be* all around the land;
He shall sap your strength from you,
And your palaces shall be plundered."

Thus says the LORD:

"As a shepherd takes from the mouth of a lion
Two legs or a piece of an ear,
So shall the children of Israel be taken out
Who dwell in Samaria–
In the corner of a bed and on the edge of a couch!

> a. **An adversary shall be all around the land**: This was fulfilled in the Assyrian invasion of Israel, less than 30 years after Amos made this prophecy. For ten years, Israel was a subject state in the Assyrian Empire.
>
> b. **As a shepherd takes from the mouth of the lion**: Exodus 22:10-13 says that if an animal dies in the care of another man – such as a shepherd – the shepherd must make restitution to the owner of the animal, *unless* he could bring remains that proved the animal was attacked by a predator.
>
>> i. "Amos' comparison, then, makes the sarcastic point that when invasion strikes Israel's devastation will be so complete that all that will be rescued is proof of death in the form of scraps of furniture." (Hubbard)
>
> c. **So shall the children of Israel be taken out who dwell in Samaria**: This was fulfilled in the Assyrian exile of Israel, less than 40 years after Amos made this prophecy. After a little more than ten years as a subject state in the Assyrian Empire, Israel was completely conquered by Assyria and the people of Israel were taken from their land and scattered throughout the Assyrian Empire.

2. (13-15) Judgment on wicked places.

Hear and testify against the house of Jacob,"
Says the Lord GOD, the God of hosts,
"That in the day I punish Israel for their transgressions,
I will also visit *destruction* on the altars of Bethel;
And the horns of the altar shall be cut off
And fall to the ground.
I will destroy the winter house along with the summer house;
The houses of ivory shall perish,
And the great houses shall have an end,"
Says the LORD.

a. **I will also visit destruction on the altars of Bethel; and the horns of the altar shall be cut off and fall to the ground**: The altars of dedication to idols would be destroyed by God's judgment. When we build a place of idolatry, we invite God to destroy it. The **horns of the altar** at each corner were thought to represent the strength of the altar, just as horns represent the strength of an animal.

b. **The great houses shall have an end**: God's judgment would not stop at places of idol worship; it would also extend to places built and enjoyed through oppression and robbery.

> i. In the age prior to Jeroboam II, the houses in Israel's cities were roughly the same size. But archaeologists find a change starting in the eighth-century B.C. – ancient cities like Tirzah have a neighborhood of large, expensive houses and another neighborhood of small, crowded structures, smaller than the houses from previous years. The larger houses are filled with the marks of prosperity, and the oppressive rich of Israel thought they could find safety there – but God's judgment came against those houses as well, just as Amos promised.

Amos 4 – "Yet You Have Not Returned to Me"

A. The sinful women of Israel.

1. (1) Amos describes the indulgent women of Israel.

Hear this word, you cows of Bashan, who *are* **on the mountain of Samaria,**
Who oppress the poor,
Who crush the needy,
Who say to your husbands,
"Bring *wine***, let us drink!"**

> a. **You cows of Bashan**: Amos wasn't trained as a prophet, he was a simple herdsman and farmer. When he wanted to get the point across to the indulgent women of Israel, he called them *fat* **cows**. The area of **Bashan** – in the northern part of Israel, the modern-day Golan Heights – was known for producing fat and healthy livestock.
>
>> i. Psalm 22:12 mentions the *strong bulls of Bashan*; Ezekiel 39:18 mentions the large livestock, the *fatlings of Bashan*. It's no exaggeration to say that Amos calls these women "fat cows." Though it is true that the very skinny ideal of female beauty is a modern phenomenon and especially in ancient times plumpness was a valued sign of affluence, we can count on it that at no time in human history has a woman appreciated being called a *fat cow*.
>
>> ii. "The sarcastic epithet *cows of Bashan* seems to refer both to the luxury that the wealthy women enjoyed and to a certain voluptuousness and sensuality which their extravagant life-style afforded them." (Hubbard)
>
>> iii. "The prophet here represents the iniquitous, opulent, idle, lazy drones, whether men or women, under the idea of fatted bullocks, which were shortly to be led out to the slaughter." (Clarke)
>
> b. **Who oppress the poor, who crush the needy**: It wasn't that these women were plump and affluent; it was that they gained their wealth and

affluence by oppressing and crushing the less fortunate. God saw this and promised to hold them to account.

> i. "These women may not have been directly involved in mistreating the poor. But their incessant demands for luxuries drove their husbands to greater injustices." (McComiskey)
>
> ii. "David complains of the strong bulls of Bashan (Psalm 22:12), but those he might better deal with than these cursed cows of Bashan." (Trapp)

c. **Who say to your husbands, "Bring wine, let us drink"**: It wasn't that these women were plump and affluent; it was that they used their affluence in the complete, self-focused pursuit of pleasure. God saw this and promised to hold them to account.

2. (2-3) God's promise of judgment against the women of Israel.

The Lord GOD has sworn by His holiness:
"Behold, the days shall come upon you
When He will take you away with fishhooks,
And your posterity with fishhooks.
You will go out *through* broken walls,
Each one straight ahead of her,
And you will be cast into Harmon,"
Says the LORD.

> a. **The Lord GOD has sworn by His holiness**: This is an exceedingly solemn and sure oath. God's **holiness** is core to His very being, and so here God swore by His own existence.
>
> i. "When he swore by his holiness in Amos 4:2, he guaranteed that the judgment would become a reality, because the holy God does not lie, nor can his holiness allow sin to go unpunished." (McComiskey)
>
> b. **He will take you away with fishhooks**: God told unrepentant Israel of their coming agony when they would be conquered and exiled by the Assyrians. When the Assyrians depopulated and exiled a conquered community, they led the captives away on journeys of hundreds of miles, with the captives naked and attached together with a system of strings and **fishhooks** pierced through their lower lip. God would make sure they were led in this humiliating manner **through** the **broken walls** of their conquered cities. This would thoroughly humble the *fat cows* of Israel.

B. God's answer to Israel's vain sacrifices.

1. (4-5) The vain sacrifices of Israel.

"Come to Bethel and transgress,
At Gilgal multiply transgression;
Bring your sacrifices every morning,
Your tithes every three days.
Offer a sacrifice of thanksgiving with leaven,
Proclaim *and* announce the freewill offerings;
For this you love,
You children of Israel!"
Says the Lord God.

> a. **Come to Bethel and transgress**: Because the kings of Israel did not want their people to go to the southern kingdom of Judah and sacrifice at Jerusalem, they set up rival centers of worship in cities like **Bethel** and **Gilgal**. They offered sacrifices at these places – supposedly to the Lord – but because the offering wasn't made in obedience to God, it was only a **transgression**.
>
> > i. **Your tithes every three days**: There was a tithe that was to be brought every three years (Deuteronomy 14:28). Amos says, even if you were to bring **your tithes every three days** it would not matter, because it would only be an outward show.
>
> b. **Offer a sacrifice of thanksgiving with leaven**: Only one offering in Israel included **leaven**, the wave offering made on the day of Pentecost. Here the prophet either refers to this one offering, or to mock their corrupt sacrifices, he suggests they bring offerings polluted by **leaven**.
>
> c. **For this you love**: The children of Israel *loved* their corrupted worship. It was disobedient both in heart and action, but they *loved* it. It's always wrong to measure worship by how it pleases *us* because it is possible for corrupt and disobedient worship to be "wonderfully" pleasing.
>
> > i. Of course, we don't want to get into the thinking that worship must hurt or be unpleasant to be holy and acceptable. That isn't the point. The point is that we don't *first* measure worship by how it makes us feel, we measure it by how it honors God.

2. (6-8) God withholds rain from idolatrous Israel.

"Also I gave you cleanness of teeth in all your cities.
And lack of bread in all your places;
Yet you have not returned to Me,"
Says the Lord.
"I also withheld rain from you,
When *there were* still three months to the harvest.
I made it rain on one city,

I withheld rain from another city.
One part was rained upon,
And where it did not rain the part withered.
So two *or* three cities wandered to another city to drink water,
But they were not satisfied;
Yet you have not returned to Me,"
Says the LORD.

> a. **I gave you cleanness of teeth in all your cities**: Because Israel seems to have enjoyed financial prosperity at the time that Amos preached, this was probably set in the "prophetic perfect tense" – future events spoken of in the present tense. God would so humble prosperous Israel that their clean teeth would not be made "dirty" by food, because there would be no food to eat in the drought that God would send.

> b. **I made it rain on one city, I withheld rain from another city**: God made the provision of rain so specific, they would know it was from His hand. Yet the message did not get through to them.

>> i. "To prove to them that this rain did not come *fortuitously* or of *necessity*, God was pleased to make these *most evident distinctions*. One city had rain, and could fill all its tanks or cisterns, while a neighbouring city had none.... in these instances a *particular providence* was most evident." (Clarke)

> c. **Yet you have not returned to Me**: This was the greatest tragedy. Anyone can stumble into sin and feel the correcting hand of God, but we are in far greater trouble when we feel God's correction and still will not return to Him.

3. (9-11) Further judgment on idolatrous Israel.

"I blasted you with blight and mildew.
When your gardens increased,
Your vineyards,
Your fig trees,
And your olive trees,
The locust devoured *them*;
Yet you have not returned to Me,"
Says the LORD.

"I sent among you a plague after the manner of Egypt;
Your young men I killed with a sword,
Along with your captive horses;
I made the stench of your camps come up into your nostrils;

Yet you have not returned to Me,"
Says the LORD.

"I overthrew *some* of you,
As God overthrew Sodom and Gomorrah,
And you were like a firebrand plucked from the burning;
Yet you have not returned to Me,"
Says the LORD.

> a. **I blasted you.... the locust devoured.... I sent among you a plague...I made the stench of your camps come up**: Because Israel would not listen to the chastisement of the LORD, His hand grew more and more heavy upon them.
>
>> i. This wasn't a demonstration of God's anger, but of His *love*. He starts His chastisement slow and increases it incrementally, so that God can use the smallest amount of discipline necessary to turn our hearts back to Him. If we will not turn back, the hand of chastisement grows heavier and heavier, out of loving desire to see our repentance.
>>
>> ii. "*Blight* is the work of the east wind that dries and scorches the grain prematurely so that it turns brown. *Mildew* is the product of parasitic worms which turn pale the tips of green grain." (Hubbard)
>
> b. **You were like a firebrand plucked from the burning; yet you have not returned to Me**: God saw Israel as a glowing ember **plucked** from the fires of judgment, like the judgment that consumed Sodom and Gomorrah. Even though God spared them, they did not respond in gratitude – they **have not returned to** God.

4. (12-13) God vows to perform what He has promised.

"Therefore thus will I do to you, O Israel;
Because I will do this to you,
Prepare to meet your God, O Israel!"

For behold, He who forms mountains,
And creates the wind,
Who declares to man what his thought *is*,
And makes the morning darkness,
Who treads the high places of the earth–
The LORD God of hosts *is* His name.

> a. **Prepare to meet your God**: This is a sober warning, appropriate for all men at all times, because we never know when we will **meet** our **God** in eternity. Because we don't know when, we must always be prepared **to meet** our God – but this is *especially* true for those facing the judgment of God.

i. We can apply this text in three ways. **Prepare to meet your God** as a *challenge*, an *invitation*, and a *summons*.

ii. As a *challenge*, God invites His enemies to **prepare to meet** Him. A boxer prepares long and hard before stepping into the ring against a champion. If you are going to step into the ring with God, you had better prepare! "The prophet may be understood as in irony challenging the proud rebels to meet in arms the God whom they have despised. Let them prepare to fight it out with him whom they have made to be their enemy, and against whose laws they have so continually revolted." (Spurgeon)

iii. As an *invitation*, this is a blessing. The summons, **prepare to meet your God** was nothing but a *blessing* to Adam. Ever since the fall, it is our nature to hide from God, so the call **prepare to meet your God** has a different sense entirely. Still, if we will come to God we must **prepare** ourselves.

iv. As a *summons*, we recognize that one day all will give account to God. "Think awhile upon who it is that you have to meet! You must meet, your God – your God! That is, offended Justice you must meet whose laws you have broken, whose penalties you have ridiculed; justice righteously indignant with its sword drawn you must confront. You must meet your God; that is, you must be examined, by unblinded omniscience. He who has seen your heart, and read your thoughts, and jotted down your affections, and remembered your idle words, you must meet him; and infinite discernment you must meet; those eyes that never yet were duped; the God who will see through the veils of hypocrisy and all the concealments of formality. There will be no making yourself out to be better than you are before him." (Spurgeon)

b. **The LORD God of hosts is His name**: God highlighted the point by emphasizing Who it is that makes the point, a God we should never consider lightly.

- He is the God of all creation (**He who forms mountains, and creates the wind**).
- He is the God who is absolutely sovereign over man (**who declares to man what his thought is**).
- He is the God with all power over nature (**makes the morning darkness**).
- He is the God who rules above all (**who treads the high places of the earth**).

Amos 5 – The Offerings God Hates

A. Seek the LORD in a time of impending judgment.

1. (1-3) Coming exile and captivity.

Hear this word which I take up against you, a lamentation, O house of Israel:

The virgin of Israel has fallen;
She will rise no more.
She lies forsaken on her land;
There is **no one to raise her up.**

For thus says the Lord GOD:

"The city that goes out by a thousand
Shall have a hundred left,
And that which goes out by a hundred
Shall have ten left to the house of Israel."

> a. **The virgin of Israel has fallen**: Amos saw Israel as a tragic young woman who was **fallen** and **forsaken**, with no one coming to her aid. In her rebellion against God, Israel was as helpless as a young woman among violent men.
>
>> i. **Virgin** "depicts the vulnerability of Israel and the special sadness that accompanies her death, as though she should have had a whole life to live and fruitfulness before her." (Hubbard)
>
> b. **The city that goes out by a thousand shall have a hundred left**: Amos predicted that things would become so bad for Israel that when the enemy came, a city that would have before sent out **a thousand** soldiers would only send out **a hundred**.
>
>> i. "Only a handful of ragged, war-weary men will be left of Israel's proud army." (McComiskey)

2. (4-9) An invitation to seek the LORD.

For thus says the LORD to the house of Israel:

**"Seek Me and live;
But do not seek Bethel,
Nor enter Gilgal,
Nor pass over to Beersheba;
For Gilgal shall surely go into captivity,
And Bethel shall come to nothing.
Seek the LORD and live,
Lest He break out like fire** *in* **the house of Joseph,
And devour** *it,*
With no one to quench *it* **in Bethel–
You who turn justice to wormwood,
And lay righteousness to rest in the earth!"**

**He made the Pleiades and Orion;
He turns the shadow of death into morning
And makes the day dark as night;
He calls for the waters of the sea
And pours them out on the face of the earth;
The LORD** *is* **His name.
He rains ruin upon the strong,
So that fury comes upon the fortress.**

    a. **Seek Me and live**: When Israel was ripe for judgment, the key to survival was to simply **seek** the LORD. However, they could not **seek** the LORD unless they first would **not seek** places of disobedience and self-will (exemplified by **Bethel** and **Gilgal** and other rival centers of worship).

        i. **Bethel, Gilgal**, and **Beersheba** were once places associated with great privilege and spiritual heritage. Now they were places of *vain, empty worship*.

- **Bethel** was the place where God met Jacob (Genesis 28:11-19, Genesis 35:1-7).
- **Gilgal** was the place where Israel's spiritual reproach was rolled away in the days of Joshua (Joshua 5:1-12).
- **Beersheba** was connected to Abraham, Isaac, and Jacob (Genesis 21:22-33, 26:23-33, 46:1-5).

        ii. There is a play on words in the phrase **for Gilgal shall surely go into captivity, and Bethel shall come to nothing**. It doesn't come across in the English translation, but in Hebrew it is a clever pun.

b. **You who turn justice to wormwood, and lay righteousness to rest**: Amos again confronted the corrupt legal system of Israel. **Justice** had been thoroughly spoiled, and **righteousness** was as good as dead.

c. **He made the Pleiades and Orion**: Amos explained *why* God was worthy to be sought, and *why* He could deliver Israel from their coming doom. He could do it because He is the God mighty enough and wise enough to make and uphold the starry constellations in the sky, and to manage the creation.

> i. This means that God is strong enough to save, but also plenty strong enough to bring judgment (**He rains ruin upon the strong, so that fury comes upon the fortress**). If the **strong** and the **fortress** can't stand before God's power, no one can.

3. (10-15) The cause, the curse, and the cure.

They hate the one who rebukes in the gate,
And they abhor the one who speaks uprightly.
Therefore, because you tread down the poor
And take grain taxes from him,
Though you have built houses of hewn stone,
Yet you shall not dwell in them;
You have planted pleasant vineyards,
But you shall not drink wine from them.
For I know your manifold transgressions
And your mighty sins:
Afflicting the just *and* **taking bribes;**
Diverting the poor *from justice* **at the gate.**
Therefore the prudent keep silent at that time,
For it *is* **an evil time.**

Seek good and not evil,
That you may live;
So the Lord God of hosts will be with you,
As you have spoken.
Hate evil, love good;
Establish justice in the gate.
It may be that the Lord God of hosts
Will be gracious to the remnant of Joseph.

a. **They hate the one who rebukes in the gate**: Amos told us the *cause* of coming judgment – the terrible way that the people of Israel treated one another, especially how the strong took advantage of the weak. The weak had no voice **in the gate** and were robbed by oppressive **taxes**. The rich took advantage with **bribes** so they could drive **the poor from justice**.

i. The **gate** was the law court in ancient cities. Israel's courts were so corrupt that they silenced the poor and righteous. The effect of this culture of injustice was that **the prudent keep silent at that time, for it is an evil time** – godly and righteous people did not speak out either fearing retribution or knowing it would do no good.

ii. "Judicial decisions for each community were taken at the gate of the city, where the heads of families and other elders assembled to hear witnesses, arbitrate disputes, decide controversies and generally dispense justice. The space on the inner side of the gate together with rooms or alcoves in the gate area itself were used as courtrooms." (Hubbard)

b. **Though you have built houses of hewn stone, yet you shall not dwell in them**: Amos told us God's *curse* for Israel's wickedness. Though the wicked in Israel gained fancy **houses** and **vineyards** from their oppression of the poor and railroading of justice, the gains were only temporary. God would evict them from their dishonestly gained **houses** and **vineyards**.

c. **Seek good and not evil, that you may live; so the LORD God of hosts will be with you**: Amos proclaimed God's *cure* for Israel's sin. They must begin to simply **seek good and not evil**. They must transform their corrupt courts and **establish justice in the gate**.

B. Wailing and woe upon Israel.

1. (16-20) Wailing and woe in the day of the LORD.

Therefore the LORD God of hosts, the Lord, says this:

"*There shall be* wailing in all streets,
And they shall say in all the highways,
'Alas! Alas!'
They shall call the farmer to mourning,
And skillful lamenters to wailing.
In all vineyards *there shall be* wailing,
For I will pass through you,"
Says the LORD.
Woe to you who desire the day of the LORD!
For what good *is* the day of the LORD to you?
It *will be* darkness, and not light.
It *will be* as though a man fled from a lion,
And a bear met him!
Or *as though* he went into the house,
Leaned his hand on the wall,
And a serpent bit him!

Is not the day of the LORD darkness, and not light?
Is it not very dark, with no brightness in it?

> a. **They shall call the farmer to mourning, and skillful lamenters to wailing**: This referred to the Jewish practice of hiring professional mourners to wail at a funeral. Amos described judgment so widespread that there would be a shortage of **skillful lamenters**, so they would have to hire **the farmer to mourning**.
>
>> i. Because the prophet Amos was a farmer, he often related the judgments of God to how they affected the farmers of Israel.
>
> b. **For what good is the day of the LORD to you? It will be darkness, and not light**: In their religious ritualism, the people of Israel still claimed they longed for **the day of the LORD**. Amos rightly warned them that they didn't know what they were asking for because **the day of the LORD** would bring them judgment, not mercy. They would end up worse off than before; it **will be as though a man fled from a lion, and a bear met him!**
>
>> i. "The illustrative parable makes it clear that darkness and light do not speak here of wickedness and righteousness but of disaster and safety." (Hubbard)

2. (21-27) Israel's religious ceremonies will not save them from the wailing and woe to come.

"I hate, I despise your feast days,
And I do not savor your sacred assemblies.
Though you offer Me burnt offerings and your grain offerings,
I will not accept *them*,
Nor will I regard your fattened peace offerings.
Take away from Me the noise of your songs,
For I will not hear the melody of your stringed instruments.
But let justice run down like water,
And righteousness like a mighty stream.

"Did you offer Me sacrifices and offerings
In the wilderness forty years, O house of Israel?
You also carried Sikkuth your king
And Chiun, your idols, the star of your gods,
Which you made for yourselves.
Therefore I will send you into captivity beyond Damascus,"
Says the LORD, whose name *is* the God of hosts.

> a. **I hate, I despise your feast days**: This would have amazed – and offended – those in Israel who heard Amos say this. They told themselves that they were really honoring God and pleasing Him by their observance of the

feasts and **sacred assemblies**. But God was offended by their religious ceremonialism, which was disconnected from their hearts and meaningless in light of the injustice that they practiced.

i. Amos expressed the same idea Jesus did in Matthew 5:23-24: *Therefore if you bring your gift to the altar, and there remember that your brother has something against you, leave your gift there before the altar, and go your way. First be reconciled to your brother, and then come and offer your gift.* God thought all that Israel did – their **feast days**, their **sacred assemblies**, their **burnt offerings**, their **grain offerings**, their **peace offerings**, and their **songs** – all this was nothing as long as there was no **justice** or **righteousness** in their dealings with others.

b. **Let justice run down like water, and righteousness like a mighty stream**: It is easy to separate our religious ceremonies from the way we treat others, and to think that God should be happy if we give Him "His due" without regard to **justice** and **righteousness** towards others. God won't have it. He says, "Keep your annoying religious ceremonies, and **let justice run down like water, and righteousness like a mighty stream**."

i. "A momentary flow of justice and righteousness will not do; these virtues are to keep on in the social order like a stream that does not dry up with summer heat." (McComiskey)

c. **You also carried Sikkuth your king and Chiun, your idols, the star of your gods, which you made for yourselves**: Apparently, these were pagan deities Israel brought with them from Egypt into the Promised Land. God reminded Israel that though they sacrificed to Him in the wilderness, they also hung on to their idolatry. It didn't please Him then and it doesn't please Him now.

i. The NIV translates **Sikkuth** and **Chiun** as *shrine* and *pedestal*. It's simply a difficult passage to translate. The Septuagint has *Moloch* for **Sikkuth** and *Rephan* (an Egyptian deity related to the planet Saturn) for **Chiun**.

d. **Therefore I will send you into captivity**: Israel's extreme sin merited an extreme correction, nothing less than exile and **captivity**.

Amos 6 – Woe to the Pride of Jacob

A. Woe to those who are at ease in Zion.

1. (1-2) Comparing Israel to her pagan neighbors.

Woe to you *who are* at ease in Zion,
And trust in Mount Samaria,
Notable persons in the chief nation,
To whom the house of Israel comes!
Go over to Calneh and see;
And from there go to Hamath the great;
Then go down to Gath of the Philistines.
***Are you* better than these kingdoms?**
Or is their territory greater than your territory?

> a. **Woe to you who are at ease in Zion**: In her pride and indulgence, all Israel sought was **ease**. This indulgent lust for comfort and luxury is a sin, and God promised to judge Israel for it.
>
>> i. Rest can be a good and godly thing. Jesus wants to give us rest (Matthew 11:28-29). There is a rest waiting for the people of God (Hebrews 4:9-11). There is rest for us in heaven (Revelation 14:13). Then there is another kind of rest, a sinful kind of rest – connected to indifference, laziness, and indulgence.
>>
>> ii. Yet the prophet Amos spoke of "a carnal ease, a fleshly security, it is not the confidence of a man who is pardoned, but the ease of a hardened wretch who has learned to despise the gibbet. It is not the assurance of one who is on the rock, but the ease of a senseless drunkard, whose house is tottering from its sandy foundations, and yet he riots at full speed; it is not the calm of a soul at peace with God, but the ease of a madman, who, because he has hidden his sin from his own eyes, thinks he has concealed it from God. It is the ease and peace of one who has grown callous, hardened, brutalized, stupid, sullen, and careless, who has begun a sleep which God grant may soon be

broken, or else it will surely bring him where he shall make his bed in hell." (Spurgeon)

iii. How did this sinful **ease** of God's people show itself?

- Israel's sinful ease was shown in *presumption*, because she trusted in the might of Mount Samaria.
- Israel's sinful ease was shown in *procrastination*, because she *put far off the day of doom* (Amos 6:3).
- Israel's sinful ease was shown in *cruelty to men*, because she caused *the seat of violence to come near* (Amos 6:3).
- Israel's sinful ease was shown in *love of self*, through all the self-indulgence described in Amos 6:4-6.
- Israel's sinful ease was shown in *carelessness*, in the willful, drunken ignorance of Amos 6:6.

iv. "Self-indulgence! Oh, this is the God of many! They live not for Christ – What do they for him? They live not for his Church – What care they for that? They live for self, and for self only. And mark there are such among the poor as well as among the rich, for all classes have this evil leaven." (Spurgeon)

v. King David had an ungodly ease when he stayed behind when it was the time for kings to go out to war – and he fell into sin with Bathsheba, eventually murdering her husband to cover up his immorality (2 Samuel 11).

b. **Are you better than these kingdoms?** God wanted to rebuke the pride of Israel by making them compare themselves to some of their pagan neighbors. God wanted them to see that these pagan cities and **kingdoms** were not so great after all. These cities may have already suffered the judgment of God, and God wanted Israel to know they would be next because they were no better.

2. (3-7) The high-standing people in Israel will be brought low.

***Woe to* you who put far off the day of doom,**
Who cause the seat of violence to come near;
Who lie on beds of ivory,
Stretch out on your couches,
Eat lambs from the flock
And calves from the midst of the stall;
Who sing idly to the sound of stringed instruments,
***And* invent for yourselves musical instruments like David;**
Who drink wine from bowls,

And anoint yourselves with the best ointments,
But are not grieved for the affliction of Joseph.
Therefore they shall now go captive as the first of the captives,
And those who recline at banquets shall be removed.

> a. **Woe to you who put far off the day of doom…who sing idly to the sound of stringed instruments…who drink wine from bowls… but are not grieved**: Amos prophesied during a time of economic prosperity in Israel, and the successful in Israel used that prosperity for pure self-indulgence. When God makes us prosperous, we have an absolute obligation to use what He gives us in a way that glorifies Him, not that pampers ourselves.

> b. **Therefore they shall now go captive as first of the captives**: God warned the leading men of Israel that they would lead in the train of **captives** when the Assyrians conquered Israel.

B. The coming destruction of Israel.

1. (8-11) The city is delivered to destruction.

The Lord God has sworn by Himself,
The Lord God of hosts says:
"I abhor the pride of Jacob,
And hate his palaces;
Therefore I will deliver up *the* city
And all that is in it."

Then it shall come to pass, that if ten men remain in one house, they shall die. And when a relative *of the dead*, with one who will burn *the bodies*, picks up the bodies to take them out of the house, he will say to one inside the house, "*Are there* any more with you?" Then someone will say, "None." And he will say, "Hold your tongue! For we dare not mention the name of the Lord."

For behold, the Lord gives a command:
He will break the great house into bits,
And the little house into pieces.

> a. **I abhor the pride of Jacob**: As much as their sinful conduct, God hated the **pride of Jacob**. In their season of prosperity and success they lifted their hearts high in pride, and God will send a destroying army to bring them low.

> > i. This principle is so important to the Lord that He repeats it three times: *God resists the proud, but gives grace to the humble* (1 Peter 5:5, James 4:6, Proverbs 3:34).

b. **Hold your tongue! For we dare not mention the name of the LORD**: The people would be so terrified at the judgment of God that they would fear to hear even the name of the LORD mentioned.

> i. "When a relative of one of the dead comes to burn the corpses, should he find one person still alive, that person will not permit his mentioning the name of the Lord for fear that the Lord will turn his wrath on him." (McComiskey)

2. (12-14) The injustice and pride of Israel make it a target of judgment.

Do horses run on rocks?
Does *one* plow *there* with oxen?
Yet you have turned justice into gall,
And the fruit of righteousness into wormwood,
You who rejoice over Lo Debar,
Who say, "Have we not taken Karnaim for ourselves
By our own strength?"
"But, behold, I will raise up a nation against you,
O house of Israel,"
Says the LORD God of hosts;
"And they will afflict you from the entrance of Hamath
To the Valley of the Arabah."

> a. **Do horses run on rocks?** You can't expect a good result if you run a horse over rough rocks, because the horse will be injured. In the same way, Israel could not expect a good result when they turned **justice into gall, and the fruit of righteousness into wormwood**.

> > i. Here, Amos "puts together two proverbs which were commonly used to signify that men do not, as a rule, continue to labour in vain, and spend their strength for nought. Wise men do not send their horses to run upon the rocks; and they do not send their oxen to plough where all their toil would be wasted: 'Shall horses run upon the rock?' 'Will one plough rocks with oxen?' The answer implied is, 'Certainly not,' and it meant that, if a thing cannot be done, or it is not worth doing if it can, it will be well for us not to attempt to do it." (Spurgeon)

> b. **I will raise up a nation against you, O house of Israel**: Amos came back to this constant theme – because of Israel's great and deep sin, judgment would come to them through a conquering nation.

> > i. "The Lord points to other cities which had been destroyed, – to Calneh, and Hamath, and Gath, which he had smitten because of the sin of the people who had lived there; and he says, 'Ye that dwell at Jerusalem, and ye that live at Samaria, do not imagine that ye will

escape the consequences of your sin. I was able to reach the inhabitants of these proud cities, despite their strong fortifications and their powerful armies; and I can reach you also.' So, when we look back upon the judgments of God upon guilty men, we may conclude that no sinner has any right to think that he shall escape. The proudest and mightiest have been brought down by God and so will men, who dare to resist the Most High, continue to be humble, even to the world's end." (Spurgeon)

Amos 7 – Visions of Judgment and the Power of the Prophet's Prayer

A. Judgment seen in three visions.

1. (1-3) The vision of locusts.

Thus the Lord GOD showed me: behold, He formed locust swarms at the beginning of the late crop; indeed *it was* the late crop after the king's mowings. And so it was, when they had finished eating the grass of the land, that I said:

"O Lord GOD, forgive, I pray!
Oh, that Jacob may stand,
For he *is* small!"
So the LORD relented concerning this.
"It shall not be," said the LORD.

> a. **Thus the Lord GOD showed me**: The prophet Amos will relate a vision from the LORD. This was something he *saw*, something the LORD **showed** him.

> b. **He formed locust swarms at the beginning of the late crop**: Late in the harvest, Amos saw a swarm of locusts coming to devour the crops of Israel. It came **after the king's mowings**, so the royal court had already taken their taxes. This left the Israelites with nothing at all.

>> i. "If the first cutting went to the court and the second crop to the locusts, Israel would be left destitute indeed." (Hubbard)

> c. **Oh, that Jacob may stand, for he is small**: At this vision of terrible judgment, the prophet's heart was moved with pity and compassion for Israel, and he asked God to consider Israel's frailty.

>> i. "Israel is called *Jacob*, a reminder that he was the smaller, younger one to Esau in Isaac's family; God had deliberately chosen him and therefore was obligated to stand by him in his helplessness." (Hubbard)

d. **So the LORD relented**: In response to the prophet's prayer, the LORD relented. This seems remarkably simple. What if Amos had not prayed, or if he had not prayed with the same earnestness? The sense of this passage is that the LORD would *not* have **relented**.

> i. This is another amazing example of how much rests upon prayer. We may debate endlessly how this incident reflects on the issues of predestination and human responsibility, but clearly we are left with the impression that the plague either came or was held back based on the prophet's prayer.

2. (4-6) The vision of fire.

Thus the Lord GOD showed me: behold, the Lord GOD called for conflict by fire, and it consumed the great deep and devoured the territory. Then I said:

"O Lord GOD, cease, I pray!
Oh, that Jacob may stand,
For he *is* small!"
So the LORD relented concerning this.
"This also shall not be," said the Lord GOD.

> a. **The Lord GOD called for conflict by fire**: After the vision of locusts, now Amos saw a vision of a great consuming fire upon the land of Israel. In response, he did what he did before: he pled for mercy (**Oh, that Jacob may stand, for he is small!**).
>
> b. **So the LORD relented concerning this**: As happened with the vision of locusts, God **relented** at the prayer of the prophet.

3. (7-9) The vision of the plumb line.

Thus He showed me: Behold, the Lord stood on a wall *made* with a plumb line, with a plumb line in His hand. And the LORD said to me, "Amos, what do you see?" And I said, "A plumb line." Then the Lord said:

"Behold, I am setting a plumb line
In the midst of My people Israel;
I will not pass by them anymore.
The high places of Isaac shall be desolate,
And the sanctuaries of Israel shall be laid waste.
I will rise with the sword against the house of Jeroboam."

> a. **I am setting a plumb line in the midst of My people Israel**: A **plumb line** measures if a wall is built straight. God held this measure against Israel, to see if they were straight against His standard.

i. **The high places of Isaac shall be desolate**: "The references to *Isaac* are the only places in the Old Testament where *Isaac* stands for the nation of his descendants rather than for the patriarch himself. Amos seems to have in mind the special veneration for Isaac which the members of the Northern Kingdom displayed…. Amos may be announcing and lamenting the tragic break with the covenantal past." (Hubbard)

b. **I will rise with the sword against the house of Jeroboam**: Because Israel was chronically crooked against the **plumb line** of God, Israel and her leadership would be judged **with the sword**.

B. Hearing from all sides.

1. (10-13) Amaziah's words against Amos.

Then Amaziah the priest of Bethel sent to Jeroboam king of Israel, saying, "Amos has conspired against you in the midst of the house of Israel. The land is not able to bear all his words. For thus Amos has said:

'Jeroboam shall die by the sword,
And Israel shall surely be led away captive
From their own land.'"

Then Amaziah said to Amos:

"Go, you seer!
Flee to the land of Judah.
There eat bread,
And there prophesy.
But never again prophesy at Bethel,
For it *is* the king's sanctuary,
And it *is* the royal residence."

a. **Then Amaziah the priest of Bethel sent to Jeroboam king of Israel**: This **Amaziah** was a wicked man because he was identified as a **priest of Bethel**, which was one of the centers of Israel's idolatrous worship. He sent a message to **Jeroboam king of Israel**, who was a successful king by worldly standards, but a wicked king before God.

b. **Saying, "Amos has conspired against you"**: Amaziah implicated the prophet in a conspiracy to undermine King Jeroboam and the people of Israel. He also said that the message of Amos was too hard (**the land is not able to bear all his words**).

c. **Flee to the land of Judah. There eat bread, and there prophesy**: Amaziah was offended that Amos came to Bethel and prophesied, so he did his best to send him back to Judah.

> i. "Hireling priests of this kind have ever been the great enemies of the true prophets of God; and when they could bring no charge of false doctrine or immorality against them, have accused them of conspiring against the government; and because they have preached against *sin*, have held them up as exciting insurrection among the people." (Clarke)

2. (14-15) The answer from Amos.

Then Amos answered, and said to Amaziah:

**"I *was* no prophet, nor was I a son of a prophet,
But I *was* a sheepbreeder
And a tender of sycamore fruit.
Then the LORD took me as I followed the flock,
And the LORD said to me,
Go, prophesy to My people Israel.'**

a. **I was no prophet, nor was I a son of a prophet**: Amos replied to Amaziah by noting that he was a reluctant, unprofessional prophet – only a farmer by trade. Amos was hardly the type to launch a conspiracy.

b. **Then the LORD took me as I followed the flock**: Like many others in the Bible, God called Amos as he faithfully performed his present calling. It was because Amos was an honorable **sheepbreeder and a tender of sycamore fruit** that God made him an honorable prophet.

> i. We see also that God used Amos *as* a **sheepbreeder and a tender of sycamore fruit**. With so many allusions and illustrations from the world of agriculture, Amos spoke as a farmer and God used it. "Every prophet has a manner and style peculiarly his own. Although God speaketh through them all, yet they lose not their individuality or originality of character. The breath which causes the music is the same, but no two of the instruments give forth precisely the same sound. It is true they all utter the words of God; but each voice has its own special cry, so that though God is pre-eminently seen, yet the man is not lost." (Spurgeon)

3. (16-17) The answer from the LORD.

**Now therefore, hear the word of the LORD:
You say, 'Do not prophesy against Israel,
And do not spout against the house of Isaac.'**

"Therefore thus says the LORD:

'Your wife shall be a harlot in the city;
Your sons and daughters shall fall by the sword;
Your land shall be divided by *survey* line;
You shall die in a defiled land;
And Israel shall surely be led away captive
From his own land.'"

> a. **Your wife shall be a harlot in the city; your sons and daughters shall fall by the sword**: God's word to Amaziah – through the prophet Amos, no less – was that the calamity he wanted to silence Amos about would certainly come upon him.

> b. **And Israel shall surely be led away captive from his own land**: This was exactly what Amaziah accused Amos of saying as part of the so-called conspiracy. Amos was bold enough to speak for the Lord and to tell Amaziah and everyone else that Israel's impending captivity is indeed true. This was a difficult word in most difficult circumstances, but Amos was faithful to deliver it.

Amos 8 – Like a Basket of Ripe Fruit

A. Rotting and corruption in Israel.

1. (1-3) The basket of summer fruit.

**Thus the Lord God showed me: behold, a basket of summer fruit.
And He said, "Amos, what do you see?"
So I said, "A basket of summer fruit."
Then the Lord said to me:**

**"The end has come upon My people Israel;
I will not pass by them anymore.
And the songs of the temple
Shall be wailing in that day,"
Says the Lord God–
"Many dead bodies everywhere,
They shall be thrown out in silence."**

> a. **A basket of summer fruit**: This was fruit that was *ripe*, and would not keep long. Just as the time is short for **summer fruit**, so the time was short for Israel.
>
>> i. In the original Hebrew, the prophet's point was far more emphatic because he used a play on words that is difficult to communicate in English. "The overt connection between the vision and Israel's fate was in the word-play based on the similar sounds [between **summer** and **end**]… The point of this vision, then, is the finality of judgment." (Hubbard)
>>
>> ii. "So when Amos replies to the Lord that he sees a basket of ripe *qayis*, God replied '*Qes!*' An end is to come upon Israel." (Boice)
>
> b. **The end has come upon My people Israel…. many dead bodies everywhere, they shall be thrown out in silence**: Ripe fruit is close to being **thrown out**, and a similar judgment will come upon rotten Israel.

2. (4-6) Dishonesty and cheating the poor in Israel.

Hear this, you who swallow up the needy,
And make the poor of the land fail,
Saying:

"When will the New Moon be past,
That we may sell grain?
And the Sabbath,
That we may trade wheat?
Making the ephah small and the shekel large,
Falsifying the scales by deceit,
That we may buy the poor for silver,
And the needy for a pair of sandals—
Even sell the bad wheat?"

>   a. **Who swallow up the needy, and make the poor of the land fail**: Amos returned to his familiar theme of justice, decrying those in Israel who made their money from the unjust treatment of the poor and vulnerable.

>   b. **When will the New Moon be past, that we may sell grain?** Israel *kept* the **New Moon** and **Sabbath**, but only outwardly. Inside, they rejected these special days appointed by God and they couldn't wait until they were over.

>   c. **Making the ephah small and the shekel large**: There was chronic corruption and cheating in the business world, and God saw it and was angry. When they sold wheat (sometimes **bad wheat**), they used a **small** measure. When they bought or gave change, they used a **large** measure for the **shekel**.

>>   i. Cheating and dishonesty in business is not a small sin, nor is it a sin excused of necessity. God sees it and takes account.

B. How God will judge Israel.

1. (7-8) The certainty of judgment.

The Lord has sworn by the pride of Jacob:
"Surely I will never forget any of their works.
Shall the land not tremble for this,
And everyone mourn who dwells in it?
All of it shall swell like the River,
Heave and subside
Like the River of Egypt.

>   a. **Surely I will never forget any of their works**: This reminds us that *time* can never erase sin. We often feel that if we, or if others, forget the sins of

our youth, then God must forget about them also, but that is not the case. Only the atoning work of Jesus can cover sin, not time.

> i. We can make a contrast between Amos 8:7 and Hebrews 6:10: *For God is not unjust to forget your work and labor of love which you have shown toward His name, in that you have ministered to the saints, and do minister.* God does not forget the *good* works of His people, and He does not forget the *evil* works of those who reject Him.

b. **All of it shall swell like the River, heave and subside like the River of Egypt**: Amos knew that the Nile River rose and fell regularly. He pictured the land and people of Israel so shaken by judgment that they would **heave and subside** like the rising and receding of the Nile River.

2. (9-10) The extent of judgment.

"And it shall come to pass in that day," says the Lord God,
"That I will make the sun go down at noon,
And I will darken the earth in broad daylight;
I will turn your feasts into mourning,
And all your songs into lamentation;
I will bring sackcloth on every waist,
And baldness on every head;
I will make it like mourning for an only *son*,
And its end like a bitter day.

a. **That I will make the sun go down at noon, and I will darken the earth in broad daylight**: Because of the reference to celestial catastrophe, many think Amos now looked forward to the circumstances surrounding the ultimate day of the Lord.

> i. Though, some think Amos only referred to an eclipse. "Two such eclipses have been calculated to have occurred in Amos' lifetime: one in 784 b.c., the other in 763 b.c." (Hubbard)

b. **I will make it like mourning for an only son**: Amos tried to capture the depth of the mourning with this metaphor. We also remember the connection to Zechariah 12:10, which describes repentant Israel's humble return to the Messiah in the last days: *And I will pour on the house of David and on the inhabitants of Jerusalem the Spirit of grace and supplication; then they will look on Me whom they pierced. Yes, they will mourn for Him as one mourns for his only son, and grieve for Him as one grieves for a firstborn.*

3. (11-14) The famine of hearing the word of God.

"Behold, the days are coming," says the Lord God,
"That I will send a famine on the land,
Not a famine of bread,

Nor a thirst for water,
But of hearing the words of the Lord.
They shall wander from sea to sea,
And from north to east;
They shall run to and fro, seeking the word of the Lord,
But shall not find *it*.

"In that day the fair virgins
And strong young men
Shall faint from thirst.
Those who swear by the sin of Samaria,
Who say,
'As your god lives, O Dan!'
And, 'As the way of Beersheba lives!'
They shall fall and never rise again."

a. **I will send a famine on the land, not a famine of bread, nor a thirst for water, but of hearing the words of the Lord**: Most people think the worst kind of famine is **a famine of bread**, but Amos reminded Israel that the worst kind of famine is a **famine…of hearing the words of the Lord**.

i. Notice carefully the nature of this **famine**. It is not a lack of God's word, but a **famine…of *hearing* the words of the Lord**. "The condition described is that of being deaf to the words of Jehovah, not able to hear them. It is not a case of God withholding His revelation; but of people being in such a state that they do not see it, do not hear the words." (Morgan)

ii. It is true that there may come times when there is a famine of God's word, either through neglect or unfaithfulness. But that isn't what Amos meant here. This was a problem with the *hearer*, not with the *preacher*. The preacher may have his own problems and the hearer as well may have his.

iii. 1 Thessalonians 2:13 describes the right way to hear the word of God: *When you received the word of God which you heard from us, you welcomed it not as the word of men, but as it is in truth, the word of God, which also effectively works in you who believe.*

iv. "We may question ourselves, whether we feed enough on God's Word. If we would grow strong, we must feed, not on condiments and sweetmeats, not on tit-bits and scraps, not on versicles and pious sentences; but on the strong meat of the Word, on the doctrines, histories, types of Scripture. Oh for more hunger and thirst for these!" (Meyer)

v. Since it is true that *man does not live by bread alone, but by every word that proceeds from the mouth of God* (Matthew 4:4), then it is true that a famine of hearing God's word is ultimately worse than a famine of bread.

b. **They shall wander…seeking the word of the Lord, but shall not find it**: When we push away God's word for a long time, we may find ourselves in the place where we **shall not find it** even if we wanted to.

i. We remember that the ability to hear God's word and *benefit* by it is a gift from God, and a gift not to be despised.

ii. Jesus alluded to this principle in the parable of the soils and the sower: *Take heed what you hear. With the same measure you use, it will be measured to you; and to you who hear, more will be given. For whoever has, to him more will be given; but whoever does not have, even what he has will be taken away from him* (Mark 4:24-25). When we seek God, it generally becomes easier to find Him. When we push away God, it generally becomes more difficult to hear and receive His word.

c. **Those who swear by the sin of Samaria…. shall fall and never rise again**: God promised that the idolaters of Israel would face judgment, and it would be lasting judgment.

Amos 9 – Raising Up the Ruins

A. Judgment brings ruin.

1. (1-4) God's judgment is inescapable.

I saw the Lord standing by the altar, and He said:
"Strike the doorposts, that the thresholds may shake,
And break them on the heads of them all.
I will slay the last of them with the sword.
He who flees from them shall not get away,
And he who escapes from them shall not be delivered.

"Though they dig into hell,
From there My hand shall take them;
Though they climb up to heaven,
From there I will bring them down;
And though they hide themselves on top of Carmel,
From there I will search and take them;
Though they hide from My sight at the bottom of the sea,
From there I will command the serpent, and it shall bite them;
Though they go into captivity before their enemies,
From there I will command the sword,
And it shall slay them.
I will set My eyes on them for harm and not for good."

> a. **I saw the Lord standing by the altar**: In this final vision of Amos, he saw the Lord right at the temple, supervising the work of judgment. Amos wanted Israel to know that God wasn't detached from even His hard work of judgment.
>
>> i. "Like the boss of a demolition squad or the commander of an invading enemy, he snaps his orders for the smashing of the temple and takes personal responsibility for seeing that the last offender is brought to justice." (Hubbard)

b. **Strike the doorposts, that the thresholds may shake**: Often, the **threshold** is the structurally strongest part of a house. If the **doorposts** are broken, it shows that the whole house has fallen in. This is a poetic and powerful way to describe complete destruction.

c. **He who flees from them shall not get away**: This was God's way of telling Israel that they could run, but they could not hide from Him and His judgment. Even if they tried to **dig into hell** or **climb up to heaven**, they could not escape their responsibility before God. A high mountain (**Carmel**) or the **bottom of the sea** could not hide them from judgment.

d. **I will set My eyes on them for harm and not for good**: An essential part of the old covenant was the promise of blessing or cursing (Deuteronomy 28, Leviticus 26) based on Israel's obedience. If Israel was in chronic, systemic disobedience, they could expect that God's eye toward them would be **for harm and not for good**.

> i. *But it shall come to pass, if you do not obey the voice of the Lord your God.... And it shall be, that just as the* Lord *rejoiced over you to do you good and multiply you, so the* Lord *will rejoice over you to destroy you and bring you to nothing; and you shall be plucked from off the land which you go to possess.* (Deuteronomy 28:15, 63)

> ii. *And if by these things you are not reformed by Me, but walk contrary to Me, then I also will walk contrary to you, and I will punish you yet seven times for your sins. And I will bring a sword against you that will execute the vengeance of the covenant.* (Leviticus 26:23-25a)

> iii. How much better to live under the blessing of the new covenant! The promise of Romans 8:31 stands: *If God is for us, who can be against us?* We know that because of our standing in grace by faith, *God is for us*. All the **harm** we deserve was completely poured out on Jesus Christ.

2. (5-10) Israel sifted among the nations.

The Lord God of hosts,
He who touches the earth and it melts,
And all who dwell there mourn;
All of it shall swell like the River,
And subside like the River of Egypt.
He who builds His layers in the sky,
And has founded His strata in the earth;
Who calls for the waters of the sea,
And pours them out on the face of the earth–
The Lord *is* **His name.**

"Are you not like the people of Ethiopia to Me,
O children of Israel?" says the LORD.
"Did I not bring up Israel from the land of Egypt,
The Philistines from Caphtor,
And the Syrians from Kir?

"Behold, the eyes of the Lord GOD *are* on the sinful kingdom,
And I will destroy it from the face of the earth;
Yet I will not utterly destroy the house of Jacob,"
Says the LORD.

"For surely I will command,
And will sift the house of Israel among all nations,
As *grain* is sifted in a sieve;
Yet not the smallest grain shall fall to the ground.
All the sinners of My people shall die by the sword,
Who say, 'The calamity shall not overtake nor confront us.'

> a. **The Lord GOD of hosts, He who touches the earth and it melts**: This wasn't just a poetic introduction. When Israel remembered *who God is* – understanding all His might and glory – then they acted in a way that brought Him glory. Constantly, Amos and the other prophets teach us *what we should do* based on understanding *who God is*.
>
>> i. Amos uses the title **Lord GOD** again – used 12 times in Amos 7-9 – emphasizing the *sovereignty* of God. "That sovereignty is symbolized in the name of God that dominates this section – *Lord God*, literally 'My Master Yahweh.'" (Hubbard)
>>
>> ii. "What counts is that God's presence is at home everywhere in the universe from top to bottom, and that presence is utterly dependable and permanently to be reckoned with." (Hubbard)
>
> b. **He who builds layers in the sky, and has founded His strata in the earth**: This is a difficult passage to translate, and the New King James does it about as well as any other translation.
>
>> i. "It is hard to catch the exact picture of what Yahweh is building in Amos 9: 6. The heavenly construction may be a 'staircase' or a 'roof-chamber'…. The earthly component is even more difficult to define precisely." (Hubbard)
>
> c. **Behold, the eyes of the Lord GOD are on the sinful kingdom**: It is striking – and terrible – to hear Israel called **the sinful kingdom**. God wants all His people to be deeply impressed that they cannot presume upon His mercy or their "chosenness."

i. Israel thought the Ethiopians were a remote and insignificant people, so God says, "**Are you not like the people of Ethiopia to Me?**" God also reminds Israel, "Yes, I brought you up out of Egypt, but I also brought **the Philistines from Caphtor, and the Syrians from Kir**. Don't think you are so special that you become proud and presumptuous. You are a **sinful kingdom**."

d. **And will sift the house of Israel among all nations**: God will use Israel's exile among the nations to **sift** His people – not to destroy them, but to purify them. In it all, **not the smallest grain shall fall to the ground**. God's sifting only eliminates the *chaff*, never the **grain** – not even **the smallest grain**. It is only **all the sinners of My people** who shall be guilty under judgment, those who presume too much and never humble themselves.

i. "I think I see you, poor believer, tossed about like that wheat, up and down, right and left, in the sieve, and in the air, never resting. Perhaps it is suggested to you, 'God is very angry with me.' No, the farmer is not angry with his wheat when he casts it up and down in the sieve, and neither is God angry with you; this you shall see one day when the light shall show that love ruled in all your griefs." (Spurgeon)

B. Israel restored to blessing and abundance.

1. (11-12) Restoring the house of David to Israel.

**"On that day I will raise up
The tabernacle of David, which has fallen down,
And repair its damages;
I will raise up its ruins,
And rebuild it as in the days of old;
That they may possess the remnant of Edom,
And all the Gentiles who are called by My name,"
Says the Lord who does this thing.**

a. **I will raise up the tabernacle of David**: Long before the time of Amos, the northern kingdom of Israel rejected the royal house of David. Here God promised to restore David's royal line – fulfilled in the Messiah, Jesus Christ, who is of **the tabernacle of David**.

i. This is an abrupt change from the strong message of rebuke and judgment. "The transition from verse 10 to verse 11 is the most abrupt and surprising in the entire book. The sword of judgment gives way to the trowel of reconstruction." (Hubbard)

ii. Without this last passage and change of tone, the book of Amos would be incomplete. "It is now declared that the reason of the divine judgment is not revenge, but the only way in which it is possible to usher in the restored order on which the heart of God is set." (Morgan)

b. **I will raise up its ruins, and rebuild it as in the days of old**: God promised to take what was ruined and to **repair** and **rebuild** it. Sometimes God works in a completely new way, letting the old die and doing a work of new creation (2 Corinthians 5:17, Isaiah 43:19). Other times God works to **raise up…ruins, and rebuild**. Both are glorious works of the LORD!

i. Amos knew that Israel was ruined because he speaks of restoring **the tabernacle of David** instead of the *house of David*. A **tabernacle** is a house, but a humble one. This "Pictures the 'house' of David that was becoming a dilapidated shack; in Amos' time the Davidic dynasty had fallen so low that it could no longer be called a house." (McComiskey)

c. **And all the Gentiles who are called by My name**: God announced that even **Gentiles who are called by My name** would come under **the tabernacle of David**, a promise fulfilled in Jesus.

i. James, the brother of Jesus, quoted Amos 9:11-12 at the Council of Jerusalem. He used this passage to demonstrate that God promised to reach the Gentiles and to bring them into His kingdom under the Messiah, not under Israel.

ii. Acts 15:17 reads *So that the rest of mankind* instead of what we have in Amos 9:12 (**that they may possess the remnant of Edom**). This is because the Septuagint, the ancient translation of the Old Testament from Hebrew to Greek, translated **Edom** as "*Adam*" – "mankind."

2. (13-15) Restoring abundance to Israel.

"Behold, the days are coming," says the LORD,
"When the plowman shall overtake the reaper,
And the treader of grapes him who sows seed;
The mountains shall drip with sweet wine,
And all the hills shall flow *with it*.
I will bring back the captives of My people Israel;
They shall build the waste cities and inhabit *them*;
They shall plant vineyards and drink wine from them;
They shall also make gardens and eat fruit from them.
I will plant them in their land,
And no longer shall they be pulled up
From the land I have given them,"
Says the LORD your God.

a. **The days are coming**: Under God's inspiration, the prophet Amos ends the book on a note of high hope, looking forward to a day of great prosperity and abundance in Israel. Under the reign of Jeroboam II, they *had* material abundance, but it was not in the LORD. God promised to restore them to prosperity *from Him* and *in Him*.

b. **When the plowman shall overtake the reaper**: Amos described how miraculous and amazing God's blessing and restoration would be.

i. When God releases blessing and restoration, fruit comes *quickly*. "*Ploughman* and *reaper* laboured separately.... but here they bump into each other, so abundant are the crops and so eager is the land to grow more." (Hubbard)

ii. When God releases blessing and restoration, fruit comes from *unexpected places*. Normally, grapevines don't grow well on mountains or high hills, but in the days of Israel's restoration even **the mountains shall drip with sweet wine and all the hills shall flow with it**.

iii. When God releases blessing and restoration, fruit comes with great quality (**drip with sweet wine**).

iv. When God releases blessing and restoration, the work is blessed – but it is still *work*. The **plowman**, the **reaper**, the **treader of grapes**, and **him who sows seed** still have their work to do. God doesn't just do it all for them, but under God's blessing and restoration the work is done with energy and joy. The **plowman** doesn't just wait around; he gets busy even if he starts bumping into the **reaper**! "One sign of a true revival, and indeed an essential part of it is the increased activity of God's labourers" (Spurgeon)

v. However, even if it is not a time of remarkable blessing and restoration, the work of God still deserves our energy and effort. "The duty of the Church is not to be measured by her success. It is as much the minister's duty to preach the gospel in adverse times as in propitious seasons. We are not to think, if God withholds the dew, that we are to withhold the plough. We are not to imagine that, if unfruitful seasons come, we are therefore to cease from sowing our seed. Our business is with action, not with result. The Church has to do her duty, even though that duty should bring her no present reward." (Spurgeon)

c. **I will plant them in their land, and no longer shall they be pulled up from the land**: So many of the warnings from the prophet Amos were about the threat of coming captivity and exile. God promised restoration and looked forward to the day when Israel would never again **be pulled up from the land**.

Obadiah – Judgment Against Israel's Brother

A. Judgment against Edom.

Obadiah 1:1-9 is paralleled remarkably in Jeremiah 49:7-22, so Jeremiah probably had Obadiah's prophecy before him as he wrote and ministered.

1. (1-4) Obadiah announces judgment against Edom and her pride.

The vision of Obadiah.

Thus says the Lord GOD **concerning Edom**
(We have heard a report from the LORD**,**
And a messenger has been sent among the nations, *saying,*
"Arise, and let us rise up against her for battle"):
"Behold, I will make you small among the nations;
You shall be greatly despised.
The pride of your heart has deceived you,
You **who dwell in the clefts of the rock,**
Whose habitation is high;
You **who say in your heart, 'Who will bring me down to the ground?'**
Though you ascend *as* **high as the eagle,**
And though you set your nest among the stars,
From there I will bring you down," says the LORD**.**

    a. **The vision of Obadiah**: The Hebrew name **Obadiah** means "Worshiper of Yahweh" or "Servant of Yahweh." There are 13 "Obadiahs" in the Old Testament, and one of these may be the Obadiah who wrote this book.

- An Obadiah was an officer in King Ahab of Israel's court and hid God's prophets in a cave (1 Kings 18:3).

- An Obadiah was sent out by King Jehoshaphat of Judah to teach the law in the cities of Judah (2 Chronicles 17:7).

- An Obadiah was one of the overseers who helped repair the temple in the days of Josiah, king of Judah (2 Chronicles 34:12).

- An Obadiah was a priest in the days of Nehemiah (Nehemiah 10:5).

b. **Thus says the Lord GOD concerning Edom**: Obadiah's prophecy is unique because he doesn't deal with Judah or Israel much at all. His focus is on the sin of Edom and the judgment coming upon them. Who were the Edomites?

- The Edomites were the people descended from Esau, the son of Isaac and Rebekah and the brother of Jacob (Genesis 25:19-34). Esau was nicknamed "Edom" (which means, "red") probably because he had red hair.
- Esau eventually settled in the area of Mount Seir and absorbed a people known as the Horites (see Genesis 36:8-43, which refers to Edomite rulers as *dukes* in the King James Version).
- When Israel came out of Egypt and wanted to pass through the land of the Edomites to enter into the Promised Land, the Edomites wouldn't let them (Numbers 20:14-21).
- The Edomites opposed Saul and were conquered under David and Solomon (1 Samuel 14:47, 2 Samuel 8:14, 1 Kings 9:26).
- In the days of King Jehoshaphat of Judah, Edom joined with Moab and Ammon to attack Judah, but the Lord fought for Judah and defeated them (see 2 Chronicles 20:1-27, which describes the famous battle that was led with praise).
- The Edomites successfully rebelled against King Jehoram of Judah (2 Kings 8:16-22).
- King Amaziah of Judah brought them back under subjugation (2 Kings 14:9-11).
- The Edomites again attacked Judah in the days of King Ahaz (2 Chronicles 28:17).
- The Edomites fought side by side with the Jews in the rebellion against Rome in A.D. 66-70 and were crushed by Rome, never to be heard of as a people again. The predictions of Obadiah 1:10 and 1:18 were proven true.

c. **Concerning Edom**: Because of what this book says of Edom and Jerusalem, we can arrive at a date for Obadiah's ministry. The only time markers we have in the book are the attack against Jerusalem (Obadiah 1:10-14) and the fact that this passage also seems to indicate that Edom was not under Judah's rule at the time.

- 2 Chronicles 21:16-17 describes an attack against Jerusalem during the reign of Jehoram (848-841 B.C.) by the Philistines and the Arabians.
- 2 Kings 24-25 describes the attack of the Babylonians against Jerusalem in 586 B.C.

   i. Probably the better choice is the earlier attack because Obadiah 1:10-14 doesn't seem to indicate that Jerusalem was totally destroyed, as it was under the Babylonian attack. If Obadiah's prophecy concerns this time period under Jehoram (848-841 B.C.), it makes him a contemporary of the prophet Elisha and also makes him the earliest of the prophets, probably before Joel by a few years. It also means that this prophet Obadiah *may* be the same man mentioned in 2 Chronicles 17:7.

d. **A report from the LORD…arise, and let us rise up against her for battle**: Obadiah gave a **report from the LORD**, announcing that God would bring nations against Edom in battle. As a result of this coming battle, God will **make** Edom **small among the nations** and **greatly despised**.

e. **The pride of your heart has deceived you**: This helps explain *why* God is bringing judgment against Edom. They are filled with **pride**, and it **has deceived** them.

   i. **Pride** is very *deceptive*. It makes us think things about ourselves and others that simply are not true. The Edomites were not the last people **deceived** by **pride**.

f. **You who dwell in the clefts of the rock**: The Edomites didn't have all that much to be proud about. They were a small, relatively poor and insignificant nation. Yet what they could be proud about, they were – they lived in an area of great natural fortifications and strength, so they boasted in the **clefts of the rock** around them.

   i. **Though you ascend as high as the eagle**: In their pride, the Edomites thought themselves to be **as high as the eagle**, Pride is so ingrained in fallen human nature that even if we don't have much to be proud about, we'll find *something* to exalt ourselves. This also reminds us that we don't have to be rich or powerful or great to be filled with pride. Sometimes those who have the least reason for pride have the most of it.

   ii. The Edomites also boasted of their secure defenses. The ancient city of Petra – once the capital city of Edom, known as Sela – had amazing defenses. It is a city carved into the rock, accessible by a narrow canyon almost a mile long. At the end of the canyon there is a spectacular city carved in stone, and seemingly incapable of being conquered by any army.

iii. The Edomites also boasted of their wisdom. The men of Edom – especially of the city **Teman** – were noted for their wisdom. The phrase *men of the East* in the Old Testament often refers to men from Edom, and passages like 1 Kings 4:30 declare the great wisdom of the *men of the East*. As well, Jeremiah 49:7 says of Edom: *Is wisdom no more in Teman? Has counsel perished from the prudent? Has their wisdom vanished?* This was another source of pride for the Edomites.

iv. The Edomites boasted of their alliances and they trusted in their allies – their *confederacy*, the *men at peace with you* (Obadiah 1:7). They thought that their alliances made them strong, and they were proud because of that strength.

g. **From there I will bring you down**: The sobering truth about our pride is that God can **bring** us **down** anytime. He can shatter our proud deception and bring us low.

2. (5-9) God's judgment against Edom will be complete.

"If thieves had come to you,
If robbers by night–
Oh, how you will be cut off!–
Would they not have stolen till they had enough?
If grape-gatherers had come to you,
Would they not have left *some* gleanings?

"Oh, how Esau shall be searched out!
How his hidden treasures shall be sought after!
All the men in your confederacy
Shall force you to the border;
The men at peace with you
Shall deceive you *and* prevail against you.
Those who eat your bread shall lay a trap for you.
No one is aware of it.

"Will I not in that day," says the LORD,
"Even destroy the wise *men* from Edom,
And understanding from the mountains of Esau?
Then your mighty men, O Teman, shall be dismayed,
To the end that everyone from the mountains of Esau
May be cut off by slaughter.

a. **Would they not have stolen till they had enough?** Obadiah says that the judgment coming upon Edom will be far worse than what happens when **robbers** come and steal because they usually stop when they have **enough**. The judgment coming against Edom will be far more complete (**everyone from the mountains of Esau may be cut off by slaughter**).

    i. The Edomites were proud of their great natural defenses, but God would break their pride and bring them low.

b. **Men at peace with you shall deceive you**: When God brings judgment against Edom, they will know the sting of treachery against them. The alliances that they once trusted in would come to nothing, and they would be double-crossed by their former friends.

    i. The Edomites were proud of their political alliances, but God would break their pride and bring them low.

c. **Destroy the wise men from Edom, and understanding from the mountains of Esau**: The Edomites were renowned for their great wisdom, but God would bring such great judgment that even their wise men would be destroyed.

    i. The Edomites were proud of their reputation for wisdom, but God would break their pride and bring them low.

3. (10-14) Why judgment is coming against Edom.

"For violence against your brother Jacob,
Shame shall cover you,
And you shall be cut off forever.
In the day that you stood on the other side—
In the day that strangers carried captive his forces,
When foreigners entered his gates
And cast lots for Jerusalem—
Even you *were* **as one of them.**

But you should not have gazed on the day of your brother
In the day of his captivity;
Nor should you have rejoiced over the children of Judah
In the day of their destruction;
Nor should you have spoken proudly
In the day of distress.
You should not have entered the gate of My people
In the day of their calamity.
Indeed, you should not have gazed on their affliction
In the day of their calamity,
Nor laid *hands* **on their substance**
In the day of their calamity.
You should not have stood at the crossroads

To cut off those among them who escaped;
Nor should you have delivered up those among them who remained
In the day of distress."

> a. **For violence against your brother Jacob**: The family lines of both Israel and Edom go back to a common ancestor – Isaac. Esau (Edom) was the **brother** of **Jacob** (Israel). This made Edom's sin against Israel all the worse.
>
>> i. Some sins become worse depending on whom we sin against. It is sin to treat someone else badly; it is *worse* to treat *a brother or sister in Jesus* badly. It is sin to speak harshly to anyone; it is *worse* to speak harshly to your *husband* or *wife*.
>
> b. **In the day you stood on the other side**: What did Edom do when **strangers** attacked Judah and **foreigners entered his gates**? *Nothing*. They stood by and cheered for Judah's misery (**nor should you have rejoiced**).
>
>> i. Sometimes doing *nothing* is a great sin. Numbers 32:23 speaks of the sin that *will find you out*, and the sin it speaks of is the sin of doing *nothing*.
>
>> ii. Edom actually did worse than nothing; they **rejoiced** over another's misfortune and suffering and used it as an occasion to exalt themselves (**nor should you have spoken proudly in the day of distress**).
>
> c. **Nor laid hands on their substance**: Edom's sin started with doing *nothing*. Then progressed to *pride* over Judah's distress. Finally, they took advantage of their brother Judah's misfortune and **laid hands on their substance**.
>
> d. **You should not have stood at the crossroads to cut off those among them who escaped**: The final progression of Edom's sin was worst of all – they joined in the attack against vulnerable Judah. When they encountered people from Judah fleeing southward from the attacking army, they killed them (**cut off**) or gave them over to the enemy as prisoners (**delivered up those among them who remained**).
>
>> i. "Sin proceeds by degrees; neither is any man at his worst at first." (Trapp)
>
> e. **In the day of his captivity…in the day of distress…. In the day of their calamity**: All in all, Edom treated God's people terribly when **distress** and **calamity** came upon them. For all this, God's judgment was coming upon them.
>
>> - First, they did nothing.
>> - Then they rejoiced in their distress and calamity.
>> - Then they took advantage of their vulnerable state.

- Then they joined in the violence against God's people.

    i. Are we guilty of the same – or worse – when we see others in **distress** or **calamity**? If so, God sees it as sin, and He must deal with it in our lives.

B. Deliverance on Mount Zion.

1. (15-16) A promise of judgment against Edom.

"For the day of the LORD upon all the nations *is* near;
As you have done, it shall be done to you;
Your reprisal shall return upon your own head.
For as you drank on My holy mountain,
***So* shall all the nations drink continually;**
Yes, they shall drink, and swallow,
And they shall be as though they had never been.

   a. **The day of the LORD upon all the nations is near**: God wants Edom to know that though distress and calamity came upon Judah, it can and will come upon Edom also. That day is **near**.

   b. **As you have done, it shall be done to you**: God will give simple *justice* to the Edomites, no more and no less. What they did to the people of Judah will also be done to them. The same principle is true for us, so if we want mercy from God, we do well to give mercy to others.

   i. There is a sense in which God's judgment against Edom was just the fulfillment of His promise to Abraham in Genesis 12:3: *I will bless those who bless you, and I will curse him who curses you.* The Edomites cursed Israel, so they were cursed. If we want to be blessed, we should bless the Jewish people.

2. (17-20) God will use Israel to bring judgment against Edom.

"But on Mount Zion there shall be deliverance,
And there shall be holiness;
The house of Jacob shall possess their possessions.
The house of Jacob shall be a fire,
And the house of Joseph a flame;
But the house of Esau *shall be* stubble;
They shall kindle them and devour them,
And no survivor shall *remain* of the house of Esau,"
For the LORD has spoken.

The South shall possess the mountains of Esau,
And the Lowland shall possess Philistia.
They shall possess the fields of Ephraim

And the fields of Samaria.
Benjamin *shall possess* Gilead.
And the captives of this host of the children of Israel
Shall possess the land of the Canaanites
As far as Zarephath.
The captives of Jerusalem who are in Sepharad
Shall possess the cities of the South.

> a. **On Mount Zion there shall be deliverance**: The trials and burdens among God's people are only temporary because among them **there shall be deliverance**. However, the attack coming against Edom will be different – Israel will be the **fire** and they will be the **stubble**, and Edom will be completely devoured.
>
>> i. The word of the LORD through Obadiah proved true. The Edomites fought side by side with the Jews in the rebellion against Rome in A.D. 66-70 and were crushed by Rome, never to be heard of as a people again. The predictions of Obadiah 1:10 and 1:18 were precisely fulfilled. You just won't meet an Edomite today.
>
> b. **The South shall possess the mountains of Esau**: Obadiah looks forward to a coming day when Israel will occupy and **possess** the land that once belonged to **Esau**. Though the modern borders of Israel do not encompass the ancient lands of Edom, we can trust that they one day will, either in this age or in the age to come.
>
>> i. **The house of Jacob shall possess their possessions**: Possessing these other lands can only happen when we first possess what is ours. God has given us a rich heritage of *every spiritual blessing in the heavenly places in Christ* (Ephesians 1:3), but how much do we actually **possess**? God wants His people to **possess their possessions**.

3. (21) Saviors come to Mount Zion.

Then saviors shall come to Mount Zion
To judge the mountains of Esau,
And the kingdom shall be the LORD's.

> a. **Saviors shall come to Mount Zion**: The idea isn't that there are many **saviors** in an ultimate sense. Here, the word "**saviors**" has the sense of "deliverers." The contrast is plain; Edom will be completely destroyed, and no **saviors** shall help her, but **saviors shall come to Mount Zion**.
>
> b. **To judge the mountains of Esau**: They will **judge the mountains of Esau** in at least three ways:
>
> - The presence of deliverers is a judgment against Edom because Edom will have no deliverers.

- The judges will rule over the territory of Edom.
- The judges will actually sit in judgment over Edom and their sins.

c. **And the kingdom shall be the Lord's:** The brief prophecy of Obadiah ends on this high note. The Edomites seemed to have their day against God's people but at the end of it all, **the kingdom shall be the Lord's**. He knows how to take care of God's people and to advance His kingdom in a glorious way.

> i. This note of encouragement may be the central purpose for this prophecy of Obadiah. We wonder if it ever had much of a reading in the streets or palaces of Edom; it certainly was received as welcome encouragement among the suffering people of God. Obadiah tells all God's people: "Don't worry about those who ignore your need, those who rejoice at your problems, those who take advantage of your crises, those who join their hands with others in attacking you. I will take care of them."

Jonah 1 – Jonah Runs from God

A. Jonah's attempted escape.

1. (1-2) God's call to Jonah.

Now the word of the LORD came to Jonah the son of Amittai, saying, "Arise, go to Nineveh, that great city, and cry out against it; for their wickedness has come up before Me."

> a. **The word of the LORD came to Jonah**: God spoke to Jonah in His own unique and powerful way and He told Jonah to do two things. First, **go to Nineveh**; second, **cry out against it** – that is, rebuke them for their sin and call them to repentance.
>
> b. **Go to Nineveh**: The city of **Nineveh** was the capital of the Assyrian Empire and was a large and prominent city in its day. It was not a city of Israel at all; God called Jonah to go to a pagan, Gentile city and call *them* to repentance.
>
> > i. Ancient historians say that Nineveh was the foremost city in the world at that time. It was the large, important capital of a dominating empire – surely an intimidating place to go.
>
> c. **For their wickedness has come up before Me**: God wanted Jonah to go because He saw their **wickedness**. None of man's wickedness is hidden before God. He sees it all, and it may come to a point where it demands the specific warning and judgment of God.

2. (3) Jonah's attempt to flee from God's call.

But Jonah arose to flee to Tarshish from the presence of the LORD. He went down to Joppa, and found a ship going to Tarshish; so he paid the fare, and went down into it, to go with them to Tarshish from the presence of the LORD.

> a. **But Jonah arose to flee**: Jonah was a reluctant prophet. He didn't want to do what God told him to do. Several reasons for this have been suggested.

i. It may have been because he was given a *difficult job to do*. Nahum 3:1-4 gives us a good idea of how wicked the people of Nineveh were. Jonah had every reason to expect that at the very best, he would be mocked and treated as a fool. He might be attacked and killed if he did what the LORD told him to do.

ii. It was also because Jonah didn't *want* the Assyrians in Nineveh to escape God's judgment. Imagine a Jewish man in New York during World War II hearing God say, "I'm going to bring terrible judgment on Germany. I want you to go to Berlin and tell Nazi Germany to repent." Instead of doing it, the man heads for San Francisco and then gets on a boat for Hong Kong.

iii. We may speculate on why Jonah did not want to do what God told him to do, but it is even better to think about why we don't do what God tells *us* to do. God told Jonah to *go* and preach; every Christian has the same command in Matthew 28:19-20. With Jonah's example before us, we have *even less reason than Jonah* for our disobedience.

b. **To flee to Tarshish**: The distant city of **Tarshish** was thought to be towards the end of the earth and in the Bible is always associated with ships. Jonah wanted to go as far as he could to escape God's presence, but this was a futile attempt.

i. Nineveh was to the east of Israel and **Tarshish** was about as far as you could go west, on the coast of what is today Spain, past the straits of Gibraltar. In heading for **Tarshish**, Jonah intended to get as far away from Nineveh, and the calling of God to go there, as he possibly could.

c. **Found a ship going to Tarshish**: We don't doubt that Jonah *felt* like going **to Tarshish**. There was an impulse within him driving him there, but it was a dangerous impulse. We may take Jonah as an example of the danger of doing things solely on the basis of mere impulse or feelings.

i. "Now, I very commonly meet with persons who say, 'I felt that I must do so and so. It came upon me that I must do so and so.' I am afraid of these impulses - very greatly afraid of them. People may do right under their power, but they will spoil what they do by doing it out of mere impulse, and not because the action was right in itself." (Spurgeon)

- An impulse may be very brave, yet wrong (Jonah was very brave in embarking on such a long sea journey).
- An impulse may appear to be self-denying, yet wrong (it cost Jonah much in money and comfort to go on this long sea journey).

- An impulse may lay claim to freedom, yet be wrong (wasn't Jonah free to go to Tarshish?).
- An impulse may lead someone to do something that they would condemn in others (what would Jonah say to another prophet disobeying God?).
- An impulse can make us do to God or others what we would never want to be done to ourselves.

ii. Many people take their inner impulses and say, "The LORD told me this or that." This is dangerous even when it doesn't seem so immediately. "What have you to do with the devices and desires of your own hearts? Are these to be a law to you? I pray you, be not among the foolish ones who will be carried about with every wind of fancy and perversity. 'To the law and to the testimony,' should be your cry, and you may not appeal to inward movements and impulses." (Spurgeon)

d. **So he paid the fare**: It seemed *easy* enough. Perhaps even Jonah felt that the LORD provided the money for **the fare**! This shows the danger of being guided by *circumstances*.

i. "Providence or no providence, the Word of the Lord is to be our guide, and we must not depart from it under pretext of necessity or circumstances. *It is very easy to make up a providence when you want to do so*. If you sit down and try to find in the ways of God to you an excuse for the wrong which you mean to commit, the crafty devil and your deceitful heart together will soon conjure up a plea for providence." (Spurgeon)

ii. Nevertheless, when you run away from the LORD, you never get to where you are going and you always pay your own fare. When you go the LORD's way, you not only get to where you are going, but He provides the fare.

e. **From the presence of the LORD**: Jonah should have read Psalm 139:7-10: *Where can I go from Your Spirit? Or where can I flee from Your presence? If I ascend into heaven, You are there; if I make my bed in hell, behold, You are there. If I take the wings of the morning, and dwell in the uttermost parts of the sea, even there Your hand shall lead me, and Your right hand shall hold me.* You can't escape the presence of God.

i. "All the while the ship sailed smoothly over the sea, Jonah forgot his God. You could not have distinguished him from the veriest heathen on board. He was just as bad as they were." (Spurgeon)

B. God prevents Jonah's escape.

1. (4) God sends a storm.

But the LORD sent out a great wind on the sea, and there was a mighty tempest on the sea, so that the ship was about to be broken up.

    a. **The LORD sent out a great wind**: It was the LORD who stirred up the storm. We often think of Jesus calming the waters, and He can do that. But God can also stir up the storm.

    b. **So that the ship was about to be broken up**: The ship and the sailors were in a dangerous place. This was all due to Jonah being on the ship. There was nothing wrong with the sailors being on the ship, but Jonah had no business there – though in other circumstances it might have been fine for him to go to Tarshish.

        i. Jonah might have wondered: "I can go to Tarshish if I want to. I paid the fare. I'm not a stowaway." Yet, "Apologies for disobedience are mere refuges of lies. If you do a wrong thing in the rightest way in which it can be done, it does not make it right. If you go contrary to the Lord's will, even though you do it in the most decent, and, perhaps, in the most devout manner, it is, nevertheless, sinful, and it will bring you under condemnation." (Spurgeon)

2. (5-6) The sailors of the ship seek their superstitious gods.

Then the mariners were afraid; and every man cried out to his god, and threw the cargo that *was* in the ship into the sea, to lighten the load. But Jonah had gone down into the lowest parts of the ship, had lain down, and was fast asleep.

So the captain came to him, and said to him, "What do you mean, sleeper? Arise, call on your God; perhaps your God will consider us, so that we may not perish."

    a. **Every man cried out to his god**: When in trouble, man does his best to fix the problem. In this case, they threw the cargo overboard. When that isn't enough, man also instinctively turns to **his god**. If we don't know the true God – the God of the Bible – *before* we are in trouble, we may sincerely turn to a false and imaginary god, one of our own making.

        i. Many people assume that they can put off doing their business with God until they choose a "better" time to do it. Nevertheless, it is presumptuous to think that in the moment of crisis we will be able to call upon the true God if we have not dealt with Him before.

b. **Was fast asleep**: While the storm raged, Jonah slept. Perhaps because the storm *outside* seemed insignificant to him in comparison to the storm *inside*, the storm that came from his resistance against God.

i. What a curious and tragic scene! All the sailors were religious men, devout in their prayers to their gods. Yet their gods were really *nothing* and could do *nothing*. There was one man on board who had a relationship with the true God, who knew His word, and who worshiped Him – *yet he was asleep!*

ii. "Jonah was asleep amid all that confusion and noise; and, O Christian man, for you to be indifferent to all that is going on in such a world as this, for you to be negligent of God's work in such a time as this is just as strange. The devil alone is making noise enough to wake all the Jonahs if they only want to awake…. All around us there is tumult and storm, yet some professing Christians are able, like Jonah, to go to sleep in the sides of the ship." (Spurgeon)

iii. The nature of Jonah's sleep is also instructive, and too much like the sleep of the careless Christian:

- Jonah slept in a place where he hoped no one would see him or disturb him. "Sleeping Christians" like to "hide out" among the Church.
- Jonah slept in a place where he could not help with the work that needed to be done. "Sleeping Christians" stay away from the work of the Lord.
- Jonah slept while there was a prayer meeting up on the deck. "Sleeping Christians" don't like prayer meetings!
- Jonah slept and had no idea of the problems around him. "Sleeping Christians" don't know what is really going on.
- Jonah slept when he was in great danger. "Sleeping Christians" are in danger, but don't know it.
- Jonah slept while the heathen needed him. "Sleeping Christians" snooze on while the world needs their message and testimony.
- iv. Some sleeping Christians protest that they are not asleep at all.
- "We talk about Jesus" – but you can *talk* in your sleep.
- "We walk with Jesus" – but you can *walk* in your sleep.
- "We have passion for Jesus – I just wept in worship the other day" – but you can *cry* in your sleep.

- "We have joy and rejoice in Jesus" – but you can *laugh* in your sleep.
- "We think about Jesus all the time" – but you can *think* while you are asleep; we call it *dreaming*.

v. Charles Spurgeon described how the believer might know that he is *not* asleep. "What do you mean by a man's being really awake? I mean two or three things. I mean, first, his having a thorough consciousness of the reality of spiritual things. When I speak of a wakeful man, I mean one who does not take the soul to be a fancy, nor heaven to be a fiction, nor hell to be a tale, but who acts among the sons of men as though these were the only substances, and all other things the shadows. I want men of stern resolution, for no Christian is awake unless he steadfastly determines to serve his God, come fair, come foul."

c. **What do you mean, sleeper? Arise, call on your God**: The captain knew that his crew cried to their gods, but it did nothing. Perhaps Jonah's God could do something in the crisis.

i. It must have seemed ironic to Jonah that the sailors demanded that he call on his God. His only reason for being on that ship was to *escape* from his God.

3. (7-8) The sailors discover that Jonah is the source of the trouble.

And they said to one another, "Come, let us cast lots, that we may know for whose cause this trouble *has come* upon us." So they cast lots, and the lot fell on Jonah.

Then they said to him, "Please tell us! For whose cause *is* this trouble upon us? What is your occupation? And where do you come from? What is your country? And of what people are you?"

a. **That we may know for whose cause this trouble *has come* upon us**: It is hard to know what motivated the sailors to think that the storm was sent because one of them had wronged their god. Perhaps it was because of some spiritual insight, and they sensed a *spiritual* power in the storm. Or, perhaps it was just an accidentally correct superstition.

b. **The lot fell on Jonah**: Once the lot fell on Jonah, the sailors wanted to know as much as they could from Jonah, so they could solve the problem and save their lives.

c. **What is your occupation?** 2 Kings 14:25 says that Jonah was a recognized prophet. When he was asked, "**What is your occupation?**" and he answered, "I am a prophet" then the sailors must have been even more terrified.

4. (9-10) Jonah tells them about who he is and what he has done.

So he said to them, "I *am* a Hebrew; and I fear the LORD, the God of heaven, who made the sea and the dry *land*."

Then the men were exceedingly afraid, and said to him, "Why have you done this?" For the men knew that he fled from the presence of the LORD, because he had told them.

> a. **The God of heaven, who made the sea and the dry land**: Jonah knew the truth about God, even though his claim to **fear the LORD** was only partly true because he was running from the LORD.
>
> > i. Even a believer who is in a state of rebellion can give glory to God if he will only tell the truth about God. Although, it is tragic that Jonah's *life* contradicted his knowledge of God.
> >
> > ii. However, at the moment when Jonah said, "**I fear the LORD**," he may have already repented of running away; turning back to God because of the present circumstances.
>
> b. **Why have you done this?** Even an unbeliever who knows *some* truth about God can rightly rebuke a Christian who is resisting God. "**Why have you done this?**" is the most logical question in the world, even for an unbeliever to ask a believer.

5. (11-16) Jonah, at his own request, asks to be thrown into the sea, and the sailors reluctantly agree.

Then they said to him, "What shall we do to you that the sea may be calm for us?"–for the sea was growing more tempestuous.

And he said to them, "Pick me up and throw me into the sea; then the sea will become calm for you. For I know that this great tempest *is* because of me."

Nevertheless the men rowed hard to return to land, but they could not, for the sea continued to grow more tempestuous against them. Therefore they cried out to the LORD and said, "We pray, O LORD, please do not let us perish for this man's life, and do not charge us with innocent blood; for You, O LORD, have done as it pleased You."

So they picked up Jonah and threw him into the sea, and the sea ceased from its raging. Then the men feared the LORD exceedingly, and offered a sacrifice to the LORD and took vows.

a. **What shall we do to you that the sea may be calm for us?** The more the sailors hear, the worse the situation gets – **the sea was growing *more* tempestuous**.

b. **Pick me up and throw me into the sea**: Jonah was willing to sacrifice his life to save everyone else on the ship. We may consider what his motive might have been.

- Perhaps it was compassion for the sailors.
- Perhaps it was a desire to be forced into complete dependence upon God alone. After all, there is no safer place than casting yourself totally upon God.
- Perhaps it was a feeling that *anything* was better than his continual resistance against, and running from, God.
- Perhaps because he had already truly repented. If this is the case, it illustrates that repentance is not only a matter of heart and mind but also a matter of *action*.

i. In all this, Jonah is a wonderful picture of the Messiah that would come after him, Jesus Christ. Jesus threw Himself into the fury of God's storm to rescue those far from God. However, there are many differences between Jonah and Jesus, and one of the greatest is that Jonah was disobedient and guilty, and Jesus was completely obedient and innocent.

c. **Nevertheless the men rowed hard to return to land**: The sailors did not want to throw Jonah into the sea, because they believed his God truly existed and they feared the consequences of throwing a prophet, even a disobedient prophet, into the sea. Still, when all hope seemed to be lost they took precautions ("**We pray, O LORD, please do not let us perish for this man's life, and do not charge us with innocent blood**") and threw Jonah into the sea.

d. **The sea ceased from its raging**: The immediate end of the storm proved that Jonah's God did exist, and that Jonah's resistance to God was the real problem. In a logical response, the sailors **feared the LORD exceedingly**, sacrificed to God and made promises to serve Him.

i. The sailors moved from fearing the storm to fearing the LORD, just as the disciples in the boat did when Jesus calmed the storm (Mark 4:35-41).

ii. "Brethren, I wish I had meet words with which I could fitly describe the peace which comes to a human heart when we learn to see Jesus cast into the sea of divine wrath on our account. Conscience accuses no longer. Judgment now decides for the sinner instead of against him.

Memory can look back upon past sins, with sorrow for the sin it is true, but yet with no dread of any penalty to come. It is a blessed thing for a man to know that he cannot be punished, that heaven and earth may shake, but he cannot be punished for his sin." (Spurgeon)

e. **And took vows**: Notice that the vows of the sailors came *after* they were delivered. Based on this, many commentators believe that the sailors came to true faith in God.

i. Spurgeon preached a sermon with four wonderful points based on the actions of the crew in this chapter.

- Sinners, when they are tossed upon the sea of conviction, make desperate efforts to save themselves.
- The fleshly efforts of awakened sinners must inevitably fail.
- The soul's sorrow will continue to increase as long as it relies on its own efforts.
- The way of safety for sinners is to be found in the sacrifice of another on their behalf.

Jonah 1:17 is examined in the commentary on Jonah chapter 2.

Jonah 2 – In the Belly of the Fish

A. Jonah in the fish.

1. (1:17) Jonah's three days and nights in the fish.

Now the Lord had prepared a great fish to swallow Jonah. And Jonah was in the belly of the fish three days and three nights.

a. **The Lord had prepared a great fish to swallow Jonah**: Some people question if this could happen as the Bible says it did; but surely it is not a difficult thing for God to have **prepared a great fish**, even if that particular fish was a special creation for that moment.

i. We don't know what kind of **fish** this was. Some speculate it was a species of whale, others say it was a large fish known as the "sea-dog." All we can say for certain is that for Jonah, it was a "lifeboat fish."

ii. There is a story of a whaler named James Bartley, who in 1891 reportedly fell into the sea while harpooning a large sperm whale. When the whale was killed and dissected, Bartley was found in the whale's stomach, unconscious but alive. While some have argued that the incident was carefully investigated and true, the widow of the ship's captain denied that it ever happened.

iii. It may be questioned if the story of James Bartley is true or not, but certainly the story of Jonah is true because *Jesus* said it was true. In Matthew 12:40 we read that Jesus said *Jonah was three days and three nights in the belly of the great fish.*

b. **Jonah was in the belly of the fish three days and three nights**: Though Jonah was a rebellious, resistant, believer, God was not finished with him yet – so the Lord preserved his life.

i. God could have rescued Jonah in any number of ways. He chose this specific way because of the effect it would have on Jonah's heart.

ii. The book of Jonah shows us important principles about the sovereignty of God. What happens when God wants a person to do something, but the person doesn't want to do it? Jonah shows us that God has a way of bringing us to the place where we want what God wants.

c. **Three days and three nights**: Apparently, Jonah did nothing for three days and three nights in the belly of the fish; it was only after that period was over that he prayed the prayer following.

i. Some have wondered if Jonah spent the time sulking, and finally decided he had to repent fully and seek God – perhaps this was the case. However, the *starting point* of the prayer in Jonah 2 seems to show that Jonah had cried out to God all the time. The prayer of Jonah 2 came *after* Jonah received assurance from God that he would be delivered.

2. (2:1-2) Jonah praises God for His deliverance.

Then Jonah prayed to the Lord his God from the fish's belly. And he said:

**"I cried out to the Lord because of my affliction,
And He answered me.**

**"Out of the belly of Sheol I cried,
And You heard my voice.**

a. **Jonah prayed to the Lord his God from the fish's belly**: Jonah was still in the belly of the fish but he knew it was enough that the Lord had heard his cry (**You heard my voice**). In faith, Jonah knew that he would be delivered.

i. Jonah knew God heard him before the answer came. This shows that Jonah had faith and that God can give total peace and assurance that prayer is answered, even before the actual answer comes.

b. **I cried out to the Lord**: In this and the rest of the chapter, Jonah's prayer uses many phrases and figures of speech from the Psalms. This shows that Jonah was a man who knew God's word, and knew it by *heart* because there was no Bible and no candle in **the fish's belly**.

- *In my distress I called upon the Lord, and cried out to my God; He heard my voice from His temple.* (Psalm 18:6)

- *Deep calls unto deep at the noise of Your waterfalls; all Your waves and billows have gone over me.* (Psalm 42:7)

- *For I said in my haste, "I am cut off from before Your eyes"; nevertheless You heard the voice of my supplications when I cried out to You.* (Psalm 31:22)

3. (3-7) Jonah describes his trouble, his cry to God, and God's faithful answer.

For You cast me into the deep,
Into the heart of the seas,
And the floods surrounded me;
All Your billows and Your waves passed over me.
Then I said, 'I have been cast out of Your sight;
Yet I will look again toward Your holy temple.'
The waters surrounded me, *even* **to my soul;**
The deep closed around me;
Weeds were wrapped around my head.
I went down to the moorings of the mountains;
The earth with its bars *closed* **behind me forever;**
Yet You have brought up my life from the pit,
O LORD, my God.

"When my soul fainted within me,
I remembered the LORD;
And my prayer went *up* **to You,**
Into Your holy temple.

a. **You cast me into the deep**: Jonah realized that it wasn't the sailors who cast him into the sea – it was God Himself. Jonah saw that he had never been out of God's hands, though he tried to run from Him.

b. **I have been cast out of Your sight**: Jonah's greatest pain was not the calamity, but his separation from God – his feeling that he was **cast out of Your sight**. Still, he was determined – even in the belly of a fish – to turn his heart towards God and His **temple**. Simply, Jonah **remembered the LORD**.

c. **Yet You have brought up my life from the pit, O LORD, my God**: Again, Jonah could praise God for the answer to prayer before the answer came because God gave him assurance.

4. (8-9) Jonah declares his commitment to God.

"Those who regard worthless idols
Forsake their own Mercy.
But I will sacrifice to You
With the voice of thanksgiving;
I will pay what I have vowed.
Salvation *is* **of the LORD."**

a. **Those who regard worthless idols forsake their own Mercy**: Jonah realized that resisting God, running from Him, was like being an idolater.

b. **But I will sacrifice to You**: Jonah repented from running away from God, and he turned to God with sacrifice and thanksgiving. He promised to pay his vows to God, and do whatever God told him to do,

> i. At one time or another, Jonah had probably said what we all have said: "Lord, I'll do whatever You want me to do." Now Jonah realized fully that he must stop resisting God and he should pay his vows to God.

c. **Salvation is of the LORD**: This was more than a statement of fact; it was Jonah's triumphant declaration. God had saved and would save, and Jonah meant it *personally*. Jonah's **salvation is of the LORD**.

> i. Jonah knows this in the *close-up* picture; he knew that *his* **salvation is of the LORD**. He also now knew it in the *big picture*; that salvation is not of a nation or a race or a language. Salvation is not of man at all; **salvation is of the LORD**.

d. At the end of Jonah 2:9 it is clear that Jonah has repented, but we might wonder *when* did Jonah repent? Jonah showed several marks of true repentance.

- Jonah proclaimed his fear of the LORD and he was honest about his sin and rebellion, no longer covering it up (Jonah 1:9).
- Jonah allowed himself to be cast into the sea (Jonah 1:12).
- Jonah began to pray; he called out to God during the three days and three nights in the belly of the fish (Jonah 2:2, 2:4, and 2:7).
- Jonah had a new heart of gratitude (Jonah 2:9).
- Jonah renewed the commitment to his vow (Jonah 2:9).
- Jonah gave glory to God in all of this (Jonah 2:9).

> i. In all this we see repentance as more than a one-time event. Though it begins at one time, it must continue and mature. Repentance is an event, but it is also a process.

B. Jonah out of the fish.

1. (10a) God speaks to the fish.

So the LORD spoke to the fish,

a. **The LORD spoke to the fish**: The fish worked at the command of God. Just as much as the fish was under the command of God when it swallowed Jonah, it was under His command when it let him go.

b. **To the fish**: If God can speak to a **fish**, He can speak to us. Then again, **fish** probably don't *resist* the will of God as we do.

2. (10b) Jonah is expelled from the fish.

And it vomited Jonah onto dry *land*.

a. **Vomited Jonah**: Sometimes we don't have much of a choice about *how* we will be delivered. Jonah might have preferred another method, but God had a purpose in this also.

>   i. Jonah's deliverance came after Jonah's repentance was complete. Jonah wasn't just *sorry* for what he did; he was now *trusting* God again. In many believers today, there is a work of God, or an aspect of His deliverance, that will remain undone as long as that believer resists Him and refuses to trust God.
>
>   ii. Jonah's deliverance came after three days and nights had passed, providing a foreshadowing of Jesus' resurrection. Jesus said, *For as Jonah was three days and three nights in the belly of the great fish, so will the Son of Man be three days and three nights in the heart of the earth* (Matthew 12:40).
>
>   iii. When Jesus spoke of *three days and three nights* in Matthew 12:40, it does make a Thursday crucifixion necessary. Rabbinic literature from the time of Jesus explains that the phrase "so many days and so many nights" was a figure of speech that could refer to any part of a day and night. Ellison notes that Rabbi Eleazar ben Azariah (around the year A.D. 100) said: "A day and a night make a whole day, and a portion of a whole day is reckoned as a whole day." This demonstrates how in Jesus' day, the phrase *three days and three nights* did not necessarily mean a 72-hour period, but a period including at least the portions of three days and three nights.
>
>   iv. Pointing towards the Messiah to come, Jesus Christ, we see that Jonah's deliverance came after a remarkable demonstration of laying down one's life. Jonah gave his life to appease the wrath of God coming upon others. But death did not hold him; after three days and nights of imprisonment, he was alive and free.

b. **Onto dry land**: It is commonly thought that Jonah was vomited out on the shores of Nineveh – but we are not told that this was the case, especially because Nineveh is about 375 miles from the Mediterranean Sea. If Jonah did walk into Nineveh right from the belly of the fish, it would have been a miraculous projection of the fish's vomit.

Jonah 3 – Jonah Preaches Repentance in Nineveh, the City Repents

A. Jonah's ministry in Nineveh.

1. (1-2) The second call to Jonah.

Now the word of the LORD came to Jonah the second time, saying, "Arise, go to Nineveh, that great city, and preach to it the message that I tell you."

> a. **Now the word of the LORD came to Jonah the second time**: This shows the amazing love of God to His wayward people. Though Jonah did everything he could to resist the first call of God, after Jonah repented God called him again – though God was under no obligation to do it. He did it out of mercy and grace.
>
> > i. "By paralleling here the book's opening remarks, almost word for word, the author skillfully conveys the idea that Jonah is being offered a new beginning." (Alexander)
> >
> > ii. "How many of us who have been called to deliver the word of Jehovah, would still be doing it, if it were not for this patient and perfecting grace of God? Surely not many! How have we failed Him, and broken down in our ministry; and often not on ground so high as that of Jonah's failure." (Morgan)
> >
> > iii. God was determined to do the work through Jonah, so He did not give up on the reluctant prophet. God is often just this committed to doing His work through a man. "Suppose that the problem had been given to us to solve - how shall this city be moved to repentance? How shall its vice be forsaken and the God of Israel worshipped by all its inhabitants from the highest to the lowest? If we had not been paralysed with despair, which is the most probable, we should, nevertheless, have sat down carefully to consider our plans. We should have parcelled it out into missionary districts; we should have needed at least several

hundreds, if not thousands, of able ministers; at once, expenses would have to be incurred, and we should have considered ourselves bound to contemplate the erection of innumerable structures in which the Word of God might be preached. Our machinery would necessarily become cumbrous; we should find that we, unless we had the full resources of an empire, could not even begin the work. But what saith the Lord concerning this? Putting aside the judgments of reason, and all the plans and schemes which flesh and blood so naturally do follow, he raises up one man. By a singular providence he qualifies that one man for his mission." (Spurgeon)

b. **Preach to it the message that I tell you**: Instead of telling Jonah to *cry out against* Nineveh, this time God simply tells Jonah to go there and wait for further instructions. God frequently works this way, and our flesh often finds it irritating that He does.

i. The story of Jonah demonstrates *why* many times God leads us one step at a time without telling us more. When God told Jonah what he would say in Nineveh, Jonah rejected the call. God often only tells us what we can handle at the time.

2. (3-4) Jonah preaches in Nineveh.

So Jonah arose and went to Nineveh, according to the word of the LORD. Now Nineveh was an exceedingly great city, a three-day journey *in extent*. And Jonah began to enter the city on the first day's walk. Then he cried out and said, "Yet forty days, and Nineveh shall be overthrown!"

a. **Jonah arose and went to Nineveh, according to the word of the LORD**: Having learned the lesson that resisting the will of God is both futile and counter-productive, Jonah now obeys the call and goes to Nineveh.

b. **Nineveh was an exceedingly great city, a three-day journey in extent**: The idea behind this statement probably refers to how long it would take to walk around the city of "Greater Nineveh" – the metropolitan area around the city.

c. **Yet forty days, and Nineveh shall be overthrown**: Jonah emphasized to the people of Nineveh what would happen if they did not repent – the city would be **overthrown** in judgment. Undoubtedly, this was not Jonah's *whole* message to the people of Nineveh; but clearly it was his emphasis.

i. "**Overthrown**" is a word applied to the destruction of Sodom and Gomorrah (Genesis 19:25, Lamentations 4:6, and Amos 4:11).

ii. We see that Jonah preached this message with earnestness. "And such earnestness becomes a ministry that has to do with immortal souls, asleep and dead in sin, hanging on the brink of perdition, and insensible of their state. The soft-speaking, gentle-intoned, unmoved preacher, is never likely to awaken souls…. But this earnestness is widely different from that noisy, blustering, screaming rant, that manifests more of a turbulence of disorderly passions, than of the real inspired influence of the Spirit of God." (Clarke)

B. The response of the people of Nineveh to Jonah's message.

1. (5-9) The response of the people: repentance.

So the people of Nineveh believed God, proclaimed a fast, and put on sackcloth, from the greatest to the least of them. Then word came to the king of Nineveh; and he arose from his throne and laid aside his robe, covered *himself* with sackcloth and sat in ashes. And he caused *it* to be proclaimed and published throughout Nineveh by the decree of the king and his nobles, saying,

Let neither man nor beast, herd nor flock, taste anything; do not let them eat, or drink water. But let man and beast be covered with sackcloth, and cry mightily to God; yes, let every one turn from his evil way and from the violence that is in his hands. Who can tell *if* God will turn and relent, and turn away from His fierce anger, so that we may not perish?

a. **So the people of Nineveh**: The *word* "repentance" isn't in this passage; but repentance isn't really a word, it is something you *do* – and these people *did* repent. One can have repentance without the word itself being spoken, and one can say the word "repentance" and never truly repent.

b. **The people of Nineveh believed God**: Repentance begins with believing God. As we believe Him and His word, we have the power to transform our lives as He wills. You can do many other things associated with repentance, but if they do not begin with believing on and trusting God, they are all useless works of the flesh.

i. You can't *believe God* apart from the word of God. Therefore, any real revival or repentance will begin with faithful preaching and faithful hearing of God's Word, just as it was in Nineveh.

c. **The people of Nineveh…proclaimed a fast, and put on sackcloth**: Repentance means *doing* something. The people of Nineveh fasted, mourned as if for the dead, and they did it from the highest to the lowest (**from the greatest to the least of them**).

i. If repentance is anything, it is *not* business as usual. When repentance comes, something has to change, and something has to be *different*. In their case, the people of Nineveh took off their normal clothes and put on **sackcloth** – a thick coarse cloth, normally made from goat's hair. Wearing it displayed the rejection of earthly comforts and pleasures.

ii. **Let man and beast be covered with sackcloth**: They even repented on behalf of their animals, dressing them as if the animals were in mourning for the dead.

d. **But let man and beast…cry mightily to God**: Repentance means crying **mightily to God**. It means coming to God with passion and seriousness about your sin and your need for His mercy and forgiveness.

i. Many modern expressions of repentance, making excuses and justifying reasons for the sin, are really not repentance at all. Often they are only attempts to justify and excuse sin. Nevertheless, you sinned or you didn't; if you did, *there is no excuse*, and if you didn't, *there is no need to repent*. Repentance and excuses simply don't belong together.

e. **Yes, let every one turn from his evil way and from the violence that is in his hands**: Repentance means turning from your **evil way and from the violence that is in** your **hands**. Repentance means to change your mind and turn from your previous sinful actions.

i. In the Christian life, repentance does not describe what you must do to turn to God; it describes the very process of turning to God. When we truly turn to Him, we turn away from the things that displease Him.

f. **Who can tell if God will turn and relent, and turn away from His fierce anger**: Repentance has hope in the mercy and love of God. It hopes that God will **relent** and that the repentant people will **not perish**.

i. Jonah could more effectively preach the message of repentance because he knew his own need to repent and was himself a model of repentance (Jonah 2:8-9). Being a repentant sinner didn't disqualify Jonah from preaching repentance; it made his preaching all the more effective.

2. (10) God's response to the people's repentance.

Then God saw their works, that they turned from their evil way; and God relented from the disaster that He had said He would bring upon them, and He did not do it.

a. **God saw their works…and God relented**: God honored Nineveh's repentance, even though their *past* sin was reason enough for an outpouring of judgment. The state would never forgive a cold-blooded murderer who vowed to never do it again, but God mercifully relented from judgment against the people of Nineveh.

    i. We do not *obligate* God to forgive us when we repent. Instead, repentance appeals to God's mercy, not His justice.

b. **God relented from the disaster that He had said He would bring upon them, and He did not do it**: Did God's relenting make Jonah a false prophet, when he prophesied *Yet forty days and Nineveh shall be overthrown*? Not at all, for two good reasons.

    i. First, God acted in total consistency with His word: *The instant I speak concerning a nation and concerning a kingdom, to pluck up, to pull down, and to destroy it, if that nation against whom I have spoken turns from its evil, I will relent of the disaster that I thought to bring upon it* (Jeremiah 18:7-8). Jonah's preaching was like all warnings of judgment: it was an invitation to repent and avert the promised judgment. His words had an implied "if you do not repent" in front of them. Remember that we are not told the sum total of Jonah's preaching; though we should assume that the statement in Jonah 3:4 is the central theme of what Jonah said, we should not assume it was *all* that he said.

    ii. Second, God did judge Nineveh (as recorded in the book of Nahum). Nevertheless, in light of their repentance He delayed the promised judgment for another 150 years.

Jonah 4 – God Deals with a Prophet's Heart

A. Jonah's complaint.

1. (1) Jonah's displeasure at the repentance of the people of Nineveh.

But it displeased Jonah exceedingly, and he became angry.

> a. **It displeased Jonah**: This was strange because usually the preacher is pleased when the congregation repents, but Jonah wasn't. There was something about the whole matter that **displeased Jonah**.
>
> b. **Exceedingly, and he became angry**: Not only was this strange, it was *very strange*, because Jonah was *very* upset at the success of his preaching. We should not miss Jonah's intensity here, because the language in the original Hebrew is strong.

2. (2-3) Jonah explains his anger.

So he prayed to the LORD**, and said, "Ah, L**ORD**, was not this what I said when I was still in my country? Therefore I fled previously to Tarshish; for I know that You** *are* **a gracious and merciful God, slow to anger and abundant in lovingkindness, One who relents from doing harm. Therefore now, O L**ORD**, please take my life from me, for** *it is* **better for me to die than to live!"**

> a. **I know that You are a gracious and merciful God, slow to anger and abundant in lovingkindness, One who relents from doing harm**: Jonah was angry because God granted repentance to the Ninevites, and the Assyrians were enemies of Judah and Israel. Jonah wanted God to bring judgment upon these people he hated.
>
> > i. Jonathan Swift wrote a verse that expressed Jonah's frame of mind:
> > *We are God's chosen few,*
> > *All others will be damned;*
> > *There is no place in heaven for you,*
> > *We can't have heaven crammed.*

b. **Ah, Lord, was not this what I said when I was still in my country?** Jonah knew that God was full of grace and mercy, and *that* was why he was afraid to tell the people of Nineveh. This was at least part of the reason why Jonah did not want to go to Nineveh – he was afraid they would repent, when all along he wanted God to judge the Assyrian capital.

i. Jonah himself called on the mercy of God and enjoyed the mercy of God when it was extended to Jonah. Now he resents it when it is extended to others. What if God treated Jonah the way Jonah wanted God to treat the people of Nineveh?

c. **For it is better for me to die than to live**: The repentance and salvation of the people of Nineveh were so painful to Jonah that he would have rather died than think about it. He also states that this was the reason that he fled the call – not out of fear that he would be ineffective, but fear that he *would* be effective!

B. God confronts a prophet.

1. (4) God questions Jonah's heart.

Then the Lord said, "Is it right for you to be angry?"

a. **Is it right for you to be angry?** Jonah, in expressing his anger against God, was being honest about his feelings – something good but we should not for a moment think that all of our feelings towards God are justified.

i. God likes to ask us questions because they reveal our hearts. It also puts us on proper ground before God, because He has every right to question us and we owe Him answers.

- Where are you? Who told you that you were naked? What is this you have done? (Genesis 3:9-13)
- Where is Abel your brother? What have you done? (Genesis 4)
- What have you done? (1 Samuel 13:11)
- Why have you despised the word of the Lord, to do evil in His sight? (2 Samuel 12:9)
- Whom shall I send? Who will go for Us? (Isaiah 6:8)
- Who do you say that I am? (Matthew 16:15)
- What do you want Me to do for you? (Matthew 20:32)
- Are you betraying the Son of Man with a kiss? (Luke 22:48)
- Saul, Saul, why are you persecuting Me? (Acts 9:4)

b. **Is it right for you to be angry?** This is the question we should and even must ask ourselves if we find ourselves angry with God. The answer must always be "No, Lord. All Your ways are right even if I don't understand them."

> i. Yes, Jonah was angry towards God, and yes, it was all right for Jonah to state his anger towards God; but he must also repent of his anger towards God.

2. (5-8) God prepares an object lesson for Jonah.

So Jonah went out of the city and sat on the east side of the city. There he made himself a shelter and sat under it in the shade, till he might see what would become of the city. And the Lord God prepared a plant and made it come up over Jonah, that it might be shade for his head to deliver him from his misery. So Jonah was very grateful for the plant. But as morning dawned the next day God prepared a worm, and it *so* damaged the plant that it withered. And it happened, when the sun arose, that God prepared a vehement east wind; and the sun beat on Jonah's head, so that he grew faint. Then he wished death for himself, and said, *"It is* better for me to die than to live."

> a. **Jonah went out of the city.... till he might see what would become of the city**: Jonah seemed to hope that the repentance of Nineveh was not enough to hold back God's judgment, and hoped that he would see the city destroyed after all. He went **out of the city** for safety.
>
> b. **The Lord God prepared a plant and made it come up over Jonah**: Just as God prepared a great fish to swallow Jonah, now He prepared a particular plant to shelter Jonah as he waited, hoping that the city would be destroyed.
>
>> i. This is the first time we find Jonah happy. "Jonah was pleased because at last, after all the compassion of God for other people, God was finally doing something for Jonah. Selfish? Of course, it was. And petty too!" (Boice)
>>
>> ii. We could say that Jonah's happiness was just as fleshly as his anger. Both were all about *self*.
>
> c. **The sun beat on Jonah's head, so that he grew faint**: Jonah was angry with God because He brought the people of Nineveh to repentance (Jonah 4:1). The ancient Hebrew word for "angry" is literally "to be hot." Now God would let *Jonah* feel some of the heat!
>
> d. **Jonah was very grateful for the plant.... It is better for me to die than to live**: When God took the plant and its pleasant shelter away from Jonah, he missed the plant so much that he wanted to die.

i. "If, dear friends, like Jonah, you want to complain, you will soon have something to complain of. People who are resolved to fret, generally make for themselves causes for fretfulness." (Spurgeon)

ii. Jonah allowed even a silly thing like a plant to become an idol. "How often our gourds are allowed to perish, to teach us these deep lessons. In spite of all we can do to keep them green, their leaves turn more and more sere and yellow, until they droop and die." (Meyer)

3. (9-11) God applies the object lesson.

Then God said to Jonah, *"Is it* right for you to be angry about the plant?"

And he said, *"It is* right for me to be angry, even to death!"

But the LORD said, "You have had pity on the plant for which you have not labored, nor made it grow, which came up in a night and perished in a night. And should I not pity Nineveh, that great city, in which are more than one hundred and twenty thousand persons who cannot discern between their right hand and their left–and much livestock?"

a. **Is it right for you to be angry about the plant?** Jonah, in response to God's question, felt totally justified in his anger about the sheltering plant's destruction. Even though the plant was just a plant, and Jonah had no personal interest or investment in the plant except for what it provided for him at the moment.

i. Jonah made three errors that angry people often make. Each of these things put Jonah in a worse place, not a better place.

- Jonah quit serving God and others.
- Jonah separated himself from others.
- Jonah became a spectator.

b. **It is right for me to be angry, even to death**: These are the last words of Jonah recorded in this book, but thankfully they are not the last words of the book. God's mercy and compassion still worked with Jonah, teaching him and guiding him to God's heart.

c. **And should I not pity Nineveh**: How much more should God be concerned about the destruction of *people* – those made in His image, even if they are Assyrians. God's response to Jonah showed the prophet that he really didn't know God as well as he thought he did.

i. Those **who cannot discern between their right hand and their left** are those who are unable to make moral judgments.

ii. The lesson is clear: not only does God's concern for people go beyond Israel, but He is totally justified in calling the nations to account. The lesson of Jonah reminds us that God is the God of all people.

iii. The lesson of Jonah is what he proclaimed before being freed from the great fish: *Salvation is of the LORD* (Jonah 2:9), and not of any race or nation or class. This is the same message God made clear to Peter in Acts 10:34-35: *In truth I perceive that God shows no partiality. But in every nation whoever fears Him and works righteousness is accepted by Him.*"

d. **Should I not pity Nineveh, that great city**: Jewish tradition says that after God said the words of Jonah 4:11, Jonah then fell on his face and said: "Govern your world according to the measure of mercy, as it is said, *To the Lord our God belong mercy and forgiveness.*" (Daniel 9:9) We can only hope that Jonah – and we – would have such a humble response.

i. God showed His mercy to Jonah through a lot of *preparation*.

- The LORD prepared a great fish (Jonah 1:17).
- The LORD prepared a plant (Jonah 4:6).
- The LORD prepared a worm (Jonah 4:7).
- The LORD prepared a wind (Jonah 4:8).

ii. Nevertheless, the real work of preparation happened in *Jonah*. What God really prepared was a *person*, a *prophet*. "I would suggest to some of you here who have to bear double trouble that God may be preparing you for double usefulness, or he may be working out of you some unusual form of evil which might not be driven out of you unless his Holy Spirit had used these mysterious methods with you to teach you more fully his mind." (Spurgeon)

Micah 1 – Coming Judgment on Israel and Judah

A. Coming judgment on Israel.

1. (1) Introduction to the prophecy of Micah.

The word of the LORD that came to Micah of Moresheth in the days of Jotham, Ahaz, *and* Hezekiah, kings of Judah, which he saw concerning Samaria and Jerusalem.

> a. **Micah of Moresheth**: The city of **Moresheth** (also called *Moresheth Gath* in Micah 1:14) was about 25 miles (40 kilometers) southwest of Jerusalem on the borderlands between Judah and the Philistines. This means that the prophet **Micah** was like the prophet Amos, a man from the country sent to the cities to bring **the word of the LORD**.
>
>> i. We really don't know anything about Micah's background or call, but we do know that he had a strong sense of his calling as a prophet, and he said so in Micah 3:8.
>
> b. **In the days of Jotham, Ahaz, and Hezekiah**: This means that Micah ministered as a prophet some time between the years 739 B.C. (the start of the reign of **Jotham**) and 686 B.C. (the end of the reign of **Hezekiah**). Since Hezekiah was a noted reformer, we can suppose that the sin Micah confronted mainly concerns the time before the important reforms of Hezekiah (2 Kings 18-20).
>
> c. **Concerning Samaria and Jerusalem**: The city of **Samaria** was the capital of the northern kingdom of Israel, and **Jerusalem** was the capital of the southern kingdom of Judah. Micah addressed both the northern and southern kingdoms in his prophecy.
>
>> i. In Judah during this time, King **Ahaz** was a particularly evil ruler. In Israel, there was a succession of evil kings.

2. (2-5) The LORD comes to judge Israel and Judah.

Hear, all you peoples!

Listen, O earth, and all that is in it!
Let the Lord GOD be a witness against you,
The Lord from His holy temple.

For behold, the LORD is coming out of His place;
He will come down
And tread on the high places of the earth.
The mountains will melt under Him,
And the valleys will split
Like wax before the fire,
Like waters poured down a steep place.
All this is for the transgression of Jacob
And for the sins of the house of Israel.
What *is* the transgression of Jacob?
Is it not Samaria?
And what *are* the high places of Judah?
Are they not Jerusalem?

> a. **The LORD is coming out of His place**: In vivid images, Micah saw the LORD descending from heaven to earth, and coming with judgment. If the **mountains** and **valleys** could not stand before Him, what hope does sinful, rebellious man have?
>
> b. **All this is for the transgression of Jacob and for the sins of the house of Israel**: This dramatic, powerful descent of the LORD was only because of the **sins of** His people.
>
> > i. It is easy to imagine that the people of Judah and Israel thought this was unfair. They looked around at the pagan nations surrounding them and saw that they were even more corrupt than themselves. Nevertheless, the principle stands: *For the time has come for judgment to begin at the house of God* (1 Peter 4:17). However, we also do well to remember the second part of that verse: *And if it begins with us first, what will be the end of those who do not obey the gospel of God?*

3. (6-7) Samaria is left desolate in judgment.

"Therefore I will make Samaria a heap of ruins in the field,
Places for planting a vineyard;
I will pour down her stones into the valley,
And I will uncover her foundations.
All her carved images shall be beaten to pieces,
And all her pay as a harlot shall be burned with the fire;
All her idols I will lay desolate,
For she gathered *it* from the pay of a harlot,
And they shall return to the pay of a harlot."

a. **I will make Samaria a heap of ruins in the field**: Micah prophesied the coming judgment on **Samaria**, the capital city of Israel, the kingdom of the ten northern tribes. This was fulfilled in 722 B.C. when Samaria fell to the Assyrians and was completely destroyed.

b. **All her pay as a harlot shall be burned with the fire**: Micah combined the ideas of idolatry and spiritual adultery. Money spent on idols and their worship would be brought to nothing when the mighty army of the Assyrians would destroy Samaria.

i. "Golden images, of such monetary value yet so spiritually and politically worthless, were constructed from the wages of cult prostitutes. The conquerors will break them up and use the money to repeat the same cycle. Only the heart of depraved man could worship gods like that!" (Waltke)

B. Coming judgment on Judah.

1. (8-9) The agony of announcing judgment on the nation of Judah.

Therefore I will wail and howl,
I will go stripped and naked;
I will make a wailing like the jackals
And a mourning like the ostriches,
For her wounds *are* incurable.
For it has come to Judah;
It has come to the gate of My people–
To Jerusalem.

a. **I will wail and howl**: Micah could not prophesy in a dispassionate, detached way. When he saw judgment coming upon his people, it made him **wail and howl** like **the jackals.**

i. Micah didn't just announce judgment and then yawn. He cared so deeply that he wept with God's people. The preacher's duty is more than to just announce judgment and to walk away. He has to *care*. "Many who have rejected a Christian's logic have been won by his tears." (Boice)

b. **For her wounds are incurable**: Our only **incurable** wounds are the ones we refuse to bring to God. With Him, all things are possible (Luke 18:27), but when we refuse to bring our sin to Him, then our **wounds are incurable.**

2. (10-16) The shame of Judah's judgment is evident among the nations.

Tell *it* not in Gath,
Weep not at all;

In Beth Aphrah
Roll yourself in the dust.
Pass by in naked shame, you inhabitant of Shaphir;
The inhabitant of Zaanan does not go out.
Beth Ezel mourns;
Its place to stand is taken away from you.

For the inhabitant of Maroth pined for good,
But disaster came down from the LORD
To the gate of Jerusalem.
O inhabitant of Lachish,
Harness the chariot to the swift steeds
(She *was* the beginning of sin to the daughter of Zion),
For the transgressions of Israel were found in you.

Therefore you shall give presents to Moresheth Gath;
The houses of Achzib *shall be* a lie to the kings of Israel.
I will yet bring an heir to you, O inhabitant of Mareshah;
The glory of Israel shall come to Adullam.
Make yourself bald and cut off your hair,
Because of your precious children;
Enlarge your baldness like an eagle,
For they shall go from you into captivity.

>   a. **Tell it not in Gath**: The city of **Gath** belonged to the Philistines, and it hurt Micah to think that the Philistines would rejoice at the pain of God's people.
>
>   b. **In Beth Aphrah roll yourself in the dust**: Continuing to the end of the chapter, Micah uses puns and plays on words to talk about the judgment coming upon the cities of Judah. These towns were clustered in the *Shephelah* – the lowlands between the coastal region and the mountains of Judah.
>
>> i. Though Micah used puns, this wasn't about clever word games – it went back to the ancient idea that a name wasn't just your name but that it described your *character* and your *destiny*, sometimes prophetically. In showing how the name of these cities was in some way a prophecy of their destiny, Micah showed how our character becomes our future.
>
>   c. **Beth Aphrah**: To Micah, **Aphrah** sounded like the Hebrew word for *dust*, so he told the citizens of **Beth Aphrah** to roll in the dust in anticipation of coming judgment.

d. **Shaphir**: The name of this town sounded like the word for *beautiful*. It wouldn't be beautiful for long, and Micah warned the citizens of **Shaphir** to prepare for judgment.

e. **Zaanan**: The name of this town sounded like the Hebrew word for *exit* or *go out*. When the enemy's siege armies would come, the Jewish people would not *exit* at all – they would be shut up in the city until they fell.

f. **Beth Ezel**: The name of this town means *the nearby city*. When the army of judgment comes, it won't be near and helpful to any other city.

g. **Maroth**: The name of this town means *bitterness*, and when the army of judgment comes, the citizens of **Maroth** will know plenty of bitterness.

h. **Lachish**: The name of this town sounded like the Hebrew word for *to the horses*. **Lachish** was an important fortress city, and its people should go *to the horses* to fight, but ironically, they would go *to the horses* [**Lachish**] to flee the army of judgment.

i. **Moresheth**: The name of this place – Micah's hometown – sounded like the Hebrew word for *betrothed*. Here he spoke of giving the city wedding gifts as she passed from the rule of one "husband" (Judah) to another (the invading army).

j. **Aczib**: The name of this town sounds like the Hebrew word for *deceitful* or *disappointing*. This city would fall so quickly it would be a deception and a disappointment for Israel.

k. **Mareshah**: The name of this town is related to the Hebrew word for *possessor* or *heir*. The invading army would soon possess this city.

l. **Adullam**: This was the place of refuge for David when he fled from King Saul. It would again be a place of refuge for the high and mighty among Israel, when they would be forced to hide out in **Adullam**.

Micah 2 – God's Sinful People

A. The sins of covetousness and pride.

1. (1-2) Covetousness among God's people.

Woe to those who devise iniquity,
And work out evil on their beds!
At morning light they practice it,
Because it is in the power of their hand.
They covet fields and take *them* **by violence,**
Also houses, and seize *them.*
So they oppress a man and his house,
A man and his inheritance.

> a. **Woe to those who devise iniquity**: All sin is bad before God, but *premeditated* sin is worse. Here Micah spoke plainly to those who **devise iniquity** – in this case – those who oppress others through their greed and covetousness.
>
> b. **At morning light they practice it**: These wicked people spent all night thinking of evil things to do, and eagerly woke up early, **at morning light**, to carry out violence and oppression against their neighbor.
>
> > i. This could also be a reference to ancient legal practices. In the ancient world, law courts opened for business **at morning light** because the rising sun demonstrated light dispelling darkness. Micah saw the corruption of Israel's law courts and explained that they practiced their theft and evil **at morning light**, when the courts opened.
>
> c. **Because it is in the power of their hand**: There are some sins we never commit because we are never put in a place where we *can* commit them. The real test comes when **it is in the power of** our **hand** to sin and we remain faithful to the Lord.

2. (3-5) God's proud people brought low.

Therefore thus says the LORD:

"Behold, against this family I am devising disaster,
From which you cannot remove your necks;
Nor shall you walk haughtily,
For this *is* an evil time.
In that day *one* shall take up a proverb against you,
And lament with a bitter lamentation, saying:
'We are utterly destroyed!
He has changed the heritage of my people;
How He has removed *it* from me!
To a turncoat He has divided our fields.'"

**Therefore you will have no one to determine boundaries by lot
In the assembly of the LORD.**

> a. **Against this family I am devising disaster**: The people devised iniquity; God devised disaster upon them. In His justice, He gave to them what they gave to others.
>
> b. **Nor shall you walk haughtily, for this is an evil time**: Micah rebuked God's people for their pride among God's people and announced that in the **evil time** to come – the time of judgment coming on God's people – they would be brought low and would no longer **walk haughtily**.
>
> c. **To a turncoat He has divided our fields**: In the coming judgment – in particular, the judgment coming on Israel by the conquering Assyrian Empire – they would leave their land in the possession of strangers.

B. Though they sin against His word, God promises restoration to His people.

1. (6-9) God's people reject the word of His prophets.

"Do not prattle," *you say to those* who prophesy.
So they shall not prophesy to you;
They shall not return insult for insult.
You who are named the house of Jacob:
"Is the Spirit of the LORD restricted?
Are these His doings?
Do not My words do good
To him who walks uprightly?

"Lately My people have risen up as an enemy–
You pull off the robe with the garment
From those who trust *you*, as they pass by,

Like men returned from war.
The women of My people you cast out
From their pleasant houses;
From their children
You have taken away My glory forever.

a. **Do not prattle**: When God's prophets came to His people, they didn't receive their message. They disregarded God's word as mere **prattle**. As a result, God stopped sending prophets (**so they shall not prophesy to you**). Fortunately, God's people responded to Micah's warning before God stopped sending him, but it took a while.

i. Micah began his ministry in the reign of Jotham, but nobody listened. Then he prophesied during the reign of Ahaz, but nobody listened. Finally, he prophesied during the reign of Hezekiah and the leaders and the people repented. Micah didn't give up, even though the results were slow in coming. Micah preached for anywhere between 16 and 25 years before there was any response.

b. **Is the Spirit of the LORD restricted?** In their foolishness, the people of Israel thought that *God* was the problem. They needed to understand that there was no restriction on **the Spirit of the LORD**; instead *they* provided all the restrictions.

i. "Do you not think, again, that we very much act as if the Spirit of the Lord were straitened *when we only look for little blessing*s? I am very glad to see three hundred or four hundred persons in a year converted and added to this church, and this has long been the case; but if I ever imbibed the idea that this was all that might be done, I should be straitening the Spirit of God." (Spurgeon)

c. **Do not My words do good to him who walks uprightly?** The key to their preservation in the midst of judgment was to stick tightly to God's **words**. When they rejected God's **words**, they were left poor and destitute, both materially and spiritually.

2. (10-11) God's people embrace false prophets.

"Arise and depart,
For this *is* not *your* rest;
Because it is defiled, it shall destroy,
Yes, with utter destruction.
If a man should walk in a false spirit
And speak a lie, *saying*,
'I will prophesy to you of wine and drink,'
Even he would be the prattler of this people.

a. **This is not your rest**: Micah exposed the lies of false prophets showing that they could never really give **rest**. The words of false prophets are **defiled**, and bring **utter destruction** instead of the peace, rest, and restoration of God's word.

b. **If a man should walk in a false spirit and speak a lie**: With judgment looming on the horizon – especially for the northern kingdom of Israel – there were false prophets who spoke of days of **wine and drink**, giving false comfort and hope to a deceived people. These were the real "prattlers," not the true prophets of God, as they were falsely called by the ungodly in Micah's day (Micah 2:6). The only prophet they wanted was one to tell them there would be plenty of alcohol (**I will prophesy to you of wine and drink**).

3. (12-13) A promise of restoration.

"I will surely assemble all of you, O Jacob,
I will surely gather the remnant of Israel;
I will put them together like sheep of the fold,
Like a flock in the midst of their pasture;
They shall make a loud noise because of *so many* people.
The one who breaks open will come up before them;
They will break out,
Pass through the gate,
And go out by it;
Their king will pass before them,
With the Lord at their head."

a. **I will surely assemble all of you, O Jacob**: Though judgment was promised because of the great sin of God's people, they were still not beyond the grace and goodness of God. He still promised restoration to **the remnant of Israel**.

b. **They shall make a loud noise because of so many people**: The remnant would not be few; there would be **many people** brought back to the Lord and His ways – **with the Lord at their head**.

c. **The one who breaks open**: This can be translated as a title; the King James Version has it as *the Breaker*. We can see this as a more obscure, but no less precious messianic title of Jesus: *the Breaker*. In this office, He is the captain and leader of His people, advancing in front of His flock. We need a *Breaker*, a trailblazer for our lives.

Micah 3 – Against Princes and Prophets

A. God against the princes of His people.

1. (1-3) The violence of leaders against God's people.

And I said:

"Hear now, O heads of Jacob,
And you rulers of the house of Israel:
Is it **not for you to know justice?**
You who hate good and love evil;
Who strip the skin from My people,
And the flesh from their bones;
Who also eat the flesh of My people,
Flay their skin from them,
Break their bones,
And chop *them* **in pieces**
Like *meat* **for the pot,**
Like flesh in the caldron."

> a. **Hear now, O heads of Jacob**: Previously, Micah addressed his comments to God's people in general. Next he specifically spoke to their leaders, because they had both a special responsibility and accountability before God.

> b. **You who hate good and love evil**: If this description wasn't bad enough, Micah went on to illustrate how terribly the leaders of Israel and Judah used the people – as if they were cannibals feasting on the people of God (**who also eat the flesh of My people**).

>> i. "Since the grinding poverty of the poor was leading them into an early grave, the prophet, in a sustained metaphor, depicts the magistrates responsible for creating these conditions as acting like cannibals. This grotesque figure aims to awaken the conscience of the reprobates." (Waltke)

ii. This reminds us the people never exist for the sake of the leaders, but leaders are there for the sake of the people. A leader should never serve God's people dominated by the question, "What is in it for me?" When they do, they are like the cannibalistic leaders described by Micah.

2. (4) God's judgment of silence against corrupt leaders.

Then they will cry to the LORD,
But He will not hear them;
He will even hide His face from them at that time,
Because they have been evil in their deeds.

a. **Then they will cry to the LORD, but He will not hear them**: This was one example of God's judgment against the corrupt leaders. When they cried out for God's help, the LORD would remain silent.

b. **He will even hide His face from them at that time**: One aspect of the blessing pronounced by the priests of Israel was asking the LORD to *make His face shine upon* them (Numbers 6:25). Here, Micah promised the opposite of this blessing – that God would **even hide His face from them at that time**.

B. God against the false prophets to His people.

1. (5-7) The sin and promised judgment of false prophets.

Thus says the LORD concerning the prophets
Who make my people stray;
Who chant "Peace"
While they chew with their teeth,
But who prepare war against him
Who puts nothing into their mouths:
"Therefore you shall have night without vision,
And you shall have darkness without divination;
The sun shall go down on the prophets,
And the day shall be dark for them.
So the seers shall be ashamed,
And the diviners abashed;
Indeed they shall all cover their lips;
For *there is* no answer from God."

a. **The prophets who make my people stray**: Micah returned to a theme first mentioned in Micah 2:11, speaking of the false **prophets** who brought hollow comfort and pretend peace to God's people.

b. **The sun shall go down on the prophets**: Through Micah, God announced that He would bring the false prophets into complete confusion and disrepute. They will have **no answer from God** and therefore they **shall be ashamed**.

2. (8) Micah's confidence as a true prophet of God.

But truly I am full of power by the Spirit of the Lord,
And of justice and might,
To declare to Jacob his transgression
And to Israel his sin.

> a. **I am full of power by the Spirit of the Lord**: In contrast to the coming shame of the false prophets, Micah had justified confidence in the Lord who called him as a prophet. Because he knew God and was close to God and His word, Micah knew that he was **full of power by the Spirit of the Lord**.
>
>> i. Micah also knew that the **power** came **by the Spirit of the Lord**, not by anything in Micah. The power also came from **justice and might** because Micah knew he was on the side of God's word and God's strength.
>>
>> ii. "We must have the Holy Spirit, and if we have him not, all our machinery will stand still; or if it goes on, it will produce no effect whatever. I heard of a Christian man whose mill-wheel was noticed to be in motion on a certain Sunday. The people going to worship greatly wondered thereat; but one who went by set their minds at rest by pointing out that the wheel was only turning idly round, because the water, by accident, was allowed to flow over it. But the man said, 'It is very like our minister and his sermons. There is no work being done, but the wheel goes round, clickety click, clickety click, though it is not grinding anything.' Therein it also greatly resembles many an organisation for spiritual service: the water is passing over it, glittering as it flows; but the outside motion does not join on to any human need, nor produce any practical result, and nothing comes of the click and hum." (Spurgeon)
>
> b. **To declare to Jacob his transgression**: Like most prophets in the Old Testament, Micah's job was to expose the sin of God's people.
>
>> i. We might say that under the new covenant, prophets have a somewhat different calling. Under the old covenant, the law was not written on the heart of the believer and the Holy Spirit did not indwell each believer in the same way as under the new covenant.
>>
>> ii. Therefore, there was a greater need for the convicting work of the Spirit of God coming from the "outside," from prophets such as Micah. In the New Testament, the Apostle Paul described the ministry

of the prophet like this: *But he who prophesies speaks edification and exhortation and comfort to men* (1 Corinthians 14:3). This certainly doesn't mean that under the new covenant prophecy will never be used to expose sin, but it isn't its central purpose.

3. (9-12) Unrepentant Jerusalem will share Samaria's fate of destruction.

Now hear this,
You heads of the house of Jacob
And rulers of the house of Israel,
Who abhor justice
And pervert all equity,
Who build up Zion with bloodshed
And Jerusalem with iniquity:
Her heads judge for a bribe,
Her priests teach for pay,
And her prophets divine for money.
Yet they lean on the LORD, and say,
"Is not the LORD among us?
No harm can come upon us."
Therefore because of you
Zion shall be plowed *like* **a field,**
Jerusalem shall become heaps of ruins,
And the mountain of the temple
Like the bare hills of the forest.

a. **Now hear this…who build up Zion with bloodshed and Jerusalem with iniquity**: In this chapter, Micah first spoke to the judges, then to the prophets. Next he speaks to the princes, **you heads of the house of Jacob**. The rulers of Jerusalem were not much better than the rulers of Israel and could expect similar judgment unless they repented.

b. **Yet they lean on the LORD, and say, "Is not the LORD among us? No harm can come upon us"**: The leaders of Jerusalem had false confidence in religious ritual and form. All the while, judgment was appointed for Jerusalem unless they repented.

i. The great thing about the prophet Micah was that he was listened to. Hosea was ignored, and so was Amos. They threw Jeremiah in jail for his prophetic message of coming judgment. In contrast, King Hezekiah and the leadership of Judah listened to the prophet Micah.

ii. Jeremiah 26:17-19 describes how even a hundred years later the impact of Micah was remembered: *Then certain of the elders of the land rose up and spoke to all the assembly of the people, saying: "Micah of Moresheth prophesied in the days of Hezekiah king of Judah, and spoke to all the people of Judah, saying, 'Thus says the* Lord *of hosts: "Zion shall be plowed like a field, Jerusalem shall become heaps of ruins, And the mountain of the temple like the bare hills of the forest. Did Hezekiah king of Judah and all Judah ever put him to death? Did he not fear the* Lord *and seek the* Lord'*s favor? And the* Lord *relented concerning the doom which He had pronounced against them. But we are doing great evil against ourselves."*

iii. "He was heard in the days of Hezekiah. A revival followed. Then, one hundred years later, his words were still remembered, and the memory of what happened earlier was used of God to spare the life of Jeremiah." (Boice)

Micah 4 – The Lord Reigns over Restored Zion

A. The character of restored Zion.

1. (1-3) Zion is the center of a renewed earth.

Now it shall come to pass in the latter days
That **the mountain of the LORD's house**
Shall be established on the top of the mountains,
And shall be exalted above the hills;
And peoples shall flow to it.
Many nations shall come and say,
"Come, and let us go up to the mountain of the LORD,
To the house of the God of Jacob;
He will teach us His ways,
And we shall walk in His paths."
For out of Zion the law shall go forth,
And the word of the LORD from Jerusalem.
He shall judge between many peoples,
And rebuke strong nations afar off;
They shall beat their swords into plowshares,
And their spears into pruning hooks;
Nation shall not lift up sword against nation,
Neither shall they learn war anymore.

    a. **The mountain of the LORD's house…shall be exalted above the hills**: This speaks of the ultimate exaltation of Jerusalem, the City of Zion, in the LORD's final restoration. This will be fulfilled completely in the millennium, when the **peoples shall flow to** a restored and redeemed Jerusalem as the capital of the millennial earth (**out of Zion the law shall go forth, and the word of the LORD from Jerusalem**).

        i. Micah 4:1-3 is repeated in Isaiah 2:1-3. Since Isaiah and Micah were contemporary prophets, it isn't surprising that the same Spirit of the

Lord could give these two prophets the same word, to establish and emphasize His word.

ii. The glorious transformation of the mountain of the Lord is especially wonderful in light of what the sinning people of God did to it: *Therefore because of you Zion shall be plowed like a field, Jerusalem shall become heaps of ruins, and the mountain of the temple like the bare hills of the forest* (Micah 3:12).

b. **He will teach us His ways**: With the prophet's eye, Micah saw the world streaming into Jerusalem to meet with the Lord GOD, and to know Him better.

c. **He shall judge between many peoples**: During the reign of the Messiah, there will be no more war. There will still be conflicts between nations and individuals, but they will be justly and decisively resolved by the Messiah and those who reign with Him (**He shall judge between many peoples, and rebuke strong nations**).

i. It isn't the reign of the Messiah itself that will change the heart of man. Citizens of the Earth will still need to trust in Jesus and His work on their behalf for their personal salvation during the millennium. But war and armed conflict will not be tolerated.

d. **Nation shall not lift up sword against nation, neither shall they learn war anymore**: It is important to see that this is not the peace of capitulation. This is the peace of enforced righteousness. There will be no more war, and no more need for **swords** – so it makes sense to transform them into **plowshares**. There will be no more war because there will be a new ruler on earth, Jesus Christ.

i. Psalm 2:9 tells us what the Messiah will do to the disobedient in that day: *You shall break them with a rod of iron; You shall dash them to pieces like a potter's vessel.*

ii. We long for the day when there is no more need for a military budget; when the money that goes for weapons and armies can go to schools and parks. But we are only safe doing that when the Messiah reigns among us!

e. **It shall come to pass in the latter days**: In 1941 Franklin Roosevelt gave a famous speech about four freedoms: freedom of *speech*, freedom of *religion*, freedom from *want*, and freedom from *fear*. Micah 4:1-5 describes four freedoms:

- Freedom from *ignorance* (**He will teach us His ways**).
- Freedom from *war* (**neither shall they learn war anymore**).

- Freedom from *want* (**everyone shall sit under his vine and under his fig tree**).
- Freedom from *fear* (**no one shall make them afraid**).

2. (4-5) The blessed people of restored Zion.

But everyone shall sit under his vine and under his fig tree,
And no one shall make *them* afraid;
For the mouth of the L ORD **of hosts has spoken.**
For all people walk each in the name of his god,
But we will walk in the name of the L ORD **our God**
Forever and ever.

> a. **Everyone shall sit under his vine and under his fig tree**: This is a proverbial expression that means prosperity and peace (1 Kings 4:25, 2 Kings 18:31).
>
> b. **We will walk in the name of the** L ORD **our God forever and ever**: In the millennial reign, the inhabitants of the Earth will not be compelled to follow the L ORD. Some will **walk each in the name of his god**; those who do **walk in the name of the** L ORD will enjoy great blessing and peace.

3. (6-8) The gathering of restored Zion.

"In that day," says the L ORD ,
"I will assemble the lame,
I will gather the outcast
And those whom I have afflicted;
I will make the lame a remnant,
And the outcast a strong nation;
So the L ORD **will reign over them in Mount Zion**
From now on, even forever.
And you, O tower of the flock,
The stronghold of the daughter of Zion,
To you shall it come,
Even the former dominion shall come,
The kingdom of the daughter of Jerusalem."

> a. **I will make the lame a remnant, and the outcast a strong nation**: God's restoration will not be just for the strong, but also for the weak and disadvantaged. They will especially know the blessing of His restoration.
>
> b. **To you shall it come**: These promises are so glorious that it would be easy for Israel to think they were too good to be true. Therefore, God gave them a special promise, vowing **to you it shall come**.

B. The birth of restored Zion.

1. (9-10) The pain before Zion's restoration.

Now why do you cry aloud?
***Is there* no king in your midst?**
Has your counselor perished?
For pangs have seized you like a woman in labor.
Be in pain, and labor to bring forth,
O daughter of Zion,
Like a woman in birth pangs.
For now you shall go forth from the city,
You shall dwell in the field,
And to Babylon you shall go.
There you shall be delivered;
There the Lord **will redeem you**
From the hand of your enemies.

> a. **Pangs have seized you like a woman in labor**: After describing the glory of restored Zion, Micah told them of some of the pain they would experience before it comes. Part of the pain would be a lack of leadership (**no king in your midst…. counselor perished**).
>
> b. **To Babylon you shall go. There you shall be delivered**: As is common in the prophets, Micah combined promises fulfilled in different eras of God's work. Having just spoken of the millennial earth, now he spoke of Israel's deliverance from Babylonian captivity.

2. (11-13) The strength of restored Zion among the nations.

Now also many nations have gathered against you,
Who say, "Let her be defiled,
And let our eye look upon Zion."
But they do not know the thoughts of the Lord,
Nor do they understand His counsel;
For He will gather them like sheaves to the threshing floor.

"Arise and thresh, O daughter of Zion;
For I will make your horn iron,
And I will make your hooves bronze;
You shall beat in pieces many peoples;
I will consecrate their gain to the Lord,
And their substance to the Lord of the whole earth."

> a. **Many nations have gathered against you**: Though the nations were set against Israel, the Lord was for them (**they do not know the thoughts of**

the LORD). The LORD will deal with Israel's enemies as easily as a farmer deals with the **sheaves** of grain on the **threshing floor**.

b. **I will make your horn iron**: When the LORD restores Zion, He will restore them in strength – as strong as an ox with an **iron** horn. This has its ultimate fulfillment in the millennium when Israel will be lifted up as a superpower among the nations.

i. "The ox pulling the threshing-sledge represents the people of God. She is supernaturally equipped with *horns of iron*, symbolizing her invincibility, and with *hoofs of bronze*, with which she treads the pride and pretensions of the enemy exceedingly fine." (Waltke)

Micah 5 – A Ruler from Bethlehem

A. The birth and the work of the Ruler from Bethlehem.

1. (1-2) From the lowly and humble in Israel comes a Ruler.

Now gather yourself in troops,
O daughter of troops;
He has laid siege against us;
They will strike the judge of Israel with a rod on the cheek.

"But you, Bethlehem Ephrathah,
***Though* you are little among the thousands of Judah,**
***Yet* out of you shall come forth to Me**
The One to be Ruler in Israel,
Whose goings forth *are* from of old,
From everlasting."

> a. **He has laid siege against us**: Micah announced that Israel will be humbled by foreign powers, and even her judges will bear insults.
>
> b. **But you, Bethlehem Ephrathah...out of you shall come forth to Me the One to be Ruler in Israel**: In the coming time of humiliation under foreign powers, God would raise up a great **Ruler** from a humble place – **Bethlehem**.
>
>> i. **Bethlehem** was well known as the hometown of David, Israel's greatest king, yet it was never a great or influential city. It was truly **little among the thousands of Judah**. Yet God chose it as the birthplace of the Messiah, the **Ruler in Israel**.
>>
>> ii. This passage from Micah 5 was quoted by the chief priests and teachers of the law when Herod asked about the birth of the Messiah (Matthew 2:5-6).
>>
>> iii. **Bethlehem** means *House of Bread*, and Jesus is the bread of life (John 6:35). "And now for that word *Ephrata*h. That was the old name of the place which the Jews retained and loved. The meaning of it is,

'fruitfulness,' or 'abundance.' Ah! well was Jesus born in the house of fruitfulness; for whence cometh my fruitfulness and thy fruitfulness, my brother, but from Bethlehem? Our poor barren hearts never produced one fruit or flower, till they were watered with the Saviour's blood." (Spurgeon)

c. **Whose goings forth are from of old, from everlasting**: This glorious promise was fulfilled in Jesus Christ, and Micah's prophetic voice declared that though Jesus came from Bethlehem, He did not *begin* there. His **goings forth** are from before the foundation of the world.

i. The Bible tells us that Jesus is the Alpha and the Omega, the Beginning and the End (Revelation 22:13). This means from the very beginning, Jesus was there. There was never a time when Jesus did not exist.

ii. Before Jesus was born in Bethlehem, He existed as the *Second Person of the Trinity* (John 17:5, 17:24). These passages tell us that there was a relationship of love, fellowship, and shared glory that the Father and the Son shared before the creation of all things. The name "Jesus" was not known as a name for the Second Person of the Trinity until the angel Gabriel announced it to Mary (Luke 1:31). But the eternal Son existed before He revealed Himself as "Jesus."

iii. Before Bethlehem, Jesus was the creator of all things (Colossians 1:16-17, John 1:1-3). "He was *before* all things. As he is the *Creator* of all things, so he is the *Eternal*, and *no part* of what was *created*. [Every] *being* but God has been *created*. Whatever has *not been created* is God. But Jesus is the *Creator* of all things; therefore he is God; for he cannot be a *part* of his *own work*." (Clarke)

iv. In the Old Testament, Jesus appeared as God made visible or the Angel of the LORD. There are many instances in the Old Testament where individuals are shown to have had a face-to-face encounter with the LORD (Genesis 16:7-13, Genesis 18, Genesis 32:24-32, Joshua 5:13-15, Judges 6:11-24, Judges 13:8-24, Daniel 3). In each situation, the Person is given different titles, but in all cases the person is plainly referred to as the LORD Himself but appearing in a human form.

v. From before the creation of all things, God's plan of the ages included Jesus (1 Peter 1.20, Ephesians 1.4).

vi. Knowing that Jesus' **goings forth are from of old, from everlasting** shows us some important things:

- It shows us the glory of Jesus, that He is far more than a man.

- It shows us the love of Jesus, that He would leave the glory of heaven for us.
- It shows us the nature of Jesus, that He would add humanity to His deity.
- It shows us the sympathy of Jesus, that He remains fully man and fully God.

2. (3-5a) The Ruler serves His flock.

Therefore He shall give them up,
Until the time *that* **she who is in labor has given birth;**
Then the remnant of His brethren
Shall return to the children of Israel.
And He shall stand and feed *His flock*
In the strength of the LORD,
In the majesty of the name of the LORD His God;
And they shall abide,
For now He shall be great
To the ends of the earth;
And this *One* **shall be peace.**

a. **He shall give them up, until the time**: Micah anticipated a future time, one that was partially fulfilled in the Babylonian exile and return, but will be ultimately fulfilled in the great tribulation and restoration of Israel. In both those eras, the LORD will seem distant from Israel **until the time** for restoration is ready.

b. **Then the remnant of His brethren shall return.... He shall stand and feed His flock in the strength of the LORD**: After the time of Israel's trial, the LORD will restore gloriously. The *Ruler* born in Bethlehem will tenderly care for **His flock in the strength of the LORD**.

c. **They shall abide, for now He shall be great to the ends of the earth**: The greatness of the *Ruler* from Bethlehem guarantees the standing of His people. They **abide** because of His greatness.

d. **This One shall be peace**: It isn't just that the *Ruler* from Bethlehem *brings* **peace**; He *is* peace. As Paul wrote of Jesus in Ephesians 2:14, *He Himself is our peace*.

3. (5b-6) The Ruler delivers Jacob from Assyria.

When the Assyrian comes into our land,
And when he treads in our palaces,
Then we will raise against him
Seven shepherds and eight princely men.

They shall waste with the sword the land of Assyria,
And the land of Nimrod at its entrances;
Thus He shall deliver *us* from the Assyrian,
When he comes into our land
And when he treads within our borders.

> a. **When the Assyrian comes into our land**: After the pattern of the prophets, Micah blended near and distant ages in his prophecy. The threat of the **Assyrian** would come against both kingdoms shortly, but Micah also used the *idea* of the **Assyrian** for any pagan nation or empire set against God's people.
>
> b. **We will raise against him seven shepherds and eight princely men**: Though the enemies of God's people would come against them, under God's blessing leaders will **raise against** them mighty men. God often works this way to **deliver us** from our enemies.

B. The triumph of the remnant of Jacob.

1. (7-9) The remnant is large and triumphant.

Then the remnant of Jacob
Shall be in the midst of many peoples,
Like dew from the LORD,
Like showers on the grass,
That tarry for no man
Nor wait for the sons of men.
And the remnant of Jacob
Shall be among the Gentiles,
In the midst of many peoples,
Like a lion among the beasts of the forest,
Like a young lion among flocks of sheep,
Who, if he passes through,
Both treads down and tears in pieces,
And none can deliver.
Your hand shall be lifted against your adversaries,
And all your enemies shall be cut off.

> a. **The remnant of Jacob shall be…like dew from the LORD**: When God delivers Zion it won't be a small deliverance. It will spread as wide as the **dew** and **showers on the grass**.
>
> b. **Like a young lion among flocks of sheep**: When God delivers Zion, it won't be a weak deliverance. It will strengthen Israel so that she will triumph over her enemies like a **lion** against **sheep**. This has its ultimate

fulfillment in the millennial earth, when it is said that the lion will lie down with the lamb – but still, it's better to be the lion!

2. (10-15) The LORD is exalted among the remnant.

"And it shall be in that day," says the LORD,
"That I will cut off your horses from your midst
And destroy your chariots.
I will cut off the cities of your land
And throw down all your strongholds.
I will cut off sorceries from your hand,
And you shall have no soothsayers.
Your carved images I will also cut off,
And your sacred pillars from your midst;
You shall no more worship the work of your hands;
I will pluck your wooden images from your midst;
Thus I will destroy your cities.
And I will execute vengeance in anger and fury
On the nations that have not heard."

> a. **I will cut off your horses…. the cities of your land…your strongholds…. sorceries…. your carved images…your sacred pillars**: In restored Zion, the LORD will not allow any of the idolatries Israel once indulged in. Instead, He will **cut off** all of those things, whether they are basically good (**horses** or **cities**) or fundamentally evil (**sorceries** or **sacred pillars**).

> b. **I will execute vengeance…on the nations that have not heard**: God will not only look after Israel's purity; in the millennial earth **the nations** will also need to walk in purity before Him.

Micah 6 – In the Court of the LORD

A. The LORD's complaint against His people.

1. (1-2) In court with the LORD.

Hear now what the LORD says:

"Arise, plead your case before the mountains,
And let the hills hear your voice.
Hear, O you mountains, the LORD's complaint,
And you strong foundations of the earth;
For the LORD has a complaint against His people,
And He will contend with Israel.

> a. **Arise, plead your case**: Micah pictured a court of law, with Israel on trial before the LORD. In the presence of unshakable witnesses (**the mountains** and **the hills** and the **strong foundations of the earth**), the court comes to order.

> b. **The LORD has a complaint against His people, and He will contend with Israel**: In His court, God will bring His case – His **complaint** against Israel.

2. (3-5) The LORD's complaint against His people.

"O My people, what have I done to you?
And how have I wearied you?
Testify against Me.
For I brought you up from the land of Egypt,
I redeemed you from the house of bondage;
And I sent before you Moses, Aaron, and Miriam.
O My people, remember now
What Balak king of Moab counseled
And what Balaam the son of Beor answered him,
From Acacia Grove to Gilgal,
That you may know the righteousness of the LORD."

a. **Testify against Me**: As Israel stepped to the witness stand, God asked them, "**What have I done to you?**" He had done nothing but good to Israel and had been repaid with rejection and rebellion.

b. **I redeemed you from the house of bondage**: Not only did God *not* do evil to Israel, He also did them an enormous amount of *good*. He **redeemed** them and gave them godly leaders. God's case against Israel was strong and Israel was guilty in the prophet's court.

c. **Remember now what Balak king of Moab counseled**: Numbers 22-24 tells the story of **Balak** and **Balaam**. After meeting with King Balak of Moab, Balaam prophesied over Israel four times. As he spoke God's word, he did not curse Israel – but he blessed them each time. When he was unsuccessful in cursing Israel, Balaam **answered** Balak on how to bring Israel under a curse. Instead of trying to have a prophet curse them, the Moabites would lead them into fornication and idolatry, and thus God would curse idolatrous and disobedient Israel. Balak did just that, sending his young women into the camp of Israel to lead Israel into sexual immorality and idolatry. Because of their sin, God did curse Israel – He brought a plague of judgment upon Israel that killed 24,000.

> i. In light of this, Israel must **remember** that God could never be persuaded to curse Israel, except if they brought curses on themselves through their own idolatry and disobedience. In the prophet's courtroom God showed Israel that if they felt cursed in any way, it was entirely their responsibility.

3. (6-7) The answer of His people: "What can I do?"

With what shall I come before the Lord,
***And* bow myself before the High God?**
Shall I come before Him with burnt offerings,
With calves a year old?
Will the Lord be pleased with thousands of rams,
Ten thousand rivers of oil?
Shall I give my firstborn *for* my transgression,
The fruit of my body *for* the sin of my soul?

> a. **With what shall I come before the Lord**: This was a question asked out of bitterness and resentment. In Micah's imagined courtroom, Israel called out to God from the witness stand, and said: "Just what do You want from me?"
>
> b. **Will the Lord be pleased with thousands of rams, ten thousand rivers of oil?** We can almost hear Israel shouting at God from the witness stand. "You ask too much, God. Nothing will satisfy You. If we brought

thousands of rams or rivers of oil or even our own firstborn it would not be enough to please You. You are unreasonable."

i. "Blinded to God's goodness and character, he reasons within his own depraved frame of reference. He need not change; God must change.... His willingness to raise the price does not reflect his generosity but veils a complaint that God demands too much." (Waltke)

4. (8) The reply of the Lord: "He has shown you."

He has shown you, O man, what *is* good;
And what does the Lord require of you
But to do justly,
To love mercy,
And to walk humbly with your God?

a. **He has shown you**: In Micah the prophet's imagined courtroom God stopped the shouting of the angry defendant from the witness box. God essentially said, "You act as if what I require of you is some mystery. In fact, it is no mystery at all. I have **shown you** clearly **what is good** and what I **require of you**."

b. **To do justly, to love mercy, and to walk humbly with your God**: The Lord answered the contentious witness in open court. "What I require of you isn't complicated. Simply do three things."

- **Do justly**: "Act in a just, fair way towards others. Treat them as you would want to be treated."

- **Love mercy**: "Don't just show mercy, but **love** to show it. Give others the same measure of mercy you want to receive from Me."

- **Walk humbly with your God**: "Remember who I am – *your God*. If you keep that in mind, you will *walk humbly* before Me."

  i. "I would not advise any of you to *try* to be humble, but to *be* humble. As to acting humbly, when a man forces himself to it, that is poor stuff. When a man talks a great deal about his humility, when he is very humble to everybody, he is generally a canting hypocrite. Humility must be in the heart, and then it will come out spontaneously as the outflow of life in every act that a man performs." (Spurgeon)

  ii. Spurgeon's sermon *Micah's Message for Today* applied the idea of how to **walk humbly with your God**:

  - Walk humbly when you are spiritually strong.
  - Walk humbly when you have much work to do.
  - Walk humbly in all your motives.

- Walk humbly when studying God's word.
- Walk humbly when under trials.
- Walk humbly in your devotions.
- Walk humbly with your brothers and sisters in Christ.
- Walk humbly when dealing with sinners.

iii. "True humility is thinking rightly of thyself, not meanly. When you have found out what you really are, you will be humble, for you are nothing to boast of. To be humble will make you safe. To be humble will make you happy. To be humble will make music in your heart when you go to bed. To be humble here will make you wake up in the likeness of your Master by-and-by." (Spurgeon)

c. **He has shown you**: In Micah the prophet's imagined courtroom God has proven His case before the court. Israel was afflicted, but it was not because of the neglect or disregard of God. Their own sin brought their affliction upon them. In addition, what God required of them was not mysterious or too difficult – they simply did not do it.

B. The voice of the LORD cries out in the city.

1. (9-12) God sees the injustice and deceit of Israel.

The LORD's voice cries to the city—
Wisdom shall see Your name:

"Hear the Rod!
Who has appointed it?
Are there yet the treasures of wickedness
In the house of the wicked,
And the short measure *that is* an abomination?
Shall I count pure *those* with the wicked scales,
And with the bag of deceitful weights?
For her rich men are full of violence,
Her inhabitants have spoken lies,
And their tongue is deceitful in their mouth.

a. **Hear the Rod! Who has appointed it?** Israel *felt* the rod of God, but they did not **hear** it. God tells them to **hear the Rod**, both in the sense of the *rod* as a picture of the corrective discipline of God, and in the sense that **the Rod** can be personified as the voice of God Himself.

i. "We can rest contentedly in our sins and in our stupidities; and anyone who has watched gluttons shoveling down the most exquisite foods as if they did not know what they were eating, will admit that we can ignore even pleasure. But pain insists on being attended to. God whispers to us in our pleasures, speaks to us in our conscience, but shouts in our pains: it is His megaphone to rouse a deaf world." (C.S. Lewis, *The Problem of Pain*)

b. **The short measure that is an abomination.... wicked scales... deceitful weights**: God was angry with Israel for cheating in their business dealings. They lied and stole and cheated one another, all for the sake of making some money from each other.

c. **Her rich men are full of violence**: The sin of Israel went further than just cheating others in business and commerce; they also made themselves rich through plain **violence**. They could expect the judgment of God for such sin.

i. "No society is ever entirely upright or godly; there are always evil people in it. But in a well-functioning society the evil are suppressed and those of good character are prominent and rule the land. In times of moral breakdown this is inverted." (Boice)

2. (13-16) God's judgment on greedy and wicked Israel.

"Therefore I will also make *you* sick by striking you,
By making *you* desolate because of your sins.
You shall eat, but not be satisfied;
Hunger *shall be* in your midst.
You may carry *some* away, but shall not save *them;*
And what you do rescue I will give over to the sword.

You shall sow, but not reap;
You shall tread the olives, but not anoint yourselves with oil;
And *make* sweet wine, but not drink wine.
For the statutes of Omri are kept;
All the works of Ahab's house *are done;*
And you walk in their counsels,
That I may make you a desolation,
And your inhabitants a hissing.
Therefore you shall bear the reproach of My people."

a. **You shall eat, but not be satisfied.... what you do rescue I will give over to the sword**: God promised a tragic end for their ill-gotten gains. He would allow them no satisfaction or blessing in what they possessed.

b. **All the works of Ahab's house are done; and you walk in their counsels**: Instead of walking in the ways of the LORD, they walked in the sinful example of wicked kings before them, and in the **counsels** of the ungodly.

i. "*Omri*, king of Israel, the father of Ahab, was one of the worst kings the Israelites ever had; and *Ahab* followed in his wicked father's steps. The *statutes* of those kings were the very grossest *idolatry*." (Clarke)

Micah 7 – Israel's Confession and Comfort

A. God's people humbly confess their sin.

1. (1-4) An honest confession of their sinful state.

Woe is me!
For I am like those who gather summer fruits,
Like those who glean vintage grapes;
There is no cluster to eat
Of the first-ripe fruit *which* my soul desires.
The faithful *man* has perished from the earth,
And *there is* no one upright among men.
They all lie in wait for blood;
Every man hunts his brother with a net.

That they may successfully do evil with both hands—
The prince asks *for gifts,*
The judge *seeks* a bribe,
And the great *man* utters his evil desire;
So they scheme together.
The best of them *is* like a brier;
The most upright *is sharper* than a thorn hedge;
The day of your watchman and your punishment comes;
Now shall be their perplexity.

> a. **Woe is me**: On behalf of the sinful nation, the prophet Micah confessed the sin of God's people. First, he recognized that their sin had left them *impoverished* (**there is no cluster to eat of the first-ripe fruit which my soul desires**). Then he described some of their specific sins and their general character, revealing their deeply ingrained sin against others.

> b. **The day of your watchman and your punishment comes; now shall be their perplexity**: When the sinner is immersed in sin and feeling successful, they feel like there is no price to pay for their sin. Nevertheless,

there will come **the day of your watchman and your punishment**. The assured self-confidence of the sinner will be turned to **perplexity**.

2. (5-7) Crumbling relationships among God's people.

Do not trust in a friend;
Do not put your confidence in a companion;
Guard the doors of your mouth
From her who lies in your bosom.
For son dishonors father,
Daughter rises against her mother,
Daughter-in-law against her mother-in-law;
A man's enemies *are* **the men of his own household.**
Therefore I will look to the Lord**;**
I will wait for the God of my salvation;
My God will hear me.

> a. **Do not trust in a friend**: Because of their rampant sin and selfishness, personal relationships had crumbled among God's people. One could not **trust in a friend** or put **confidence in a companion**, and even blood relatives were at war with each other.
>
> b. **Therefore I will look to the** Lord**…my God will hear me**: In this sin-immersed culture, there were few people to inspire confidence or offer compassion – so one could only **look to the** Lord.
>
>> i. This was a *bad* thing because people should be honorable and trustworthy enough so that we can have confidence in them and expect compassion from them. Nevertheless, God can use this as a *good* thing, because it forces us to put our trust in the only One who can never let us down – the **God of my salvation**.

3. (8-10) The humble state of God's people.

Do not rejoice over me, my enemy;
When I fall, I will arise;
When I sit in darkness,
The Lord *will be* **a light to me.**
I will bear the indignation of the Lord**,**
Because I have sinned against Him,
Until He pleads my case
And executes justice for me.
He will bring me forth to the light;
I will see His righteousness.
Then *she who is* **my enemy will see,**
And shame will cover her who said to me,

"Where is the LORD your God?"
My eyes will see her;
Now she will be trampled down
Like mud in the streets.

> a. **Do not rejoice over me, my enemy**: Micah spoke for those brought low by personal sin and the sin of the community. In spite of their humiliation, he warned their enemies to not **rejoice** over their condition because **when I fall, I will arise** and **when I sit in darkness, the LORD will be a light to me**. "You see me brought low now, but you should know that it isn't for long. God will lift me up."
>
> b. **I will bear the indignation of the LORD, because I have sinned against Him**: Speaking for the sinful people, Micah honorably took responsibility for their sin. The idea is, "I know that I have sinned, and so I will accept my correction." Micah knew that God's people would stay in their low place **until He pleads my case and executes justice for me**. They were totally dependent on God's care.
>
>> i. "Herein is discovered the difference between remorse and penitence. In remorse a man is sorry for himself; he mourns over his sin because it has brought suffering to him. In penitence he is grieved by the wrong sin has done to God; he yields his personal suffering in the confidence that by it God is setting him free from his sin." (Morgan)
>
> c. **He will bring me forth to the light; I will see His righteousness**: At the same time, there was complete confidence in the salvation of God and their vindication before their enemies. This shows that God's people knew their sinful state, but they also knew the greatness of God's redemption.

B. God's comfort and pardon for His people.

1. (11-13) The restored city of the people of God.

In **the day when your walls are to be built,**
In **that day the decree shall go far and wide.**
In **that day they shall come to you**
From Assyria and the fortified cities,
From the fortress to the River,
From sea to sea,
And mountain *to* **mountain.**
Yet the land shall be desolate
Because of those who dwell in it,
And for the fruit of their deeds.

> a. **In the day when your walls are to be built, in that day the decree shall go far and wide**: When the time comes for Israel's restoration, God will send a call out **far and wide** to gather and restore His people.
>
> b. **Yet the land shall be desolate because of those who dwell in it**: When God gathers Israel for restoration, they will come to a **desolate** land, ruined because of the judgment of God on the sin of His people.

2. (14-15) God cares for His people as in days of old.

Shepherd Your people with Your staff,
The flock of Your heritage,
Who dwell solitarily *in* a woodland,
In the midst of Carmel;
Let them feed *in* Bashan and Gilead,
As in days of old.

"As in the days when you came out of the land of Egypt,
I will show them wonders."

> a. **Shepherd Your people with Your staff**: After God's people will be brought back to the place they belong, they will be lovingly cared for by the Lord Himself. The Lord *shepherds* them and *feeds* them.
>
> b. **As in the days of old**: There was a time when God's people enjoyed this kind of close relationship with Him. Now, that previous relationship will be restored, and He will **show them wonders**. The **wonders** will come *out of* the close relationship with the Shepherd.

3. (16-17) The nations are brought low before restored Israel.

The nations shall see and be ashamed of all their might;
They shall put *their* hand over *their* mouth;
Their ears shall be deaf.
They shall lick the dust like a serpent;
They shall crawl from their holes like snakes of the earth.
They shall be afraid of the Lord our God,
And shall fear because of You.

> a. **The nations shall see and be ashamed**: When Israel is restored to the land and enjoys a restored relationship with the Lord, then those who opposed God's people will see how wrong they were to fight against them.
>
> b. **They shall be afraid of the Lord our God, and shall fear because of You**: Seeing the greatness of God's restoration will make the nations respect the Lord in a way they didn't before. They will see the power and love of God *in action*.

4. (18-20) The glorious mercy and pardon of God.

Who *is* a God like You,
Pardoning iniquity
And passing over the transgression of the remnant of His heritage?

He does not retain His anger forever,
Because He delights *in* mercy.
He will again have compassion on us,
And will subdue our iniquities.

You will cast all our sins
Into the depths of the sea.
You will give truth to Jacob
***And* mercy to Abraham,**
Which You have sworn to our fathers
From days of old.

a. **Who is a God like You**: In light of the glorious restoration given by the Lord to Israel, Micah glorified the God of such great forgiveness (**pardoning iniquity and passing over the transgression of the remnant of His heritage**). Micah saw that God's forgiveness was so great, that it can't even be compared to what often passes for forgiveness among men.

i. Boice on **who is a God like You**: "It is a theme verse and appropriately ends the book. For it is a play on Micah's name. Micah means 'Who is like Yahweh?'"

b. **Because He delights in mercy**: *Why* does God have such great mercy and forgiveness for His people? The reasons are in *Him*, not in His people. It is simply **because He delights in mercy**.

i. If God **delights in mercy**, *then why are some men lost?* Because God doesn't delight in mercy so as to shame His justice. God opens His hand of mercy to all who will receive it, but those who will not receive His mercy can blame only themselves.

ii. If God **delights in mercy**, *then why is He not always, on every occasion merciful?* Because there comes a time when the guilty must be punished. God's judgments are in themselves expressions of mercy because they are like the cutting away of cancer. The surgery hurts but must take place or the whole body will die.

iii. If God **delights in mercy**, *then why is there an unpardonable sin?* We should be grateful that there is only one unpardonable sin – the sin of rejecting His mercy.

iv. If God **delights in mercy**, *then why do I feel that He can't have mercy on me?* In such cases, we should trust God and not our feelings. "Whatever despair may whisper or doubt may suggest, one text of Scripture is worth fifty fears and doubts, or fifty thousand either.... All objections to the delight of God in mercy are but illusions of your brain, or delusions of your heart." (Spurgeon)

v. If God is this merciful to those who sin against Him, do we have any justification for not showing mercy to those who sin against us? "To all of you I would say – take care, as you expect the mercy of God, to deal it out to others. Never say, 'I won't forgive,' for you seal your own condemnation when you do, and if you forgive not your brother his trespasses neither will your heavenly Father forgive you. You have chosen your own destruction when you shut the door against your child, or against your neighbour, and say, 'I will treasure up that enmity as long as I live.' I tell you, sirs, your offerings at God's altar are an abomination to him until you have forgiven every one of your fellows his trespasses." (Spurgeon)

c. **He will again have compassion on us**: God's people once knew His compassion, but they resisted and rejected it. Now they could know it again, confident that **He will again have compassion on us**.

i. His **compassion** is shown in that the LORD **will subdue our iniquities**. He loves us as sinners but loves us too much to leave us in our sin. His **compassion** saves us from our sin.

ii. His **compassion** is shown in that the LORD **will cast all our sins into the depths of the sea**. God will not hold on to our sin but forgive us instead. This means there is no probation with God's forgiveness. He doesn't forgive our sins just to hold onto them and hang them over our heads. In His **compassion**, He does away with our sins, casting them **into the depths of the sea** – and then He puts a "No Fishing" sign there!

iii. His **compassion** is shown in that the LORD **will give truth to Jacob**. God's people not only need His mercy, they also need His **truth** and He is compassionate enough to give His **truth** as He gives mercy and pardon.

d. **Which You have sworn to our fathers from days of old**: In concluding his prophecy, Micah saw God's future work as a continuation of His past work to the **fathers** of Israel. Micah knew that the same love, compassion, and mercy He showed to their **fathers** was available to them today – if they received it in faith.

Nahum 1 – Coming Judgment on Nineveh

A. The character of the God who brings judgment.

1. (1) The burden of Nahum.

The burden against Nineveh. The book of the vision of Nahum the Elkoshite.

> a. **The burden**: In the prophets, a **burden** is a heavy message of weighty importance, heavy in the sense that it produces sorrow or grief.
>
>> i. "*Massa* comes from the verb 'to lift up' (*nasa*), and so it can mean 'to carry' or 'to lift up the voice.' From the first meaning comes the translation 'burden,' or 'load'; and from the second meaning we get the translation 'oracle,' or 'utterance.'" (Wolf, in his commentary on Isaiah). Grammatically, we may be able to say "oracle," but since these are *heavy* oracles, we are justified in calling them *burdens*.
>
>> ii. "*Massa* not only signifies a *burden*, but also a thing *lifted up, pronounced,* or *proclaimed*; also a *message*. It is used by the prophets to signify the *revelation* which they have received from God to deliver to any particular people." (Clarke)
>
> b. **Against Nineveh**: The capital of the Assyrian Empire was Nineveh, the city that heard the preaching of Jonah a hundred years before and repented. Nahum's call was to address a city that had slipped back into sin and was again ripe for judgment.
>
>> i. Among other things, the prophecy of Nahum shows us that God not only deals with individuals, He also deals with nations. "This is the prophecy which sets forth, more clearly than any other, the truth concerning the wrath of God, in its national application" (Morgan). Nations will be held to account by God.
>
>> ii. Nineveh was an ancient and famous city. It was founded by the first world dictator, Nimrod (Genesis 10:11). "From Nineveh's walls, temples, palaces, inscriptions, and reliefs, mute yet elaborate witness

is given to a city that flourished up to its destruction in 612 B.C. Accordingly, the magnificent buildings, artistic designs, and water-supply projects of Nineveh have resulted in its being likened to ancient Versailles." (*Major Cities of the Biblical World*)

c. **The book of the vision**: This was more than a message communicated to Nahum in words or phrases from God. Because this was a **vision**, in some way Nahum *saw* it. When we see the vivid, descriptive way Nahum writes we understand that **the book** records what he saw in his **vision**.

> i. Isaiah 2:1 says: *The word that Isaiah the son of Amoz saw concerning Judah and Jerusalem*. Isaiah *saw* a *word*, and in some sense Nahum also did.

d. **Nahum the Elkoshite**: We don't know anything else about **Nahum** or the city of Elkosh. The name **Nahum** is an abbreviated form of the name *Nehemiah*, which means "Comfort of Yahweh." It may be that Elkosh was in the region of Galilee because the city of Capernaum (Matthew 4:13, Mark 9:33, John 2:12) was named after **Nahum** (*Kephar-Nahum*, "City of Nahum").

> i. We don't know exactly when Nahum gave this prophecy. He mentioned the destruction of the Egyptian city *No Amon* (Thebes) in Nahum 3:8 and Thebes fell to the Assyrians in 663 B.C., so Nahum must have been written after that. Nineveh was destroyed 50 years after No Amon (612 B.C.).

> ii. It is likely that Nahum prophesied when Nineveh was a mighty city. "It was concerned with Nineveh, and was delivered almost certainly when she was at the height of her power." (Morgan)

2. (2-8) The judgments of a merciful God.

God *is* jealous, and the LORD avenges;
The LORD avenges and *is* furious.
The LORD will take vengeance on His adversaries,
And He reserves *wrath* for His enemies;
The LORD *is* slow to anger and great in power,
And will not at all acquit *the wicked.*

The LORD has His way
In the whirlwind and in the storm,
And the clouds *are* the dust of His feet.
He rebukes the sea and makes it dry,
And dries up all the rivers.
Bashan and Carmel wither,
And the flower of Lebanon wilts.

The mountains quake before Him,
The hills melt, and the earth heaves at His presence,
Yes, the world and all who dwell in it.

Who can stand before His indignation?
And who can endure the fierceness of His anger?
His fury is poured out like fire,
And the rocks are thrown down by Him.

The LORD *is* good,
A stronghold in the day of trouble;
And He knows those who trust in Him.
But with an overflowing flood
He will make an utter end of its place,
And darkness will pursue His enemies.

a. **The LORD is slow to anger and great in power, and will not at all acquit the wicked**: Nahum began his prophecy by considering the *character* of the God who brings judgment.

- **God is jealous**: How can it be said that God is **jealous**? "God's jealousy is love in action. He refuses to share the human heart with any rival, not because He is selfish and wants us all for Himself, but because He knows that upon that loyalty to Him depends our very moral life…. God is not jealous *of* us: He is jealous *for* us." (Redpath in *Law and Liberty*)

- **The LORD will take vengeance on His adversaries**: Man needs to understand that he can't fight against God and hope to prevail. Everyone who sets themselves against God will end up receiving His **vengeance**.

- **The LORD is slow to anger**: God is far more patient than man. Though there is a time and place where He does display His **anger**, it doesn't come quickly or randomly. "God's sword of justice is in its scabbard: not rusted in it – it can be easily withdrawn – but held there by that hand that presses it back into its sheath, crying, 'Sleep, O sword, sleep; for I will have mercy upon sinners, and will forgive their transgressions.'" (Spurgeon)

- **And great in power**: Knowing God's power should make us *trust* in His help (because He is able to help) and *fear* His judgment (knowing that He judges with **power**).

- **Will not at all acquit the wicked**: God is not like an unjust judge who simply lets the guilty go out of a false sense of compassion. We can't just hope that God will say, "All is forgiven" when anyone passes from this world to the next. Sin must be accounted for, because He **will not acquit the wicked**. Every sin will be paid for – either in hell or at the cross – but God **will not acquit the wicked**. "Never once has he pardoned an unpunished sin; not in all the years of the Most High, not in all the days of his right hand, has he once blotted out sin without punishment." (Spurgeon)

- **The LORD has His way in the whirlwind and in the storm**: God's power is so great that it controls the mightiest forces known to man. A huge **whirlwind** or **storm** is nothing to God because He **has His way** in them.

- **His fury is poured out like fire**: When God is resisted long enough and rejected strongly enough, eventually His judgment comes. He is **slow to anger**, but when it does come **His fury is poured out like fire**. Understanding this should make man quick to repent and wary of presuming upon God's patience.

- **The LORD is good, a stronghold in the day of trouble**: Those who love Him and trust Him see the goodness of God and find protection in His **stronghold** – which is the LORD Himself. "Remember that it is only a *day;* it is not a week, nor a month, and God will not permit the devil to add an extra hour to that day; it is a 'day *of* trouble.' There is an end to all our griefs." (Spurgeon)

- **He knows those who trust in Him**: Not only does He know them in the sense of identification, but also in the sense of *relationship*. **Trust** implies relationship, and God **knows those who trust in Him**. "Once more, dear friends, this word 'know' here means *loving communion*.... God knows us; he knows our prayers and tears, he knows our wishes, he knows that we are not what we want to be, but he knows what we do desire to be. He knows our aspirations, our sighs, our groans, our secret longings, our own chastenings of spirit when we fail; he has entered into it all. He says, 'Yes, dear child, I know all about you; I have been with you when you thought you were alone. I have read what you could not read, the secrets of your own heart that you could not decipher I have known them all, and I still know them.'" (Spurgeon)

b. **The LORD is good**: It is vitally important for everyone to know this.

- God is good in His very being – it is His very *nature* to be good.
- God is good independently – no one must *help* Him be good.
- God is eternally and unchangeably good.

- God is good in each one of His Divine Persons.
- God is good in all His acts of grace.
- God is good in all His plans and purposes for our lives.

c. **With an overflowing flood He will make an utter end of its place**: Taking into account the character of God, though He is **slow to anger** and **good**, He could not forever overlook the sin and rebellion of the Assyrians. Their end in judgment would come like **an overflowing flood**.

> i. The **overflowing flood** was fulfilled both figuratively and literally. "According to secular accounts, during the final siege of Nineveh by a rebel army of Persians, Medes, Arabians, and Babylonians, unusually heavy rains caused the rivers to flood and to undermine the city's walls, which then collapsed…the invading armies entered the city through this breach in its defenses." (Boice)
>
> ii. The **utter end of its place** was also literally fulfilled. "Not only were these people lost from history, even the city was lost until it was discovered by archaeologists, beginning in the 1840's." (Boice)
>
> iii. "The author is not expressing some personal feeling of vindication over some hurt by the oppressor, nor even a nationalistic chauvinism that pagan nations must be punished. Rather, Yahweh is applying his universal standard against evil, no matter who is responsible." (Baker)

B. Nineveh destroyed, Judah delivered.

1. (9-11) The destruction of Nineveh.

What do you conspire against the LORD?
He will make an utter end *of it*.
Affliction will not rise up a second time.
For while tangled *like* **thorns,**
And while drunken *like* **drunkards,**
They shall be devoured like stubble fully dried.
From you comes forth one
Who plots evil against the LORD,
A wicked counselor.

> a. **He will make an utter end of it**: Nineveh was ripe for a devastating judgment. This was not a harsh chastening; this was utter destruction to come upon the city. The promise **affliction will not rise up a second time** sounds encouraging, until we realize that it **will not rise up a second time** because the judgment will be so severe the *first time*.

b. **They shall be devoured like stubble fully dried**: The dry leftover stalks of grass were ready to be **devoured** by the smallest flame. This was how ripe Nineveh was for judgment, and how complete the fire of judgment will be when it comes.

2. (12-13) The deliverance of Zion.

Thus says the Lord:

"Though *they are* safe, and likewise many,
Yet in this manner they will be cut down
When he passes through.
Though I have afflicted you,
I will afflict you no more;
For now I will break off his yoke from you,
And burst your bonds apart."

a. **Though they are safe**: The enemies of Zion looked mighty; they were **safe** and **many**. Yet they would be devastated by the judgment that the Lord promised.

b. **Though I have afflicted you, I will afflict you no more**: God's people looked weak and **afflicted** yet God promised that they would be strengthened and restored. The power of their oppressors would be broken (**I will break off his yoke from you**).

i. Could not the believer today, who is trapped or oppressed by sin, ask God to break the yoke of sin? It must be done with a complete willingness to *walk* in the freedom God gives, but only God can **break off** the power of the things that bind us.

3. (14) The end of the wicked in Assyria.

The Lord has given a command concerning you:

"Your name shall be perpetuated no longer.
Out of the house of your gods
I will cut off the carved image and the molded image.
I will dig your grave,
For you are vile."

a. **Your name shall be perpetuated no longer**: The city of Nineveh was once instantly recognized as one of the great power cities of the world. God promised to bring this wicked city so low that they would lose their legacy and **name** among the nations.

b. **I will dig your grave, for you are vile**: In this vivid – almost extreme – imagery, God warned Nineveh of its coming judgment and destruction.

4. (15) Blessing in Judah.

Behold, on the mountains
The feet of him who brings good tidings,
Who proclaims peace!
O Judah, keep your appointed feasts,
Perform your vows.
For the wicked one shall no more pass through you;
He is utterly cut off.

> a. **Behold, on the mountains the feet of him who brings good tidings, who proclaims peace!** The contrast between the fate of the godly and wicked was nothing but *good news* to Nahum and the people of God.
>
>> i. Isaiah 52:7 uses a similar expression, but Isaiah marvels at the *beauty* of the *feet of him who brings good news*. Nahum would certainly agree because those who bring **good tidings** have beautiful feet; they partner with God for the salvation of men. The **feet** speak of activity, motion, and progress, and those who are active and moving in the work of preaching the gospel have *beautiful* **feet**.
>>
>> ii. In Isaiah, the good news is the coming of the Messiah. In Nahum, the good news is the defeat of the enemies of God's people. Revelation 17 and 18 describe the fall of Babylon, representing the world system and all of its support structures. Revelation 18:9-19 shows how the kings and merchants of the earth mourned the fall of Babylon, but Revelation 18:20 through 19:6 shows how heaven rejoiced over the fall of the world system. What was mourned on earth was applauded in heaven, and the same principle applies in Nahum's prophecy of Nineveh's fall.
>>
>> iii. "Rejoicing is not in this context gleeful gloating at the misfortune of others.... Rather it is pleasure at the vindication of God and his promises." (Baker)
>
> b. **O Judah, keep your appointed feasts, perform your vows**: Knowing the grace and mercy of God to His people should not make the believer *careless* in obedience, it should make the believer more careful to obey every word of the LORD.

Nahum 2 – Nineveh Conquered

"This chapter is a masterpiece of ancient literature, unsurpassed for its graphic portrayal of a military assault." (James Montgomery Boice)

A. The battle of Nineveh.

1. (1-2) A call to battle.

He who scatters has come up before your face.
Man the fort!
Watch the road!
Strengthen *your* flanks!
Fortify *your* power mightily.
For the LORD will restore the excellence of Jacob
Like the excellence of Israel,
For the emptiers have emptied them out
And ruined their vine branches.

> a. **He who scatters**: Nahum spoke from a vision he saw (Nahum 1:1). Now he saw a mighty army coming against the city of Nineveh.
>
> b. **For the LORD will restore the excellence of Jacob**: In this case, part of God's restoration for His people was connected to judgment and destruction on their enemies, those who **have emptied them out and ruined their vine branches**. They would now face destruction from **he who scatters**.

2. (3-7) The battle decided.

The shields of his mighty men *are* made red,
The valiant men *are* in scarlet.
The chariots *come* with flaming torches
In the day of his preparation,
And the spears are brandished.
The chariots rage in the streets,
They jostle one another in the broad roads;

They seem like torches,
They run like lightning.

He remembers his nobles;
They stumble in their walk;
They make haste to her walls,
And the defense is prepared.
The gates of the rivers are opened,
And the palace is dissolved.
It is decreed:
She shall be led away captive,
She shall be brought up;
And her maidservants shall lead *her* as with the voice of doves,
Beating their breasts.

 a. **The chariots come with flaming torches**: Nahum could see it all in his vision. The battle for Nineveh was fierce and bloody, and though **the defense is prepared** they would be conquered.

 b. **The chariots rage in the streets, they jostle one another in the broad roads; they seem like torches, they run like lightning**: Chuck Smith noted that some have taken this – erroneously – as a prophecy of the automobile and traffic congestion.

 c. **She shall be led away captive**: The prophet not only saw the battle, but he also saw the outcome – Nineveh would fall before this mighty army, and she would be humbled and **led away captive** even as the Assyrians led other nations in captivity.

B. Nineveh in defeat.

1. (8-12) Nineveh brought low and spoiled.

**Though Nineveh of old *was* like a pool of water,
Now they flee away.
"Halt! Halt!" *they cry;*
But no one turns back.
Take spoil of silver!
Take spoil of gold!
There is no end of treasure,
Or wealth of every desirable prize.
She is empty, desolate, and waste!
The heart melts, and the knees shake;
Much pain *is* in every side,
And all their faces are drained of color.**

Where *is* the dwelling of the lions,
And the feeding place of the young lions,
Where the lion walked, the lioness *and* lion's cub,
And no one made *them* afraid?
The lion tore in pieces enough for his cubs,
Killed for his lionesses,
Filled his caves with prey,
And his dens with flesh.

> a. **Nineveh of old was like a pool of water**: Nahum said the troops defending Nineveh would be like a pool of water that drains away to no use. They would be useless in defending the city.
>
>> i. **Take spoil of silver! Take spoil of gold!** "An impressive confirmation of this prophecy is that nothing of all this gold and silver has been discovered in the ruins of Nineveh by archaeologists. Nineveh was indeed stripped bare." (Boice)
>
> b. **Where is the dwelling of the lions**: The **lion** was one of the national emblems of the Assyrian Empire, and they crushed and plundered other nations like lions destroying prey. Nahum now asked, "**Where is the dwelling of the lions?**" God would bring them low, who once were so mighty.

2. (13) The LORD vows to conquer Nineveh.

"Behold, I *am* against you," says the LORD of hosts, "I will burn your chariots in smoke, and the sword shall devour your young lions; I will cut off your prey from the earth, and the voice of your messengers shall be heard no more."

> a. **Behold, I am against you**: What a terrible thing to hear from God! The principle of Romans 8:31 is true for the believer: *If God is for us, who can be against us?* Accordingly, the opposite is also true – if God is **against you**, then who can be for you?
>
> b. **Says the LORD of hosts**: It is bad when God is against you; it is even worse when **the LORD of hosts** is against you. This title refers to God's place as commander in chief over all the armies of heaven.
>
> c. **The voice of your messengers shall be heard no more**: Nineveh enjoyed its status as a power center of the world and gloried in the fact that the **voice** of her **messengers** commanded attention in palaces all over the world. That day would come to an end under the judgment of God.

Nahum 3 – Nineveh, the Wicked City

A. The sin within Nineveh.

1. (1-4) The violence and immorality in Nineveh.

Woe to the bloody city!
It *is* all full of lies *and* robbery.
***Its* victim never departs.**
The noise of a whip
And the noise of rattling wheels,
Of galloping horses,
Of clattering chariots!
Horsemen charge with bright sword and glittering spear.
***There is* a multitude of slain,**
A great number of bodies, countless corpses—
They stumble over the corpses—
Because of the multitude of harlotries of the seductive harlot,
The mistress of sorceries,
Who sells nations through her harlotries,
And families through her sorceries.

    a. **Woe to the bloody city**: In his prophetic vision, Nahum took a tour of the city of Nineveh and observed how ripe it was for judgment. He saw it was a busy city, full of the **noise of a whip and the noise of rattling wheels, of galloping horses, of clattering chariots**. Yet it was busy with violence, deception, and idolatry.

        i. Not only were the rulers of Assyria terribly cruel, but they also *boasted* of their cruelty on monuments that exist in museums to this day. Boice quotes some of the boasts from various monuments:

- "I cut off their heads and formed them into pillars."
- "Bubo, son of Buba, I flayed in the city of Arbela and I spread his skin upon the city wall."

- "I flayed all the chief men who had revolted, and I covered the pillar with their skins."
- "Many within the border of my own land I flayed, and spread their skins upon the walls."
- "I cut off the limbs of the officers, the royal officers who had rebelled."
- "3,000 captives I burned with fire."
- "Their corpses I formed into pillars."
- "From some I cut off their hands and their fingers, and from others I cut off their noses, their ears, and their fingers, of many I put out their eyes."
- "I made one pillar of the living, and another of heads, I bound their heads to posts round about the city."

b. **Who sells the nations through her harlotries**: It was bad enough that Nineveh indulged in this sin for herself; it was worse that she led the **nations** into violence, deception, and idolatry. For this, the judgment of God was coming.

i. "Thousands of tablets uncovered in the Mesopotamian valley show abysmal superstition. Hundreds of sorcery incantations have been brought to light." (Maier, cited in Boice)

2. (5-7) The wicked city is humbled.

"Behold, I *am* against you," says the LORD of hosts;
"I will lift your skirts over your face
I will show the nations your nakedness,
And the kingdoms your shame.
I will cast abominable filth upon you,
Make you vile,
And make you a spectacle.
It shall come to pass *that* all who look upon you
Will flee from you, and say,
'Nineveh is laid waste!
Who will bemoan her?'
Where shall I seek comforters for you?"

a. **I am against you**: Nahum repeated this phrase, first mentioned in Nahum 2:13. In the first mention, the emphasis was on the military defeat of Nineveh. Here, the emphasis was on the *humbling* of the city.

i. This reminds us of the principle of 1 Peter 5:5: *Be clothed with humility, for "God resists the proud, but gives grace to the humble."* Nineveh walked in pride, and as a result, had the LORD **against** them. How much better to be humble and receive the grace of God.

b. **I will cast abominable filth upon you, make you vile, and make you a spectacle**: The strength of the word of the LORD almost surprises us here. He will take the idols of Nineveh (**abominable filth**, the Hebrew word *shiqquts* often translated "abomination") and throw them back in their faces.

c. **Make you vile**: The idea behind the Hebrew word for **vile** (*nabel*) is that something is made weak, foolish, and contemptible. Nineveh walked high in their pride, but would certainly be brought low – with no one to comfort them (**Where shall I seek comforters for you?**).

i. Again, this was literally fulfilled. The ancient Greek historian Diodorus Siculus wrote of the destruction of Nineveh: "So great was the multitude of the slain that the flowing stream, mingled with their blood, changed its color for a considerable distance.... They plundered the spoil of the city, a quantity beyond counting." (Boice)

ii. Adam Clarke, writing before the discovery of the ruins in Nineveh in 1840, quotes an author commenting on the disappearance of the city: "What probability was there that the capital city of a great kingdom, a city which was *sixty* miles in compass, a city which contained so many *thousand* inhabitants, a city which had walls a *hundred* feet high.... And yet so totally was it destroyed that the place is hardly known where it was situated.... Great as it was formerly, so little of it is remaining, that authors are not agreed even about its situation."

B. Nineveh is ripe for judgment.

1. (8-11) Because of the way God judged other cities, Nineveh is ripe.

Are you better than No Amon
***That was* situated by the River,**
That had the waters around her,
Whose rampart *was* the sea,
Whose wall *was* the sea?
Ethiopia and Egypt *were* her strength,
And *it was* boundless;
Put and Lubim were your helpers.
Yet she *was* carried away,
She went into captivity;
Her young children also were dashed to pieces

At the head of every street;
They cast lots for her honorable men,
And all her great men were bound in chains.
You also will be drunk;
You will be hidden;
You also will seek refuge from the enemy.

> a. **Are you better than No Amon**: The Hebrew name for the Egyptian city of Thebes is **No Amon**. Thebes was another wealthy, mighty city that was destroyed completely. The Assyrians in Nineveh knew this well because it was their armies that destroyed Thebes. Nahum said to the Assyrians, "Remember what you did to **No Amon**? The same is coming on you."

> b. **You also**: We are like the Ninevites. We see empires and nations judged in our own day and in history, just like the Assyrians saw Thebes destroyed. Yet we, like the Ninevites, somehow think that we will be spared, despite our sinful arrogance and rebellion.

2. (12-15) Because of her own weakness, Nineveh is ripe.

All your strongholds *are* fig trees with ripened figs:
If they are shaken,
They fall into the mouth of the eater.
Surely, your people in your midst *are* women!
The gates of your land are wide open for your enemies;
Fire shall devour the bars of your *gates*.

Draw your water for the siege!
Fortify your strongholds!
Go into the clay and tread the mortar!
Make strong the brick kiln!
There the fire will devour you,
The sword will cut you off;
It will eat you up like a locust.

Make yourself many– like the locust!
Make yourself many– like the *swarming* locusts!

> a. **Your strongholds are fig trees with ripened figs**: As easily as ripe fruit falls from a shaken tree, so would the **strongholds** of Nineveh fall before the judgment of God. We often have our **strongholds** of sin and pride that we put great confidence in, but they are ready to be shaken and fall to the ground.

> b. **Fire shall devour the bars of your gates**: Archaeologists document the burning of Nineveh. "The excavators of Nineveh have remarked on

the large deposits of ash, which are evidence of a gigantic conflagration." (Boice)

c. **Draw your water for the siege**: Nahum practically mocked the people of Nineveh, cheering them on to do the best they could in light of the coming judgment. They could prepare as many provisions and people as they pleased, but it would all come to nothing against the judgment of God.

3. (16-19) Because her leaders are weak, Nineveh is ripe.

You have multiplied your merchants more than the stars of heaven.
The locust plunders and flies away.
Your commanders *are* **like** *swarming* **locusts,**
And your generals like great grasshoppers,
Which camp in the hedges on a cold day;
When the sun rises they flee away,
And the place where they *are* **is not known.**

Your shepherds slumber, O king of Assyria;
Your nobles rest *in the dust.*
Your people are scattered on the mountains,
And no one gathers them.
Your injury *has* **no healing,**
Your wound is severe.
All who hear news of you
Will clap *their* **hands over you,**
For upon whom has not your wickedness passed continually?

a. **Merchants.... commanders...generals.... shepherds...nobles**: Each of these classes of leaders were numerous in Nineveh, but they would all be ineffective and come to nothing in the day of judgment. Despite their numbers, **your people are scattered on the mountains, and no one gathers them**. The sinful and rebellious leadership of Nineveh would be powerless against the judgment of God.

b. **All who hear news of you will clap their hands over you**: Nahum ended his prophecy with a view of the righteous and their triumph over the unrighteous. This is something that the people of God need to be repeatedly reminded of, because it often goes against present appearances.

i. Because Nineveh was so known – even renowned – for its violence and cruelty, no wonder Nahum sees the nations applauding when the city is judged and destroyed.

ii. In Psalm 73, Asaph dealt with this same problem. It seemed to him that the wicked constantly prospered and lived at ease. It troubled him so much that he doubted his own walk with God, *Until I went into the sanctuary of God; then I understood their end. Surely You set them in slippery places; You cast them down to destruction. Oh, how they are brought to desolation, as in a moment! They are utterly consumed with terrors.* (Psalm 73:17-19)

iii. For Nahum, Asaph, and for us today, we take comfort in knowing that the judgments of the Lord are faithful and true. We don't need to envy the unrighteous or seek vengeance against them ourselves. Nahum and Asaph each show us that God is more than able to take care of them and us, each according to His promise.

Habakkuk 1 – The Prophet's Problem

A. The first problem: "How long, O LORD?"

1. (1) Habakkuk and his burden.

The burden which the prophet Habakkuk saw.

> a. **The prophet Habakkuk**: We don't know much about the **prophet Habakkuk** from any other book in the Bible. Since he prophesied the coming Babylonian army and its destruction of Judah, he prophesied some time before that invasion. Many think that Habakkuk ministered sometime during the reign of King Jehoiakim, perhaps around the year 607 B.C.
>
> > i. It's hard to say with certainty when Habakkuk prophesied. Since he speaks of God *raising up* the Babylonians (Habakkuk 1:6), we can guess that he wrote in the 25-year period between the time when Babylon conquered Nineveh and the Assyrian Empire (612 B.C.) and the time when Babylon conquered Jerusalem (587 B.C.).
> >
> > ii. We don't know how old Habakkuk was when he gave this prophecy, but it is likely that he lived during the time of the godly King Josiah (640 to 609 B.C.) and then gave this prophecy during the reign of one of Josiah's successors. Habakkuk knew what it was like to live during a time of revival, and then to see God's people and the nation slip into lethargy and sin. "Habakkuk had a problem. He had lived through a period of national revival followed by a period of spiritual decline." (Boice)
>
> b. **The burden which the prophet Habakkuk saw**: Habakkuk had a **burden** – not only in the sense of a message from God but also in the sense of a heavy weight. It was heavy in its *content* because Habakkuk announced coming judgment on Judah. It was also heavy in its *source* because Habakkuk brought a message from God, and every word of God is heavy with meaning and relevance.

i. The name **Habakkuk** is derived from the Hebrew verb "embrace." His name probably means, *he who embraces* or *he who clings*. It is an appropriate name for both the prophet and the book because Habakkuk comes to a firm faith through grappling with tough questions.

ii. **The prophet**: "This title is rare in book headings (see Haggai 1:1; Zechariah 1:1), and is taken by some to indicate that Habakkuk was a professional prophet, one who earned his living serving as a prophet at the Temple or court, unlike Amos (*cf.* Amos 7:14)." (Baker)

2. (2-4) Habakkuk asks God why He seems to delay judgment.

O Lord, how long shall I cry,
And You will not hear?
Even cry out to You, "Violence!"
And You will not save.
Why do You show me iniquity,
And cause *me* to see trouble?
For plundering and violence *are* before me;
There is strife, and contention arises.
Therefore the law is powerless,
And justice never goes forth.
For the wicked surround the righteous;
Therefore perverse judgment proceeds.

a. **Even cry out to You, "Violence!" and You will not save**: Habakkuk looked at the **violence** and injustice around him in the nation of Judah. He wondered where God was, and why God did not set things right.

b. **Why do You show me iniquity, and cause me to see trouble?** This was, and is, an excellent question. Why does God allow us to see iniquity and trouble, in ourselves or in others?

i. Some reasons why God allows us to see iniquity in ourselves:

- To keep us humble.
- To keep us submissive to Him in the hour of trouble.
- To make us value salvation even more.

ii. Some reasons why God allows us to see iniquity in others:

- To show us what we might have been ourselves.
- To make us see the wickedness of sin, that we might pass by it and hate it, and not indulge in it ourselves.
- To make us admire the grace of God when He saves sinners.

- To set us more earnestly to work that God can use us to save others and extend God's kingdom. "Ah, my brethren, we need to know more of the evil of men, to make us more earnest in seeking their salvation; for if there be anything in which the Church is lacking more than in any other matter, it is in the matter of earnestness." (Spurgeon)

c. **Iniquity…trouble…. plundering and violence…strife…contention …. the law is powerless…justice never goes forth…perverse judgment proceeds**: Habakkuk saw trouble and sin everywhere, from personal relationships to the courts of law. This distressed him so much that he cried out to God and asked God why He didn't bring judgment and immediately correct things.

i. Habakkuk dealt with the questions that come up when someone really believes God, yet looks around and sees that the world doesn't seem to match up with how God wants it. Habakkuk saw this – especially remembering the prior times of revival under King Josiah – and asked, "LORD, why are you allowing this?"

ii. "This prophecy deals with the problems created by faith; and with the Divine answers to the questions which express those problems." (Morgan)

B. God's answer to the first problem.

1. (5-6) God's astounding work: bringing the Babylonians to judge Judah.

**"Look among the nations and watch–
Be utterly astounded!
For *I will* work a work in your days
Which you would not believe,
Though it were told *you.*
For indeed I am raising up the Chaldeans,
A bitter and hasty nation
Which marches through the breadth of the earth,
To possess dwelling places *that are* not theirs.**

a. **Be utterly astounded**: God told the troubled prophet, "Don't worry about it. Look at the surrounding nations and from them will come a nation that will be My instrument of judgment on sinful Judah."

b. **I will work a work in your days which you would not believe**: We understand the idea of something "too good to be true," but that isn't what God meant here. This was something "too bad to be true," a work of judgment so astounding that Habakkuk would have a hard time believing it.

c. **I am raising up the Chaldeans**: When the Babylonians (**the Chaldeans**) eventually came against Judah, they came as sent by the LORD. It wasn't that they themselves did not want to come, but God allowed their sinful desire to conquer Judah to come to fruition. If God had not allowed them to do it, they never could have conquered Judah and exiled God's people from the Promised Land.

2. (7-11) The strength and speed of the Babylonian army.

They are terrible and dreadful;
Their judgment and their dignity proceed from themselves.
Their horses also are swifter than leopards,
And more fierce than evening wolves.
Their chargers charge ahead;
Their cavalry comes from afar;
They fly as the eagle *that* **hastens to eat.**

"They all come for violence;
Their faces are set *like* **the east wind.**
They gather captives like sand.
They scoff at kings,
And princes are scorned by them.
They deride every stronghold,
For they heap up earthen *mounds* **and seize it.**
Then *his* **mind changes, and he transgresses;**
He commits offense,
Ascribing **this power to his god."**

a. **They are terrible and dreadful**: Habakkuk wondered where God's judgment was against sinful Judah. The LORD told him that the judgment would indeed come, and when it came through the Babylonians it would be **terrible and dreadful**.

b. **He commits offense, ascribing this power to his god**: When the Babylonians would come and overwhelm the land of Judah, they would wrongly give the credit to their false gods. The LORD knew and said they would do this before it ever happened.

C. The second problem: "Why do it this way, O LORD?"

1. (12-17) Habakkuk wonders why God would use a nation more wicked than Judah to bring judgment on Judah.

Are You not from everlasting,
O Lord my God, my Holy One?
We shall not die.
O Lord, You have appointed them for judgment;
O Rock, You have marked them for correction.
You are of purer eyes than to behold evil,
And cannot look on wickedness.
Why do You look on those who deal treacherously,
And hold Your tongue when the wicked devours
A *person* more righteous than he?
Why do You make men like fish of the sea,
Like creeping things *that have* no ruler over them?

They take up all of them with a hook,
They catch them in their net,
And gather them in their dragnet.
Therefore they rejoice and are glad.
Therefore they sacrifice to their net,
And burn incense to their dragnet;
Because by them their share *is* sumptuous
And their food plentiful.
Shall they therefore empty their net,
And continue to slay nations without pity?

> a. **Why do You look on those who deal treacherously**: Habakkuk was first troubled that there was no judgment against Judah; God answered by telling him judgment was on the way. Then Habakkuk was troubled by the *agent* of judgment, the Babylonians – who were an even more wicked people than the people of Judah.
>
>> i. It would be like crying out to God about the state of the church in America, and hearing God respond by saying, "I'll fix the problem by an enemy invasion of America." We might say, "Wait a minute Lord – the problem is bad, but Your cure is worse than the disease!"
>>
>> ii. Some people face crisis times like this all the wrong way. They withdraw from the church and from fellowship and they pull back into a little spiritual corner. Others give up on God altogether. D. Martyn Lloyd-Jones suggested a better response (cited in Boice):
>>
>> - *Stop to think* – before talking about it, think about it.
>>
>> - *Restate basic principles* – as you think about the problem, don't begin with the problem. Go back further to basic principles about God and His dealing with man.

- *Apply the principles to the problem* – now, think about your problem in light of these basic principles.
- *Commit the matter to God in faith* – whether you know what to do or not.

b. **You are of purer eyes than to behold evil, and cannot look on wickedness**: This is even more problematic to Habakkuk because he knew the character of God. Since he understood the holy character of God, he was more troubled than ever as to why God would judge wicked Judah by exalting even more wicked Babylon.

c. **Shall they therefore empty their net, and continue to slay nations without pity?** Habakkuk wondered how long God would allow the Babylonians to continue their cruel conquest of nations. It was as if God's people were conquered as easily as fish are captured in a net.

i. "Easily are we taken and destroyed. We have no *leader* to guide us, and no *power* to defend ourselves. Nebuchadnezzar is here represented as a fisherman, who is constantly casting nets into the sea, and enclosing multitudes of fishes; and being always successful, he sacrifices to his own net." (Clarke)

2. (2:1) Habakkuk resolutely waits for God's reply.

I will stand my watch
And set myself on the rampart,
And watch to see what He will say to me,
And what I will answer when I am corrected.

a. **And watch to see what He will say to me**: Habakkuk has raised two important questions with God, yet he asked both with a proper attitude. He anticipated an answer from God and was willing to **watch** – that is, *wait* for it. Often when we question God we don't expect Him to answer, but Habakkuk did. Other times we not only *expect* God will answer, but we *demand* that He answer, and answer according to our schedule. Habakkuk approached this with the correct attitude.

i. "How often God's answers come, and find us gone! We have waited for a while, and, thinking there was no answer, we have gone our way but as we have turned the first corner the post has come in. God's ships touch at our wharves; but there is no one to unload them.... It is not enough to direct your prayer unto God; look up, and look out, until the blessing alights on your head." (Meyer)

b. **And what I will answer when I am corrected**: Habakkuk's attitude was also right because he *expected* God to correct him. From this, we see that Habakkuk didn't ask God this question because he thought God was wrong and had to explain Himself. He asked it because he knew that he was wrong and he needed to be corrected. His questions were his invitation to God saying, "God, I don't understand what You are doing, but I know that You are right in all things. Please speak to me and correct me."

Habakkuk 2 – God Justifies His Judgment

A. The proud rebuked.

In respect of the context, Habakkuk 2:1 is considered at the end of the commentary on Habakkuk 1.

1. (2-3) Preparation for the answer: how to publish the vision.

Then the LORD answered me and said:

"Write the vision
And make *it* plain on tablets,
That he may run who reads it.
For the vision *is* yet for an appointed time;
But at the end it will speak, and it will not lie.
Though it tarries, wait for it;
Because it will surely come,
It will not tarry.

a. **Write the vision and make it plain**: God told Habakkuk to record this "question and answer" time for the benefit of others – **that he may run who reads it**. Habakkuk's revelation wasn't just for himself, but also to strengthen others. Those who read it would make rapid progress (**may run**), but they couldn't make this progress if Habakkuk did not **make it plain**.

i. Habakkuk first had to *see the vision*. The preacher cannot make anyone else see what he does not see for himself.

ii. Habakkuk then had to *make it known*. The preacher must do what he can to make the word of God known, and make it known in as many ways as possible.

iii. Habakkuk had to make it known as *permanently as possible* – he was told to **write the vision**. The preacher must do what he can to make a permanent impact on his listeners.

iv. Habakkuk had to *make it plain*. The preacher must proclaim God's truth as clearly as possible. "I have sometimes thought that certain ministers fancied that it was their duty to make the message elaborate, to go to the very bottom of the subject, and stir up all the mud they could find there, till you could not possibly see them, nor could they see their own way at all.... They tell people all the difficulties they have discovered in the Bible, – which difficulties most of their hearers would never have heard of unless their ministers had told them." (Spurgeon)

v. Habakkuk had to *make it practical* – **that he may run who reads it**. It doesn't say, "that he who runs may read it," but "**that he may run who reads it**." The *running* – the activity and progress – comes from God's word. The preacher must seek to make God's truth relate to the real life of those who listen.

b. **For the vision is yet for an appointed time**: Habakkuk spoke to an age beyond his own. The Babylonian conquest would not be evident in his day but in the future.

2. (4-8) God knows how to deal with the proud.

"Behold the proud,
His soul is not upright in him;
But the just shall live by his faith.

"Indeed, because he transgresses by wine,
He is a proud man,
And he does not stay at home.
Because he enlarges his desire as hell,
And he *is* like death, and cannot be satisfied,
He gathers to himself all nations
And heaps up for himself all peoples.

"Will not all these take up a proverb against him,
And a taunting riddle against him, and say,
'Woe to him who increases
What is not his– how long?
And to him who loads himself with many pledges'?
Will not your creditors rise up suddenly?
Will they not awaken who oppress you?
And you will become their booty.
Because you have plundered many nations,
All the remnant of the people shall plunder you,
Because of men's blood
And the violence of the land *and* the city,
And of all who dwell in it.

a. **Behold the proud**: Habakkuk wondered why Babylon – a nation even more sinful than Judah – would be used to bring judgment against Judah. In answering the prophet, God first assured him that He saw **the proud**, and knew that **his soul is not upright in him**.

i. Pride is everywhere and takes all manner of shapes.

- Here is the rich man, proud of what he has.
- There is the poor man, proud of his "honor" in having less.
- Here is the talented man, proud of what he can do.
- There is the man of few talents, proud of his hard work.
- Here is the religious man, proud of his religion.
- There is the unbeliever, proud of his unbelief.
- Here is the establishment man, proud of his place in society.
- There is the counter-cultural man, proud of his "outcast" status.
- Here is the learned man, proud of his intelligence and learning.
- Here is the simple man, proud of his simplicity.

ii. "If there is a sin that is universal, it is this. Where is it not to be found? Hunt among the highest and loftiest in the world, and you shall find it there; and then go and search amongst the poorest and the most miserable, and you shall find it there. There may be as much pride inside a beggar's rags as in a prince's robe; and a harlot may be as proud as a model of chastity. Pride is a strange creature; it never objects to its lodgings. It will live comfortably enough in a palace, and it will live equally at its ease in a hovel. Is there any man in whose heart pride does not lurk?" (Spurgeon)

iii. Pride can be especially dangerous among the people of God. Once a man came to John Bunyan after a sermon and told him what a fine sermon he preached. "You're too late," Bunyan answered. "The devil told me that before I stepped down from the pulpit." Satan can tell the praying brother to be proud of his ability to pray, the growing brother to be proud of his growth, and even the humble brother to be proud of his humility.

iv. "*Wherever pride is found, it is always hateful to God.* Why! pride is even hateful to men. Men cannot bear a proud man; and hence it is that a proud man, who has any sense left, often sees that it is so, and he therefore tries to affect manners of modesty. He will seem to be humble, when he really is not, if he has the suspicion that all about him will dislike him if they know him to be proud. But God cannot bear pride; it is a part of his daily business to put down the proud." (Spurgeon)

b. **But the just shall live by his faith**: In contrast to **the proud**, there are **the just**. The principle of their life is **faith**, instead of pride that looks to self. True **faith** looks outside of self to the LORD God, while pride always looks to self.

i. This brief statement from the prophet Habakkuk is one of the most important, and most quoted Old Testament statements in the New Testament. Paul used it to show that the **just** live **by faith**, not by law. Being under the law isn't the way to be found **just** before God, only living by faith is.

ii. If you are declared **just** – that is, *approved* – before God, you have been accepted because of a relationship of **faith**. If your life is all about living under the law, then God does not find you approved.

iii. In Hebrew, the important part of the verse has only three words: "the justified man," "by his faith," and "will live." Every word in Habakkuk 2:4 is important, and the Lord quotes it three times in the New Testament just to bring out the fullness of the meaning

- Romans 1:17 is the commentary on *the justified man* – "The **just** shall live by faith."
- Hebrews 10:38 is the commentary on *faith* – "The just shall live by **faith**."
- Galatians 3:11 is the commentary on the Christian *life* – "The just shall **live** by faith."

iv. Before his bold declaration of the truth of the gospel, Martin Luther was an Augustinian monk. As a monk, he went on a pilgrimage to Rome and as he crossed the Alps he fell deathly ill. As he lay sick he felt great turmoil, both physical and spiritual, and a verse that had previously touched him came to mind: *The just shall live by his faith*, from Romans 1:17 and Habakkuk 2:4. When Luther recovered he went on to Rome and did the tourist things that all the pilgrims did. One day he came to the church of Saint John's Lateran, where there is a staircase said to be from Pilate's judgment hall. It was the custom of pilgrims to climb this staircase, but never on their feet – they painfully climbed a step at a time on their knees, saying prayers and kissing the steps where it was thought the blood of Jesus fell. Luther came to this place and started doing just as all the pilgrims did because the pope promised an indulgence to all who climbed the steps on their knees and said the prayers. As he did this, Luther remembered the words from Romans, quoting Habakkuk: *The just shall live by his faith*. It is said that when he remembered this he stopped, stood up, walked down and went straight home to Germany. Some say the Reformation began on those stairs.

v. "Before those words broke upon my mind I hated God and was angry with him because, not content with frightening us sinners by the law and by the miseries of life, he still further increased our torture by the gospel. But when, by the Spirit of God, I understood those words – 'The just shall live by faith!' 'The just shall live by faith!' – then I felt born again like a new man; I entered through the open doors into the very Paradise of God." (Luther, cited in Boice)

vi. We are called to live by faith and nothing else.

- Some Christians live by devotions.
- Some Christians live by works.
- Some Christians live by feelings.
- Some Christians live by circumstances.

Each of these is meaningless and perhaps *dangerous* without faith.

c. **He enlarges his desire as hell, and he is like death, and cannot be satisfied**: God sees the proud man and how the proud man **cannot be satisfied**. The one who is declared just by faith is satisfied, but the proud man keeps grasping.

d. **Because you have plundered many nations, all the remnant of the people shall plunder you**: Here, God assured Habakkuk that He knew how to deal with nations like Babylon. He promised the Babylonians that just as they **plundered many nations**, so one day others would **plunder** them.

i. The Babylonians were perfect examples of the proud who set themselves against those who are declared just by faith – and Habakkuk could take comfort in the fact that God would deal with them.

ii. "The immediate value of the word was that Habakkuk learned that God's employment of the Chaldeans did not mean the permanent power of this evil people." (Morgan)

B. Four woes to silence sinful man.

1. (9-11) Woe to the greedy.

**"Woe to him who covets evil gain for his house,
That he may set his nest on high,**

That he may be delivered from the power of disaster!
You give shameful counsel to your house,
Cutting off many peoples,
And sin *against* your soul.
For the stone will cry out from the wall,
And the beam from the timbers will answer it.

> a. **Woe to him who covets evil gain for his house**: God addressed the greedy man, and told him that he was ripe for judgment. The greedy man did his best to protect himself (**set his nest on high**), yet all his best defense would come to nothing.
>
> b. **You…sin against your own soul**: The greedy man thinks in terms of nothing but gain, but ends up losing his own soul. Jesus' parable in Luke 12:16-21 is the perfect example of the greedy man who sinned against his **own soul**.
>
> c. **For the stone will cry out from the wall**: Habakkuk pictured a beautiful house built by a greedy man, but the very stones of the house would **cry out from the wall** against the man's greed.

2. (12-14) Woe to the violent.

"Woe to him who builds a town with bloodshed,
Who establishes a city by iniquity!
Behold, *is it* not of the LORD of hosts
That the peoples labor to feed the fire,
And nations weary themselves in vain?
For the earth will be filled
With the knowledge of the glory of the LORD,
As the waters cover the sea.

> a. **Woe to him who builds a town with bloodshed**: The LORD was not only displeased with the greedy man, He also pronounced a woe against the *violent* man.
>
> b. **The earth will be filled with the knowledge of the glory of the LORD**: The violent man thinks that *his* power gives him the right to abuse others for his gain. As a correction and a rebuke, the LORD reminded the violent man of *His* ultimate triumph.

3. (15-17) Woe to the drunk.

"Woe to him who gives drink to his neighbor,
Pressing *him to* your bottle,
Even to make *him* drunk,
That you may look on his nakedness!
You are filled with shame instead of glory.

You also – drink!
And be exposed as uncircumcised!
The cup of the LORD's right hand *will be* turned against you,
And utter shame will be on your glory.
For the violence *done to* Lebanon will cover you,
And the plunder of beasts *which* made them afraid,
Because of men's blood
And the violence of the land *and* the city,
And of all who dwell in it.

> a. **Woe to him who gives drink to his neighbor.... You also – drink!** Through the prophet Habakkuk, the LORD rebuked both the drunk and those who promoted drunkenness. Though they thought that alcohol made them feel good, God rightly says they were **filled with shame instead of glory**.
>
>> i. In Ephesians 5:18 the Apostle Paul called drunkenness *dissipation*; drunkenness is a *waste* of resources that should be submitted to Jesus. John Trapp writes of drinking "all the three outs" – "that is, ale out of the pot, money out of the purse, and wit out of the head" (Trapp's commentary on Galatians 5:21).
>>
>> ii. The damage of drunkenness goes beyond the act itself and into what effects it has in lives and families. In the 1990s it was recorded that yearly in the United States alcohol was responsible for almost 100,000 deaths (25,000 by drunk drivers alone), 6 million non-fatal injuries, and more than $100 billion in economic losses such as unemployment and loss of productivity.
>
> b. **The cup of the LORD's right hand will be turned against you**: The drunk and those who promote drunkenness loved their cup full of drink; now God promises a **cup** for them, a cup of judgment and just recompense for their sin.

4. (18-20) Woe to the idolater.

"What profit is the image, that its maker should carve it,
The molded image, a teacher of lies,
That the maker of its mold should trust in it,
To make mute idols?
Woe to him who says to wood, 'Awake!'
To silent stone, 'Arise! It shall teach!'
Behold, it is overlaid with gold and silver,
Yet in it there is no breath at all.

"But the Lord is in His holy temple.
Let all the earth keep silence before Him."

> a. **Woe to him who says to wood, "Awake!"** Having dealt with the greedy man, the violent man, and the drunk then God spoke to the idolater – who treated inanimate objects as if they had life and intelligence.
>
> b. **In it there is no breath at all. But the Lord is in His holy temple**: In contrast to lifeless idols, the Lord was alive and well **in His holy temple**. The folly of the idolater will be exposed by the majesty of the living God.
>
>> i. Through it all, the point is proven. Habakkuk couldn't understand why God would judge a sinful nation (Judah) by an even *more* sinful nation (Babylon). Yet God reminds Habakkuk of His wisdom and strength, and of His ultimate triumph over the wicked. God knew that Babylon was filled with the proud, the greedy, the violent, the drunk, and the idolater – and the Lord knew how to deal with them all.

Habakkuk 3 – The Prophet's Prayer

A. Seeking revival from the God of all power.

1. (1-2) A plea for revival.

A prayer of Habakkuk the prophet, on Shigionoth.

O LORD, I have heard your speech *and* was afraid;
O LORD, revive Your work in the midst of the years!
In the midst of the years make *it* known;
In wrath remember mercy.

> a. **A prayer of Habakkuk the prophet**: The first two chapters of Habakkuk presented the prophet's question and answer time with God. Now that God had answered Habakkuk, the prophet brought a prayer to close the book.
>
> b. **O LORD, revive Your work in the midst of the years**: Habakkuk simply prayed for *revival*. He knew how God once worked and how His people once responded, and Habakkuk wanted to see that again.
>
>> i. The prayer of Habakkuk shows us that revival is a work of God, not the achievement of man. There is something man can and must do for revival – simply cry out to God and plead for His reviving work.
>>
>> ii. Notice the prayer: **revive Your work**. Often, my prayer is really "revive *my* work," but I must have a heart and mind for God's work, far bigger than my portion of it. "Shake off all the bitterness of everything that has to do with self, or with party, and now pray, 'Lord, revive thy work, and if thy work happen to be more in one branch of the church than in another, Lord, give that the most reviving. Give us all the blessing, but do let thine own purposes be accomplished, and thine own glory come of it, and we shall be well content, though we should be forgotten and unknown.'" (Spurgeon)
>>
>> iii. At the same time, this must be a *personal* prayer: "LORD, revive *me*." We too often blame the church for sin, corruption, laziness,

prayerlessness, lack of spiritual power, or whatever – and we forget that *we are the church*. Pray for personal revival and diligently search yourself:

- Check your conduct – does your walk glorify the LORD as it should? How about your *private* conduct, which only the LORD sees?
- Check your conversation – is your speech profane or impure? Do you talk about Jesus with others?
- Check your communion – are you living a growing, abiding life with Jesus?

c. **In the midst of the years make it known**: Habakkuk longed for God to do a work that was *evident* to everyone as a work of God. He prayed that revival would be **known** at a definite *time and place* (**in the midst of the years**), not just as an idea in someone's head.

d. **In wrath remember mercy**: Habakkuk prayed knowing well that they didn't *deserve* revival, so he prayed for **mercy**. The idea is, "LORD, I know that we deserve your **wrath**, but in the midst of your **wrath remember mercy** and send revival among us."

> i. "Sorrowfully, not wishing to be an accuser of the brethren, it does seem to me that considering the responsibilities which were laid upon us, and the means which God has given us, the church generally, (there are blessed exceptions!) has done so little for Christ that if 'Ichabod' were written right across its brow, and it were banished from God's house, it would have its deserts. We cannot therefore appeal to merit, it must be mercy." (Spurgeon)

> ii. "O God, have mercy upon thy poor church, and visit her, and revive her. She has but a little strength; she has desired to keep thy word; oh, refresh her; restore to her thy power, and give her yet to be great in this land." (Spurgeon)

2. (3-15) The power of God on behalf of His people.

God came from Teman,
The Holy One from Mount Paran. *Selah*.

His glory covered the heavens,
And the earth was full of His praise.
His **brightness was like the light;**
He had rays *flashing* **from His hand,**
And there His power *was* **hidden.**

Before Him went pestilence,
And fever followed at His feet.

He stood and measured the earth;
He looked and startled the nations.
And the everlasting mountains were scattered,
The perpetual hills bowed.
His ways *are* everlasting.
I saw the tents of Cushan in affliction;
The curtains of the land of Midian trembled.

O LORD, were *You* displeased with the rivers,
Was Your anger against the rivers,
Was Your wrath against the sea,
That You rode on Your horses,
Your chariots of salvation?
Your bow was made quite ready;
Oaths were sworn over *Your* arrows. *Selah*.

You divided the earth with rivers.
The mountains saw You *and* trembled;
The overflowing of the water passed by.
The deep uttered its voice,
And lifted its hands on high.
The sun and moon stood still in their habitation;
At the light of Your arrows they went,
At the shining of Your glittering spear.

You marched through the land in indignation;
You trampled the nations in anger.
You went forth for the salvation of Your people,
For salvation with Your Anointed.
You struck the head from the house of the wicked,
By laying bare from foundation to neck. *Selah*.

You thrust through with his own arrows
The head of his villages.
They came out like a whirlwind to scatter me;
Their rejoicing was like feasting on the poor in secret.
You walked through the sea with Your horses,
Through the heap of great waters.

> a. **His glory covered the heavens, and the earth was full of His praise**: As Habakkuk prayed for revival he began to praise the God who brings revival. In this song of praise (punctuated by several expressions of **Selah**, as in the Psalms) Habakkuk glorified God for His power and majesty.

> i. It is good to praise God like this, and God's people need to do more of it. It is good to praise God:
>
> - Because it gives appropriate honor and glory to God.
> - Because it declares God's specific works.
> - Because it teaches and reminds us of who God is and what He has done.
> - Because it places man in his proper position under God.
> - Because it builds confidence in the power and works of God.

b. **You went forth for the salvation of Your people, for salvation with Your Anointed**: As Habakkuk remembered how God had saved in the past, it made him full of faith for what God could do in the present and in the future. He also declared that salvation is **with Your Anointed** – and the LORD's **Anointed** is none other than the Messiah, Jesus Christ.

B. The triumph of the prophet's faith.

1. (16-18) Knowing God's strength, Habakkuk can trust the LORD even in a crisis.

When I heard, my body trembled;
My lips quivered at *the* voice;
Rottenness entered my bones;
And I trembled in myself,
That I might rest in the day of trouble.
When he comes up to the people,
He will invade them with his troops.

Though the fig tree may not blossom,
Nor fruit be on the vines;
Though the labor of the olive may fail,
And the fields yield no food;
Though the flock may be cut off from the fold,
And there be no herd in the stalls–
Yet I will rejoice in the LORD,
I will joy in the God of my salvation.

> a. **When I heard, my body trembled**: Habakkuk showed the proper response of a man under the sovereign power of God. He recognized his own weakness and low standing before this God of all majesty and power.
>
> b. **He will invade them with his troops**: The prophet remembered that the Babylonians were coming and that this God of sovereign power and majesty would direct their work against Judah.

c. **Though the fig tree may not blossom, nor fruit be on the vines… yet I will rejoice in the LORD, I will joy in the God of my salvation**: In what was almost a vision, Habakkuk saw the Judean countryside desolate, perhaps from the invading Babylonian army or perhaps from natural calamity. In the midst of this almost complete loss, Habakkuk could still **rejoice in the LORD**.

> i. He knew that this God of majesty and power is not *diminished* because man faces difficult trials. Sometimes we think, "If God is so great and powerful, how come I am going through a hard time?" Habakkuk knew this was the wrong question and the wrong attitude. Instead, he said: "I know You are strong and mighty, and if we are in desolate circumstances it is because we deserve it. I will praise You still, and even rejoice in You."

> ii. **Rejoice in the LORD…joy in the God of my salvation**: With desolate circumstances like he just described, Habakkuk could find no joy in the **fig tree** or in the **vines** or in the **fields** or **flock**; yet God was unchanged. He could still **rejoice in the LORD** because He is unchanging.

> iii. Habakkuk didn't just practice positive thinking and shut out the idea of the barren fig tree and the empty cattle stalls. Instead, he saw those problems for what they were and remembered that God was greater than them all.

> iv. Benjamin Franklin – who was not a Christian, though he had great respect for the Bible – used Habakkuk 3:17-19 to confound a group of sophisticated, cultured despisers of the Bible. When he was in Paris he heard this group mocking the Bible, and mocking Franklin for his admiration of it. One evening he came among them and said that he had a manuscript containing an ancient poem, that he was quite impressed by the poem and he wanted to read it to them. When he read Habakkuk 3:17-19, his listeners received it with praise and admiration – "What a magnificent poem!" they said, and wanted to know where they could get copies. Franklin told them to just look in Habakkuk chapter 3. (Boice)

2. (19) Knowing God's strength, Habakkuk can trust God for strength.

The LORD God is my strength;
He will make my feet like deer's *feet,*
And He will make me walk on my high hills.

To the Chief Musician. With my stringed instruments.

a. **The Lord God is my strength**: Habakkuk could only properly declare this after he prayed the prayer of faith in the previous verses. He rightly declared that his strength was *not* in fig trees or vines or fields or flocks, but only in the **Lord God**.

> i. We might even say that *what we praise is our strength*. If by his words, life, or heart a man lives to praise his own achievements and resources, then those are his *strength*. If by words, life, or heart one praises a person or an idea, then those are his *strength*. We demonstrate that the **Lord God** is our **strength** when we praise Him.

b. **He will make my feet like deer's feet**: Habakkuk thought of the deer running about on the **high hills**, never losing a step and never falling. More than that, the deer positively dance and leap on the hills – they are full of life and joy. With that in mind the prophet proclaimed, "God will also set my steps firmly and full of life. As I trust in Him, He will not allow me to slip or fall, and I will do more than merely plod along – I will skip about with life and joy."

Zephaniah 1 – Coming Judgment and the Reasons for It

A. God's promised judgment.

1. (1) Zephaniah: The man and his times.

The word of the LORD which came to Zephaniah the son of Cushi, the son of Gedaliah, the son of Amariah, the son of Hezekiah, in the days of Josiah the son of Amon, king of Judah.

a. **The word of the LORD which came to Zephaniah**: This first verse of the prophecy of Zephaniah sets it apart from most other prophets, in that he told us both his time and his lineage. Zephaniah was an unusual prophet, in that he was of royal lineage, descending from the godly King **Hezekiah**.

i. The name **Zephaniah** means "Yahweh hides" or "Yahweh has hidden." Zephaniah was almost certainly born during the long, wicked reign of Manasseh, whose reign began 55 years before the start of Josiah's reign. Zephaniah was probably hidden for his own protection.

b. **In the days of Josiah**: Josiah was a godly, young king who brought great revival and reform to Judah but Josiah reigned for 10 years before he led his great revival. Zephaniah was probably written in the years before the revival, and God used this prophecy to bring and to further revival.

i. Since Zephaniah predicts the destruction of Nineveh (which happened in 612 B.C.) we know that his prophecy belongs to the first part of the reign of King Josiah.

ii. The 12 books of the Minor Prophets are divided into two groups: pre-exilic and post-exilic. The first 9 are *pre-exilic*, writing before the Babylonians conquered and exiled Judah. The last 3 are *post-exilic*, writing during and after the return of Israel from Babylon to the Promised Land. Zephaniah is the last of the pre-exilic prophets and can be said to "sum up" the messages of the previous 8. Zephaniah seems unoriginal to some scholars because he quotes the words and ideas of many previous prophets.

2. (2-3) The promise of judgment.

"I will utterly consume everything
From the face of the land,"
Says the Lord;
"I will consume man and beast;
I will consume the birds of the heavens,
The fish of the sea,
And the stumbling blocks along with the wicked.
I will cut off man from the face of the land,"
Says the Lord.

a. **I will utterly consume everything**: Zephaniah didn't waste any time getting to the point. Delivering the message of the Lord, he warned of harsh and complete judgment that would consume everything before the Lord.

3. (4-6) Judgment is promised to idolaters.

"I will stretch out My hand against Judah,
And against all the inhabitants of Jerusalem.
I will cut off every trace of Baal from this place,
The names of the idolatrous priests with the *pagan* priests—
Those who worship the host of heaven on the housetops;
Those who worship and swear *oaths* by the Lord,
But who *also* swear by Milcom;
Those who have turned back from *following* the Lord,
And have not sought the Lord, nor inquired of Him."

a. **Against Judah**: The promise of judgment in Zephaniah 1:2-3 was broad enough to include the whole earth, and to allow some to think that God didn't really mean *them*. Now God focused in on His people in the land of **Judah**, and He would not allow them to think that He spoke just to others.

b. **I will cut off every trace of Baal**: King Josiah inherited a corrupt nation from his father Amon and grandfather Manasseh; a nation almost wholly given over to idolatry (2 Kings 21:3-7). Here, God announced judgment against the idol worshippers in Israel. Apparently, both the leadership and the people heeded this announcement of judgment because in the days of Josiah this kind of gross idolatry was eliminated (2 Kings 23:4-15).

i. Considering the complete uprooting of idolatry described in 2 Kings 23, we can see that God's promise to **cut off every trace of Baal** and destroy the rest of the expressions of idolatry was fulfilled. We also see that this prophecy was an invitation, as if God said: "Baal and the idols are going to go. You can get rid of them in righteousness, or I will get rid of them in judgment but rest assured that they are going to go." King Josiah directed the war on idolatry and the nation was blessed.

4. (7-9) Judgment is promised to royalty.

Be silent in the presence of the Lord God;
For the day of the Lord *is* at hand,
For the Lord has prepared a sacrifice;
He has invited His guests.

"And it shall be,
In the day of the Lord's sacrifice,
That I will punish the princes and the king's children,
And all such as are clothed with foreign apparel.
In the same day I will punish
All those who leap over the threshold,
Who fill their masters' houses with violence and deceit.

a. **Be silent in the presence of the Lord God**: God addresses the royalty of Judah in a way they aren't used to hearing. He tells them to "shut up" and listen to His pronouncement of judgment – a **sacrifice** of judgment made against a wicked nation.

i. Boice tells the story of two gangsters, one named "Two-Gun Crowley" who cruelly murdered many including a policeman. He was captured in a shoot-out with police and wrote this note during the shoot-out, fearing he would die: "Under my coat is a weary heart, but a kind one – one that would do nobody any harm." The other gangster is Al Capone, who said: "I have spent the best years of my life giving people the lighter pleasures, and all I get is abuse, the existence of a hunted man." Our ability to proclaim our innocence when we are deep in sin is remarkable, but through it all God tells us to **be silent in the presence of the Lord God**.

b. **I will punish the princes and the king's children**: This warning came to a *godly* king during a time of reform. God warns Josiah and the whole royal community what will happen if they don't follow through on their turning to God.

c. **All such as are clothed with foreign apparel**: The priests and leaders of Judah were ashamed of their national identity, so they loved to dress in **foreign apparel**. They wanted to be as much like the worldly nations around them as they could possibly be.

d. **All those who leap over the threshold**: This probably refers to bringing pagan customs and superstitions into the house of God, in the same way that the worshippers of Dagon honored silly and offensive superstitions (1 Samuel 5:5).

5. (10-11) Judgment is promised to merchants.

"And there shall be on that day," says the LORD,
"The sound of a mournful cry from the Fish Gate,
A wailing from the Second Quarter,
And a loud crashing from the hills.
Wail, you inhabitants of Maktesh!
For all the merchant people are cut down;
All those who handle money are cut off.

a. **All the merchant people are cut down**: Merchants and those with money trusted in their riches, and now God promises to cut down those steeped in that kind of idolatry. Colossians 3:5-6 shows this isn't just an Old Testament concept: *Therefore put to death your members which are on the earth…covetousness, which is idolatry. Because of these things the wrath of God is coming upon the sons of disobedience.*

6. (12-13) Judgment is promised to the complacent.

"And it shall come to pass at that time
***That* I will search Jerusalem with lamps,**
And punish the men
Who are settled in complacency,
Who say in their heart,
'The LORD will not do good,
Nor will He do evil.'
Therefore their goods shall become booty,
And their houses a desolation;
They shall build houses, but not inhabit *them*;
They shall plant vineyards, but not drink their wine."

a. **I will search Jerusalem with lamps**: No one will be able to hide against the judgment of God. It is coming, and even if God must get out the **lamps** or searchlights, He will find them.

i. "Unlike Diogenes, the pre-Christian Greek philosopher who was searching for an honest man, Yahweh in this context does not seek righteousness but sin to *punish* and eradicate." (Baker)

b. **Punish the men who are settled in complacency**: The LORD promised judgment against those who felt that God was distant or detached from their lives, and had thus become complacent.

c. **The LORD will not do good, nor will He do evil**: Some people believe in God as a great "clockmaker" who created the universe, wound it up and then left it ticking without any further intervention from Him. Those who believe there is no God, or that if God exists He has nothing to do with man, are terribly and tragically wrong.

i. Edward Gibbon in his book *The Decline and Fall of the Roman Empire* described the attitudes towards religion in the last days of the Roman Empire – attitudes remarkably like our own today.

- The people regarded all religions as equally true.
- The philosophers regarded all religions as equally false.
- The politicians regarded all religions as equally useful.

B. The description of judgment.

1. (14-16) The intensity of judgment.

The great day of the LORD *is* near;
***It is* near and hastens quickly.**
The noise of the day of the LORD is bitter;
There the mighty men shall cry out.
That day *is* a day of wrath,
A day of trouble and distress,
A day of devastation and desolation,
A day of darkness and gloominess,
A day of clouds and thick darkness,
A day of trumpet and alarm against the fortified cities
And against the high towers.

a. **The great day of the LORD is near**: The term **day of the LORD** (used more than 25 times in the Bible) does not necessarily refer to one specific day; it speaks of "God's time." The idea is that now is the *day of man*, but the day of man will not last forever. One day, the Messiah will end the day of man and herald the **day of the LORD**.

b. **That day is a day of wrath**: It is a **day of wrath** because man will not give up without a fight, and because mankind will receive the just penalty for his rebellion against the LORD. Zephaniah paints the picture powerfully with the repeated description, "**a day of…**"

i. **That day is a day of wrath**: "This passage in the Vulgate forms the first line of the medieval sequence *Dies irae*." (Walker)

2. (17-18) The certainty of judgment.

"I will bring distress upon men,

And they shall walk like blind men,
Because they have sinned against the LORD;
Their blood shall be poured out like dust,
And their flesh like refuse."

Neither their silver nor their gold
Shall be able to deliver them
In the day of the LORD's wrath;
But the whole land shall be devoured
By the fire of His jealousy,
For He will make speedy riddance
Of all those who dwell in the land.

> a. **I will bring distress upon men**: God wants to make it plain and certain that He will judge a rebellious Judah. If they do not repent, there will be no holding back from the completion of His judgment.
>
> b. **Neither their silver nor their gold shall be able to deliver them**: Men trust in **silver** and **gold**, but it will do them no good on the day of God's judgment.

Zephaniah 2 – Judgment Against the Nations

A. The last chance.

1. (1-2) Repent while there is still time.

Gather yourselves together, yes, gather together,
O undesirable nation,
Before the decree is issued,
Or **the day passes like chaff,**
Before the LORD's fierce anger comes upon you,
Before the day of the Lord's anger comes upon you!

> a. **Gather yourselves together**: The idea is gathering together in a solemn demonstration of national mourning and repentance.
>
> b. **Before the decree is issued**: All the announcement of judgment in the previous chapter is understood as a warning and as an invitation to repentance. The often-unwritten theme behind almost every prophecy of judgment is, "This is what will happen if you *do not repent*." Here the prophet pleads with the nation to repent **before** it is too late.
>
> c. **Before…the day passes like chaff**: Here the prophet called for a sense of *urgency* in repentance. Each day **passes like chaff**, and there is nothing to show for the day if we neglect what is most important: getting right and staying right with God.
>
>> i. How easy it is to let the days pass **like chaff**, and never get right with God! Often the devil's most powerful lie isn't that there is no God, or no Bible, or no truth – often his most powerful lie is that *there is no hurry*. Nevertheless, *today is the day of salvation*.

2. (3) The last chance.

Seek the LORD, all you meek of the earth,
Who have upheld His justice.
Seek righteousness, seek humility.

It may be that you will be hidden
In the day of the LORD's anger.

> a. **Seek the LORD, all you meek**: Even the righteous must take heed to this warning. It would do them no good to say, "The LORD speaks to my wicked neighbor and not to me." At a critical moment of national danger, even the righteous must **seek the LORD**.

> b. **It may be that you will be hidden in the day of the LORD's anger**: In more than one place, God promises to *hide* His righteous people in the day of great judgment. This is especially relevant to the time of the Great Tribulation, when Jesus warned us to *Watch therefore, and pray always that you may be counted worthy to escape all these things that will come to pass, and to stand before the Son of Man.* (Luke 21:36)

B. Judgment against the nations.

1. (4-7) Judgment against the Philistines.

For Gaza shall be forsaken,
And Ashkelon desolate;
They shall drive out Ashdod at noonday,
And Ekron shall be uprooted.
Woe to the inhabitants of the seacoast,
The nation of the Cherethites!
The word of the LORD *is* against you,
O Canaan, land of the Philistines:
"I will destroy you;
So there shall be no inhabitant."

The seacoast shall be pastures,
With shelters for shepherds and folds for flocks.
The coast shall be for the remnant of the house of Judah;
They shall feed *their* flocks there;
In the houses of Ashkelon
They shall lie down at evening.
For the LORD their God will intervene for them,
And return their captives.

> a. **For Gaza shall be forsaken**: Judgment will come against an unrepentant Judah, but it will also come against the pagan nations neighboring Judah. God promises to destroy the cities of the Philistines and give their land as pasture **for the remnant of the house of Judah**.

> b. **The nation of the Cherethites**: The name **Cherethites** is "a reference to their early geographical links with Crete." (Baker)

2. (8-11) Judgment against the Moabites and Ammonites.

"I have heard the reproach of Moab,
And the insults of the people of Ammon,
With which they have reproached My people,
And made arrogant threats against their borders.
Therefore, as I live,"
Says the LORD of hosts, the God of Israel,
"Surely Moab shall be like Sodom,
And the people of Ammon like Gomorrah–
Overrun with weeds and saltpits,
And a perpetual desolation.
The residue of My people shall plunder them,
And the remnant of My people shall possess them."

This they shall have for their pride,
Because they have reproached and made arrogant threats
Against the people of the LORD of hosts.
The LORD *will be* awesome to them,
For He will reduce to nothing all the gods of the earth;
***People* shall worship Him,**
Each one from his place,
Indeed all the shores of the nations.

> a. **I have heard the reproach of Moab, and the insults of the people of Ammon**: First, God looked to the west and saw the Philistines; then He looked to the east and saw the Moabites and the Ammonites. God promised to judge these peoples and bring them to **perpetual desolation**.
>
>> i. "The comparison of Moab and Ammon to Sodom and Gomorrah is not surprising in view of their origin: Moab and Ammon were the offspring of the incestuous relations of Lot's daughters with their drunk father after he fled the destruction of Sodom and Gomorrah." (Walker)
>
> b. **The LORD will be awesome to them, for He will reduce to nothing all the gods of the earth; people shall worship Him**: God would glorify Himself among the nations, and one way He would do it was to bring the idols of the nations low. All would see that their idols were vain and that the LORD alone is God.

3. (12) Judgment against Ethiopia.

"You Ethiopians also,
You shall be slain by My sword."

a. **You Ethiopians also**: Now God looked to the south, announcing judgment against the **Ethiopians**.

4. (13-15) Judgment against Assyria.

And He will stretch out His hand against the north,
Destroy Assyria,
And make Nineveh a desolation,
As dry as the wilderness.
The herds shall lie down in her midst,
Every beast of the nation.
Both the pelican and the bittern
Shall lodge on the capitals *of* **her** *pillars;*
Their voice shall sing in the windows;
Desolation *shall be* **at the threshold;**
For He will lay bare the cedar work.
This is the rejoicing city
That dwelt securely,
That said in her heart,
"I *am it,* **and** *there is* **none besides me."**
How has she become a desolation,
A place for beasts to lie down!
Everyone who passes by her
Shall hiss and shake his fist.

a. **And He will stretch out His hand against the north**: God completed the circle of judgment against Israel's neighbors by looking at **Assyria** and her capital city of **Nineveh**, which would be made a desolate city fit only for the habitation of animals and birds.

b. **This is the rejoicing city that dwelt securely**: Nineveh felt strong and confident, but God knew how to bring her low. Here the LORD fulfilled the principle of James 4:6: *God resists the proud, but gives grace to the humble.*

i. Zephaniah never mentions *why* the nations were ripe for judgment. Perhaps he assumed his readers were already familiar with the prophecies of Amos, Isaiah, and Nahum, which described the sins of these neighboring nations.

Zephaniah 3 – The LORD Rejoices Over the Restoration of His People

A. A contrast between a wicked city and a righteous God.

1. (1-4) Jerusalem, the wicked city.

Woe to her who is rebellious and polluted,
To the oppressing city!
She has not obeyed *His* voice,
She has not received correction;
She has not trusted in the LORD,
She has not drawn near to her God.

Her princes in her midst *are* roaring lions;
Her judges *are* evening wolves
That leave not a bone till morning.
Her prophets are insolent, treacherous people;
Her priests have polluted the sanctuary,
They have done violence to the law.

> a. **Woe to her who is rebellious and polluted, to the oppressing city**: From the way that Zephaniah 2 ended we perhaps hoped that this **oppressing city** was Nineveh. From the references to **her prophets**, **her priests**, and the **sanctuary** and the **law**, we learn that *Jerusalem* was the **oppressing city**.
>
> b. **She has not…she has not…she has not…she has not**: In repeating these words four times, the prophet told us the root of Jerusalem's sin.
>
>> i. **She has not obeyed His voice**: God called to His people, but they did not listen. If there is any voice for the sheep to obey, it is the voice of the shepherd – but **she has not obeyed His voice**.
>>
>> ii. **She has not received correction**: Correction certainly came, but she did not *receive* it as correction from the LORD. Instead, it was a

bad time, tough circumstances, whatever – but **she has not received correction**.

iii. **She has not trusted in the Lord**: God never gave Jerusalem a reason to stop trusting in Him; He never proved Himself unfaithful or untrustworthy. Now God's people will openly deny and contradict God's word and promises, showing that **she has not trusted in the Lord**.

iv. **She has not drawn near to her God**: The worst offense was saved for last. God longed for a relationship with His people, but they rejected His desire and went their own way, so **she has not drawn near to her God**.

2. (5-7) The righteous God.

The Lord *is* righteous in her midst,
He will do no unrighteousness.
Every morning He brings His justice to light;
He never fails,
But the unjust knows no shame.

"I have cut off nations,
Their fortresses are devastated;
I have made their streets desolate,
With none passing by.
Their cities are destroyed;
***There is* no one, no inhabitant.**
I said, 'Surely you will fear Me,
You will receive instruction'–
So that her dwelling would not be cut off,
***Despite* everything for which I punished her.**
But they rose early and corrupted all their deeds.

a. **The Lord is righteous in her midst**: This made the unrighteousness of His people even more criminal and tragic. God had been nothing but **righteous** to them, yet they responded with sin. Eventually, they would put themselves on the wrong side of God's righteousness and face His **justice**.

b. **Surely you will fear Me, you will receive instruction…. But they rose early and corrupted all their deeds**: God brought His justice to the nations around Judah, and it should have warned Judah what would happen if they rejected God. Instead of learning from the surrounding nations, they dedicated themselves to ungodliness all the more.

B. The promise of restoration.

1. (8-13) Judgment and restoration.

"Therefore wait for Me," says the Lord,
"Until the day I rise up for plunder;
My determination *is* to gather the nations
To My assembly of kingdoms,
To pour on them My indignation,
All My fierce anger;
All the earth shall be devoured
With the fire of My jealousy.

For then I will restore to the peoples a pure language,
That they all may call on the name of the Lord,
To serve Him with one accord.
From beyond the rivers of Ethiopia
My worshipers,
The daughter of My dispersed ones,
Shall bring My offering.
In that day you shall not be shamed for any of your deeds
In which you transgress against Me;
For then I will take away from your midst
Those who rejoice in your pride,
And you shall no longer be haughty
In My holy mountain.
I will leave in your midst
A meek and humble people,
And they shall trust in the name of the Lord.
The remnant of Israel shall do no unrighteousness
And speak no lies,
Nor shall a deceitful tongue be found in their mouth;
For they shall feed *their* flocks and lie down,
And no one shall make *them* afraid."

a. **Pour on them My indignation.... then I will restore**: In light of the repeated and chronic sin of the nations and of God's own people, God would bring judgment – and then bring *restoration*.

b. **That they all may call on the name of the Lord**: In this ultimate restoration, God will give the world a common language again (**a pure language**), and the entire world will worship the Lord, not only Israel.

i. Most Bible scholars see this as fulfilled in the days of the Millennium, when Jesus reigns for 1,000 years over this earth after His return in power and glory. From this passage, many scholars believe that in that day the world will go back to a common language – perhaps Hebrew.

c. **To serve Him with one accord**: Literally, this is *with one shoulder*. The idea is that the shoulders are working together as one to bear the load of the work.

d. **You shall no longer be haughty in My holy mountain**: In the millennial era Israel will be the world's superpower, but she will not be proud or **haughty**. Under the leadership of the Lord Jesus and His redeemed, she will know that her standing is all of grace.

e. **For they shall feed their flocks and lie down, and no one shall make them afraid**: This speaks of the peace and prosperity Israel will know in the millennial era.

2. (14-20) Restored with singing.

Sing, O daughter of Zion!
Shout, O Israel!
Be glad and rejoice with all *your* heart,
O daughter of Jerusalem!
The Lord has taken away your judgments,
He has cast out your enemy.
The King of Israel, the Lord,
***Is* in your midst;**
You shall see disaster no more.

In that day it shall be said to Jerusalem:
"Do not fear;
Zion, let not your hands be weak.
The Lord your God in your midst,
The Mighty One, will save;
He will rejoice over you with gladness,
He will quiet *you* with His love,
He will rejoice over you with singing."

"I will gather those who sorrow over the appointed assembly,
Who are among you,
***To whom* its reproach *is* a burden.**
Behold, at that time
I will deal with all who afflict you;
I will save the lame,
And gather those who were driven out;
I will appoint them for praise and fame
In every land where they were put to shame.

**At that time I will bring you back,
Even at the time I gather you;
For I will give you fame and praise
Among all the peoples of the earth,
When I return your captives before your eyes,"
Says the Lord.**

a. **Sing, O daughter of Zion**: Considering the glorious promise of restoration, Israel should sing and shout with joy. God will save and redeem them from both their enemies and their iniquities.

b. **The Lord your God in your midst, the Mighty One, will save**: This passage gives us definite reasons for consolation, as we understand that:

- The Lord is in our midst.
- The Lord is in our midst with the power to save.
- God takes joy in us.
- God gives us rest in His love.
- God sings over us.

c. **He will rejoice over you with gladness**: We often underestimate the joy God has in His people, and too often think God is annoyed or irritated with us.

i. "Faulty as the church is, the Lord rejoices in her. While we mourn, as well we may, yet we do not sorrow as those that are without hope; for God does not sorrow, his heart is glad, and he is said to rejoice with joy – a highly emphatic expression." (Spurgeon)

d. **He will rejoice over you with singing**: We don't often think of God singing, but He does – and He sings **over** His people. This is how much joy and delight we give to the Lord – that He breaks into song!

i. "Think of the great Jehovah singing! Can you imagine it? Is it possible to conceive of the Deity breaking into a song: Father, Son and Holy Ghost together singing over the redeemed? God is so happy in the love which he bears to his people that he breaks the eternal silence, and sun and moon and stars with astonishment hear God chanting a hymn of joy." (Spurgeon)

ii. "If God sings, shall not we sing? He did not sing when he made the world. No; he looked upon it, and simply said that it was good. The angels sang, the sons of God shouted for joy: creation was very wonderful to them, but it was not much to God, who could have made thousands of worlds by his mere will. Creation could not make him sing…. When all was done, and the Lord saw what became of it in the salvation of his redeemed, then he rejoiced after a divine manner." (Spurgeon)

e. **Do not fear; Zion, let not your hands be weak**: Knowing this is the tender love and care of God for us should make us respond in two ways. First, we should **not fear** – if **the Mighty One** loves us and delights in us this way, what can we be afraid of? Second, we should not **let** our **hands be weak** – knowing this mighty Lord of love is for us, we want to be for *Him* with all our energy. We will not become weak or weary in our service for Him.

> i. "'Fear thou not.' What! Not a little? No, 'Fear thou not.' But surely I may show some measure of trembling? No, 'Fear thou not.' Tie that knot tight about the throat of unbelief. 'Fear thou not': neither this day, nor any day of thy life. When fear comes in, drive it away; give it no space. If God rests in his love, and if God sings, what canst thou have to do with fear?" (Spurgeon)

f. **I will gather.... I will save**: God promised to encourage the discouraged, to defeat the enemies of His people, to heal the lame, and to gather the scattered. All this is for His **praise and fame** and for His people because they are found in Him (**I will give you fame and praise among all the peoples**).

Haggai 1 – Getting Priorities Straight

A. God rebukes the returning remnant for their misplaced priorities.

1. (1) Introduction.

In the second year of King Darius, in the sixth month, on the first day of the month, the word of the LORD came by Haggai the prophet to Zerubbabel the son of Shealtiel, governor of Judah, and to Joshua the son of Jehozadak, the high priest, saying,

a. **In the second year of King Darius**: The prophecy of Haggai gives us several specific chronological marking points (Haggai 1:1, 1:15, 2:1, 2:10, 2:20). Here we learn that the prophecy began in September, 520 B.C.

i. This makes Haggai the first among the *post-exilic* minor prophets. Of the 12 minor prophets, the first 9 spoke *before* Judah was carried away captive – exiled to Babylon. The last 3 minor prophets (Haggai, Zechariah, and Malachi) each spoke to those who returned from the 70-year exile.

ii. "Gone was the glory of the former kingdom and temple. Gone was the great population. All that was left was the rubble of Jerusalem, the remnant of the people, and the task of restoration." (Boice)

iii. In 538 B.C. King Cyrus of Persia allowed the exiled Jews to return to Jerusalem after 70 years in captivity. Two years later (536 B.C.) construction on the temple began, led by Zerubbabel. The work stopped after two years (534 B.C.). After 14 years of neglect, work on the temple resumed in 520 B.C. and was finished four years later in 516 B.C. (Ezra 6:15).

iv. We notice that the dates are reckoned by a pagan king because there was at that time no king over Israel. Yet the date was still important to God. "There is a set time for each of his messages to come to men, and God would have them give heed to every message as soon as it is delivered to them. If they do not, he keeps count of the days of their delay." (Spurgeon)

b. **The word of the Lord came by Haggai the prophet**: In the difficult years of the return from exile God spoke to His people through the prophet Haggai.

i. Haggai is also mentioned twice in the book of Ezra, the priest who oversaw the work of rebuilding the temple:

Then the prophet Haggai and Zechariah the son of Iddo, prophets, prophesied to the Jews who were in Judah and Jerusalem, in the name of the God of Israel, who was over them. So Zerubbabel the son of Shealtiel and Jeshua the son of Jozadak rose up and began to build the house of God which is in Jerusalem; and the prophets of God were with them, helping them. (Ezra 5:1-2)

So the elders of the Jews built, and they prospered through the prophesying of Haggai the prophet and Zechariah the son of Iddo. And they built and finished it, according to the commandment of the God of Israel, and according to the command of Cyrus, Darius, and Artaxerxes king of Persia. (Ezra 6:14)

ii. The name **Haggai** is probably an abbreviated form of the phrase, *festival of Yahweh*. Some speculate that he was born on the day of a major feast in Israel.

c. **Zerubbabel…Joshua**: Haggai introduced us to two leading figures in Jerusalem during these difficult days of rebuilding the temple. **Zerubbabel** was the governor of Jerusalem, and a descendant of the last legitimate ruler of Judah, Jeconiah. **Joshua** was the high priest.

2. (2) An excuse for not rebuilding the temple.

"Thus speaks the Lord of hosts, saying: 'This people says, "The time has not come, the time that the Lord's house should be built."'"

a. **The time has not come**: Haggai gave this first word in September, 520 b.c. At that time the exiles had been back in Jerusalem for 18 years – but the work of rebuilding the temple lain idle for the last 14 years.

i. The work started gloriously: *When the builders laid the foundation of the temple of the Lord, the priests stood in their apparel with trumpets, and the Levites, the sons of Asaph, with cymbals, to praise the Lord, according to the ordinance of David king of Israel. And they sang responsively, praising and giving thanks to the Lord: "For He is good, For His mercy endures forever toward Israel." Then all the people shouted with a great shout, when they praised the* LORD, *because the foundation of the house of the* LORD *was laid.* (Ezra 3:10-11)

ii. Despite the glorious beginning, after two years the work stopped, mired in discouragement and derailed by a lack of focus. When Haggai prophesied the foundation of the temple was laid and the altar was rebuilt but the temple wasn't yet rebuilt.

b. **This people says**: God's **people** – the citizens of Jerusalem – told themselves that it wasn't yet **time** to resume work on the temple. There were some good reasons why they might say this, and why the work of rebuilding the temple was hard:

- The land was still desolate after 70 years of neglect.
- The work was hard.
- They didn't have a lot of money (Haggai 1:6) or manpower.
- They suffered crop failures and drought (Haggai 1:10-11).
- Hostile enemies resisted the work (Ezra 4:1-5).
- They remembered easier times in Babylon.

c. **The time has not come, the time that the** LORD'**s house should be built**: The people made their excuse sound spiritual. They couldn't speak against the *idea* of building the temple, so they spoke against its *timing*. They said, "It isn't God's timing to rebuild the temple."

i. Because of the great obstacles against the work, God's people began to rationalize and decided that it wasn't time to rebuild after all. "If it's so hard, evidently, God doesn't want us to do it – at least not anytime soon."

ii. They may have said "**the time has not come**" because they thought that the 70 years of captivity mentioned in Jeremiah 25:11-13 and 29:10 had not yet been fulfilled. According to Usher's chronology of these events, they were in the 69th year since the last siege of Jerusalem.

iii. Even in this, the people of God lacked faith. There were three "waves" of captivity – 605 B.C., 597 B.C., and 587 B.C. In Daniel's prayer in Daniel 9, he was bold enough to ask God to take the earliest starting point to determine the 70 years – and God did. Unbelief made these returned captives think that God's mercy might not come to Israel until 18 years later.

d. **This people**: We never like to hear God speak to His people this way – saying, "**this people**" instead of "*My* people." He said this because He saw their excuses and their poor priorities and noticed that they were not living like His people.

> i. We should remember that these weren't "bad people." They were the remnant that returned from Babylon. Hundreds of thousands of people went into the Babylonian captivity and only about 50,000 returned. Those who did were the most committed to the LORD and to the restoration of Jerusalem.

3. (3-4) Haggai exposes their wrong priorities.

Then the word of the LORD came by Haggai the prophet, saying, "*Is it time for you yourselves to dwell in your paneled houses, and this temple to lie* in ruins?"

a. **Then the word of the LORD came**: God saw and heard their excuses and poor priorities – and He had something to say to them through **Haggai the prophet**.

b. **Is it time for you yourselves to dwell in your paneled houses**: The people said that it wasn't *time* to rebuild the temple. In their actions, they said that it was **time** to live in nicely rebuilt houses.

> i. "Solomon first built a house for God, and then for himself." (Trapp)

c. **And this temple to lie in ruins**: This was the real problem – not that God's people lived in **paneled houses**, but that they lived in such personal comfort and luxury while the **temple** was in **ruins**.

> i. The problem was simply wrongly ordered priorities. They were content to let the cause of the LORD suffer rather than give up their comfort. Instead, they should have felt no rest until the work of God was as prosperous as their personal lives. They should have been as willing to sacrifice for the work of God as they were for their personal comfort and luxury.
>
> ii. It is easy to see how this happened over 14 years. At first, the work is stopped because it is so difficult and some obstacle in the construction prevented progress.
>
> - "We can't get much done at the temple, and I'm tired of living in a wreck. Time to start the remodel at home."
> - "God wants me to give attention to things at home – home comes first."
> - "I would fund more construction at the temple, but all my money is tied up with my home renovation."

- "I'm not living extravagantly – look at the other houses in my neighborhood! Look at the chariots in their driveways!"
- "Someone should get to work on the temple. I hope someone steps up to the job – I've got to finish paneling my living room."
- "The temple hasn't been open for business for more than 50 years – a little while longer won't matter."
- "This isn't the right time – later will be better."
- "The altar is there, and we can at least sacrifice to the Lord. We're getting by."

iii. The excuses sound familiar – but God saw through them in the days of Haggai, and He sees through similar excuses today. The prophet Haggai was like an alarm clock: unwelcome but necessary.

iv. "Many Christians are like those ancient Hebrews, somehow convincing themselves that economy in constructing church buildings is all-important while at the same time sparing no expense in acquiring their personal luxuries." (Alden)

v. **Houses**: "It seems to intimate some of them had more than one house, a city and a country house, and whilst God's house lay waste; they thus lavish out their wealth on private worldly conveniences, but grudge their charge against God's house.... Do you owe so much to yourselves, and so little to your God?" (Poole)

4. (5-6) Consider your ways and the result of them.

Now therefore, thus says the Lord of hosts: "Consider your ways!
"You have sown much, and bring in little;
You eat, but do not have enough;
You drink, but you are not filled with drink;
You clothe yourselves, but no one is warm;
And he who earns wages,
Earns wages *to put* **into a bag with holes."**

a. **Consider your ways**: The Hebrew figure of speech for this phrase is literally "put your heart on your roads." Haggai asks God's people to consider what direction their lives were heading and if they really wanted it to continue that way.

b. **You have sown much, and bring in little**: The cause of their financial difficulties was their wrong priorities. They suffered setback after setback because the blessing of God wasn't on their pocketbook.

i. Haggai described a double curse. Instead of much, **little** was reaped; and the little that was brought home melted away without doing any good (**earns wages to put into a bag with holes**). "I do not know of any passage in the Bible that better describes the feverish yet ineffective activity of our own age." (Boice)

ii. These judgments were a fulfillment of promises God made hundreds of years before in the time of Moses (Deuteronomy 11:16-17). The people of Israel were being judged and they didn't even know it – they probably wrote it all off as bad luck or tough economic times, but God was trying to tell them something.

iii. Sometimes our priorities are out of order and we seem to suffer no financial hardship. In such times we should never presume on the mercy of God – we should turn to Him and re-order our priorities before He needs to use a crisis to get through to us.

c. **You drink, but you are not filled with drink**: If our priorities are wrong, nothing will satisfy us. Each accomplishment soon reveals that there must be something more, something that can really satisfy. Nothing fills the God-shaped void in our lives except putting Him first.

i. "Had your little been as the righteous man's little, you might have lived on it, and rejoiced in it; but it had not such a blessing upon it; it was blasted, and so was weak, and empty, and profited little." (Poole)

5. (7-11) What they must do: rebuild the temple.

Thus says the LORD of hosts: "Consider your ways! Go up to the mountains and bring wood and build the temple, that I may take pleasure in it and be glorified," says the LORD. *You* looked for much, but indeed *it came to* little; and when you brought it home, I blew it away. Why?" says the LORD of hosts. "Because of My house that *is in* ruins, while every one of you runs to his own house. Therefore the heavens above you withhold the dew, and the earth withholds its fruit. For I called for a drought on the land and the mountains, on the grain and the new wine and the oil, on whatever the ground brings forth, on men and livestock, and on all the labor of *your* hands."

a. **Go up to the mountains and bring wood**: God called them to *work*. Sometimes God's cause needs *work*, work that is supported by prayer, not work that is neglected because of in pretense of spiritual service.

i. They were not supposed to think, "Someone else will do it." William Carey (1761-1834) was a groundbreaking missionary to India. When he proposed the idea of going to India to reach the lost at a gathering of fellow British pastors, a well-known minister named John Ryland told him: "Young man, sit down. You are an enthusiast. When God pleases to convert the heathen, He will do it without your help or mine." This is not the case at all – God *will* do it, and He *wants* our participation. As far as we can perceive, God *often will wait* for our participation. William Carey had the right idea; his motto was "Expect great things from God; attempt great things for God."

b. **That I may take pleasure in it and be glorified**: It was time for God's people to start being concerned with pleasing Him instead of themselves. In their nice houses and prosperous lives they took pleasure and were glorified; now it was the LORD's turn.

i. God was also telling them to do it with the right kind of heart; a heart that wanted to please and glorify God

c. **You looked for much, but indeed it came to little**: When God was neglected, nothing worked right. They were able to accomplish some things (like building their own houses), but it didn't bring the satisfaction that it should have.

d. **For I called for a drought on the land**: We can imagine the people of God were depressed and discouraged because of the drought. They probably thought it was all an attack of Satan, and prayed fervently against what they said was Satan's plot. Yet it wasn't Satan's doing at all, but it was the LORD who **called for a drought on the land**. The problem wasn't Satan, but their priorities.

e. **On the grain and the new wine and the oil**: Because they neglected the LORD, He neglected to bless their three basic crops.

B. The response to Haggai's prophecy.

1. (12) They obeyed God and feared His presence.

Then Zerubbabel the son of Shealtiel, and Joshua the son of Jehozadak, the high priest, with all the remnant of the people, obeyed the voice of the LORD their God, and the words of Haggai the prophet, as the LORD their God had sent him; and the people feared the presence of the LORD.

a. **Then Zerubbabel…and Joshua…with all the remnant of the people, obeyed the voice of the LORD**: Obedience had to begin with the leadership. This wasn't a sermon just for the *people*, but also for the highest leaders among God's people.

b. **The voice of the LORD their God, and the words of Haggai the prophet**: The **voice** of God was expressed through **the words of Haggai**. This is the principle of the inspiration of the scriptures in action. God literally speaks, but through a man's **words**.

i. "For the word of God is not distinguished from the words of the Prophet, as though the Prophet had added anything of his own." (Calvin)

ii. In pointing out both, Haggai is distinguishing between the Author of the truth and the messenger of the truth.

c. **The words of Haggai the prophet, as the LORD their God had sent him**: Their respect for Haggai was based on his office (**prophet**) and his commission (**God had sent him**).

d. **The people feared the presence of the LORD**: Their fear of God prompted obedience. This was more than basic respect; it was recognition that God is a judge who deals with us righteously.

2. (13-15) God responds to His people.

Then Haggai, the LORD's messenger, spoke the LORD's message to the people, saying, "I *am* with you, says the LORD." So the LORD stirred up the spirit of Zerubbabel the son of Shealtiel, governor of Judah, and the spirit of Joshua the son of Jehozadak, the high priest, and the spirit of all the remnant of the people; and they came and worked on the house of the LORD of hosts, their God, on the twenty-fourth day of the sixth month, in the second year of King Darius.

a. **I am with you, says the LORD**: God was there to encourage them, and to strengthen them for the work. He always empowers and encourages us to do what He commands.

b. **So the LORD stirred up the spirit**: We long for such a stirring of **spirit** among His people today. This stirring began with the leadership (**Zerubbabel…Joshua**) and extended to the people (**all the remnant of the people**).

c. **They came and worked on the house of the LORD**: The stirring of spirit didn't come and go just as a spiritual experience. The stirring of *spirit* flourished into a stirring for the *work*.

Haggai 2 – The Glory of the Second Temple

A. The second word from God: the glory of the new temple.

1. (1-3) Is the new temple as nothing compared to Solomon's temple?

In the seventh *month*, on the twenty-first of the month, the word of the LORD came by Haggai the prophet, saying: "Speak now to Zerubbabel the son of Shealtiel, governor of Judah, and to Joshua the son of Jehozadak, the high priest, and to the remnant of the people, saying: 'Who is left among you who saw this temple in its former glory? And how do you see it now? In comparison with it, *is this* not in your eyes as nothing?'"

> a. **In the seventh month**: This message came in October of 520 B.C. It was feast time in Israel, celebrating both the Day of Atonement and the Feast of Tabernacles.
>
> b. **Who is left among you who saw this temple in its former glory?** Haggai spoke some 66 years after the temple was destroyed. Certainly, there were some old men who had seen Solomon's temple in its splendor.
>
>> i. Ezra 3:12-13 describes what those who had seen the first temple felt like 16 years before this prophecy of Haggai, when the work of rebuilding the temple first began:
>>
>> *But many of the priests and Levites and heads of the fathers' houses, old men who had seen the first temple, wept with a loud voice when the foundation of this temple was laid before their eyes. Yet many shouted aloud for joy, so that the people could not discern the noise of the shout of joy from the noise of the weeping of the people, for the people shouted with a loud shout, and the sound was heard afar off.* (Ezra 3:12-13)
>>
>> ii. The men in Ezra 3 wept because they **saw this temple in its former glory**. When Solomon built the first temple, he spared no expense in materials and hired the best talent he could find to do the work. The temple to be rebuilt couldn't match the majesty of that first temple.

c. **In comparison with it, is this not in your eyes as nothing?** These kinds of comparisons between "the good old days" and the present-day – or between the work of God in various places and times – are rarely beneficial. It didn't do the people of Haggai's day any good to think of how magnificent Solomon's temple was compared to their own rebuilding work.

> i. "The smallness of our gifts may be a temptation to us. We are consciously so weak and so insignificant, compared with the great God and his great cause, that we are discouraged, and think it vain to attempt anything.... the enemy contrasts our work with that of others, and with that of those who have gone before us. We are doing so little as compared with other people, therefore let us give up. We cannot build like Solomon, therefore let us not build at all. Yet, brethren, there is a falsehood in all this, for, in truth, nothing is worthy of God. The great works of others, and even the amazing productions of Solomon, all fell short of his glory." (Spurgeon)

> ii. A.W. Tozer suggested this prayer regarding our tendency to compare and compete:

"Dear Lord, I refuse henceforth to compete with any of Thy servants. They have congregations larger than mine. So be it. I rejoice in their success. They have greater gifts. Very well. That is not in their power nor in mine. I am humbly grateful for their greater gifts and my smaller ones. I only pray that I may use to Thy glory such modest gifts as I possess. I will not compare myself with any, nor try to build up my self-esteem by noting where I may excel one or another in Thy holy work. I herewith make a blanket disavowal of all intrinsic worth. I am but an unprofitable servant. I gladly go to the foot of the cross and own myself the least of Thy people. If I err in my self-judgment and actually underestimate myself I do not want to know it. I purpose to pray for others and to rejoice in their prosperity as if it were my own. And indeed it is my own if it is Thine own, for what is Thine is mine, and while one plants and another waters it is Thou alone that giveth the increase." (A.W. Tozer, *The Price of Neglect*)

2. (4-5) Carry on the work in strength and assurance.

"Yet now be strong, Zerubbabel," says the LORD; "and be strong, Joshua, son of Jehozadak, the high priest; and be strong, all you people of the land," says the LORD, "and work; for I *am* with you," says the LORD of hosts. "*According to* the word that I covenanted with you when you came out of Egypt, so My Spirit remains among you; do not fear!"

a. **Be strong...be strong...be strong...and work.... do not fear**: God gave the leaders and people of Israel three clear commands. Each of these three was essential to getting the work of God done. Great things are not accomplished without *action*.

> i. "What was lacking was dissatisfaction with things as they were, and the consequent drive to initiate action. Resignation killed faith." (Baldwin)

b. **I am with you.... According to the word that I covenanted with you when you came out of Egypt**: The same God that did great things in the past was among them today, so they could be encouraged.

> i. "Undoubtedly fear gripped many of the returnees – fear that God had written an eternal 'Ichabod' ['the glory has departed'] over Jerusalem." (Alden)

c. **My Spirit remains among you**: This was a wonderful promise and should have given God's people great confidence. Yet, in the new covenant, we have an even greater promise. Under the old covenant the Holy Spirit was *among* the people. Under the new covenant He would be *in* God's people.

3. (6-9) Why the rebuilt temple will be more glorious than the temple of Solomon.

"For thus says the LORD of hosts: 'Once more (it *is* a little while) I will shake heaven and earth, the sea and dry land; and I will shake all nations, and they shall come to the Desire of All Nations, and I will fill this temple with glory,' says the LORD of hosts. 'The silver *is* Mine, and the gold *is* Mine,' says the LORD of hosts. 'The glory of this latter temple shall be greater than the former,' says the LORD of hosts. 'And in this place I will give peace,' says the LORD of hosts."

a. **Once more...I will shake heaven and earth**: This is the only portion of Haggai quoted in the New Testament (Hebrews 12:26). It announces God's intention to **shake** the present order in His coming day of judgment.

b. **They shall come to the Desire of All Nations**: Many ancient commentators see this as a prophecy of the Messiah coming to this temple rebuilt in the days of Haggai and Ezra. This understanding began with the ancient rabbis and continued among Christians, and fits in well with the promise of filling the **temple with glory**.

> i. Some commentators point out that this word for **Desire** can also be translated *treasures*. We know that the Gentiles will bring tribute to the LORD in the millennium (Isaiah 60:5) – but that won't bring treasure to this temple that was rebuilt in the days of Ezra and Haggai.

ii. The true **Desire of All Nations** is Jesus, even if the nations themselves do not know it. "He is the one, the true Reformer, the true rectifier of all wrong, and in this respect the desire of all nations. Oh! if the world could gather up all her right desire; if she could condense in one cry all her wild wishes; if all true lovers of mankind could condense their theories and extract the true wine of wisdom from them; it would just come to this, we want an Incarnate God, and you have got the Incarnate God! Oh! Nations, but ye know it not! Ye, in the dark, are groping after him, and know not that he is there" (Spurgeon).

iii. Knowing that Jesus is the **Desire of All Nations** also encourages our missionary work. "Brethren, I may add, Christ is certainly the desire of all nations in this respect, that we desire him for all nations. Oh! That the world were encompassed in his gospel! Would God the sacred fire would run along the ground, that the little handful of corn on the top of the mountains would soon make its fruit to shake like Lebanon. Oh! When will it come, when will it come that all the nations shall know him? Let us pray for it: let us labour for it." (Spurgeon)

c. **"The silver is Mine, and the gold is Mine," says the Lord of hosts**: They didn't need to be discouraged if they didn't have money for the building project. They had to boldly trust the God who owned every resource, and then give generously.

i. When we really trust God, we will give generously. Hudson Taylor, the groundbreaking missionary to the interior regions of China in the second half of the nineteenth century, experienced this principle early in his life. As a young man he preached in boarding houses in the poor slums of London. A poor man asked Taylor to come back to his room and pray for his wife who suffered complications from childbirth and was near death. The man had no money at all, and couldn't afford to pay a priest to come and perform the last rites. Taylor went to the man's room and found the heartbreaking situation – several children, the afflicted mother and a three-day-old baby living in absolute filth and squalor, with absolutely no food or money. Taylor knew he had (something like) a $20 coin in his pocket that would meet their needs, but it was all the money he had in the world himself. He began to speak to the family about God when the Lord spoke to his own heart: "You hypocrite! Telling these unconverted people about a kind and loving Father in heaven, and not prepared yourself to trust Him without your $20." Taylor wished that he had two $10 pieces, and he would gladly have given them one – but all he had was one $20 coin. He was taken aback, but decided to lead the family in the Lord's Prayer. As soon as he said the words "Our Father," the Lord convicted him of his hypocrisy again. He struggled through the prayer under tremendous conviction and then gave the father the $20 piece. That provision saved the life of the mother and rescued the family.

ii. The lesson is plain. Knowing God provides should make us *more* generous, instead of less generous ("I don't have to give to their need, because God will provide for them some other way").

d. **The glory of this latter temple shall be greater than the former**: The glory of this temple was in fact **greater**. First, Herod remodeled this second temple into something **greater** than Solomon's temple. Second, the LORD of Glory – Jesus – personally visited it and worshipped there. That alone made it **greater**.

i. "Because Christ shall appear and preach in it, who is the brightness of his Father's glory." (Trapp)

ii. Some scholars speculate that Herod remodeled the temple with the intent of fulfilling **the glory of this latter temple shall be greater than the former**, so that *he* might fulfill it *instead* of the Messiah.

e. **And in this place I will give peace**: The promised **peace** is *shalom*. It means far more than stopping conflict – it is the establishment of a lasting, righteous, order.

B. The third word from God: clean and unclean.

1. (10-14) A question for the priests.

On the twenty-fourth *day* of the ninth *month,* in the second year of Darius, the word of the LORD came by Haggai the prophet, saying, "Thus says the LORD of hosts: 'Now, ask the priests *concerning the* law, saying, "If one carries holy meat in the fold of his garment, and with the edge he touches bread or stew, wine or oil, or any food, will it become holy?"'"

Then the priests answered and said, "No."

And Haggai said, "If *one who is* unclean *because* of a dead body touches any of these, will it be unclean?"

So the priests answered and said, "It shall be unclean."

Then Haggai answered and said, "'So is this people, and so is this nation before Me,' says the LORD, 'and so is every work of their hands; and what they offer there is unclean.

a. **Will it become holy?.... Will it be unclean?** Haggai questioned the priests – who were accustomed to answering such questions – about the transmission of both holiness and impurity. The priests answered correctly according to the law of Moses: holiness is not contagious, but impurity is.

    i. A sick child cannot catch health from contacting a healthy child, but the healthy child can become sick. Normally, the principle of transmission only works one way.

b. **So is this people, and so is this nation before Me**: On the same principle, living in the Holy Land and offering sacrifices would not make the people acceptable, as long as they themselves were unclean through the neglect of the house of the LORD.

    i. Since their exile to Babylon, the people of Israel focused on *getting back to the Promised Land*. By itself this was not a bad objective; yet it led to the thinking that once they made it back to the Promised Land everything else would be good. Haggai reminded them that their presence in the Promised Land didn't make everything they did holy. If the priorities of our hearts are wrong, nothing we do is holy to God.

    ii. "The ruined skeleton of the Temple was like a dead body decaying in Jerusalem and making everything contaminated." (Baldwin)

2. (15-19) God sees their change of heart and promises a harvest of blessing to come.

'And now, carefully consider from this day forward: from before stone was laid upon stone in the temple of the LORD; since those *days,* when *one* came to a heap of twenty ephahs, there were *but* ten; when *one* came to the wine vat to draw out fifty baths from the press, there were *but* twenty. I struck you with blight and mildew and hail in all the labors of your hands; yet you did not *turn* to Me,' says the LORD. Consider now from this day forward, from the twenty-fourth day of the ninth month, from the day that the foundation of the Lord's temple was laid; consider it: Is the seed still in the barn? As yet the vine, the fig tree, the pomegranate, and the olive tree have not yielded *fruit. But* from this day I will bless *you*.'"

    a. **I struck you with blight and mildew and hail in all the labors of your hands; yet you did not turn to Me**: Those experiences of God's chastening were real, but God's people did not learn from them. Difficult times don't *necessarily* bring us closer to God.

    b. **But from this day I will bless you**: God promised blessing to His people if they put their priorities back in order, with Him and His work first. Nevertheless, the blessings might not come immediately, and He did not want them to become discouraged, but to trust that **from this day I will bless you.**

C. The final word from God: God rules.

1. (20-22) God asserts His sovereignty over the nations.

And again the word of the LORD **came to Haggai on the twenty-fourth day of the month, saying, "Speak to Zerubbabel, governor of Judah, saying:**

'I will shake heaven and earth.
I will overthrow the throne of kingdoms;
I will destroy the strength of the Gentile kingdoms.
I will overthrow the chariots
And those who ride in them;
The horses and their riders shall come down,
Every one by the sword of his brother.

> a. **I will shake heaven and earth. I will overthrow the throne of kingdoms; I will destroy the strength of the Gentile kingdoms**: It was easy for the returning exiles to feel insignificant in the world, as if they were just pawns or spectators. God wanted them to know that though they were small in the eyes of the superpowers of the world, they were servants of the God of all power. They were on the winning side.
>
>> i. The writer to the Hebrews seems to refer to this line in Hebrews 12:25-26: *See that you do not refuse Him who speaks. For if they did not escape who refused Him who spoke on earth, much more shall we not escape if we turn away from Him who speaks from heaven, whose voice then shook the earth; but now He has promised, saying, "Yet once more I shake not only the earth, but also heaven."* The author of Hebrews then went on to make an application of the truth that God **will shake heaven and earth**: *Now this, "Yet once more," indicates the removal of those things that are being shaken, as of things that are made, that the things which cannot be shaken may remain.* (Hebrews 12:27)
>
> b. **I will overthrow the chariots and those who ride in them**: This word of encouragement shows us that Haggai's messages from God were a mixture of rebuke and encouragement. God promised to fight for His people in His day of restoration and rescue.

2. (23) A promise to Zerubbabel.

'In that day,' says the LORD **of hosts, 'I will take you, Zerubbabel My servant, the son of Shealtiel,' says the L**ORD**, 'and will make you like a signet** *ring;* **for I have chosen you,' says the L**ORD **of hosts."**

> a. **I will take you, Zerubbabel…and will make you like a signet ring**: The **signet ring** was a token of royal authority much like a throne, a crown, or a scepter.

i. "This is not a personal assurance only to Zerubbabel, for neither he nor his natural seed reigned in Jerusalem, or rose to any special eminence in the kingdoms of this world." (Deane)

b. **For I have chosen you**: Zerubbabel was truly chosen of God. He is included in the ancestry of Jesus, as the grandson of King Jeconiah, the descendant of Solomon. Zerubbabel was in the line leading to Joseph, the adoptive father of Jesus (Matthew 1:12). There is also a man named Zerubbabel in the line of Mary (the blood lineage of Jesus, Luke 3:27) but this seems to be a different man with the same name.

i. God used these two lines of ancestry for Jesus because He placed a curse on the seed of Jeconiah (also known as Coniah or Jehoiachin) as recorded in Jeremiah 22:30. That line was the royal line of David, so if the Messiah was to be eligible for the throne of David (Luke 1:31-33), he had to be of the legal line of David, yet not of his seed.

ii. Jeconiah was the last legitimate king of Judah and the royal House of David goes through him. His only successor was Zedekiah, his uncle who was appointed not by right, but by an occupying Babylonian ruler (2 Kings 24:17-20). Even at the end of his life, the Babylonians recognized Jeconiah as the legitimate king of Judah (2 Kings 25:27-30).

iii. Because Zerubbabel was a descendant of the last legitimate king of Judah, he could be legitimately recognized as the ruler (though not king) of the returning exiles.

Zechariah 1 – The First Two Visions

A. Introduction.

1. (1) The prophet and his times.

In the eighth month of the second year of Darius, the word of the LORD came to Zechariah the son of Berechiah, the son of Iddo the prophet, saying,

> a. **In the eighth month of the second year of Darius**: Zechariah served the LORD in the years after the remnant returned from the 70-year Babylonian exile. His prophetic career began in the reign of **Darius**, the ruler of the Medes and Persians. His career was not marked by the reign of a king over Israel or Judah, because there was no king of Israel or Judah in this period after the exile.
>
>> i. The timing of Zechariah's prophecy sets it two months after Haggai's first prophecy (Haggai 1:1) and within a month after another prophecy of Haggai (Haggai 2:1). This was between October and November of 520 B.C.
>>
>> ii. "Like Haggai, Zechariah's message is one of encouragement. But he was aware that not all the returned remnant were fully sincere in their desires to serve God, and he therefore counseled them to repent of sin and return to God with all their hearts and minds." (Boice)
>>
>> iii. If we only had Haggai to go by, we might conclude that all God was really interested in was the temple. Zechariah gave us more of the story and showed how God is interested in the lives of His people, not only buildings.
>>
>> iv. The prophecy of Zechariah is noted for its rich use of visions, pictures, and symbols. In this way, it is much like the book of Revelation or Daniel which also have significant visions. "Haggai lays down the mind of God to the people more plainly in direct and downright terms; Zechariah flies a higher pitch, abounding with types

and visions; and is therefore worthily reckoned among the [most puzzling] and profoundest penmen of Holy Scripture…. We pass from dark prophecies to that which is much more dark." (Trapp).

b. **The word of the LORD came to Zechariah**: We know little about this prophet, though "Zechariah" was a common name in the Old Testament (at least 27 different Zechariahs are mentioned in the Bible). The only details we have about this **Zechariah** come from Ezra 5 and 6.

i. *Then the prophet Haggai and Zechariah the son of Iddo, prophets, prophesied to the Jews who were in Judah and Jerusalem, in the name of the God of Israel, who was over them. So Zerubbabel the son of Shealtiel and Jeshua the son of Jozadak rose up and began to build the house of God which is in Jerusalem; and the prophets of God were with them, helping them.* (Ezra 5:1-2)

ii. *So the elders of the Jews built, and they prospered through the prophesying of Haggai the prophet and Zechariah the son of Iddo. And they built and finished it, according to the commandment of the God of Israel, and according to the command of Cyrus, Darius, and Artaxerxes king of Persia.* (Ezra 6:14)

iii. The name **Zechariah** means *the LORD remembers*, and was a fitting name for a prophet of restoration. This prophet was called to encourage and mobilize God's people to accomplish a task that they had begun yet lost the momentum before completing. He encouraged them indirectly by telling them about God's care for them and by keeping the presence of the Messiah very much in their minds. He worked with others, notably Haggai, Zerubbabel, and Ezra. He warned them of the consequences of neglecting God's work, and he emphasized that God wants to do a work through His people.

iv. Jesus mentioned the ministry and martyrdom of Zechariah in Matthew 23:35: *That on you may come all the righteous blood shed on the earth, from the blood of righteous Abel to the blood of Zechariah, son of Berechiah, whom you murdered between the temple and the altar.*

2. (2-6) God pleads with His people: "**Return to Me.**"

"The LORD has been very angry with your fathers. Therefore say to them, 'Thus says the LORD of hosts: "Return to Me," says the LORD of hosts, "and I will return to you," says the LORD of hosts. "Do not be like your fathers, to whom the former prophets preached, saying, 'Thus says the LORD of hosts: "Turn now from your evil ways and your evil deeds. But they did not hear nor heed Me," says the LORD.

"Your fathers, where *are* they?
And the prophets, do they live forever?
Yet surely My words and My statutes,
Which I commanded My servants the prophets,
Did they not overtake your fathers?

"So they returned and said:

'Just as the LORD of hosts determined to do to us,
According to our ways and according to our deeds,
So He has dealt with us.'"'"

> a. **The LORD has been very angry with your fathers**: Zechariah began his prophecy with a call to repentance, and a call that remembered the poor spiritual heritage of Israel and Judah. The sin of their fathers doomed the nation to exile, and Zechariah warned the people to remember that the same could happen to them.
>
>> i. We should remember that these weren't "bad people" – they were the remnant that returned from Babylon. Hundreds of thousands of people went into the Babylonian captivity and only about 50,000 returned. Those who did were the most committed to the LORD and to the restoration of Jerusalem. Yet even they, some 18 years after returning to the Promised Land, needed to hear and heed this warning from the LORD.
>
> b. **Return to Me...and I will return to you**: Adverse circumstances discouraged God's people, and they wondered why God seemed so far away.
>
> - The land was still desolate after 70 years of neglect.
> - The work to rebuild and restore was difficult.
> - They didn't have a lot of money (Haggai 1:6) or manpower.
> - They suffered crop failures and drought (Haggai 1:10-11).
> - Hostile enemies resisted the work (Ezra 4:1-5).
> - They remembered easier times in Babylon.
>
>> i. Each of these circumstances made them feel that God was far away; through Zechariah God assured them that He was *not* distant. They would **return** to Him, and He would **return** to them.
>>
>> ii. **Return to Me**: Sometimes we wish God would *make* us return to Him, instead of *wooing* us to return out of our own choice. Nevertheless, God wants our freely given love, so He prompts us to choose Him and **return to** Him.

iii. Zechariah's words remind us of James 4:8: *Draw near to God and He will draw near to you.* God promises to run to meet us when we return to Him. We are also reminded that if we are far from God, He hasn't distanced Himself from us, we have distanced ourselves from Him. An elderly couple drove down the road in their car with a front bench seat. As they drove, the wife noticed that in many of the other cars with couples in the front seat, the woman sat close to the man as he drove. She asked her husband, "Why is it that we don't sit that close anymore?" He simply answered, "It wasn't me who moved." If we are far from God, He hasn't moved.

c. **Yet surely My words and My statutes, which I commanded My servants the prophets, did they not overtake your fathers?** God's promises outlived and outlasted all the previous prophets and ancestors. Zechariah encouraged God's people to not only rebuild the temple (the emphasis of his contemporary prophet Haggai) but also to rebuild their relationship with the LORD and learn from the lessons of their fathers.

B. The vision of the four horses among the myrtle trees.

1. (7-10) Zechariah's vision of the four horses and their riders.

On the twenty-fourth day of the eleventh month, which is the month Shebat, in the second year of Darius, the word of the LORD came to Zechariah the son of Berechiah, the son of Iddo the prophet: I saw by night, and behold, a man riding on a red horse, and it stood among the myrtle trees in the hollow; and behind him *were* horses: red, sorrel, and white. Then I said, "My lord, what *are* these?" So the angel who talked with me said to me, "I will show you what they *are*."

And the man who stood among the myrtle trees answered and said, "These *are the ones* whom the LORD has sent to walk to and fro throughout the earth."

a. **Behold, a man riding on a red horse**: Zechariah's vision was simple enough in what he saw – one man on horseback leading other horses and their riders, patrolling **to and fro throughout the earth**. Zechariah saw them among **myrtle trees**, in a ravine (**in the hollow**).

i. Specifically, this exploration mission examined the progress of rebuilding Jerusalem and the other cities of Judah. Its purpose was to examine the work of God's people.

ii. "The troop of horsemen were emissaries of the Lord sent on world mission. Like the Persian monarchs who used messengers on swift steeds to keep them informed on all matters concerning their empire, so the Lord knew all about the countries of the earth." (Baldwin)

iii. "Just as Satan walks about the earth for evil (Job 1:7, 2:2; 1 Peter 5:8), so the Lord Jehovah has His representatives walking up and down in the earth to examine the affairs of men." (Luck)

b. **Red, sorrel, and white**: Bible commentators debate the meaning of these colors. Connecting them with the four horsemen of Revelation 6:1-8 doesn't seem to work, because these seem to be observers and not messengers of judgment as in Revelation 6. Some suggest that the different colors mean different angelic offices.

i. **Sorrel** is sort of a dirty yellow or a spotted, brownish orange.

ii. "Probably pointing out the *different orders* of angels in the heavenly host, which are employed by Christ in the defence of his Church. The different *colours* may point out the *gradations* in power, authority, and excellence, of the angelic natures which are employed between Christ and men." (Clarke)

c. **The man who stood among the myrtle trees**: The myrtle tree is a laurel, which is evergreen and possibly a symbol of the people of Israel. This **man** is the *Angel of the LORD* (Zechariah 1:11) and is no doubt an Old Testament appearance of Jesus before His incarnation in Bethlehem.

i. There are many examples in the Old Testament of an encounter with a heavenly man known as the *Angel of the LORD* who is revealed to be God Himself (Genesis 16:7-13, Genesis 22:11-18, Exodus 3:2-9, Judges 2:1-4, and many other places). Because of Zechariah 1:11, we know this **man** is the *Angel of the LORD*, and that He is God.

ii. We can assume that this was God, in the person of Jesus Christ, appearing to Abraham before His incarnation and birth at Bethlehem, because of God the Father it is said, *No one has seen God at any time. The only begotten Son, who is in the bosom of the Father, He has declared Him* (John 1:18), and no man has ever seen God in the person of the Father (1 Timothy 6:16). Therefore, if God appears to someone in human appearance in the Old Testament, and no one has seen God the Father, it makes sense the appearing is of the eternal Son, the Second Person of the Trinity, before His incarnation in Bethlehem.

iii. **Myrtle trees**: "Israel is not likened to a cedar of Lebanon, which is majestic, or an oak tree, which is strong. Having blossoms that emit a sweet fragrance when crushed, the myrtle illustrates the strange grace of Israel in affliction." (Boice)

2. (11-17) The Angel of the LORD intercedes for Jerusalem and Judah.

So they answered the Angel of the LORD, who stood among the myrtle trees, and said, "We have walked to and fro throughout the earth, and behold, all the earth is resting quietly." Then the Angel of the LORD answered and said, "O LORD of hosts, how long will You not have mercy on Jerusalem and on the cities of Judah, against which You were angry these seventy years?"

And the LORD answered the angel who talked to me, *with* **good** *and* **comforting words. So the angel who spoke with me said to me, "Proclaim, saying, 'Thus says the LORD of hosts:**

"I am zealous for Jerusalem
And for Zion with great zeal.
I am exceedingly angry with the nations at ease;
For I was a little angry,
And they helped–*but* **with evil** *intent.***"**

'Therefore thus says the LORD:

"I am returning to Jerusalem with mercy;
My house shall be built in it," says the LORD of hosts,
"And a *surveyor's* **line shall be stretched out over Jerusalem."'**

"Again proclaim, saying, 'Thus says the LORD of hosts:

"My cities shall again spread out through prosperity;
The LORD will again comfort Zion,
And will again choose Jerusalem."'"

> a. **All the earth is resting quietly**: The patrol found that the world was at peace, but it was not the right kind of peace (**I am exceedingly angry with the nations at ease**). God was angry with the nations of the world because they were at ease while God's people suffered. In God's thinking, if the earth is at rest at the expense of His people, there is no true rest at all.
>
>> i. **And they helped; but with evil intent**: The nations of the world offered some help to the returning exiles, but even their help was polluted by evil motives.
>
> b. **I am zealous for Jerusalem and for Zion with great zeal**: The **Angel of the LORD** showed His heart of compassion for Israel and Jerusalem. God relented and allowed Israel back after 70 years of exile, yet the effects of exile were still painfully evident.
>
>> i. The word for **zealous** in ancient Hebrew comes from the idea "to become intensely red" and it has the thought of a face becoming

flushed with deep emotion. God is genuinely and deeply concerned about the state of His people.

c. **My cities shall again spread out through prosperity**: God solemnly promised to restore Jerusalem and the cities of Judah. This was an especially comforting promise considering the lowly condition of the cities of the Promised Land in Zechariah's day.

i. About four years from the time of this prophecy, Zion was comforted, and Jerusalem was specially chosen. The temple was rebuilt four years after Zechariah gave this prophecy.

C. The vision of the four horns and four craftsmen.

1. (18-19) Four horns represent the nations that scattered God's people.

Then I raised my eyes and looked, and there *were* four horns. And I said to the angel who talked with me, "What *are* these?"

So he answered me, "These *are* the horns that have scattered Judah, Israel, and Jerusalem."

a. **There were four horns**: In biblical times **horns** spoke of strength and authority because the power of a bull or an ox is expressed through its **horns**.

i. "Horns, the pride of a young bull, are an obvious choice symbol to represent invincible strength.... As trophies of the hunt they represented conquest of strength." (Baldwin)

b. **These are the horns that have scattered Judah, Israel, and Jerusalem**: Since Zechariah told us there were **four** horns we wonder which four nations Zechariah spoke of here. If he spoke of scattering in a broad prophetic sense – including scattering that had yet come to God's people in his own day – then the likely **four horns** are Babylon, Medo-Persia, Greece, and Rome.

2. (20-21) God announces judgment against the nations that scatter His people.

Then the LORD showed me four craftsmen. And I said, "What are these coming to do?"

So he said, "These *are* the horns that scattered Judah, so that no one could lift up his head; but the craftsmen are coming to terrify them, to cast out the horns of the nations that lifted up *their* horn against the land of Judah to scatter it."

a. **The craftsmen are coming to terrify them**: God raised up other nations to judge the nations that scattered His people. From of old, God promised to curse those who cursed Israel (Genesis 12:3).

i. "And then he finds the right men; not four gentlemen with pens to write; not four architects to draw plans, but four mechanics to do rough work. He who wants to open an oyster, must not use a razor: there needs less of daintiness, and more of force, for some works: providence does not find gentlemen to cut off the horns, but carpenters. The work needs a man who, when he has his work to do, puts his whole strength into it, and beats away with his hammer, or cuts through the wood that lays before him with might and main. Rest assured, you who tremble for the ark of God, that when the horns grow troublesome, the carpenters will be found." (Spurgeon)

b. **To cast out the horns of the nations that lifted their horn against the land of Judah**: God promised to break the power of those who used their power against God's people. An ancient proverb puts it well: "The church of God is an anvil that has worn out many hammers."

Zechariah 2 – A City Without Walls

A. A call to return to the Promised Land.

1. (1-5) The man with the measuring line and the protection promised.

Then I raised my eyes and looked, and behold, a man with a measuring line in his hand. So I said, "Where are you going?"

And he said to me, "To measure Jerusalem, to see what *is* its width and what *is* its length."

And there *was* the angel who talked with me, going out; and another angel was coming out to meet him, who said to him, "Run, speak to this young man, saying: 'Jerusalem shall be inhabited *as* towns without walls, because of the multitude of men and livestock in it. For I,' says the LORD, 'will be a wall of fire all around her, and I will be the glory in her midst.'"

> a. **A man with a measuring line in his hand**: This was undoubtedly an angelic being and some think it was the Angel of the LORD. Angelic beings never truly become human beings, but they can take human form.
>
> b. **To see what is its width and what is its length**: Apparently, Jerusalem was measured to make sure that it is large enough for the multitudes God would bring to it. In the time of Zechariah, it seemed strange to worry about Jerusalem being big enough, because there seemed to be too few people for the city.
>
>> i. It is as if the **man with a measuring line** went into a huge old cathedral where only a few attended the church services and started to make sure it was large enough for the crowds God was sure to bring.
>
> c. **Jerusalem shall be inhabited as towns without walls.... For I...will be a wall of fire all around her**: God promised to bring so many people to Jerusalem that the crowds would overflow the walls of the city. The effect on the walls would not matter because God would be their protection. He will be **a wall of fire all around her**.

i. This prophecy had a short-term fulfillment in God's protection of the rebuilding work and blessing of the city under Ezra and Nehemiah. But clearly, its ultimate fulfillment will be rebuilding under the rule of the Messiah.

ii. Today Jerusalem is indeed a city **without walls** because in modern warfare they are useless for defending the city. Ultimately Jerusalem will be a city **without walls** because the Prince of Peace (Isaiah 9:6) will reign from Jerusalem and He will be her protection.

2. (6-7) Exiles exhorted to return.

"Up, up! Flee from the land of the north," says the LORD; "for I have spread you abroad like the four winds of heaven," says the LORD. "Up, Zion! Escape, you who dwell with the daughter of Babylon."

a. **Flee from the land of the north**: In Zechariah's day, few of those who were carried into captivity in the Babylonian Empire returned to the Promised Land when they were allowed to. Here the LORD exhorted His people to return to their land.

i. Sadly most of the exiles were comfortable in Babylon and refused to endure the challenge to build a work of God.

b. **Escape, you who dwell with the daughter of Babylon**: Throughout the Bible **Babylon** is used as an idea as well as a literal city. If Jerusalem carries the idea of "God's city" then **Babylon** carries the idea of the city of the world. Zechariah's call to come out of **Babylon** is both literal and figurative (Revelation 18:4-5).

B. Reasons for rejoicing.

1. (8-9) God promises to protect His precious people.

For thus says the LORD of hosts: "He sent Me after glory, to the nations which plunder you; for he who touches you touches the apple of His eye. "For surely I will shake My hand against them, and they shall become spoil for their servants. Then you will know that the LORD of hosts has sent Me.

a. **He who touches you touches the apple of His eye**: The phrase "**apple of His eye**" was used to describe something precious, easily injured, and demanding protection.

i. "He esteems them as much as men value their eyesight, and is as careful to protect them from injury, as men are to protect the apple of their eye. The pupil of the eye is the tenderest part of the tenderest organ, and very fitly sets forth the inexpressible tenderness of God's love." (Spurgeon)

b. **They shall become spoil for their servants**: God promises that those who enslaved the people of God would **become spoil** for the restored people of God. The enslavers would become enslaved. This will be ultimately fulfilled in the millennial reign of Jesus.

i. **I will shake My hand against them**: All God needs to do to bring such a dramatic reversal of standings is to **shake** His **hand** against the enemies of His people.

2. (10-13) The promise of the presence of the Lord.

"Sing and rejoice, O daughter of Zion! For behold, I am coming and I will dwell in your midst," says the Lord.

"Many nations shall be joined to the Lord in that day, and they shall become My people. And I will dwell in your midst. Then you will know that the Lord of hosts has sent Me to you. "And the Lord will take possession of Judah as His inheritance in the Holy Land, and will again choose Jerusalem. Be silent, all flesh, before the Lord, for He is aroused from His holy habitation!"

a. **Sing and rejoice, O daughter of Zion**: God didn't expect His people to be passive or reserved given such dramatic promises. He expected them to **sing and rejoice**.

b. **I am coming and I will dwell in your midst**: God's people should be excited because He will be *among them* in a unique and powerful way.

c. **Many nations shall be joined to the Lord in that day**: God's people should be excited because God will bring many into His kingdom. God's desire to bless Israel was never intended to stop with Israel, but to use them as a channel of blessing for **many nations**.

d. **In the Holy Land**: This is the only place where the phrase **Holy Land** is used in the Bible. The land is **holy** because it is separated to God in a unique way. Some assume that it is only the *people* of Judah and Jerusalem that are God's holy inheritance but passages like this show that the **land** itself is **holy** and precious to God.

Zechariah 3 – The Cleansing of Joshua the High Priest

A. The vision of the LORD, Satan, and Joshua the high priest.

1. (1-3) The Angel of the LORD stands against Satan on Joshua's behalf.

Then he showed me Joshua the high priest standing before the Angel of the LORD, and Satan standing at his right hand to oppose him. And the LORD said to Satan, "The LORD rebuke you, Satan! The LORD who has chosen Jerusalem rebuke you! *Is* **this not a brand plucked from the fire?"**

Now Joshua was clothed with filthy garments, and was standing before the Angel.

> a. **Then he showed me Joshua the high priest**: Joshua was the high priest at the time (Haggai 1:1). In his vision, Zechariah saw the high priest in the presence of the LORD (**standing before the Angel of the LORD**), and he was **clothed with filthy garments**.
>
> b. **Standing before the Angel of the LORD**: The phrase **standing before** has the idea of priestly service. Joshua wasn't in God's presence just as a spectator but as a ministering priest.
>
> c. **Satan standing at his right hand to oppose him**: Satan hated the whole scene. He hates it when God's people come into the presence of the LORD. He hates it when they come into God's presence to serve and honor the LORD.
>
>> i. "Satan must have been pointing to those [filthy clothes] and declaring forcefully that Joshua was unfit to stand before the Lord in this office." (Boice)
>>
>> ii. This is all according to character for **Satan**. The name **Satan** literally means *adversary* or *opponent*. He stands against us in every spiritual

battle (Ephesians 6:10-18). The only thing worse than having Satan as an adversary is to have him as a friend.

d. **The LORD rebuke you, Satan!** We see the LORD standing before **Satan** and preventing his advance; either directly, if the Angel of the LORD is Jesus in this place, or indirectly exercising authority through the Angel of the LORD.

i. God does allow Satan to attack and harass His people, but He always strictly regulates what Satan is allowed to do. Satan wanted to destroy Simon Peter, sifting him like wheat (Luke 22:31-32) but Jesus prayed for Peter and stood beside him and did not allow Satan to carry out every evil intention of his heart.

ii. "Take note that this rebuke comes at the right season. When Satan accuses, Christ pleads. He does not wait till the case has gone against us and then express his regret, but he is always a very present help in time of trouble. He knows the heart of Satan, being omniscient God, and long before Satan can accuse he puts in the demurrer, the blessed plea on our behalf, and stays the action till he gives an answer which silences for ever every accusation." (Spurgeon)

iii. **The LORD rebuke you**: Jude 1:9 tells us that Michael the archangel used this same phrase in battling against Satan. The example here of the Angel of the LORD and of Michael shows us a model for spiritual warfare – that we always should battle with the LORD's authority. In His authority we fight *from* a place of victory, more than fighting for victory.

e. **The LORD who has chosen Jerusalem rebuke you!** With this phrase, God reinforced the important standing of **Jerusalem** in His eyes. As mentioned in Zechariah 2:12 it is His *Holy Land*.

f. **Is this not a brand plucked from the fire?** Joshua the high priest had a place of high standing – next to the Angel of the LORD and protected against satanic attack. Still, this place of high privilege was not based on Joshua's own goodness or merit; he himself was rescued as a **brand plucked from the fire**. This is even more boldly stated in that Joshua stood **clothed in filthy garments**. Satan had a lot to accuse Joshua of, but Joshua had an even greater Advocate in the Angel of the LORD.

i. A **brand** is a burnt, burning, or smoldering piece of wood. Think of a campfire with a blackened, charred chunk of wood smoking in the ashes. It isn't worth much at all and will be consumed completely if it isn't **plucked from the fire**.

ii. "So it is with the child of God. What is he at the best? Till he is taken up to heaven, he is nothing but a brand plucked out of the fire. It is his daily moan that he is a sinner; but Christ accepts him as he is: and he shuts the devil's mouth by telling him, 'Thou sayest this man is black – of course he is: what did I think he was but that? He is a brand plucked out of the fire. I plucked him out of it. He was burning when he was in it: he is black now he is out of it. He was what I knew he would be; he is not what I mean to make him, but he is what I knew he would be. I have chosen him as a brand plucked out of the fire. What hast thou to say to that?' Do observe that this plea did not require a single word to be added to it from Joshua." (Spurgeon)

iii. "Such is the divine economy, that God makes much of brands, fragments, castaways. What others regard as unworthy of their heed is dear and priceless to the great Lover of souls." (Meyer)

iv. "This question, as it appears to me, will bear three renderings; first, it may be looked upon as *an exclamation of wonder:* 'Is not this a brand plucked out of the fire!' Secondly, *as an enquiry or hope:* 'Is not *this* a brand' – this one particularly, 'plucked out of the fire?' And, in the third place, it is certainly *a defiance for us, assured of our safety, to throw into the face of Satan, the accuser:* 'Is not this a brand plucked out of the fire?' " (Spurgeon)

v. When John Wesley was only six years old, he was trapped in a burning house and was only rescued when one neighbor climbed on another's shoulders and pulled him out of a window. A picture of the scene was drawn for Wesley and he kept the drawing until he died, and wrote under it Zechariah 3:2: *Is this not a brand plucked from the burning?*

2. (4-5) Joshua's iniquity is removed and he is given clean garments.

Then He answered and spoke to those who stood before Him, saying, "Take away the filthy garments from him." And to him He said, "See, I have removed your iniquity from you, and I will clothe you with rich robes."

And I said, "Let them put a clean turban on his head."

So they put a clean turban on his head, and they put the clothes on him. And the Angel of the LORD stood by.

a. **Take away the filthy garments from him**: As Joshua, the high priest, stood in the presence of the LORD, Satan accused him on seemingly solid grounds – Joshua was guilty of standing before God in **filthy garments**.

Nevertheless, the LORD addressed the problem by cleansing Joshua, taking away the **filthy garments** and the **iniquity** they represented.

    i. The Hebrew word translated **filthy** is "the strongest expression in the Hebrew language for filth of the most vile and loathsome character." (Feinberg, cited in Barker)

b. And I will clothe you with rich robes: Joshua not only enjoyed having his **iniquity** removed, but he also was given a *positive* righteousness – clothed with **rich robes**. The thought of being clothed by God in righteousness runs from Genesis (Genesis 3:7 and 3:21) to Revelation (Revelation 7:13-14).

c. Let them put a clean turban on his head: The **turban** was part of the high priest's garments and on the front, it had a gold plate inscribed with the phrase HOLINESS TO THE LORD (Exodus 28:36-38).

B. God's message to Joshua the high priest.

1. (6-7) A personal admonishment and promise to Joshua.

Then the Angel of the LORD admonished Joshua, saying, "Thus says the LORD of hosts:
'If you will walk in My ways,
And if you will keep My command,
Then you shall also judge My house,
And likewise have charge of My courts;
I will give you places to walk
Among these who stand here.

    a. If you will walk in My ways and if you will keep My command: Joshua, in Zechariah's day, was encouraged much the same way that the first Joshua was admonished. *Only be strong and very courageous, that you may observe to do according to all the law which Moses My servant commanded you; do not turn from it to the right hand or to the left, that you may prosper wherever you go.* (Joshua 1:7)

    b. Then you shall also judge My house, and likewise have charge of My courts: God promised Joshua that he would indeed continue to serve as high priest as he was diligent to stay obedient to God.

    c. I will give you places to walk among these who stand here: God promised Joshua privileged access into the presence of God. This wasn't a surprising promise for a high priest, but we have the same promise: *Let us therefore come boldly to the throne of grace, that we may obtain mercy and find grace to help in time of need.* (Hebrews 4:16)

2. (8-10) A prophetic message of Messiah and His reign.

> 'Hear, O Joshua, the high priest,
> You and your companions who sit before you,
> For they are a wondrous sign;
> For behold, I am bringing forth My Servant the BRANCH.
> For behold, the stone
> That I have laid before Joshua:
> Upon the stone *are* seven eyes.
> Behold, I will engrave its inscription,"
> Says the LORD of hosts,
> 'And I will remove the iniquity of that land in one day.
> In that day,' says the LORD of hosts,
> 'Everyone will invite his neighbor
> Under his vine and under his fig tree.'"

a. **I am bringing forth My Servant the BRANCH**: The term **Branch** is used several times as a title for the Messiah (Isaiah 4:2 and 11:1, Jeremiah 23:5 and 33:15). The **Branch** is associated with fruitfulness and life. Jesus used the same image when He said that He was the vine and we are the branches (John 15:5).

b. **For behold, the stone I have laid before Joshua**: If a branch seems weak, then God gives us another picture – a **stone**, having **seven eyes**. In the thinking of the ancient world, eyes represented knowledge because we learn more through our eyes than any other way. The **seven eyes** speak of the perfection and fullness of the knowledge and wisdom of the Messiah.

c. **I will engrave its inscription**: Early Christians saw the engraving on the stone to be a picture of Jesus' wounds. The engraving could also be a mark of identification or beautification.

d. **Everyone will invite his neighbor under his vine and under his fig tree**: This is a proverbial expression that means prosperity and peace (1 Kings 4:25, 2 Kings 18:31). Ultimately, this is the peace that the reign of the Messiah brings. This vision and word from Zechariah show how much God wanted to encourage and strengthen Joshua, and He does it in the best way: by setting his eyes on our Messiah, Jesus Christ. That is always our best encouragement.

Zechariah 4 – By My Spirit, Says the LORD

A. Zechariah's vision.

1. (1-3) Zechariah's vision of the olive trees and lampstands.

Now the angel who talked with me came back and wakened me, as a man who is wakened out of his sleep. And he said to me, "What do you see?"

So I said, "I am looking, and there *is* a lampstand of solid gold with a bowl on top of it, and on the *stand* seven lamps with seven pipes to the seven lamps. Two olive trees *are* by it, one at the right of the bowl and the other at its left."

> a. **As a man who is wakened out of his sleep**: Zechariah had that lightheaded feeling that we get if we are awakened suddenly from a deep sleep.
>
> b. **A lampstand of solid gold**: God gave Zechariah a vision of the golden lampstand that was meant to stand in the temple. Since Zechariah and his people were there to rebuild the temple, it made sense that God spoke to them in images related to the temple.
>
> c. **Seven pipes to the seven lamps…. Two olive trees**: In addition to the **lampstand**, Zechariah saw something that was never in the temple – **two olive trees** that supplied the **seven lamps** with oil through **seven pipes**.
>
>> i. One of the more tedious duties of the temple service was the constant care of the lamps on the golden lampstand. They had to be continually refilled with oil, cleaned of soot, and their wicks had to be maintained. In this vision, Zechariah sees "self-filling" lamps, fed directly from two olive trees.
>>
>> ii. In the temple, the lamps were fueled by pure, specially prepared olive oil. The lampstand Zechariah saw in his vision was fed straight from the trees.

2. (4-5) Zechariah asks for an explanation of the vision.

So I answered and spoke to the angel who talked with me, saying, "What *are* these, my lord?"

Then the angel who talked with me answered and said to me, "Do you not know what these are?"

And I said, "No, my lord."

> a. **What are these, my lord?** Zechariah saw the vision but didn't understand what it meant. What he saw was simple but unusual – a lampstand with lamps supplied with oil directly through pipes coming from two olive trees.
>
> b. **Do you not know what these are?** The angel made sure that Zechariah knew that he must come to understand the meaning of this vision.

B. The meaning of the vision.

1. (6-7) How Zerubbabel will accomplish the work: by the Spirit of God.

So he answered and said to me:

"This *is* the word of the LORD to Zerubbabel:
'Not by might nor by power, but by My Spirit,'
Says the LORD of hosts.
Who *are* you, O great mountain?
Before Zerubbabel *you shall become* a plain!
And he shall bring forth the capstone
With shouts of "Grace, grace to it!"'"

> a. **This is the word of the LORD to Zerubbabel**: Zerubbabel was the civic leader of Jerusalem and had the responsibility to finish the work of rebuilding the temple. The work had stalled, and Zerubbabel needed encouragement to carry on the work.
>
> b. **'Not by might nor by power, but by My Spirit,' says the LORD of hosts**: In the vision of Zechariah 3 God spoke to Zerubbabel about the issue of *purity*. But purity alone was not enough to accomplish the work of God – the work of God also needs *resources*, and not the resources of human **might** or **power**.
>
>> i. **Might** focuses on *collective* strength, the resources of a group or army. **Power** focuses on individual strength. God says, "not by the resources of many or one, but by My Spirit. It will not be by your cleverness, your ability, or your physical strength that the temple will be rebuilt, but by the Spirit of God."

ii. The necessary resource for God's work is the Holy Spirit and God promises Zerubbabel a rich resource in the Spirit of God to accomplish His work. When we trust in our own resources – whether they be small or great in the eyes of man – then we don't enjoy the full supply of the Spirit. "Oh! May God send us poverty; may God send us lack of means, and take away our power of speech if it must be, and help us only to stammer, if we may only thus get the blessing. Oh! I crave to be useful to souls, and all the rest may go where it will." (Spurgeon)

iii. This was the Spirit – the breath – the *ruach* of the LORD which worked in creation (Genesis 1:2), at the Red Sea, to open and close it (Exodus 15:8, 10) and that gave life to dead bones (Ezekiel 37:1-14).

iv. Looking back to the vision earlier in the chapter, we see that God wanted Zerubbabel to know that the Holy Spirit would continually supply his need, just as the oil trees in the vision continually supplied oil to the lamps on the lampstand. God wants His supply and our reliance on the Holy Spirit to be *continual*.

v. "O churches! take heed lest ye trust in yourselves; take heed lest ye say, 'We are a respectable body,' 'We are a mighty number,' 'We are a potent people;' take heed lest ye begin to glory in your own strength; for when that is done, 'Ichabod' shall be written on your walls and your glory shall depart from you. Remember, that he who was with us when we were but few, must be with us now we are many, or else we must fail; and he who strengthened us when we were but as 'little in Israel,' must be with us, now that we are like 'the thousands of Manasseh,' or else it is all over with us and our day is past." (Spurgeon)

c. **By My Spirit**: Oil is a good representation of the Holy Spirit.

- Oil *lubricates* when used for that purpose – there is little friction and wear among those who are lubricated by the Spirit of God.
- Oil *heals* and was used as a medicinal treatment in biblical times (Luke 10:34) – the Spirit of God brings healing and restoration.
- Oil *lights* when it is burned in a lamp – where the Spirit of God is there is light.
- Oil *warms* when it is used as fuel for a flame – where the Spirit of God is there is warmth and comfort.
- Oil *invigorates* when used to massage – the Holy Spirit invigorates us for His service.
- Oil *adorns* when applied as a perfume – the Holy Spirit adorns us and makes us more pleasant to be around.

- Oil *polishes* when used to shine metal – the Holy Spirit wipes away our grime, smoothing out our rough edges.

d. **Who are you, O great mountain? Before Zerubbabel you shall become a plain**: The work of rebuilding the temple was so massive it seemed like a **great mountain**. Here God promised that by His Spirit, that **great mountain** would be leveled into a **plain**.

i. In this case, the **great mountain** may have literally been the mountainous pile of rubble at the temple site. That rubble would be removed, and the work carried on.

ii. "You all get up plans and say, 'Now, if the church were altered a little bit, it would go on better.' You think if there were different ministers, or different church order, or something different, then all would be well. No, dear friends, it is not there the mistake lies, it is that we want more of the Spirit." (Spurgeon)

e. **He shall bring forth the capstone with shouts of "Grace, grace to it!"** This was God's assurance to Zerubbabel that not only will the work be finished, but *Zerubbabel* – **he** – shall finish it, setting the **capstone** and declaring that it is all a work of **grace**.

i. When the work is done through human **might** or **power**, we can take credit for it, but when the work is done by the continual supply of the **Spirit**, then it is all of **grace** and to God's glory.

2. (8-10) More encouragement for Zerubbabel.

Moreover the word of the LORD came to me, saying:

"The hands of Zerubbabel
Have laid the foundation of this temple;
His hands shall also finish *it***.**
Then you will know
That the LORD of hosts has sent Me to you.
For who has despised the day of small things?
For these seven rejoice to see
The plumb line in the hand of Zerubbabel.
They are the eyes of the LORD,
Which scan to and fro throughout the whole earth."

a. **His hands shall also finish it**: When the work is done by God's Spirit there are not only resources to *begin* the work, but also enough to **finish** the work. God is the One who *finishes* His work (Philippians 1:6).

b. **For who has despised the day of small things?** Zechariah's question rings true to us today. Almost every one of us could answer, "I have

despised the day of small things." The question provides its own answer: none of us *should* despise **the day of small things**, because God has a wonderful purpose even if it is difficult to understand.

i. It was a long **day of small things** for Zerubbabel because the work of the temple lay in ruins for almost 20 years. He might have said to God, "What do You mean '**day of small things**?' I've lived with 20 years of **small things**." Even so, God told Zerubbabel to not despise the time of **small things**, and to consider it is all as just a **day**.

ii. In many of God's choice workers He uses a powerful season of **small things**. Those days are not a mistake nor are they punishment; they are days of priceless shaping and preparation. They are not days to despise.

iii. When Satan tempts us to despise **the day of small things**, he shines as an outstanding liar because *Satan does not despise the day of small things*. Satan *fears* **the day of small things** in our lives because he sees what great things God does in them and brings out of them.

iv. Spurgeon spoke of the need for courage in **the day of small things** in our churches: "To me, it seems that it should be your glory to join the poorest and weakest churches of your denomination, and wherever you go, to say, 'This little cause is not as strong as I should like it to be; but, by the grace of God, I will make it more influential. At any rate, I will throw in my weight to strengthen the weak things of Zion, and certainly I will not despise the day of small things.' Where would have been our flourishing churches of today if our forefathers had disdained to sustain them while they were yet in their infancy?"

v. "God accepts your little works if they are done in faith in his dear Son. God will give success to your little works: God will educate you by your little works to do greater works; and your little works may call out others who shall do greater works by far than ever you shall be able to accomplish." (Spurgeon)

c. **For these seven rejoice to see the plumb line in the hand of Zerubbabel**: The **seven** are the **eyes of the L**ORD mentioned in this same context. They **rejoice** when they see Zerubbabel busy with the building work, with the **plumb line** in his hand. The **eyes of the L**ORD see it all, and they are happy to see God's people at work.

i. Though the work was empowered by the Spirit of God, Zerubbabel still needed his **plumb line**. He still needed to get to work. God could have given Zerubbabel a shortcut and instantly, miraculously finished the work. That isn't God's way of doing things, because His work in the life of Zerubbabel was as important to Him as His work through Zerubbabel.

3. (11-14) Explanation of the olive trees and lampstands.

Then I answered and said to him, "What *are* these two olive trees–at the right of the lampstand and at its left?" And I further answered and said to him, "What *are these* two olive branches that *drip* into the receptacles of the two gold pipes from which the golden *oil* drains?"

Then he answered me and said, "Do you not know what these *are?*"

And I said, "No, my lord."

So he said, "These *are* the two anointed ones, who stand beside the Lord of the whole earth."

a. **What are these two olive trees**: Zechariah understood the message of encouragement to Zerubbabel, but he didn't exactly understand how it connected to the vision of the olive trees and the lampstand.

b. **These are the two anointed ones**: In Zechariah's day, the **two anointed ones** were Zerubbabel and Joshua. It seems that they were not the entire trees, but **two olive branches** from the trees, probably one branch from each tree. The trees themselves may represent the kingly and priestly offices in Israel.

i. God had a special work for these **two anointed ones**. They would be uniquely anointed to work together and to accomplish the work of God. God often calls two men to work together:

- Moses and Aaron.
- Joshua and Caleb.
- Elijah and Elisha.
- Peter and John.
- Paul and Barnabas.
- Calvin and Luther.
- Whitefield and Wesley.
- Moody and Sankey.
- Graham and Barrows.

ii. God promises to raise up two more witnesses, anointed ones to preach the gospel to the world immediately before Jesus' return (Revelation 11:3-13). Revelation 11:4 specifically says of these witnesses: *These are the two olive trees and the two lampstands standing before the God of the earth.*

c. **The two anointed ones** had work to do and it would be so supplied by the Spirit of God that they would be like the olive trees with a continual supply of oil for the lamps on the lampstand.

i. **Anointed ones** means *sons of oil*. In Hebrew idioms, the *son of* something is radically characterized by that thing. For example, the *sons of Belial* totally represent their pagan god Belial. These two are so characterized by the ministry and the power of the Holy Spirit that they are *sons of oil*.

ii. We note that the oil came *out of* the trees. All real ministry is giving of ourselves. It doesn't matter how much we have; what matters is how much we give of ourselves. Some people are like a huge tank of oil that you might see at an oil refinery. You think, "that's enough gasoline to last a lifetime" – but you could never fill your tank there. At the refinery, there is much supply, but no delivery. A five-gallon can of gasoline at home can carry only a little supply – but it will deliver.

Zechariah 5 – Two Visions Regarding the Cleansing of God's People

A. The vision of the flying scroll.

1. (1-2) What Zechariah saw.

Then I turned and raised my eyes, and saw there a flying scroll.
And he said to me, "What do you see?"
So I answered, "I see a flying scroll. Its length *is* twenty cubits and its width ten cubits."

> a. **A flying scroll**: In this vision, Zechariah saw a scroll flying through the air. The scroll was apparently rolled open because Zechariah could see how large the scroll was.
>
> b. **Its length is twenty cubits and its width ten cubits**: The scroll was approximately 15 by 30 feet (4.5 meters by 9 meters). These were the dimensions of the porch of Solomon's temple (1 Kings 6:3).

2. (3-4) What the scroll represents.

Then he said to me, "This *is* the curse that goes out over the face of the whole earth: 'Every thief shall be expelled,' according *to* this side of *the scroll*; and, 'Every perjurer shall be expelled,' according *to* that side of it."

"I will send out *the curse*," says the LORD of hosts;
"It shall enter the house of the thief
And the house of the one who swears falsely by My name.
It shall remain in the midst of his house
And consume it, with its timber and stones."

> a. **Every thief shall be expelled…every perjurer shall be expelled**: This makes many people think that the text on the scroll contained the Ten Commandments. To steal was to injure your neighbor; to perjure was to dishonor God because you had sworn in His name.

b. **I will send out the curse**: The two sins, one from each side of the tablets of the Ten Commandments, represented all of Israel's sin. God would curse the people who committed these sins and also curse their house.

B. Vision of the woman and the basket.

1. (5-8) The woman sitting in the basket.

Then the angel who talked with me came out and said to me, "Lift your eyes now, and see what this *is* that goes forth."

So I asked, "What *is* it?" And he said, "It *is* a basket that is going forth."

He also said, "This *is* their resemblance throughout the earth: Here *is* a lead disc lifted up, and this *is* a woman sitting inside the basket"; then he said, "This *is* Wickedness!" And he thrust her down into the basket, and threw the lead cover over its mouth.

a. **It is a basket that is going forth**: The basket was an *ephah*, it and the **lead disc** were units of measurement and symbols of commerce.

i. **This is their resemblance throughout the earth**: The NIV (New International Version) translates this, *This is the iniquity of the people throughout the land.*

b. **This is Wickedness**: The woman, the basket, and the weight were associated with wickedness. They were images of greed, materialism, and dishonesty for profit.

i. The Hebrew word for **Wickedness** is feminine. This is probably why a woman was the image of evil in this vision.

ii. Zechariah prophesied to those who returned from the Babylonian exile. God's people came back from Babylon with a materialism problem, and this vision spoke of this problem.

c. **He thrust her down into the basket, and threw the lead cover over its mouth**: God first demonstrates His authority over evil and then removes the wickedness from Jerusalem.

2. (9-11) The woman and the basket are returned to Babylon.

Then I raised my eyes and looked, and there *were* two women, coming with the wind in their wings; for they had wings like the wings of a stork, and they lifted up the basket between earth and heaven.

So I said to the angel who talked with me, "Where are they carrying the basket?"

And he said to me, "To build a house for it in the land of Shinar; when it is ready, *the basket* will be set there on its base."

a. **Two women…they had wings like the wings of a stork**: This means that the **women** in Zechariah's vision had big wings, strong enough to take this basket back to Babylon. Some regard these women as agents of evil because storks were unclean animals, but here they seem to do the work of God in sending the wicked woman back to Babylon.

b. **Where are they carrying the basket?** God would cause this evil, materialistic spirit to be returned to its starting place: Babylon (**the land of Shinar**). There it would eventually be destroyed.

c. **When it is ready, the basket will be set there on its base**: The word for **base** has the thought of a pedestal for an idol. The storks set the idol of materialism where it belonged.

Zechariah 6 – A King and Priest

A. The vision of the four chariots and their horses.

1. (1-3) What Zechariah saw.

Then I turned and raised my eyes and looked, and behold, four chariots *were* coming from between two mountains, and the mountains *were* mountains of bronze. With the first chariot *were* red horses, with the second chariot black horses, with the third chariot white horses, and with the fourth chariot dappled horses–strong *steeds*.

> a. **Four chariots were coming from between two mountains**: Since the original text says *the* **two mountains**, most people assume they are the Mount of Olives and Mount Zion. **Mountains of bronze** associates these mountains with strength and judgment.
>
> b. **Four chariots.... red horses...black horses...white horses...dappled horses—strong steeds**: The horsemen of Zechariah 1 were observers on reconnaissance. These **four chariots** and their horses seem to be hostile agents of God's judgment, emissaries of His war against the earth.
>
>> i. Some commentators want to identify these **four chariots** with Daniel's four world empires (Daniel 2 and Daniel 7) but the colors essentially are the same as the four horsemen in Revelation 6, the emissaries of God's judgment. Some commentators connect these with the angelic messengers of judgment in Revelation 7:1-3.
>>
>> ii. "In the usual Scriptural symbolism *red* speaks of *war*, *black* of *famine* and *death*, *white* of *victory*, and *grizzled* of *pestilence* (Ezekiel 14:21, Revelation 6:1-8)." (Luck)

2. (4-8) What the vision means.

Then I answered and said to the angel who talked with me, "What *are* these, my lord?"

And the angel answered and said to me, "These *are* four spirits of heaven, who go out from *their* station before the Lord of all the earth. The one with the black horses is going to the north country, the white are going after them, and the dappled are going toward the south country." Then the strong *steeds* went out, eager to go, that they might walk to and fro throughout the earth. And He said, "Go, walk to and fro throughout the earth." So they walked to and fro throughout the earth. And He called to me, and spoke to me, saying, "See, those who go toward the north country have given rest to My Spirit in the north country."

a. **Four spirits of heaven**: This means that these *four chariots* were actually four angelic beings sent from God. Therefore these may not be exactly the same as the four horsemen of Revelation 6, but the idea of their mission and purpose is similar.

i. John Calvin said that these angels are compared to horsemen on chariots because "These ride swiftly as it were through the whole world to execute what God commands them." If Zechariah had reference to the technology of today, he might picture the angels in fast cars or fighter jets, showing how swiftly and powerfully they move across the earth to accomplish God's purpose.

b. **To the north country**: Two of the horses are focused on the **north**, where Babylon and Magog are. Nevertheless, each of the four also walks **to and fro throughout the earth**.

c. **Those who go toward the north country have given rest to My Spirit in the north country**: God's **Spirit** is only at rest when His enemies and the enemies of His people are judged.

B. The crowning of Joshua, the high priest.

1. (9-11) A command to make a crown for Joshua.

Then the word of the LORD came to me, saying: "Receive *the gift* from the captives–from Heldai, Tobijah, and Jedaiah, who have come from Babylon–and go the same day and enter the house of Josiah the son of Zephaniah. Take the silver and gold, make an elaborate crown, and set *it* on the head of Joshua the son of Jehozadak, the high priest.

a. **Receive the gift from the captives…who have come from Babylon**: As the refugees continued to return from exile they brought with them gifts from wealthy Babylon.

b. **Heldai, Tobijah, and Jedaiah**: Taking the meaning of the names (**Heldai** means *robust*, **Tobijah** means *God's goodness*, and **Jedaiah** means *God knows*), McGee sees in the meaning of these names the sense that God knew that through His goodness, He would put His king on the throne, and He would do it in a robust manner.

c. **Make an elaborate crown, and set it on the head of Joshua**: It was unthinkable to crown a **high priest** because priests were never crowned as kings and kings were never priests.

> i. 2 Chronicles 26 tells the tragic story of King Uzziah who tried to function as a priest, and was stricken with leprosy until the end of his life. Throughout the history of Israel God commanded a separation between the religious and the civil leadership of Israel.
>
> ii. **Elaborate crown**: This was definitely a *royal* **crown** and was not the customary headdress of the high priest.

d. **On the head of Joshua the son of Jehozadak, the high priest**: There already was a strong, godly civil leader in Jerusalem named Zerubbabel. It seems like it would have made a lot more sense to crown Zerubbabel instead of **Joshua…the high priest**. But Joshua was crowned because a coming descendant of David to rule over Israel would be Jesus, prefigured by the high priest Joshua.

> i. Liberal critics are so certain that Zerubbabel should be crowned here that they think that the text is in error. This misses the whole point because this crowning of Joshua prophesies the King-Priest Jesus.

2. (12-13) Prophecy of the BRANCH, who is both King and Priest.

Then speak to him, saying, 'Thus says the LORD of hosts, saying:
"Behold, the Man whose name *is* the BRANCH!
From His place He shall branch out,
And He shall build the temple of the LORD;
Yes, He shall build the temple of the LORD.
He shall bear the glory,
And shall sit and rule on His throne;
So He shall be a priest on His throne,
And the counsel of peace shall be between them both."'

a. **Behold, the Man whose name is the BRANCH!** We already saw this **Branch** in Zechariah 3:8, and it was a familiar title for the Messiah (Isaiah 4:2 and 11:1, Jeremiah 23:5 and 33:15). The **Branch** was associated with fruitfulness and life. Jesus used the same image when He said that He is the vine and we are the branches (John 15:5).

> i. **Behold, the Man**: "In the Hebrew text the prophecy begins 'Behold the Man,' the very words Pilate used to present the beaten Christ to the people of Jerusalem: '*Ecce homo!*'" (Boice). But in Zechariah's vision it

isn't the humiliated Jesus we are asked to **behold**, it is the triumphant Jesus.

b. **From His place He shall branch out**: This speaks of the fruitfulness and spreading life of the Messiah.

i. "He will come where there is little promise of new life, unexpectedly, like the root out of a dry ground." (Baldwin)

c. **And He shall build the temple of the LORD**: The **Branch** will rebuild the temple – not the same temple Zerubbabel worked on, but the temple of His people (Ephesians 2:19-22, 1 Peter 2:5).

d. **So He shall be a priest on His throne**: This was an unthinkable concept previously in Israel because priests did not sit on thrones and kings did not serve as priests. Nevertheless, the **Branch** is different; He rules as both a King and Priest.

3. (14-15) The crown as a memorial.

"Now the elaborate crown shall be for a memorial in the temple of the LORD for Helem, Tobijah, Jedaiah, and Hen the son of Zephaniah. Even those from afar shall come and build the temple of the LORD. Then you shall know that the LORD of hosts has sent Me to you. And *this* shall come to pass if you diligently obey the voice of the LORD your God."

a. **Now the elaborate crown shall be for a memorial**: The LORD made it clear that the **crown** for Joshua was a picture of the ruling Priest-King in the future. God never intended for Joshua to take control as king in the Jerusalem of his day.

b. **Hen the son of Zephaniah**: Earlier, *Josiah* was said to be the son of Zephaniah, and Zechariah apparently gave this prophecy in his house (Zechariah 6:10). Since the name **Hen** means "gracious," it is almost certainly another name, and an appropriate name, for this Josiah **the son of Zephaniah**.

c. **Even those from afar shall come and build the temple of the LORD**: The **elaborate crown** spoke of something that would not happen for a long time in the future. Still, God's promised blessing in the future means that He wants the work to continue right now, and that He will bless the current work.

Zechariah 7 – Obedience Is Better than Ritual

A. Confronting the sin of religious hypocrisy.

1. (1-3) A question about fasting.

Now in the fourth year of King Darius it came to pass *that* **the word of the LORD came to Zechariah, on the fourth** *day* **of the ninth month, Chislev, when** *the people* **sent Sherezer, with Regem-Melech and his men,** *to* **the house of God, to pray before the LORD,** *and* **to ask the priests who** *were* **in the house of the LORD of hosts, and the prophets, saying, "Should I weep in the fifth month and fast as I have done for so many years?"**

> a. **In the fourth year…on the fourth day of the ninth month**: On December 4, 518 B.C. a delegation came to Jerusalem with a question about fasting. At this point, the temple was somewhere around halfway completed.
>
> b. **Should I weep in the fifth month and fast**: The fast in the **fifth month** commemorated the destruction of the temple (2 Kings 25:8-9). Zechariah also mentioned a fast in the seventh month (Zechariah 7:5), which remembered the murder of Gedaliah, the last act of rebellion against the Babylonian governor of Judah (2 Kings 25:25).
>
>> i. The Law of Moses commanded that on the Day of Atonement, the people of Israel should afflict their souls (Leviticus 16:29-34). The text in Leviticus does not specifically say they should fast, but it has long been understood by Jewish teachers as a command for Jews to fast on the Day of Atonement. In addition to this, during the exile the Jewish people instituted four more fasts to remember key dates in the tragic defeat of their nation. Here are the additional fasts:

Month/Day	Reason	Reference
4/17	Mourning the capture of Jerusalem	Jeremiah 52:6-30
5/9	The burning of Jerusalem and the destruction of Solomon's temple	2 Kings 25:2-10
7/3	The assassination of Gedaliah and the massacre of 80 men	Jeremiah 41:1-10
10/10	The beginning of Nebuchadnezzar's siege against Jerusalem	2 Kings 25:1

ii. Psalm 137 beautifully – and powerfully – described the sadness of heart that made the exiles remember their sin and such tragedies with these additional days of fasting.

c. **To ask the priests who were in the house of the LORD**: These men knew that during their forced exile in Babylon they observed these fasts that commemorated the tragic fall of Jerusalem. Now since God's people were back in the land and the temple was rebuilt, they wanted to know if it was appropriate to continue to observe these fasts of mournful remembrance.

i. The matter brings up an issue relevant today: How long should we remember and mourn over our past? Should we do things to remember either our sins or the tragedies of the past?

d. **As I have done for so many years**: These additional fasts were not commanded by God but instituted by man. Yet because they were traditionally practiced for so long (at least 70 years), they developed a legitimacy of their own. They thought, "We've done this **for so many years**, we may as well keep doing it."

2. (4-7) Hypocrisy in fasting is rebuked.

Then the word of the LORD of hosts came to me, saying, "Say to all the people of the land, and to the priests: 'When you fasted and mourned in the fifth and seventh *months* during those seventy years, did you really fast for Me—for Me? When you eat and when you drink, do you not eat and drink *for yourselves? Should you* not *have obeyed* the words which the LORD proclaimed through the former prophets when Jerusalem and

the cities around it were inhabited and prosperous, and the South and the Lowland were inhabited?'"

> a. **Did you really fast for Me – for Me?** God's word through Zechariah rebuked the people of God for what their fasting had become – indulgent seasons of self-pity instead of a time to genuinely seek God. Their lives were not right when they did **eat and drink** – that they did for themselves, not for the LORD. A few days of fasting every year does not make up for the rest of the year of living **for yourselves**.
>
>> i. This also shows us that when we cling to the memory of sin or tragedy in the past, we may do it out of simple self-indulgence. We may do it for ourselves, not for the LORD.
>
> b. **Should you not have obeyed the words which the LORD proclaimed**: Because their hearts were not right with God, their rituals were not acceptable to God. Everyday obedience would make their times of fasting meaningful, but their neglect of everyday obedience made their fasting hypocritical.
>
>> i. "It was easy to spend fast-days mourning their losses, but harder to face up to God's continuing demands." (Baldwin)
>>
>> ii. Instead of actively remembering the sin or tragedy of the past, God wants us to focus on active obedience and an active walk with Him. "There is no need to observe the sad anniversaries of our sins and their accompanying punishment, if once we are assured of God's free forgiveness. When He forgives and restores, the need for dwelling on the bitter past is over.... Too many of us are always dwelling beside the graves of the dead past." (Meyer)
>>
>> iii. **Through the former prophets when Jerusalem and the cities around it were inhabited and prosperous**: If their ancestors had been obedient, they would have never needed to fast, and their land wouldn't have been conquered and desolate.
>
> c. **And the South and the Lowland were inhabited**: Here, **the South** refers to the *Negev*, the desolate desert near the Dead Sea. This area wasn't always desolate; before Israel's disobedience, it too was prosperous and **inhabited**.

B. **What God wants: people who will listen and obey.**

1. (8-10) The conduct God desires.

Then the word of the LORD came to Zechariah, saying, "Thus says the LORD of hosts:

'Execute true justice,
Show mercy and compassion
Everyone to his brother.
Do not oppress the widow or the fatherless,
The alien or the poor.
Let none of you plan evil in his heart
Against his brother.'

> a. **Execute true justice, show mercy and compassion**: In Zechariah 7:7 the prophet rebuked the people of God and their ancestors for a basic neglect of obedience. Next Zechariah described the kind of obedience God wanted, beginning with decent and loving treatment of one's neighbor.

> b. **Let none of you plan evil in his heart against his brother**: Some among the people of God found it easier to fast a few days a year instead of truly treating others in a godly way. Their bad relationship with others demonstrated a fundamentally bad relationship with the LORD.

2. (11-12) The rebellious reaction of God's people.

"But they refused to heed, shrugged their shoulders, and stopped their ears so that they could not hear. Yes, they made their hearts like flint, refusing to hear the law and the words which the LORD of hosts had sent by His Spirit through the former prophets. Thus great wrath came from the LORD of hosts.

> a. **Refused to heed, shrugged their shoulders, and stopped their ears…. made their hearts like flint**: Zechariah vividly described a *progression of rejection*. It began with simply refusing to **heed** God, then a self-justifying shrugging of **their shoulders**, then stopping **their ears**. It all ends with hearts as hard as **flint**.

>> i. When you meet people with **hearts like flint**, you know they did not become that way overnight. There was a gradual, certain progression to their present place of hardness.

>> ii. Baldwin on **shrugged their shoulders**: "Israel had *turned a stubborn shoulder*, like an animal that stiffened every muscle in its effort to refuse the yoke."

> b. **Refusing to hear the law and the words which the LORD of hosts had sent by His Spirit through the former prophets**: In their hardened state, they just didn't want to hear God's word. When we lose our hunger for God's word it is a sobering evidence of the progression of rejection and hardness of heart.

>> i. Zechariah didn't doubt that the **Spirit** of God genuinely inspired his words and the words of other prophets.

3. (13-14) God's judgment on their disobedience.

Therefore it happened, *that* **just as He proclaimed and they would not hear, so they called out and I would not listen," says the LORD of hosts. "But I scattered them with a whirlwind among all the nations which they had not known. Thus the land became desolate after them, so that no one passed through or returned; for they made the pleasant land desolate."**

a. **Just as He proclaimed and they would not hear, so they called out and I would not listen**: Since God's people refused to listen to God, God would refuse to listen to and answer their prayers. This is just another good reason to stay under the teaching of God's word – so that our prayers will be answered.

i. **I scattered them with a whirlwind**: "This refers to the swift victories and cruel conduct of the Chaldeans towards the Jews; they came upon them like a *whirlwind*; they were tossed to and fro, and up and down, everywhere scattered and confounded." (Clarke)

b. **Thus the land became desolate after them**: Their disobedience and disregard for God led to scattering and desolation. This is always our fate when we allow religious rituals to take the place of a real relationship and daily obedience towards God.

Zechariah 8 – Jerusalem Restored

A. Israel restored to God's favor.

1. (1-2) The LORD says: My passionate love for Israel has not diminished.

Again the word of the LORD of hosts came, saying, "Thus says the LORD of hosts:

**'I am zealous for Zion with great zeal;
With great fervor I am zealous for her.'**

> a. **Thus says the LORD of hosts**: God introduced Himself with a title declaring His power and majesty. He is the **LORD of hosts**, with **hosts** referring to the armies of heaven. The title itself is a wake-up call.
>
> b. **I am zealous for Zion with great zeal**: The word for **zealous** in the ancient Hebrew comes from the idea "to become intensely red." It has the thought of a face becoming flushed with deep emotion. This shows that God is passionately concerned for His people.

2. (3) The LORD says: Jerusalem will be restored.

"Thus says the LORD:

**'I will return to Zion,
And dwell in the midst of Jerusalem.
Jerusalem shall be called the City of Truth,
The Mountain of the LORD of hosts,
The Holy Mountain.'**

> a. **I will return to Zion, and dwell in the midst of Jerusalem**: God's people and city will be transformed by the presence of the LORD.
>
> b. **Jerusalem shall be called the City of Truth…the Holy Mountain**: Because of God's presence the city will be transformed into a place of truth and holiness. When God's presence is real and embraced in our lives, we become *people* **of Truth** and **Holy** *people*.

i. In 2 Corinthians 3:18 Paul describes this process of transformation: *But we all, with unveiled face, beholding as in a mirror the glory of the Lord, are being transformed into the same image from glory to glory, just as by the Spirit of the Lord.*

3. (4-5) The LORD says: Jerusalem will be a thriving, safe place.

"**Thus says the LORD of hosts:**

'**Old men and old women shall again sit
In the streets of Jerusalem,
Each one with his staff in his hand
Because of great age.
The streets of the city
Shall be full of boys and girls
Playing in its streets.**'

    a. **Old men and old women shall again sit in the streets of Jerusalem**: Because of the difficulty and hardship of returning to Jerusalem, there were probably few old people in the city, and their absence was felt. But the LORD promised that all that would change one day and young and old together would enjoy the city in safety. This was a significant promise because in Zechariah's time Jerusalem's walls were ruined and the city was not safe and secure for **old men and old women** or for **boys and girls playing in its streets**.

    b. **The streets of the city shall be full of boys and girls playing in its streets**: Dr. J. Vernon McGee took this as meaning that there would be no cars in the millennial Jerusalem.

4. (6) The LORD says: Even if it is too amazing for you, is it too hard for Me?

"**Thus says the LORD of hosts:**

'**If it is marvelous in the eyes of the remnant of this people in these days,
Will it also be marvelous in My eyes?**'
Says the LORD of hosts.

    a. **If it is marvelous in the eyes of the remnant of this people**: The promise of a transformed, prosperous, safe Jerusalem seemed a little too fantastic to believe when the city was half-built, and the walls wouldn't be completed for another 60 years.

    b. **Will it also be marvelous in My eyes?** Just because it seemed too big in the eyes of man, it was not too **marvelous** for the LORD. As Jesus said, *"With men this is impossible, but with God all things are possible."* (Matthew 19:26)

i. "I remember when a boy being taken to see the residence of one of our nobility, and the good friend who took me noticed my astonishment at the largeness of the house. I was amazed at it, having never seen anything like it, and so I said, 'What a house for a man to live in!' 'Bless you, boy,' said he, 'this is only the kitchen!' I was only looking at the servants' apartments, and was astonished at the grandeur thereof; but the mansion itself was a far nobler affair. Oftentimes when you see what the Lord has done, you are ready to cry out, 'How can all this be? His goodness, his mercy, is it as great as this?' Rest assured that you have only seen a little of his goodness, as it were the kitchen of his great house: you have not seen the palace of the Most High, where he reveals his full power and splendour." (Spurgeon)

5. (7-8) The LORD says: Israel will be gathered, far more than the few who have returned thus far.

"**Thus says the LORD of hosts:**

**'Behold, I will save My people from the land of the east
And from the land of the west;
I will bring them *back*,
And they shall dwell in the midst of Jerusalem.
They shall be My people
And I will be their God,
In truth and righteousness.'**

a. **I will save My people from the land of the east and from the land of the west**: Proportionately, few among the exiles returned to the Promised Land. God promised a gathering from exile to come that would far surpass the present gathering.

b. **They shall be My people and I will be their God, in truth and righteousness**: The gathering God promised will not just be a *geographic* gathering, but also a *spiritual* gathering. It won't just be that their address changes, but their hearts also.

6. (9-13) The LORD says: take courage; finish the work, for I will bless you.

"**Thus says the LORD of hosts:**

**'Let your hands be strong,
You who have been hearing in these days
These words by the mouth of the prophets,
Who *spoke* in the day the foundation was laid
For the house of the LORD of hosts,
That the temple might be built.
For before these days**

There were no wages for man nor any hire for beast;
There was no peace from the enemy for whoever went out or came in;
For I set all men, everyone, against his neighbor.

But now I *will* not *treat* the remnant of this people as in the former days,' says the LORD of hosts.

For the seed *shall be* prosperous,
The vine shall give its fruit,
The ground shall give her increase,
And the heavens shall give their dew–
I will cause the remnant of this people
To possess all these.
And it shall come to pass
That just as you were a curse among the nations,
O house of Judah and house of Israel,
So I will save you, and you shall be a blessing.
Do not fear,
Let your hands be strong.'

> a. **Let your hands be strong**: This encouraging command was for those who had heard the words of the prophets **in the day the foundation was laid for the house of the LORD of hosts**. The foundation was set more than fifteen years before. Though they faced a lack of resources (**no wages for man**) and opposition (**no peace from the enemy**), God wanted them to find strength for the work (**let your hands be strong**) in His promise.
>
> b. **I will not treat the remnant of this people as in the former days**: God allowed a period of difficulty but would not allow it to last forever. He would bring prosperity and blessing to the once afflicted nation.
>
> c. **You shall be a blessing. Do not fear, let your hands be strong**: Though their present state was lowly, God wanted Israel to trust in His promise of **blessing**, and let the promise encourage them to diligent, strong service.

7. (14-17) The LORD says: I am determined to bless My people.

"For thus says the LORD of hosts:

'Just as I determined to punish you
When your fathers provoked Me to wrath,'
Says the LORD of hosts,
'And I would not relent,
So again in these days
I am determined to do good
To Jerusalem and to the house of Judah.
Do not fear.

These *are* the things you shall do:
Speak each man the truth to his neighbor;
Give judgment in your gates for truth, justice, and peace;
Let none of you think evil in your heart against your neighbor;
And do not love a false oath.
For all these *are things* that I hate,'
Says the LORD."

> a. **Just as I determined to punish you when your fathers provoked Me...in these days I am determined to do good**: God promised blessing to Israel instead of cursing, and He promised it on the principle of the Mosaic covenant.
>
>> i. "God's strange work is judgment. His delight is to bless His people." (Unger)
>
> b. **These are the things you shall do**: God promised blessing to an obedient Israel and cursing to a disobedient Israel (Deuteronomy 28:1-2, 28:15). If God will bless instead of curse, they must fulfill their end of the Mosaic covenant, and gain blessing instead of curses.

B. Feasting for fasting.

1. (18-19) The LORD says: in light of your glorious future, feasting is more appropriate than fasting.

Then the word of the LORD of hosts came to me, saying, "Thus says the LORD of hosts:
'The fast of the fourth *month,*
The fast of the fifth,
The fast of the seventh,
And the fast of the tenth,
Shall be joy and gladness and cheerful feasts
For the house of Judah.
Therefore love truth and peace.'

> a. **The fast of the fourth month...shall be joy and gladness and cheerful feasts**: Each one of these fast days commemorated a tragic day around the fall of Jerusalem. God here promised blessing so wonderful that these mournful fasts would be transformed into **cheerful feasts** of celebration.
>
>> i. G. Campbell Morgan said of these man-appointed fasts: "None of these things had been in the purpose of God for His people; they had resulted from their sins. The fasts therefore were the result of their sins. In jealousy and fury, the outcome of love, Jehovah would put away their sins, and so restore them to true prosperity. In that day, let

them still remember and observe, only let the observance be a feast in celebration of God's grace, instead of a fast in memory of their sin."

b. **Therefore love truth and peace**: In light of God's promised blessing, His people should want to be more like Him – they should **love truth and peace**.

2. (20-22) The LORD says: the nations will stream into Jerusalem, to seek the LORD.

"Thus says the LORD of hosts:

'Peoples shall yet come,
Inhabitants of many cities;
The inhabitants of one *city* shall go to another, saying,
"Let us continue to go and pray before the LORD,
And seek the LORD of hosts.
I myself will go also."
Yes, many peoples and strong nations
Shall come to seek the LORD of hosts in Jerusalem,
And to pray before the LORD.'

a. **Peoples shall yet come**: In Zechariah's day not many people wanted to come to a still ruined, downtrodden city like Jerusalem. God promised a redemption so great that one day the **peoples shall yet come** to the glorified city.

b. **Yes, many peoples and strong nations shall come to seek the LORD of hosts in Jerusalem**: This promise will ultimately be fulfilled in the millennial kingdom of Jesus. Jerusalem will be the headquarters of His kingdom, and the nations will come to **seek the LORD** in Jerusalem.

3. (23) The LORD says: God will give Israel such favor that the nations will see God is with them.

"Thus says the LORD of hosts: 'In those days ten men from every language of the nations shall grasp the sleeve of a Jewish man, saying, "Let us go with you, for we have heard *that* God *is* with you."'"

a. **Ten men from every language of the nations shall grasp the sleeve of a Jewish man**: This same word **grasp** is used for grabbing a snake by the tail (Exodus 4:4) or for grabbing a lion by its beard (1 Samuel 17:35). It means to grasp something that you must not let go of.

i. "This prophecy teaches, then, that Israel will be the means of drawing the nations of the earth to the Lord in the time of the Messiah's reign of righteousness upon earth." (Feinberg, cited in Barker)

ii. "We are all clinging to the seamless robe of that *one* Jew, Jesus of Nazareth, who because of His work on the cross is the only basis on which anyone may approach God and entreat Him for spiritual blessings." (Boice)

b. **Let us go with you, for we have heard that God is with you**: When others see that God is with us, it attracts them to the LORD. When people see *Christ in you, the hope of glory* (Colossians 1:27), they want to come to Jesus.

i. "God is never idle while he dwells in his people; for he cleanses away every kind of impurity, every kind of deceit, that where he dwells may ever be a holy place." (Calvin)

Zechariah 9 – A Humble King Conquers

A. The burden against Hadrach.

1. (1-4) Judgment against the cities of Lebanon.

The burden of the word of the Lord—
Against the land of Hadrach,
And Damascus its resting place
(For the eyes of men
And all the tribes of Israel
Are on the Lord);
Also *against* Hamath, *which* borders on it,
And *against* Tyre and Sidon, though they are very wise.

For Tyre built herself a tower,
Heaped up silver like the dust,
And gold like the mire of the streets.
Behold, the Lord will cast her out;
He will destroy her power in the sea,
And she will be devoured by fire.

> a. **The burden of the word of the Lord**: The two oracles that make up the remainder of Zechariah (chapters 9 through 14) are undated, but many scholars believe they came from Zechariah's old age. Most see this **burden… against the land of Hadrach** as fulfilled by the armies of Alexander the Great when he conquered this region. The cities mentioned in Zechariah 9:1-7 trace Alexander's march through the Promised Land in 332-331 B.C.
>
>> i. **The eyes of men…are on the Lord** in the sense that they were on God's instrument of judgment, Alexander.
>
> b. **Against Tyre and Sidon**: These were the two major cities north of Israel, in the land of Lebanon. **Tyre** was an important commercial city that was thought to be impossible to conquer. The Assyrians laid siege against Tyre

for five years but never conquered the city. Nebuchadnezzar tried for 13 years to conquer Tyre, but Alexander did it in seven months.

> i. Alexander the Great conquered Tyre by laying siege for seven months, then using the rubble from the old city to make a causeway out to the island city. It was a spectacular achievement of both military and engineering strategy.

2. (5-8) Judgment against the cities of the Philistines.

Ashkelon shall see *it* and fear;
Gaza also shall be very sorrowful;
And Ekron, for He dried up her expectation.
The king shall perish from Gaza,
And Ashkelon shall not be inhabited.

"A mixed race shall settle in Ashdod,
And I will cut off the pride of the Philistines.
I will take away the blood from his mouth,
And the abominations from between his teeth.
But he who remains, even he *shall be* for our God,
And shall be like a leader in Judah,
And Ekron like a Jebusite.
I will camp around My house
Because of the army,
Because of him who passes by and him who returns.
No more shall an oppressor pass through them,
For now I have seen with My eyes.

> a. **Ashkelon shall see it and fear; Gaza also shall be very sorrowful**: The Philistine cities of **Ashkelon**, **Gaza**, **Ekron**, and **Ashdod** are south of Tyre and Sidon, and were also conquered by Alexander the Great in 332-331 B.C.
>
>> i. This passage "accurately foretells the conquest of the eastern Mediterranean coastlands by Greek armies under the command of Alexander the Great." (Boice)
>
> b. **He who remains…and Ekron like a Jebusite**: The Jebusites inhabited Jerusalem when David conquered the city (Joshua 15:8, 2 Samuel 5:6-9, 2 Samuel 24:16-18). David did not wipe out the Jebusites but merely incorporated them into Israel. The same would happen to the people of **Ekron**.
>
> c. **I will camp around My house because of the army, because of him who passes by**: When Alexander the Great marched through Lebanon and the Promised Land towards Egypt he did not conquer or attack Jerusalem.

God promised to protect and spare His **house** during this time, and He did through a remarkable chain of events connected to Alexander the Great and the high priest.

i. Josephus' account of Alexander's meeting with the high priest is fascinating (*Antiquities* 11.8.4-5):

Now Alexander, when he had taken Gaza, made haste to go up to Jerusalem; and Jaddua the high-priest, when he heard that, was in agony, and under terror, as not knowing how he should meet the Macedonians, since the king was displeased at his foregoing disobedience. He therefore ordained that the people should make supplications, and should join with him in offering sacrifices to God, whom he besought to protect that nation, and to deliver them from the perils that were coming upon them; whereupon God warned him in a dream, which came upon him after he had offered sacrifice, that he should take courage, adorn the city, and open the gates; that the rest appear in white garments, but that he and the priests should meet the king in habits proper to their order, without the dread of any ill consequences, which the providence of God would prevent. Upon which, when he rose from his sleep, he greatly rejoiced; and declared to all the warning he had received from God. According to the dream he acted entirely, and so waited for the coming of the king.

And when he understood that he was not far from the city, he went out in procession, with the priests and the multitude of the citizens. The procession was venerable, and the manner of it different from that of other nations. It reached to a place called Sapha; which name, translated in Greek, signifies a *prospect*, for you have thence a prospect both of Jerusalem and of the temple; and when the Phoenicians and the Chaldeans that followed him, thought they should have liberty to plunder the city, and torment the high-priest to death, which the king's displeasure fairly promised them, the very reverse of it happened; for Alexander, when he saw the multitude at a distance, in white garments, while the priests stood clothed with fine linen, and the high-priest in purple and scarlet clothing, with his mitre on his head having the golden plate on which the name of God was engraved, he approached by himself, and adored that name, and first saluted the high-priest. The Jews also did all together, with one voice, salute Alexander, and encompass him about: whereupon the kings of Syria and the rest were surprised at what Alexander had done, and supposed him to be disordered in his mind. However, Parmenio [Alexander's second-in-command] alone went up to him, and asked him how it came to pass, that when all others adored him, he should adore the high-priest of the Jews? To whom he replied, "I did not adore him, but that God who has honored him with that high-priesthood; for I saw this very person in a dream, in this very habit, when I was at Dios, in Macedonia, who, when I was considering with myself how I might obtain the dominion of Asia, exhorted me to make no delay, but boldly to pass over the sea thither, for that he would conduct my army, and would give me dominion over the Persians; whence it is, that having seen no other in that habit, and now seeing this person in it, and remembering my vision and the exhortation which I had in my dream, I believe that I bring this army under divine conduct, and shall therewith conquer Darius, and destroy the power of the Persians, and that all things will succeed according to what is in my own mind." And when he had said this to Parmenio, and had given the high-priest his right hand, the priests ran along by him, and he came into the city; and when he went up into the temple, he offered sacrifice to God, according to the high-priest's direction, and magnificently treated both the high-priest and the priests. And when the book of Daniel was showed him, wherein Daniel declared that one of the Greeks should destroy the empire of the Persians, he supposed that himself was the person intended; and as he was then glad, he dismissed the multitude for the present, but the next day he called them to him, and bade them ask what favors they pleased of him: whereupon the high-priest desired that they might enjoy the laws of their forefathers, and might pay no tribute on the seventh year. He granted all they desired: and when they entreated him that he would permit the Jews in Babylon and Media to enjoy their own laws also, he willingly promised to do hereafter what they desired: and when he said to the multitude, that if any of them would enlist themselves in his army on this condition, that they should continue under the laws of their forefathers, and live according to them, he was willing to take them with him, many were ready to accompany him in his wars.

B. The coming King and His deliverance.

1. (9) A lowly King comes into Jerusalem.

"Rejoice greatly, O daughter of Zion!
Shout, O daughter of Jerusalem!
Behold, your King is coming to you;
He *is* just and having salvation,
Lowly and riding on a donkey,
A colt, the foal of a donkey.

a. **Behold your King is coming to you…lowly and riding on a donkey**: This Messiah-King is **lowly**, but this wasn't indicated by the animal he rode. He doesn't ride the triumphant stallion of a conquering general, but the customary mount for royalty, coming in peace. This was quite a contrast to the conqueror Alexander the Great.

> i. "Brethren, *let us be lowly*. Did I hear one say, 'Well, I will try to be lowly'? You cannot do it in that way. We must not try to act the lowly part; we must be lowly, and then we shall naturally act in a humble manner. It is astonishing how much of pride there is in the most modest." (Spurgeon)

> ii. "How we condemn pride! We feel that it would be well if all were as humble as we are. We boast that we detest boasting. We flatter ourselves that we hate flattery. When we are told that we are singularly free from pride, we feel as proud as Lucifer himself at the consciousness that the compliment is right well deserved. We are so experienced, so solid, so discerning, so free from self-confidence, that we are the first to be caught in the net of self-satisfaction. Brethren, we must pray God to make us humble." (Spurgeon)

b. **A donkey, a colt, the foal of a donkey**: This seems to be a Hebrew expression of speech emphasizing that the animal is purebred – a truly magnificent, royal mount.

> i. "God had commanded the kings of Israel not to multiply *horses*. The kings who broke this command were miserable themselves, and scourgers to their people. Jesus came to *fulfill the law*. Had he in his title of *king* rode upon a *horse*, it would have been a *breach* of a positive command of God; therefore he rode upon an *ass*." (Clarke)

c. **Rejoice greatly…. Shout…. Behold, your King is coming**: This clearly prophesies what is known as the triumphal entry of Jesus (Matthew 21:5), when He presented Himself as the Messiah to Jerusalem and the people of Israel.

> i. Though the triumphal entry was a joyful celebration, a Roman spectator would wonder what was so triumphal about this entry. It didn't compare at all to the kind of parade Julius Caesar had when he came back to Rome from Gaul. Then there was a parade that lasted three days as he displayed all the captives and booty he brought back. In contrast to this, the procession of Jesus must have seemed pretty humble, and this showed that Jesus was a different kind of king.

2. (10) The strength and the authority of the Messiah's reign.

I will cut off the chariot from Ephraim
And the horse from Jerusalem;
The battle bow shall be cut off.
He shall speak peace to the nations;
His dominion *shall be* 'from sea to sea,
And from the River to the ends of the earth.'

> a. **The battle bow shall be cut off**: Zechariah 9:9 belongs to the first coming of Jesus, but Zechariah 9:10 is associated with the second coming of Jesus, when He comes in power and glory to reign over this earth for 1,000 years. In that day there will be enforced righteousness, and He will no longer allow war (Isaiah 2:4).
>
>> i. "Even though the Evangelists saw fulfillment of verse 9, they did not go on to quote verse 10, which may indicate that they were conscious of having only a partial fulfillment." (Baldwin)
>
> b. **His dominion shall be "from sea to sea, and from the River to the ends of the earth"**: When Jesus rules over this earth, His reign will be universal. The entire earth will be under His authority.
>
>> i. This speaks of the time many refer to as the *millennium*, the thousand-year reign of Jesus on this earth (Psalm 72, Isaiah 2:2-4, Isaiah 11:4-9, Jeremiah 23:5-6, Luke 1:32-33 and 19:12-27, Matthew 5:18).

3. (11-17) Judah's liberation and blessing.

"As for you also,
Because of the blood of your covenant,
I will set your prisoners free from the waterless pit.
Return to the stronghold,
You prisoners of hope.
Even today I declare
That I will restore double to you.
For I have bent Judah, My *bow,*
Fitted the bow with Ephraim,
And raised up your sons, O Zion,
Against your sons, O Greece,
And made you like the sword of a mighty man."

Then the LORD will be seen over them,
And His arrow will go forth like lightning.
The Lord GOD will blow the trumpet,
And go with whirlwinds from the south.
The LORD of hosts will defend them;
They shall devour and subdue with slingstones.

They shall drink *and* roar as if with wine;
They shall be filled *with blood* like basins,
Like the corners of the altar.
The LORD their God will save them in that day,
As the flock of His people.
For they *shall be like* the jewels of a crown,
Lifted like a banner over His land—
For how great is its goodness
And how great its beauty!
Grain shall make the young men thrive,
And new wine the young women.

> a. **Because of the blood of your covenant**: This probably describes God acting towards Israel in light of the blood of the covenant of Moses (Exodus 24:1-8). As Israel turns to God, He will turn to them and rescue them as if they were trapped in a dry cistern (**I will set your prisoners free from the waterless pit**).
>
> b. **Return to the stronghold, you prisoners of hope**: Because of His faithful promise, even the **prisoners** are **prisoners of hope**. They should receive encouragement from His promise and **return to the stronghold** – both in the sense of a military fortress and a spiritual fortress in the LORD Himself.
>
> c. **For I have bent Judah, My bow, fitted the bow with Ephraim, and raised up your sons, O Zion, against your sons, O Greece**: This was partially fulfilled in the days of the Maccabees, when God raised up Jews to fight against the successors of Alexander's Empire. Nevertheless, it seems that the ultimate fulfillment of this promise is yet to come.
>
> d. **The Lord GOD will blow the trumpet**: The idea is that the LORD Himself leads the battle. Both the Bible and the Koran have the idea of the *holy war* – which Islam calls *Jihad* – but there is a huge difference between the idea of the holy war in the Bible and in Islam. Jesus alone carries out the biblical holy war, and never His people. In Islam, the *Jihad* is the responsibility of every good Muslim.
>
>> i. Here, God makes it clear who does the fighting: **The LORD their God will save them in that day**. This is God's battle, not the battle of men.
>
> e. **Grain shall make the young men thrive, and new wine the young women**: As in other passages that speak of the millennium (Hosea 2:21-22, Joel 2:19) here **grain** and **new wine** are pictures of prosperity and blessing.

Zechariah 10 – A Promise to Gather Israel

A. The superiority of the Messiah's reign.

1. (1) The blessed nature of the Messiah's reign.

Ask the Lord for rain
In the time of the latter rain.
The Lord will make flashing clouds;
He will give them showers of rain,
Grass in the field for everyone.

> a. **Ask the Lord for rain in the time of the latter rain**: Ancient Israel had no irrigation system and relied on rain to water their crops. In a time of drought, nothing grew – so Israel relied on both the *former rain* (falling in autumn) and the **latter rain** (falling in spring).

> b. **He will give them showers of rain**: The Lord challenged His people saying, "Be bold enough to ask Me, and I will answer your prayer. I will provide what I alone can provide."

> c. **Grass in the field for everyone**: In man's ideas of equality, often everyone ends up equally poor. God's idea of equality means abundance for everyone.

2. (2-5) Only the people of the true God conquer in the end.

For the idols speak delusion;
The diviners envision lies,
And tell false dreams;
They comfort in vain.
Therefore *the people* wend their way like sheep;
They are in trouble because *there is* no shepherd.

"My anger is kindled against the shepherds,
And I will punish the goatherds.
For the Lord of hosts will visit His flock,
The house of Judah,

And will make them as His royal horse in the battle.
From him comes the cornerstone,
From him the tent peg,
From him the battle bow,
From him every ruler together.
They shall be like mighty men,
Who tread down *their enemies*
In the mire of the streets in the battle.
They shall fight because the LORD is with them,
And the riders on horses shall be put to shame.

    a. **For the idols speak delusion; the diviners envision lies**: The ancient Hebrew word for **idols** here is *teraphim*, meaning common household idols. **Diviners** consulted the spirits of idols to predict the future. God warns His people that there is no real help from either idols or their representatives (**they comfort in vain**).

    b. **They are in trouble because there is no shepherd**: The people had listened to false and deceptive leaders, and part of the reason was that there was a lack of godly leadership.

    c. **Will make them as His royal horse in the battle**: In mercy God would transform His people from a **flock** of sheep to a herd of war horses, ready for **battle**. All of them shall **be like mighty men** and defeat their enemies.

    d. **From him comes the cornerstone, from him the tent peg, from him the battle bow, from him every ruler together**: Though God was displeased with Israel's shepherds, He would raise up the perfect shepherd from Judah and for Judah.

        i. Jesus is the **cornerstone**: the foundation, measure, and standard (Isaiah 28:16, Psalm 118:22-23, Matthew 21:42, Acts 4:11, 1 Peter 2:4-5).

        ii. Jesus is the **tent peg**: holding all things securely (Isaiah 22:23-24).

        iii. Jesus is the **battle bow**: a strong fighter for good (Isaiah 63:1-4, Revelation 19:11-16).

        iv. Jesus is the leader over **every ruler** of His people (Revelation 19:16).

B. Israel gathered and strengthened.

1. (6-7) Israel strengthened.

"I will strengthen the house of Judah,
And I will save the house of Joseph.
I will bring them back,
Because I have mercy on them.

They shall be as though I had not cast them aside;
For I *am* the LORD their God,
And I will hear them.
***Those of* Ephraim shall be like a mighty man,**
And their heart shall rejoice as if with wine.
Yes, their children shall see *it* and be glad;
Their heart shall rejoice in the LORD.

> a. **I will strengthen the house of Judah**: The promise from the preceding passage is repeated more intensely. God will save and bless Israel and **have mercy on them**. This blessing would include *all* of the tribes of Israel, even **the house of Joseph** (those of the conquered northern kingdom).
>
>> i. God has strength for us also. Ephesians 6:10 tells us that we can draw on His resources for strength: *Finally, my brethren, be strong in the Lord and in the power of His might.*
>>
>> ii. The availability of God's strength means there will be opportunities for us to use it. "The Lord does not say, 'I will take you away from your labours,' but 'I will strengthen you, so that you will be able to perform, them.'" (Spurgeon)
>
> b. **Their children shall see it and be glad; their heart shall rejoice in the LORD**: The LORD will not only return strength to Israel, but also *joy*. Their sense of defeat and weakness will be replaced with gladness.

2. (8-12) Israel gathered into the land from across the earth.

I will whistle for them and gather them,
For I will redeem them;
And they shall increase as they once increased.
I will sow them among the peoples,
And they shall remember Me in far countries;
They shall live, together with their children,
And they shall return.
I will also bring them back from the land of Egypt,
And gather them from Assyria.
I will bring them into the land of Gilead and Lebanon,
Until no *more room* is found for them.
He shall pass through the sea with affliction,
And strike the waves of the sea:
All the depths of the River shall dry up.
Then the pride of Assyria shall be brought down,
And the scepter of Egypt shall depart.

"So I will strengthen them in the LORD,
And they shall walk up and down in His name,"
Says the LORD.

> a. **I will whistle for them and gather them**: The promise to **gather** Israel is repeated often in the prophecies concerning the new covenant (Deuteronomy 30:1-6, Jeremiah 23:1-8, Jeremiah 32:37-41, Ezekiel 11:16-20, Ezekiel 36:16-28). Though Israel was scattered to the nations, **they shall remember Me in far countries** and come back to the land.
>
>> i. In the 20th Century many Jewish people were gathered back to the land of Israel, and in 1948 Israel became a nation again – after more than 2,000 years of not being a nation. Does the 20th Century gathering of Israel fulfill this prophecy? It fulfills it in part, but only in part – because Israel will be gathered again in belief, not in rejection of the LORD and His Savior. The gathering began in unbelief but will end up in belief and trust in Jesus.
>
> b. **So I will strengthen them in the LORD, and they shall walk up and down in His name**: When God gathers Israel and defeats their enemies they shall walk in freedom and liberty again. It will be like a new exodus from Egypt, complete with exodus-like miracles (**He shall pass through the sea with affliction, and strike the waves of the sea: All the depths of the River shall dry up**).

Zechariah 11 – Thirty Pieces of Silver

A. Judgment coming on God's flock.

1. (1-3) Creation mourns because of coming judgment.

Open your doors, O Lebanon,
That fire may devour your cedars.
Wail, O cypress, for the cedar has fallen,
Because the mighty *trees* **are ruined.**
Wail, O oaks of Bashan,
For the thick forest has come down.
***There is* the sound of wailing shepherds!**
For their glory is in ruins.
***There is* the sound of roaring lions!**
For the pride of the Jordan is in ruins.

> a. **Open your doors, O Lebanon, that fire may devour your cedars**: This describes the coming of destructive armies of judgment from the north, through Lebanon. The **doors** of Lebanon are the mountain passes between Lebanon and Israel.
>
>> i. Boice comments on how this prophecy was fulfilled in the Roman campaign against Judea. "These verses might have described the Babylonian invasion if they had been written earlier; but that was past history by Zechariah's time. There is nothing in the history of the people that a comprehensive destruction of the land can refer to prior to the terrible destruction ordered by Vespasian and his successor Titus."
>
> b. **Wail, O cypress, for the cedar has fallen**: The cedar trees Illustrate Lebanon's strength. Once they fall the lesser forests of **cypress** and **oak** will also be destroyed, so they also **wail**.
>
> c. **Wailing shepherds.... roaring lions**: In addition to the trees, the **shepherds** and **lions** also mourn because of judgment on the land – coming because Israel has rejected their good shepherd.

2. (4-7) Zechariah acts out a prophecy of judgment.

Thus says the LORD my God, "Feed the flock for slaughter, whose owners slaughter them and feel no guilt; those who sell them say, 'Blessed be the LORD, for I am rich'; and their shepherds do not pity them. For I will no longer pity the inhabitants of the land," says the LORD. "But indeed I will give everyone into his neighbor's hand and into the hand of his king. They shall attack the land, and I will not deliver *them* from their hand."

So I fed the flock for slaughter, in particular the poor of the flock. I took for myself two staffs: the one I called Beauty, and the other I called Bonds; and I fed the flock.

a. **Feed the flock for slaughter**: Zechariah acted out this prophecy, feeding a literal flock of sheep that represented the people of God. As the shepherd, Zechariah represented the LORD who had appointed this flock for a season of judgment.

b. **I took for myself two staffs**: Zechariah's **two staffs** were named "**Beauty**" (*grace*) and "**Bonds**" (*unity*). The staff was a common tool for a shepherd (Psalm 23:4).

i. "*Favor* [**Beauty**] symbolizes the favored status of Israel as the chosen people of God. *Union* symbolizes the internal harmony of the people that was lost at the time of the siege of Jerusalem." (Boice)

3. (8-11) The covenant symbolically broken.

I dismissed the three shepherds in one month. My soul loathed them, and their soul also abhorred me. Then I said, "I will not feed you. Let what is dying die, and what is perishing perish. Let those that are left eat each other's flesh." And I took my staff, Beauty, and cut it in two, that I might break the covenant which I had made with all the peoples. So it was broken on that day. Thus the poor of the flock, who were watching me, knew that it *was* the word of the LORD.

a. **I dismissed the three shepherds in one month**: We know that Zechariah was acting prophetically, but it is hard to identify these **three shepherds** whom Zechariah hated, and who hated him.

i. "The best explanation is probably the oldest, which sees the three shepherds not as three individuals but as three classes of individuals, namely: the prophets, priests, and kings of Israel" (Boice). The offices of prophet, priest, and king were taken away from Israel after the Roman conquest of Judea and have never been restored – because they are now fulfilled in Jesus Christ.

b. **I will not feed you. Let what is dying die**: In bringing judgment by letting the *dying die*, God merely took away His hand of protection. At one time God had a **covenant** with **all the peoples**, preventing them from attacking His people Israel. When God decided to **break the covenant**, His people would be attacked.

c. **Let those who are left eat each other's flesh**: This really happened during the Roman siege of Jerusalem in A.D. 70

d. **The poor of the flock…knew that it was the word of the LORD**: These were the faithful remnant who knew that even these hard words were from God.

4. (12-14) The shepherd is paid with contempt.

Then I said to them, "If it is agreeable to you, give *me* my wages; and if not, refrain." So they weighed out for my wages thirty *pieces* of silver.

And the LORD said to me, "Throw it to the potter"–that princely price they set on me. So I took the thirty *pieces* of silver and threw them into the house of the LORD for the potter. Then I cut in two my other staff, Bonds, that I might break the brotherhood between Judah and Israel.

a. **Give me my wages**: Zechariah was "play-acting" this prophecy, employing himself as a shepherd over a flock. Now he asked his employer for his wages, and **they weighed out for my wages thirty pieces of silver**.

b. **That princely price they set on me**: Zechariah spoke sarcastically here. **Thirty pieces of silver** was not an insignificant amount, but it was the price of a slave (Exodus 21:32). It was the lowest they could pay, and it said that they regarded Zechariah as a slave.

i. This speaks prophetically of Jesus, who was contemptuously betrayed for **thirty pieces of silver** (Matthew 26:15 and 27:3) – the price of a slave.

ii. Matthew 27:9-10 says: *Then was fulfilled what was spoken by Jeremiah the prophet, saying, "And they took the thirty pieces of silver, the value of Him who was priced, whom they of the children of Israel priced, and gave them for the potter's field, as the LORD directed me."* This is a problem because clearly Zechariah records the passage mentioned in Matthew 27:9-10. There are generally three solutions offered for this problem:

- Some think it is an error but not by Matthew – an early copyist made a mistake. Perhaps Matthew wrote *Zechariah*, but an early copyist put *Jeremiah* instead.

- Some think that Jeremiah spoke this prophecy and Zechariah recorded it. This may be the word spoken by Jeremiah but *recorded* by Zechariah.
- Some think that Matthew refers to the *scroll* of Jeremiah, which included the book of Zechariah.

c. **Threw them into the house of the LORD for the potter**: Curiously, Zechariah said that the thirty pieces of silver were thrown **into the house of the LORD** but that they were also given to the **potter**. This is an exact fulfillment of what Judas did with his thirty pieces of silver (Matthew 27:3-10).

i. The money to betray Jesus – His purchase price – went to buy a potter's field (Matthew 27:7). A potter's field was a piece of useless land where the potter threw his broken, damaged, and rejected pots. Jesus really did purchase the potter's field – the place where broken, rejected, and useless people like us are scattered.

d. **Then I cut in two my other staff, Bonds, that I might break the brotherhood between Judah and Israel**: After the exchange of the thirty pieces of silver the staff of **Bonds** (unity) was broken. This was fulfilled when Israel was scattered by the Romans after their rejection of their Shepherd, Jesus.

B. A false shepherd to come.

1. (15-16) God will allow foolish shepherds to come to His people.

And the LORD said to me, "Next, take for yourself the implements of a foolish shepherd. For indeed I will raise up a shepherd in the land *who* will not care for those who are cut off, nor seek the young, nor heal those that are broken, nor feed those that still stand. But he will eat the flesh of the fat and tear their hooves in pieces.

a. **Take for yourself the implements of a foolish shepherd**: Now Zechariah play-acted as a **foolish shepherd** who did not care for the sheep the way that a shepherd should.

- The foolish shepherd **will not care for those who are cut off**, but a wise and godly shepherd will seek the lost.
- The foolish shepherd will not **seek the young**, but a wise and godly shepherd knows that **the young** need to come to the LORD as much as older people do.
- The foolish shepherd will not **heal those that are broken**, but a wise and godly shepherd looks for broken hearts and lives and mends them with God's love and word.

- The foolish shepherd will not **feed those that still stand**, but a wise and godly shepherd will faithfully feed the sheep.
- The foolish shepherd will **eat the flesh of the fat and tear their hooves in pieces**, but a wise and godly shepherd will lay down his life for the sheep (John 10:11).

b. **I will raise up a shepherd in the land**: This foolish shepherd was allowed and appointed by God as judgment because His people forsook the true shepherd. This was fulfilled in Israel's rejection of Jesus. They rejected the good shepherd (John 10:1-18) but received another shepherd (John 5:43).

i. We often assume all that people need is the right leader. Here we see that even the ultimate leader may be rejected, and a worthless leader chosen. Democracy's value is that it respects man's fallen nature and spreads out power – yet the majority *may be* very, very wrong and prefer a **foolish shepherd** instead of the good shepherd.

ii. The **foolish shepherd** embraced by Israel was partially fulfilled in their choice of Barabbas (Matthew 27:20-22) but will be ultimately fulfilled in their embrace of the Antichrist and their covenant with him (Daniel 9:27).

2. (17) Judgment on the worthless shepherd.

"Woe to the worthless shepherd,
Who leaves the flock!
A sword *shall be* against his arm
And against his right eye;
His arm shall completely wither,
And his right eye shall be totally blinded."

a. **Woe to the worthless shepherd**: Though God appointed the foolish shepherd in light of Israel's rejection of the good shepherd, it does not mean that God approves of the foolish shepherd. God will judge that **worthless shepherd** who injured His **flock**.

b. **A sword shall be against his arm and against his right eye**: The worthless shepherd feels the sword of God's judgment against **his arm** and **his right eye**. The **arm** expresses strength and the **eye** expresses intelligence, so this will be a harsh blow against the worthless shepherd.

i. Revelation 13:3 and 13:12-14 tell us the Antichrist will suffer a severe wound yet survive. This confirms that the **worthless shepherd** is ultimately fulfilled in the Antichrist.

Zechariah 12 – Mourning for the Pierced One

A. God defends Israel against her enemies.

1. (1-4) God supernaturally defends Israel against attack.

The burden of the word of the LORD against Israel. Thus says the LORD, who stretches out the heavens, lays the foundation of the earth, and forms the spirit of man within him: "Behold, I will make Jerusalem a cup of drunkenness to all the surrounding peoples, when they lay siege against Judah and Jerusalem. And it shall happen in that day that I will make Jerusalem a very heavy stone for all peoples; all who would heave it away will surely be cut in pieces, though all nations of the earth are gathered against it. In that day," says the LORD, "I will strike every horse with confusion, and its rider with madness; I will open My eyes on the house of Judah, and will strike every horse of the peoples with blindness."

> a. **Thus says the LORD, who stretches out the heavens**: The section begins with praise for God's creative power, reminding us that He is in control and completely able to accomplish what He predicts.
>
> b. **I will make Jerusalem a cup of drunkenness to all the surrounding peoples**: God says that in a coming day Jerusalem will intoxicate and stupefy the **surrounding peoples**. The control of the city of Jerusalem and its surrounding region has been hotly contested by rival empires, nations, peoples, and faiths for many centuries.
>
> > i. The interest nations and men have in Jerusalem has many motivations and causes, but God expresses a special interest in Jerusalem throughout the Scriptures. Jerusalem is the most named location in the Bible, mentioned more than 800 times. There is undeniably something special about Jerusalem to God and His plan of the ages.
> >
> > - God commanded men to pray for the peace of Jerusalem (Psalm 122:6).

- God chose Jerusalem as the place where He will set His name forever (2 Chronicles 6:6; 33:7; Psalms 46:4; 48:1-8; 87:3)
- God promised to bless and protect Jerusalem (Psalm 132:13–14).
- God chose Jerusalem as the place where Jesus Christ would suffer, die, be buried, rise from the dead, and ascend to heaven.

c. **I will make Jerusalem a very heavy stone for all peoples**: If Jerusalem will be a **cup of drunkenness to all the surrounding peoples**, it will be a **heavy stone** – a burden – **for all peoples**, presenting a problem that cannot be solved (**all who would heave it away will surely be cut in pieces**).

   i. "Consider how remarkable even this one prophecy is. Who could have imagined when the Old Testament was written that all the nations of the world would be involved in deciding the fate of Israel? And this involvement of all nations in dividing Israel has occurred exactly as prophesied and is still in the process of being implemented." (Hunt)

d. **I will open My eyes on the house of Judah, and will strike every horse of the peoples with blindness**: Though the nations come against Jerusalem with fury, God would protect her. This will find its ultimate fulfillment in the last battle at the end of the age, but we may also earlier fulfillments.

2. (5-9) God supernaturally empowers His people.

"And the governors of Judah shall say in their heart, 'The inhabitants of Jerusalem *are* my strength in the Lord of hosts, their God.' In that day I will make the governors of Judah like a firepan in the woodpile, and like a fiery torch in the sheaves; they shall devour all the surrounding peoples on the right hand and on the left, but Jerusalem shall be inhabited again in her own place—Jerusalem.

"The Lord will save the tents of Judah first, so that the glory of the house of David and the glory of the inhabitants of Jerusalem shall not become greater than that of Judah. In that day the Lord will defend the inhabitants of Jerusalem; the one who is feeble among them in that day shall be like David, and the house of David *shall be* like God, like the Angel of the Lord before them. It shall be in that day *that* I will seek to destroy all the nations that come against Jerusalem.

   a. **I will make the governors of Judah like a firepan in the woodpile**: In that day God will deliver Israel not only through His direct work, but also through blessing and empowering both the **governors** and **inhabitants** of Jerusalem. They will be supernaturally empowered by God to defend the city.

b. **In that day the LORD will defend the inhabitants of Jerusalem; the one who is feeble among them in that day shall be like David**: King David was renowned for his fighting ability, courage, and success. God promised a day when the *weakest* in Jerusalem will be as mighty as David – and the leaders could only be compared in might to **God**!

B. God gives Israel a spirit of humble repentance.

1. (10) Mourning for the pierced One.

"And I will pour on the house of David and on the inhabitants of Jerusalem the Spirit of grace and supplication; then they will look on Me whom they pierced. Yes, they will mourn for Him as one mourns for *his* only *son*, and grieve for Him as one grieves for a firstborn.

  a. **And I will pour on the house of David and on the inhabitants of Jerusalem the Spirit of grace and supplication**: Part of this great outpouring of strength and might to defend Jerusalem will be an outpouring of the **Spirit** – but of **grace and supplication**. God will move among Israel and bring saving grace and repentant prayer.

  b. **Then they will look on Me whom they pierced. Yes, they will mourn for Him as one mourns for his only son**: As Jerusalem is supernaturally defended and the Spirit is poured out on the nation, *they will turn to Jesus*, the **pierced** One. His head was **pierced** with thorns, His hands and feet were **pierced** with nails, and a spear **pierced** His side.

  i. **They will look**: They will turn away from their trust in the foolish, worthless shepherd and turn their focus on the good shepherd. When we see Jesus crucified – understanding why He went to the cross and what He accomplished there – we are drawn to Him in humble repentance (John 12:32).

  ii. They will look on Him **whom they pierced**. They will realize that **they** did it and that they bear responsibility – not sole responsibility, but responsibility nonetheless – for the crucifixion of their Savior.

  iii. **They will mourn**: The Jewish people will turn to Jesus in repentance, mourning their past rejection of Him. The mourning will be deep, as if for an **only son**, the **firstborn**. **Firstborn** was synonymous with the most beloved.

  iv. This will fulfill the amazing promise of Romans 11:26 (*And so all Israel will be saved*) and many other passages that tell us that before the physical return of Jesus to this earth, the Jewish people – as a whole – will welcome Him as their Lord and Savior. The whole context of

Zechariah 12 puts this radical conversion in the setting of miraculous deliverance from an attack from the nations.

c. **They will look…. they will mourn**: Here we see the pattern for coming to Jesus and true repentance. *First*, we look to Jesus, *then* we mourn for our sins. *Looking to Jesus must come first.*

> i. "A great mistake is very common among all classes of men – it is currently believed that we are first of all to mourn for our sins, and then to look by faith to our Lord Jesus Christ. Most persons who have any concern about their souls, but are not as yet enlightened by the Spirit of God, think that there is a degree of tenderness of conscience, and of hatred of sin, which they are to obtain somehow or other, and then they will be permitted and authorised to look to Jesus Christ. Now you will perceive that this is not according to the Scripture, for, according to the text before us men first look upon him whom they have pierced, and then, but not till then, they mourn for their sin." (Spurgeon)

> ii. "It is a beautiful remark of an old divine, that eyes are made for two things at least; first, to look with, and next, to weep with. The eye which looks to the pierced One is the eye which weeps for him." (Spurgeon)

d. **They will look on Me**: Comparing Zechariah 12:10 with Zechariah 12:1 and 12:4 (*Thus says the* Lord…. *says the* Lord) makes it clear that the **Me** they look upon is the Lord God – Yahweh – Himself. This is astounding and wonderful evidence that Jesus the **pierced** One is God, and that Yahweh is the triune God.

> i. Simply said, the Father sends the Spirit so that men will look upon the Son.

2. (11-14) The great mourning of repentance.

In that day there shall be a great mourning in Jerusalem, like the mourning at Hadad Rimmon in the plain of Megiddo. And the land shall mourn, every family by itself: the family of the house of David by itself, and their wives by themselves; the family of the house of Nathan by itself, and their wives by themselves; the family of the house of Levi by itself, and their wives by themselves; the family of Shimei by itself, and their wives by themselves; all the families that remain, every family by itself, and their wives by themselves.

a. **A great mourning in Jerusalem**: The repentance that comes to Israel in that day will be like a **great mourning**, the ultimate fulfillment of the

Day of Atonement, the day of national mourning over their greatest sin – rejecting Jesus.

b. **Like the mourning at Hadad Rimmon**: This refers to the mourning over King Josiah's death (2 Kings 23:29 and 2 Chronicles 35:20-25). He was such a godly king that the whole nation wept bitterly at his death.

c. **And the land shall mourn, every family by itself**: This indicates there will be both great *individual* repentance and great *corporate* repentance. It seems fantastic to us that Israel as a whole would turn to Jesus and repent of their sin of rejecting their Savior – it is so amazing that we would not believe it unless the Bible so clearly taught it.

> i. "We know of a surety, because God has said it, that the Jews will be restored to their own land, and that they shall inherit the goodly country which the Lord has given unto their fathers by a covenant of salt for ever; but, better still, they shall be converted to the faith of our Lord Jesus Christ, and shall see in him the house of David restored to the throne of Israel." (Spurgeon)

Zechariah 13 – The Nation Purified

A. The purification of the people.

1. (1) A fountain to cleanse sin.

"In that day a fountain shall be opened for the house of David and for the inhabitants of Jerusalem, for sin and for uncleanness."

a. **In that day**: Zechariah 12 ended with Israel's return to the LORD through the once rejected but now embraced Messiah. Flowing from their embrace of the Messiah, they will then enjoy **a fountain** of cleansing **for sin and for uncleanness**. The cleansing comes after their mourning for the One whom they have pierced.

i. **Shall be opened**: "The fountain shall be not simply opened, but shall remain open." (Pusey)

ii. "The idea of God being a fountain to His people is found frequently in the Old Testament, but Zechariah's treatment is possibly the richest of all." (Boice)

iii. The idea of the sin-cleansing fountain has also been a part of famous hymns:

There is a fountain filled with blood,
Drawn from Immanuel's veins;
And sinners, plunged beneath that flood,
Lose all their guilty stains.
(William Cowper)

Foul, I to the Fountain fly;
Wash me, Saviour, or I die.
Rock of Ages, cleft for me,
Let me hide myself in thee.
(Augustus Toplady)

iv. "According to the verse before us this provision is inexhaustible. There is a *fountain* opened; not a cistern nor a reservoir, but a fountain. A fountain continues still to bubble up, and is as full after fifty years as at the first; and even so the provision and the mercy of God for the forgiveness and the justification of our souls continually flows and overflows." (Spurgeon)

v. "The means by which sin and sinfulness can be put away are at this moment accessible to the sons of men. The atonement is not a fountain hid and concealed, and closed and barred and bolted, it is a fountain open." (Spurgeon)

b. **For sin and for uncleanness**: The only thing that can cleanse **sin and uncleanness** is God's **fountain**. It is His supply, and nothing else can cleanse. Our own works at reform or restitution can't cleanse us; our past, present, or promised works can't cleanse – only His **fountain**.

i. "Sin and uncleanness must be put away. They cannot be excused, condoned, or compromised with. The foundations of the throne of God are righteousness and justice." (Morgan)

2. (2-6) Cleansing from idolatry and false prophets.

"It shall be in that day," says the LORD of hosts, *"that* I will cut off the names of the idols from the land, and they shall no longer be remembered. I will also cause the prophets and the unclean spirit to depart from the land. It shall come to pass *that* if anyone still prophesies, then his father and mother who begot him will say to him, 'You shall not live, because you have spoken lies in the name of the LORD.' And his father and mother who begot him shall thrust him through when he prophesies.

"And it shall be in that day *that* every prophet will be ashamed of his vision when he prophesies; they will not wear a robe of coarse hair to deceive. But he will say, 'I *am* no prophet, I *am* a farmer; for a man taught me to keep cattle from my youth.' And *one* will say to him, 'What are these wounds between your arms?' Then he will answer, *'Those* with which I was wounded in the house of my friends.'

a. **I will cut off the names of the idols.... I will also cause the prophets and the unclean spirit to depart from the land**: Idolatry and false prophecy were the two main ways Israel was led astray from God. God would not only provide a fountain to cleanse, but He also promised to cut off the source of uncleanness – in this case, idolatry and false prophecy.

      i. The gaudy and ornate shrines that supposedly mark holy sites in Israel today are evidence that idolatry is still alive and well in the Holy Land. God promised to cleanse the land from such idolatry completely.

      ii. **They shall no longer be remembered**: God promises ultimately to take away even the *memory* of our sin.

b. **His father and mother who begot him shall thrust him through when he prophesies**: Zechariah prophesied a coming day when public opinion would not tolerate false prophets. There would be such a commitment to the LORD and His truth that even the family of a false prophet would condemn the false prophet.

c. **Every prophet will be ashamed of his vision when he prophesies**: Those who had been false messengers of God would be **ashamed** of their message. They will put away the clothing of the prophets (**a robe of coarse hair**) and earn an honest living.

      i. "Those who posed as prophets will so fear exposure that they will deny ever having made such a claim." (Baldwin)

      ii. This does not say that true prophets will be silent but only those who **deceive** and have **spoken lies in the name of the LORD**.

d. **Those with which I was wounded in the house of my friends**: The man accused of being a false prophet insists the scars on his body are not the self-inflicted wounds often associated with false prophets, but merely the result of a brawl in his friend's house.

      i. The unlikely, ironic explanation shows just how desperately people will avoid being identified with false prophets in this coming day Zechariah speaks of.

      ii. It wasn't unusual for false prophets to wound or mutilate themselves in the service of idols (1 Kings 18:28, Jeremiah 48:37).

e. **I was wounded in the house of my friends**: Some take this as another Messianic prophecy in Zechariah, because Jesus was clearly **wounded** by those who should have been His **friends**. Nevertheless, the context and the original Hebrew argue against this referring to Jesus and His wounds.

      i. The translation from the King James Version makes it seem that this refers to Jesus: *What are these wounds in thine hands?* But the Hebrew is more literally *between your hands*, that is on the body, whether the chest or the back.

      ii. "Some apply this to Christ, because Zechariah has mentioned wounds on the hands; but this is very puerile; for it is quite evident that he speaks here of false teachers, who had for a time falsely pretended God's name." (Calvin)

iii. "I do not think that these words are spoken at all concerning Jesus Christ. I have heard them quoted this way; but I cannot hear such an application of them without horror." (Clarke)

B. The Shepherd struck; the nation scattered.

1. (7) Striking the Man who is the Companion of the LORD.

"Awake, O sword, against My Shepherd,
Against the Man who is My Companion,"
Says the LORD of hosts.
"Strike the Shepherd,
And the sheep will be scattered;
Then I will turn My hand against the little ones.

a. **Against My Shepherd**: In the context, and especially in light of the quotation of this passage in Matthew 26:31, we understand that the **Shepherd** is Jesus the Messiah – and it is God the Father Himself who calls for the **Shepherd** to be struck.

i. Zechariah relates a thought also stated in Isaiah 53:10: *Yet it pleased the LORD to bruise Him; He has put Him to grief.* The prophets Isaiah and Zechariah gloriously and emphatically, state that the LORD ordained the Servant of the LORD's suffering. This was *God's doing!* He gave the command to **strike the Shepherd**. Jesus was no victim of circumstance or at the mercy of political or military power. It was the planned, ordained work of the LORD God, prophesied by Isaiah hundreds of years before it happened. This was *God's victory*, not Satan's or man's triumph.

ii. As Paul says in 2 Corinthians 5:19, *God was in Christ reconciling the world to Himself.* The Father and the Son worked together at the cross. Though Jesus was *treated* as if He were an enemy of God, He was not. Even as Jesus was punished as if He were a sinner, He was performing the most holy service to God the Father ever offered.

b. **The Man who is My Companion**: The ancient Hebrew word for **My Companion** is used in Leviticus 6:2 and 18:20 to mean a "near neighbor." According to Baldwin, this describes someone who is more than a *friend* of the LORD; this **Shepherd** "dwells side by side with the Lord, His equal."

i. "God would not apply this epithet to any godly or ungodly man whom he might have appointed shepherd over a nation. The idea of nearest one (or fellow) involves not only similarity in vocation, but community of physical or spiritual descent, according to which he whom God calls his neighbor cannot be a mere man, but can only be one who participates in the divine nature, or is essentially divine." (Keil)

c. **Strike the Shepherd, and the sheep will be scattered**: Jesus quoted this phrase from Zechariah 13:7 in Matthew 26:31 in reference to the scattering of His disciples during His arrest and suffering. There is also a sense in which the disciples were a type of Israel as a whole being scattered.

2. (8-9) Israel scattered, smitten, refined, and saved.

And it shall come to pass in all the land,"
Says the LORD,
"*That* two-thirds in it shall be cut off *and* die,
But *one*-third shall be left in it:
I will bring the *one*-third through the fire,
Will refine them as silver is refined,
And test them as gold is tested.
They will call on My name,
And I will answer them.
I will say, 'This *is* My people';
And each one will say, 'The LORD *is* my God.'"

a. **I will bring the one-third through the fire**: After the dispersion of Israel, there will come a time of devastation and purification through fiery trials. Two-thirds will be destroyed and the remaining third will be put **through the fire** but preserved.

i. This seems to suggest that only one-third of the Jewish people will survive the great tribulation. If this is the case, no wonder these years are called *the time of Jacob's trouble* (Jeremiah 30:7), and why Jesus said the great tribulation will be the most horrific time in human history (Matthew 24:21).

b. **They will call on My name, and I will answer them**: This prophetically refers to the Jewish people who survive the great tribulation, come to salvation in the second half of that final period and welcome Jesus in the name of the LORD. This group – which includes the 144,000 of Revelation 7 and 14 but is not limited to that number – will make up the core of a restored Israel as Jesus establishes His millennial rule over the earth.

Zechariah 14 – Holiness to the LORD

A. Israel attacked but defended by the returning Messiah.

1. (1-2) Jerusalem under siege from the nations.

Behold, the day of the LORD is coming,
And your spoil will be divided in your midst.
For I will gather all the nations to battle against Jerusalem;
The city shall be taken,
The houses rifled,
And the women ravished.
Half of the city shall go into captivity,
But the remnant of the people shall not be cut off from the city.

> a. **I will gather all the nations to battle against Jerusalem**: Zechariah seems to have the very end times in view, when Jerusalem will be surrounded and attacked by some type of international force. When the Romans came against Jerusalem in A.D. 70 they came with a multinational army and brought terrible destruction on the city and its people. Yet there was none of the deliverance that Zechariah will describe in the following verses, so it is difficult to say that this was fulfilled in the Roman attack upon Jerusalem in A.D. 70.

> b. **Half the city shall go into captivity**: This attack against Jerusalem will be severe, but the city itself will not be overthrown (**the remnant of the people shall not be cut off from the city**).

2. (3-5) The Messiah intervenes for His people.

Then the LORD will go forth
And fight against those nations,
As He fights in the day of battle.
And in that day His feet will stand on the Mount of Olives,
Which faces Jerusalem on the east.
And the Mount of Olives shall be split in two,

From east to west,
Making a very large valley;
Half of the mountain shall move toward the north
And half of it toward the south.

Then you shall flee *through* My mountain valley,
For the mountain valley shall reach to Azal.
Yes, you shall flee
As you fled from the earthquake
In the days of Uzziah king of Judah.

Thus the LORD my God will come,
And all the saints with You.

> a. **Then the LORD will go forth and fight**: Just when it seems that all hope will be gone for Jerusalem and the people of Israel, then the LORD will fight for His people.
>
> > i. "God is said to *go forth* when he manifests his power by delivering his people and punishing their enemies." (Deane)
>
> b. **His feet will stand on the Mount of Olives.... And the Mount of Olives shall be split in two, from east to west**: This speaks of the LORD – Jesus, as God the Son – materially returning to a material earth and setting His feet on **the Mount of Olives**. At that time a great split will cut the Mount of Olives in two, and the persecuted people of Jerusalem will **flee through** the valley made by the split.
>
> c. **Thus the LORD my God will come, and all the saints with You**: Jesus will touch His feet on the Mount of Olives when He returns in glory with **all the saints**, the *armies of heaven* described in Revelation 19:14.
>
> > i. This was the type of arrival the Jews in Jesus' day hoped for. Indeed, when the Roman armies surrounded Jerusalem in A.D. 70 a mistaken assurance from prophecies like this made the Jews utterly confident that the Messiah would return from heaven and wipe out the Roman armies surrounding Jerusalem. They could not see that the Messiah must first be rejected, and the nation brought to repentance as Zechariah mentioned in 11:12-13 and 12:10.

B. The kingdom of the Messiah.

1. (6-11) The Messiah's rule changes the earth.

It shall come to pass in that day
That there will be no light;
The lights will diminish.
It shall be one day

Which is known to the LORD—
Neither day nor night.
But at evening time it shall happen
That it will be light.

And in that day it shall be
That living waters shall flow from Jerusalem,
Half of them toward the eastern sea
And half of them toward the western sea;
In both summer and winter it shall occur.
And the LORD shall be King over all the earth.
In that day it shall be—
"The LORD *is* one,"
And His name one.

All the land shall be turned into a plain from Geba to Rimmon south of Jerusalem. *Jerusalem* shall be raised up and inhabited in her place from Benjamin's Gate to the place of the First Gate and the Corner Gate, and *from* the Tower of Hananel to the king's winepresses.

The people shall dwell in it;
And no longer shall there be utter destruction,
But Jerusalem shall be safely inhabited.

a. **At evening time it shall happen that it will be light**: Now Zechariah looked forward to the glory of Jerusalem in the Messiah's kingdom. The lights we guide our lives by **will diminish**, but God will establish His own light.

b. **Living waters shall flow from Jerusalem**: Jerusalem will no longer be a dry city, but a glorious river will flow from the city and branch off both east and west, and it will be a never-ending flow (**in both summer and winter it shall occur**).

i. All over the world people want to know what will happen to Jerusalem. Zechariah knows the answer – God will gloriously save and restore Jerusalem, making it the capital city of the millennial earth.

ii. Ezekiel 47 records a vision that may describe this scene. Ezekiel saw a river flowing from the throne of God and down to the Dead Sea, bringing life and vitality everywhere.

c. **All the land shall be turned into a plain from Geba to Rimmon south of Jerusalem**: Since the mountains around Jerusalem would no longer be needed as a defense, they could be flattened into a plain.

d. **Jerusalem shall be safely inhabited**: This will be the first time in a long time that Jerusalem will be a safe place to live.

2. (12-15) Enemies are forever plagued.

And this shall be the plague with which the LORD will strike all the people who fought against Jerusalem:

**Their flesh shall dissolve while they stand on their feet,
Their eyes shall dissolve in their sockets,
And their tongues shall dissolve in their mouths.**

It shall come to pass in that day
That **a great panic from the LORD will be among them.
Everyone will seize the hand of his neighbor,
And raise his hand against his neighbor's hand;
Judah also will fight at Jerusalem.
And the wealth of all the surrounding nations
Shall be gathered together:
Gold, silver, and apparel in great abundance.**

**Such also shall be the plague
On the horse** *and* **the mule,
On the camel and the donkey,
And on all the cattle that will be in those camps.
So** *shall* **this plague** *be.*

> a. **Their flesh shall dissolve while they stand on their feet**: In the glorious deliverance the Messiah brings, the enemies of God and His people will be destroyed by plague, mutual slaughter, and by the sword of Judah (**Judah also will fight at Jerusalem**).
>
>> i. The description of flesh dissolving makes some think that Zechariah is describing the effects of a neutron or nuclear bomb.
>
> b. **The wealth of all the surrounding nations shall be gathered together**: In the glorious deliverance the Messiah brings, Jerusalem will become a wealthy and influential city again.

3. (16-19) All the nations come to Jerusalem to worship the LORD.

And it shall come to pass *that* **everyone who is left of all the nations which came against Jerusalem shall go up from year to year to worship the King, the LORD of hosts, and to keep the Feast of Tabernacles. And it shall be** *that* **whichever of the families of the earth do not come up to Jerusalem to worship the King, the LORD of hosts, on them there will be no rain. If the family of Egypt will not come up and enter in, they** *shall have* **no** *rain***; they shall receive the plague with which the LORD strikes the nations who do not come up to keep the Feast of Tabernacles. This**

shall be the punishment of Egypt and the punishment of all the nations that do not come up to keep the Feast of Tabernacles.

> a. **Shall go up from year to year to worship the King**: Instead of coming to Jerusalem for battle, now the nations come to honor God and to remember His faithfulness to Israel in the wilderness by keeping the **Feast of Tabernacles**.
>
>> i. Jesus told us to go to the ends of the earth with the gospel but in the millennium the earth will come to Jerusalem to worship and honor God.
>
> b. **Whichever of the families of the earth do not come up to Jerusalem… on them there will be no rain**: God won't *make* people worship Him during the millennium, but the advantages of worshipping and honoring God will be more evident than ever.
>
> c. **If the family of Egypt will not come up and enter in, they shall have no rain**: Egypt is specifically mentioned because they were a nation not especially dependent on rain, yet they too would be punished if they were disobedient.

4. (20-21) The common is made holy.

In that day "HOLINESS TO THE LORD" shall be *engraved* on the bells of the horses. The pots in the Lord's house shall be like the bowls before the altar. Yes, every pot in Jerusalem and Judah shall be holiness to the LORD of hosts. Everyone who sacrifices shall come and take them and cook in them. In that day there shall no longer be a Canaanite in the house of the LORD of hosts.

> a. **In that day "HOLINESS TO THE LORD" shall be engraved on the bells of the horses**: This was the great inscription on the metal band around the high priest's headpiece (Exodus 28:36). In the glory of the Messiah's kingdom horses won't be needed for war any longer – then even they can wear the emblems of **HOLINESS TO THE LORD**.
>
> b. **The pots in the LORD's house**: These were the cooking utensils used by worshipers to cook the sacrificial meat intended for them from the peace offerings. The **bowls before the altar** were used to gather and sprinkle sacrificial blood on the altar. This shows that animal sacrifice will continue in the millennium, but *not as atonement for sin* – which was perfectly satisfied by the atoning work of Jesus. Sacrifice in the millennium will look back to the perfect work of Jesus.
>
> c. **Every pot in Jerusalem and Judah shall be holiness to the LORD of hosts**: In the glory of the Messiah's kingdom, what was previously common is made holy; the holy is made holier and the irreclaimably profane is

forever shut out. At the end of it all, there is no longer any distinction between the holy and the profane. All is set apart to God and His purposes.

i. "The point is that the people and the city will be so holy that even these insignificant things will be fully dedicated to the Lord." (Boice)

ii. There is a right way and a wrong way to eliminate the line between the holy and the profane: you can make everything *holy* (set apart to the LORD), or you can make everything *profane* (set apart to sin and self). Zechariah ends his prophecy making it clear that God's way is to make everything that was once common or profane *holy* instead.

Malachi 1 – "I Have Loved You"

A. God's love for a rebellious Israel.

1. (1-2a) God declares His love for Israel through the prophet Malachi.

The burden of the word of the LORD to Israel by Malachi.

"I have loved you," says the LORD.

    a. **To Israel by Malachi**: Malachi spoke to the exiles some 100 years after their initial return, after the days of Zechariah and Haggai. Malachi served God either at the time of Nehemiah or immediately afterwards.

        i. We know this because in Malachi's day the temple was already rebuilt (Malachi 1:13, 3:10).

        ii. We know this because the Jews were under a civil ruler (the *governor* of Malachi 1:8), and Nehemiah was the last civil ruler over Jerusalem.

        iii. We know this because the sins that Malachi condemned were the same sins Nehemiah spoke against.

- The priesthood was defiled (Nehemiah 13:29, Malachi 1:6-2:9).
- Marriage was corrupt in Israel (Nehemiah 13:23-25, Malachi 2:14-15).
- The tithe that should have gone to the Levites was kept from them (Nehemiah 13:10-11, Malachi 3:8-12).

        iv. By now, the temple was rebuilt, sacrifice and feasts had resumed but the dramatic promises of the prophets like Haggai and Zechariah were still far from fulfillment. This left the nation discouraged and disappointed in what they thought were unfulfilled promises. This led them towards a low regard for God. Israel needed an assurance of God's love and a challenge to their disobedience.

    b. **"I have loved you," says the LORD**: Malachi would bring a lot of specific correction for Israel, but before God corrected them, He assured them of

His love. This set a foundation for their obedience because if they loved Him, they would keep His commandments (as in John 14:15).

> i. Morgan translates this as "'I have loved you, I do love you, I will love you,' says the Lord."

2. (2b-5) Their first question: How has God demonstrated His love to Israel?

> "Yet you say, 'In what way have You loved us?'
> *Was* not Esau Jacob's brother?"
> Says the LORD.
> "Yet Jacob I have loved;
> But Esau I have hated,
> And laid waste his mountains and his heritage
> For the jackals of the wilderness."
>
> Even though Edom has said,
> "We have been impoverished,
> But we will return and build the desolate places,"
> Thus says the LORD of hosts:
> "They may build, but I will throw down;
> They shall be called the Territory of Wickedness,
> And the people against whom the LORD will have indignation forever.
> Your eyes shall see,
> And you shall say,
> 'The LORD is magnified beyond the border of Israel.'

> a. **In what way have You loved us?** This is the kind of question rarely spoken, but often kept in the heart. It asks, "God, if you really love me, then why are things the way they are?"

> > i. The prophecy of Malachi is built around seven questions the people asked God. These questions revealed their doubting, discouraged, sinful hearts.
> >
> > - *In what way have You loved us?* (Malachi 1:2)
> > - *In what way have we despised Your name?* (Malachi 1:6)
> > - *In what way have we defiled You?* (Malachi 1:7)
> > - *In what way have we wearied Him?* (Malachi 2:17)
> > - *In what way shall we return?* (Malachi 3:7)
> > - *In what way have we robbed You?* (Malachi 3:8)
> > - In *what way have we spoken against You?* (Malachi 3:13)

b. **Yet Jacob I have loved; but Esau I have hated**: God asked Israel to find assurance in His election, His choice of them. He wanted them to understand that they were chosen and remained His chosen and favored people. When the people of Israel compared themselves to their neighbors the Edomites (the descendants of **Esau**), they saw that God chose to preserve Israel and He punished the Edomites.

  i. Obadiah promised judgment against the land and people of Edom. Apparently, by Malachi's time it had happened, and God's choice of Israel assured His love for them.

  ii. Understanding our election can bring a wonderful assurance of God's love. It means that God chose us before we existed and that the reasons for His choosing and loving us are based on Him, not on us. Knowing God chose us gives us a sense of boldness and confidence in our walk with Him.

  iii. Understanding our election gives assurance of love but the greatest demonstration of His love is found in the finished work of Jesus: *But God demonstrates His own love toward us, in that while we were still sinners, Christ died for us.* (Romans 5:8)

c. **Jacob I have loved; but Esau I have hated**: The choice of Jacob over Esau is a strong and classic example of God's election. God chose Jacob instead of Esau to carry the blessing promised to their grandfather Abraham. In some ways, Esau was a more likely candidate because though Jacob and Esau were twins, Esau was born first. Nevertheless, Jacob was chosen, and chosen before he and Esau were ever born (Genesis 25:23).

d. **Jacob I have loved; but Esau I have hated**: God did not hate Esau in the sense of cursing him or striking out against him. Indeed, Esau was a blessed man (Genesis 33:9, 36:1-43). Yet when God *chose* Jacob, He left Esau *unchosen* in regard to receiving the blessing given to Abraham.

  i. In his commentary on Romans (where Paul quoted this Malachi passage in Romans 9:13) Leon Morris cited examples where *hate* clearly seems to mean something like "loved less" (Genesis 29:31-33, Deuteronomy 21:15, Matthew 6:24, Luke 14:26, John 12:25). Yet he agreed with Calvin's idea that the real thought here is much more like "accepted" and "rejected" rather than our understanding of the terms "loved" and "hated."

  ii. We should remember the reason why election is brought up here: not to exclude, but to comfort and reassure. "A woman once said to Mr. Spurgeon, 'I cannot understand why God should say that He hated Esau.' 'That,' Spurgeon replied, 'is not my difficulty, madam. My trouble is to understand how God could love Jacob.'" (Newell)

iii. Malachi *isn't* teaching double predestination. "Malachi is not speaking of the predestination of the one brother and reprobation of the other; he is contrasting the histories of the two peoples represented by them.... Both nations sinned; both are punished; but Israel by God's free mercy was forgiven and restored, while Edom was left in the misery which it had brought upon itself by its own iniquity." (Deane)

e. **Jacob I have loved; but Esau I have hated**: Our greatest error in considering God's election is to think that God chooses for arbitrary reasons, as if He made choices in a random way. We may not understand God's reasons for choosing and they may be reasons He alone knows, but God's choices are not crazy, without reason, or capricious. They make perfect sense knowing everything God knows and seeing everything God sees.

i. Some consider God's election as *conditional*, in the sense that it is based upon foreknowledge. Others consider God's election *unconditional*, based on God's sovereign choice. Here, it seems that the election of Jacob was *unconditional*. Though God knew what sort of men Jacob and Esau would become His election was not based on that.

ii. One might say, "I don't believe in Jesus; therefore, I must not be chosen." That is fine, but then that person must not blame God at all for not choosing them if they refuse to choose Him.

f. **And laid waste his mountains and his heritage for the jackals of the wilderness**: The idea of God's preference for **Jacob** over **Esau** also extended to their descendants. The nation descended from Jacob (Israel) was conquered by the Babylonian Empire, and so was the nation descended from Esau (Edom). Yet God restored Israel from exile and at this point Edom had not been restored. God chose to show greater favor to Jacob and his descendants.

g. **They may build, but I will throw down**: God promised that Edom would be permanently ruined and that their status as "unchosen" would not change. As a reflection of God's steadfast commitment to Israel, this was a comfort to God's people – once He chose Israel they stayed chosen, and God would not forsake them and choose another.

B. Sacrifices dishonoring to God are exposed and condemned.

1. (6-8) Their second and third questions: How have we despised the LORD? How have we defiled His ministry?

"A son honors *his* father,
And a servant *his* master.
If then I am the Father,
Where *is* My honor?
And if I *am* a Master,
Where *is* My reverence?
Says the LORD of hosts
To you priests who despise My name.
Yet you say, 'In what way have we despised Your name?'

You offer defiled food on My altar.
But say,
'In what way have we defiled You?'
By saying,
'The table of the LORD is contemptible.'
And when you offer the blind as a sacrifice,
Is it not evil?
And when you offer the lame and sick,
Is it not evil?
Offer it then to your governor!
Would he be pleased with you?
Would he accept you favorably?"
Says the LORD of hosts.

a. **Where is My honor?** Through Malachi, God asked the priests of Israel why they showed so little respect and honor to Him in their sacrifices. They called God **Father**, they called Him **Master**, yet they did not honor Him and show Him reverence with their sacrifices.

b. **To you priests who despise My name**: The priests of Israel brought the sacrifices and it was their duty to uphold the honor and dignity of the sacrificial system. Yet they offered **defiled food** to God and offered animals that were **blind**, **lame**, or **sick**.

i. Passages such as Leviticus 22:20-23 and Deuteronomy 15:21 clearly prohibited offering blemished sacrifices.

c. **In what way have we despised Your name?** The priests weren't even aware that they **despised** God with their actions. This meant that it came by degrees; they probably did not know the extent of their offense and simply carried on as before. They slowly slid into despising God's name.

i. In ministry, it is easier than many people think to blindly continue serving God and His people while in sin, and to do it in mechanical indifference. God wanted Israel's priests to think about their service to Him, and He wants today's ministers to think just as carefully.

ii. Richard Baxter, a great Puritan writer, carefully considered the walk of the minister: "But consider plainly that the great and lamentable sin of ministers of the Gospel is that *they are not fully devoted to God*. They do not give themselves up wholly to the blessed work they have undertaken to do. Is it not true that flesh-pleasing and self-seeking interests – distinct from that of Christ – make us neglect our duty and lead us to walk unfaithfully in the great trust that God has given us? Is it not true that we serve God too cheaply? Do we not do so in the most applauded way? Do we not withdraw ourselves from that which would cost us the most suffering? Does not all this show that we seek earthly rather than heavenly things? And that we mind the things which are below? While we preach for the realities which are above, do we not idolize the world? So what remains to be said, brethren, but to cry that we are all guilty of too many of the aforementioned sins. Do we not need to humble ourselves in lamentation for our miscarriages before the Lord?" (Baxter)

d. **You offer defiled food on My altar**: The altar was the place of sacrifice, and it belonged to God. Yet the priests of Malachi's day disgraced God and His altar by offering **defiled food** to Him. Spiritually speaking, ministers today must never present **defiled food** to God in their ministry.

i. If the pastor's sermon is filled with funny jokes, clever anecdotes, and emotional stories but it lacks God's word – this is like **defiled food**. To throw in a few Bible verses here and there to illustrate or back up the preacher's stories, but to really make the sermon all about the preacher is to offer **defiled food**. If the sermon isn't about Jesus, if it isn't about God's word, then the preacher is setting **defiled food on** God's **altar**.

ii. If the pastor's sermon is sloppy, if he has not done the work in the study when there was the opportunity to do that work, that is like offering **defiled food** before God. When the preacher will not labor in prayer and meditation over God's word and seek His message for the people, the sermon can be an offering of **defiled food**. If the preacher does not hold fast the pattern of sound words and rightly divide the word of truth, it is all like setting **defiled food on** God's **altar**.

iii. If the preacher's sermon is cold, refusing to show any concern or passion in the pulpit; if his passion is reserved for other things in life, then the sermon can be like **defiled food**. If the preacher can pontificate or argue with the best of them, but his messages have no deep passion for God or his people, the message may be like **defiled food**. If the preacher does his job and collects his paycheck but with a heart for Jesus that is cold, that preacher sets **defiled food on** God's **altar**.

e. **The table of the LORD is contemptible**: The priests weren't grateful for their ministry, for their work before the LORD. They complained about what the people gave and the trouble of being a priest.

f. **Offer it then to your governor**: The priests and the people tried to give to God things that the government wouldn't accept as taxes. King David had a completely different heart, saying *nor will I offer burnt offerings to the Lord my God with that which costs me nothing* (2 Samuel 24:24).

2. (9-11) God will be glorified but will it be by His present people?

"But now entreat God's favor,
That He may be gracious to us.
***While* this is being *done* by your hands,**
Will He accept you favorably?"
Says the LORD of hosts.
Who *is there* even among you who would shut the doors,
So that you would not kindle fire *on* My altar in vain?
I have no pleasure in you,"
Says the LORD of hosts,
"Nor will I accept an offering from your hands.
For from the rising of the sun, even to its going down,
My name *shall be* great among the Gentiles;
In every place incense *shall be* offered to My name,
And a pure offering;
For My name shall be great among the nations,"
Says the LORD of hosts.

a. **Entreat God's favor, that He may be gracious to us**: This phrase is rich with irony. Moffatt's paraphrase gives the sense: *Try to pacify God and win his favour? How can he favour any one of you, says the Lord of hosts, when you offer him such sacrifices?*

b. **Who would shut the doors**: God thought it was better to **shut the doors** rather than to continue worthless worship. Not everything that is offered to God as worship is accepted by God as worship. Sometimes God would prefer that it would just stop and He simply says, "**I have no pleasure in you.**"

i. We are often concerned with church growth, evangelism, and planting churches. Yet in some cases, the best thing we could do for the cause of the LORD is to **shut the doors** of many churches.

ii. "I am more afraid of profanity of the sanctuary than I am of the profanity of the street." (Morgan)

c. **My name shall be great among the Gentiles**: Yet, God will not go without worship. If the priests and people among Israel would not worship Him in Spirit and in truth, God would find worshippers **among the Gentiles**.

d. **In every place incense shall be offered to My name**: This is a glorious promise that the true worship of God will extend all over the earth. Jesus' command to spread the gospel and to go to every nation is part of God's way of fulfilling this promise.

i. "It is, therefore, inconceivable that a prophet should suggest that the nations of his own day were worshipping the Lord under another name (Isaiah 42:8). Rather is he proclaiming that the nations will come to know the God revealed in the Scriptures." (Baldwin)

3. (12-14) God promises to curse shallow, selfish, false worship.

"But you profane it,
In that you say,
'The table of the LORD is defiled;
And its fruit, its food, *is* contemptible.'
You also say,
'Oh, what a weariness!'
And you sneer at it,"
Says the LORD of hosts.
"And you bring the stolen, the lame, and the sick;
Thus you bring an offering!
Should I accept this from your hand?"
Says the LORD.
"But cursed *be* the deceiver
Who has in his flock a male,
And takes a vow, but sacrifices to the LORD what is blemished–
For I *am* a great King,"
Says the LORD of hosts,
"And My name *is to be* feared among the nations.

a. **Contemptible.... Oh, what a weariness**: Their selfish, insincere worship was also unsatisfying to the worshippers. Because they did not meet God in their worship it was as hollow for them as it was for God. True worship is never **contemptible** or **a weariness**.

b. **Cursed be the deceiver**: In bringing God less than their best, they were deceivers, like Ananias and Sapphira who pretended to surrender everything to God but did not (Acts 5).

c. **I am a great King**: They simply did not treat God like a great King, one to be feared and honored. When we offer shallow, insincere worship to God we don't honor Him as a **great King**.

Malachi 2 – Unfaithful Priests and Broken Marriages

A. God exposes and condemns the unfaithful priesthood of Israel.

1. (1-4) God threatens to severely rebuke a wicked priesthood.

"And now, O priests, this commandment is for you.
If you will not hear, and if you will not take *it* **to heart,**
To give glory to My name,"
Says the LORD of hosts,
"I will send a curse upon you,
And I will curse your blessings.
Yes, I have cursed them already,
Because you do not take *it* **to heart.**

Behold, I will rebuke your descendants
And spread refuse on your faces,
The refuse of your solemn feasts;
And *one* **will take you away with it.**
Then you shall know that I have sent this commandment to you,
That My covenant with Levi may continue,"
Says the LORD of hosts.

> a. **If you will not hear**: If the priests would not hear and repent, God promised to **curse** their **blessings**. This was either a reference to the gifts or blessings brought to the priests by the people, or the priestly **blessings** they gave to the people.
>
> b. **Because you do not take it to heart**: Their sin all went back to a hollow formalism. It was a religion of surface emotions and outward signs, but not of the **heart**.
>
> c. **Spread refuse on your faces**: Sacrificed animals still had excrement in their systems, and God said this should be burned outside the camp

(Exodus 29:14). Here, God said He would **spread** that **refuse** on their **faces**, so that *they* would have to be taken outside the camp.

    d. **That My covenant with Levi may continue**: This shows the *motive* for God's discipline of these ungodly priests. The LORD hoped that this would warn the priests to properly respect His **covenant**.

2. (5-7) What a priest should be – the example of Levi.

"My covenant was with him, *one* of life and peace,
And I gave them to him *that he might* fear *Me*;
So he feared Me and was reverent before My name.
The law of truth was in his mouth,
And injustice was not found on his lips.
He walked with Me in peace and equity,
And turned many away from iniquity.

"For the lips of a priest should keep knowledge,
And *people* should seek the law from his mouth;
For he is the messenger of the LORD of hosts.

    a. **My covenant was with him**: God promised Levi that his descendants would be scattered in Israel. This was turned into a wonderful blessing when Levi was designated as the priestly tribe and the priests were sprinkled throughout Israel.

    b. **So he feared Me**: God used Levi as an example for the priests in the days of Malachi. Levi was shown to be an example of:

- Reverence: **He feared Me and was reverent before My name**.
- Knowing God's word: **The law of truth was in his mouth**.
- Godly character: **He walked with Me in peace and equity**.
- Preserving and promoting God's word: God's servant **should keep knowledge, and people should seek the law from his mouth**.

    c. **The law of truth was in his mouth**: The priests had a special responsibility to study and spread the word of God (2 Chronicles 31:4, Nehemiah 8:7-9). God's word was given to the priests for **life and peace**, and so they would be **reverent before** the LORD.

    d. **The lips of a priest should keep knowledge**: Because the priests had to study and spread God's word they had to do it with **knowledge**, so the people could **seek the law from his mouth**. Leaders should be knowledgeable messengers of God's word.

3. (8-9) Contrast between the ideal and the real.

But you have departed from the way;

You have caused many to stumble at the law.
You have corrupted the covenant of Levi,"
Says the LORD of hosts.

"Therefore I also have made you contemptible and base
Before all the people,
Because you have not kept My ways
But have shown partiality in the law."

> a. **You have departed from the way**: The priests *should have* kept the word of God with knowledge, reverence, and obedience. Instead, they **departed from the way** and therefore **caused many to stumble at the law**.
>
> b. **Therefore I also have made you contemptible and base before all the people**: Because the priests of Malachi's day fell so far short of God's ideal for them, the people held them in contempt.

B. God exposes and condemns their treachery, especially in their marriages.

1. (10) God rebukes the priests of Israel for their treacherous dealing.

Have we not all one Father?
Has not one God created us?
Why do we deal treacherously with one another
By profaning the covenant of the fathers?

> a. **Have we not all one Father?** This does not teach the idea of the universal fatherhood of God, the doctrine that all are inherently right with God, or that God is everyone's father in the same way. This is a simple assertion that because we are all made in the image of God, we must respect and deal honorably with all.
>
>> i. In addition, this may have reference to their common **Father** in Abraham.
>
> b. **Why do we deal treacherously with one another**: Malachi will apply this specifically to marriage, but their sin of treachery went beyond their unfaithfulness in marriage.
>
>> i. "All betrayals, from the slightest unkindness to the grossest injustice, merit God's disapproval." (Alden)

2. (11-12) The first offense of the priests: marrying foreign wives.

Judah has dealt treacherously,
And an abomination has been committed in Israel and in Jerusalem,
For Judah has profaned
The LORD's holy *institution* which He loves:
He has married the daughter of a foreign god.

May the LORD cut off from the tents of Jacob
The man who does this, being awake and aware,
Yet who brings an offering to the LORD of hosts!

> a. **The LORD's holy institution which He loves**: This tells us exactly how God feels about marriage. It is **holy** to Him; it is an **institution** to Him and God **loves** marriage.
>
>> i. When we sin by breaking our marriage vows or by taking God's gift of marriage lightly, we sin against something **holy** to God. He has *set apart* marriage for a special meaning, a special purpose in the life of His people.
>>
>> ii. When we sin by breaking our marriage vows or by taking God's gift of marriage lightly, we sin against an **institution** that God has established. Marriage is God's idea, not man's; He formed and established the first marriage as a pattern for every one afterwards (Genesis 2:20-25). Because it is an **institution**, we are not allowed to define marriage in any way that pleases us; God has established marriage and we must conform to what He has established.
>>
>> iii. When we sin by breaking our marriage vows or by taking God's gift of marriage lightly, we sin against something that God **loves**.
>>
>> - God **loves** marriage for what it displays about His relationship with us.
>> - God **loves** marriage for the good it does in society.
>> - God **loves** marriage for the way it meets the needs of men, women, and children.
>> - God **loves** marriage as a tool for conforming His people into the image of His Son.
>
> b. **He has married the daughter of a foreign god**: The first *treachery* and **abomination** God addressed was the intermarriage between the people of God and their ungodly neighbors. The dangers of an ungodly intermarriage are well documented in the Old and New Testaments.
>
> - Israel married women from Moab and brought the curse of God upon the people (Numbers 25).
> - Solomon married foreign women who took his heart away from God (1 Kings 11:1-10).
> - Ahab married Jezebel – a foreign woman given over to pagan gods – who led Israel into new depths of depravity (1 Kings 16:29-33).

- Paul says that believers and unbelievers should not be joined together (2 Corinthians 6:11-18).

c. **May the LORD cut off from the tents of Jacob the man who does this, being awake and aware, yet who brings an offering**: God promised to punish the priests who married foreign, pagan wives and thought that it would not affect their service to the LORD.

i. **Awake and aware** is a difficult phrase to translate. Other translations have "master and scholar," "tempter and tempted," "witness and advocate," "kith and kin," or even "nomads and settlers." "Obviously, the Hebrew idiom is just another way of saying 'everyone.'" (Alden)

ii. God's command against mixed marriages in Israel had nothing to do with race, but with faith. There is even a foreign wife in the genealogy of Jesus – Ruth was a Moabite who married a Jewish man named Boaz but she forsook Moab's gods for the LORD. (Ruth 1:16)

3. (13-16) The second offense of the priests: a low regard of marriage.

And this is the second thing you do:
You cover the altar of the LORD with tears,
With weeping and crying;
So He does not regard the offering anymore,
Nor receive *it* **with goodwill from your hands.**
Yet you say, "For what reason?"
Because the LORD has been witness
Between you and the wife of your youth,
With whom you have dealt treacherously;
Yet she is your companion
And your wife by covenant.
But did He not make *them* **one,**
Having a remnant of the Spirit?
And why one?
He seeks godly offspring.
Therefore take heed to your spirit,
And let none deal treacherously with the wife of his youth.

"For the LORD God of Israel says
That He hates divorce,
For it covers one's garment with violence,"
Says the LORD of hosts.
"Therefore take heed to your spirit,
That you do not deal treacherously."

a. **You cover the altar of the LORD with tears...so He does not regard the offering anymore**: The neglected and divorced wives of the priests came and wept at God's altar. When their priestly husbands then offered sacrifice to God at the same altar it offended God.

> i. "They cover the altar of Jehovah with tears, namely, by compelling the wives who have been put away to lay their trouble before God in the sanctuary." (Keil)
>
> ii. It is a disgrace if a pastor or preacher's harsh, neglectful, or unkind treatment of his wife causes her to cry out before God. "You caused your poor wives, when they should have been cheerful in God's service.... to cover the Lord's altar with tears, with weeping, and with crying out." (Trapp)

b. **Because the LORD has been witness between you and the wife of your youth, with whom you have dealt treacherously**: The priests sinned by forsaking the wife they married in their youth, by breaking the goal of marriage (**she is your companion**) and by breaking the bond of marriage (**your wife by covenant**).

> i. "They kept their wives till they had *passed their youth*, and then put them away, that they might get *young ones* in their place." (Clarke)

c. **Did He not make them one**: The Bible continually points back to God's goal and plan for marriage as revealed in Genesis 2:18-25. Fundamental to God's plan for marriage is the essential oneness between husband and wife. One important reason for this oneness is to establish a proper environment for raising **godly offspring**.

d. **He hates divorce**: There is no doubt that God **hates divorce** because it destroys what He *loves* – marriage is *the LORD's holy institution which He loves* (Malachi 2:11). Specifically, we can say that God **hates divorce** for at least three reasons:

- God hates divorce because it breaks a solemn vow.
- God hates divorce because it is harmful.
- God hates divorce because it illustrates apostasy and damnation.

> i. There is no doubt that God *allows* divorce in particular circumstances, though divorce is *never* commanded. God's heart is *always* for repentance, forgiveness, and reconciliation in marriage. We have sinned against God far worse than any spouse could sin against us, and God does not divorce us – though He has every right to.
>
> ii. Yet because we are fallen and suffer from hardness of heart, God gives *permission* for divorce in two circumstances. Sexual immorality is

valid grounds (Matthew 19:1-9), and so is desertion by an unbelieving spouse (1 Corinthians 7:10-16).

iii. Significantly, *misery*, *unhappiness*, *poverty*, or *incompatibilities* are never given as grounds for divorce. Where there is danger or abuse separation is often in order in accordance with 1 Corinthians 7:10-11, but the separated couple must live in complete faithfulness to their marriage vows, though they live as separately.

iv. If someone does not have biblical grounds for divorce, God regards them as still married and any subsequent relationship is considered adultery (Matthew 19:8-9). It isn't that you *shouldn't* divorce for unbiblical grounds; you *can't* divorce for unbiblical grounds. Nevertheless, if someone divorces having proper grounds, then they are free to remarry (1 Corinthians 7:15).

e. **It covers one's garment with violence**: Part of the marriage ceremony in Bible times involved the husband covering his wife with his garment as a symbol of the protection he brought her. But now, their garments were covered with violence. When a wife is forsaken or mistreated the man covers *his own* **garment with violence**. This is because the husband and wife are one, and he cannot mistreat his wife without bringing misery and destruction to himself.

i. This was Paul's point in Ephesians 5:28: *So husbands ought to love their own wives as their own bodies; he who loves his wife loves himself.* Simply said, when you love your wife, *you benefit yourself.* Perhaps it is better to put it in the negative: *when you neglect your wife, you neglect yourself, and it* will *come back to hurt you.*

ii. We all know what it is like to neglect something – like a noise or a maintenance issue on an automobile – and it comes back to hurt you. This is even more true in regard to husbands because the wife is actually *part of* the husband. He neglects and does damage to himself, not only to her.

f. **Therefore take heed to your spirit**: This phrase is repeated twice because it is so important. The reason why the priests dealt treacherously against their wives is that they did not **take heed** to their **spirit**. They allowed their hearts to become hard, critical, and embittered against the woman they were supposed to regard as their special, God-given companion in oneness.

i. It is important to realize that we can *change* our feelings towards our spouse. If we do not feel loving or connected or caring about them, *that can be changed* if we will **take heed to** our **spirit**.

4. (17) The fourth question: Where is the God of justice in this unjust world?

You have wearied the Lord with your words;
Yet you say, "In what way have we wearied *Him?*"
In that you say,
"Everyone who does evil
***Is* good in the sight of the Lord,**
And He delights in them,"
Or, "Where *is* the God of justice?"

> a. **Everyone who does evil is good in the sight of the Lord**: The people of God in Malachi's day were depressed and discouraged because it seemed like the wicked prospered and had it better than the godly. This filled them with doubt and unbelief, and they grumbled that **everyone who does evil is good in the sight of the Lord**.
>
> b. **Where is the God of justice?** When they compared themselves with others, they thought it was unjust of God to bless others and not them. Nevertheless, their question shows that they didn't understand what **the God of justice** would give to them.
>
> c. **You have wearied the Lord with your words**: This kind of ignorant, unbelieving talk from God's people is wearisome to God. It shows how much His people resist His truth and His work.
>
>> i. "God is offended when people accuse Him of injustice." (Boice)

Malachi 3 – The Messenger of the Covenant

A. The coming of the two messengers.

1. (1) The two messengers are introduced.

**"Behold, I send My messenger,
And he will prepare the way before Me.
And the Lord, whom you seek,
Will suddenly come to His temple,
Even the Messenger of the covenant,
In whom you delight.
Behold, He is coming,"
Says the Lord of hosts.**

> a. **Behold, I send My messenger**: This prophesied **messenger** is none other than John the Baptist. Matthew 11:10, Mark 1:2, and Luke 7:27 all show this promise was fulfilled in John the Baptist.
>
>> i. At the end of Malachi 2, Israel complained that God seemed to reward the wicked and did not exercise His justice in the world. God responds to their complaint by saying, "I will set things right with My Messiah, and before Him will come **My messenger**."
>
> b. **And he will prepare the way before Me**: In an ancient royal procession, the messenger went before the king to announce his arrival, to indicate the route, and to remove any obstacles in the road. John the Baptist fulfilled this exact ministry for Jesus. The same idea is indicated in Isaiah 40:3-5.
>
>> i. God's purpose for bringing this specific prophecy through Malachi in his day was probably because Israel complained that the Messianic promises of Haggai and Zechariah were not fulfilled. Here Malachi showed that the way for the Messiah must be *prepared*, and they were not ready yet.
>
>> ii. **Before Me**: The Lord promised that He Himself would come – not merely a new or better prophet, but the Lord Himself.

c. **Even the Messenger of the covenant**: This second messenger is the LORD Himself – Jesus coming to **His temple** as the fulfillment of the old covenant and to institute a new covenant.

2. (2-5) This second Messenger will also come with purifying judgment; it will be a fearful coming.

"But who can endure the day of His coming?
And who can stand when He appears?
For He *is* **like a refiner's fire**
And like launderer's soap
He will sit as a refiner and a purifier of silver,
He will purify the sons of Levi,
And purge them as gold and silver,
That they may offer to the LORD
An offering in righteousness.

Then the offering of Judah and Jerusalem
Will be pleasant to the LORD,
As in the days of old,
As in former years.
And I will come near you for judgment;
I will be a swift witness
Against sorcerers,
Against adulterers,
Against perjurers,
Against those who exploit wage earners and widows and orphans,
And against those who turn away an alien–
Because they do not fear Me,"
Says the LORD **of hosts.**

a. **Who can endure the day of His coming?** Malachi 3:1 spoke of two messengers to come – one to prepare the way of the LORD, and one to be the *Messenger of the covenant*. The **coming** that man must **endure** is the coming of the *Messenger of the covenant*, but it is His *second coming*.

i. "Like most Old Testament prophets, Malachi, in his picture of the coming Christ, mingled the two advents." (Alden)

b. **He is like a refiner's fire and like launderer's soap**: The coming of this second Messenger will be awesome and terrible, but with a purpose. Both the launderer and the refiner work to clean, not to destroy.

i. **He will sit as a refiner and a purifier of silver**: "The beauty of this picture is that the refiner looks into the open furnace, or pot, and knows that the process of purifying is complete, and the dross all burnt away, when he can see his image plainly reflected in the molten metal." (Baldwin)

ii. "If any of you, my hearers, are seeking the Lord at this time, I want you to understand what it means: you are seeking a fire which will test you, and consume much which has been dear to you. We are not to expect Christ to come and save us in our sins, he will come and save us from our sins; therefore, if you are enabled by faith to take Christ as a Saviour, remember that you take him as the purger and the purifier, for it is from sin that he saves us." (Spurgeon)

iii. We note that **He will sit as a refiner**. "What a comfort it is that He surrenders this work to no other hands than his own. He may give his angels charge concerning us when we are in danger; but he keeps our purification beneath his special superintendence." (Meyer)

iv. At the same time, notice that **He will sit as a refiner**. The *sitting* posture shows that the refiner may seem indifferent, but He is not. He is carefully working with the silver, burning off and scraping away the dross that the flames bring to the top. "I think I see in the sitting down of the refiner a settled patience...for it will need care, and time, and constant watchfulness.'" (Spurgeon)

v. "If you are just now in the fire, dear soul, be of good cheer – it shows at least that you are silver, and are capable of performing more acceptable service in God's holy Temple." (Meyer)

c. **He will purify the sons of Levi**: In the first two chapters of Malachi, the LORD spoke out against the corruption of the priesthood. Here, God gave His ultimate answer for that corruption – the Messiah **will purify the sons of Levi**.

i. "Have you ever reflected upon the fact that when Christ's refining work is done upon us there will never be any need for it again? Blessed be God, there is no purgatorial fire. We need not dread that we have yet to pass through purging flames in another world." (Spurgeon)

d. **I will be a swift witness against sorcerers**: God's ultimate purpose is to cleanse society, and to change the hearts of men. When Jesus returns in glory and rules on this earth, evil will be quickly punished.

i. **Sorcerers**: This sin is mentioned first because the Jews became familiar with sorcery and other magical arts during their captivity in Babylon.

B. Returning to God instead of robbing God.

1. (6-7) While declaring His mercy, God asks for repentance.

"For I *am* the Lord, I do not change;
Therefore you are not consumed, O sons of Jacob.
Yet from the days of your fathers
You have gone away from My ordinances
And have not kept *them.*
Return to Me, and I will return to you,"
Says the Lord of hosts.
"But you said,
'In what way shall we return?'

> a. **I am the Lord, I do not change; therefore you are not consumed**: If it were *possible* for God to change His mind about us, He might very well do it and we would be **consumed**. Fortunately, the Lord does **not change** in His love for us or His choice of us.
>
> b. **Yet from the days of your fathers you have gone away from My ordinances**: God's unchanging love for Israel should have made them more obedient and submitted to Him, but they presumed upon His faithfulness and patience.
>
> c. **Return to Me, and I will return to you**: This was a simple call to repentance. Those who have once walked with God and been committed to His covenant must **return** to Him. When they do, they will find that He **will return to** them with blessing and the marks of His presence.
>
>> i. In its most basic sense, repentance is turning away from sin and turning to God. It isn't so much *required* if we want to return to God; repentance describes what the very act of returning is.
>
> d. **In what way shall we return?** Israel didn't know how to return to God. Either they *chose* not to know, or they simply were ignorant.

2. (8-12) How Israel needed to repent.

"Will a man rob God?
Yet you have robbed Me!
But you say,
'In what way have we robbed You?'
In tithes and offerings.
You are cursed with a curse,
For you have robbed Me,
Even this whole nation.
Bring all the tithes into the storehouse,
That there may be food in My house,
And try Me now in this,"
Says the Lord of hosts,

"If I will not open for you the windows of heaven
And pour out for you *such* blessing
That *there will* not *be room* enough *to receive it.*

And I will rebuke the devourer for your sakes,
So that he will not destroy the fruit of your ground,
Nor shall the vine fail to bear fruit for you in the field,"
Says the LORD of hosts;

"And all nations will call you blessed,
For you will be a delightful land,"
Says the LORD of hosts.

a. **Will a man rob God?** It seems strange to think that a man could rob God. What could someone possibly steal from God? The LORD explained how it could happen – they **robbed** God by withholding their **tithes and offerings**.

i. It was an expression of astonishment: **Will a man rob God?**

- Astonishing because it is such a daring thing to do.
- Astonishing because it is shamefully ungrateful.
- Astonishing because it is senselessly self-destructive.
- Astonishing because it will certainly be punished.

ii. God called it robbery because they had unlawful possession of what belonged to God. It wasn't because *only* the **tithes and offerings** belonged to God. In fact, *everything* we have belongs to God (Psalm 24:1). Yet God does not normally command us to give everything that belongs to Him; He allows us to keep some as managers on His behalf. But the **tithes and offerings** are different; they are not given to us to manage – they belong to what the LORD calls **My house**, the **house** of the LORD.

iii. If we give a tithe – that is, 10% of your income or assets – to God, it isn't as if the remaining 90% is yours to do with as you please. It all belongs to God, but He allows us to directly manage the remaining 90%.

iv. The Law of Moses had a detailed system of giving based on the tithe (Deuteronomy 14:22-29 is one passage describing this system). If you failed to pay your tithe, you had to pay a 20% penalty (Leviticus 5:14-16; 22:14; 27:31-32). Nevertheless, the practice and principle of tithing came long before the law (Genesis 14:18-20).

b. **You are cursed with a curse, for you have robbed Me**: Because God's people did not give as He commanded, God did not bless them materially or spiritually the way He would have otherwise. Their stingy ways proved that their hearts were far from God because God is the greatest giver (John 3:16).

i. Many people with financial problems fail to do the most important thing first: obey and honor God with their resources. When we put God and His kingdom first, He promises to meet our other needs (Matthew 6:33).

c. **Bring all the tithes into the storehouse**: This was the answer to their problems – to actually *do* what God commanded them to do, and to **bring *all* the tithes** to God. It wasn't that they didn't give anything to God; they simply did not **bring *all* the tithes** to Him. They must not fall short in giving God everything that He asked for.

i. Under the new covenant, are we under a similar command to tithe? The New Testament nowhere specifically commands tithing, but it certainly does speak of it in a positive light if it is done with a right heart (Luke 11:42).

ii. It is also important to understand that tithing is not a principle that depends on the Law of Moses. Hebrews 7:5-9 explains that tithing was practiced and honored by God long before the Law of Moses.

iii. What the New Testament does speak with great clarity on is the principle of *giving*. 1 Corinthians 16:1-4 makes it clear that our giving must be:

- Periodic (done at regular periods).
- Planned (thought of in advance of the giving).
- Proportional (giving in proportion to our blessings).
- Private (not done to make us known as generous givers).

iv. As well, 2 Corinthians 9 tells us that giving must be:

- Generous (giving more rather than less).
- Freely given (not done out of guilt or manipulation).
- Cheerful (given happily and with rejoicing in God).

v. Since the New Testament doesn't emphasize tithing, one might not be strict on it for Christians (though some Christians sadly argue against tithing on the basis of self-interest). Nevertheless, because giving is to be proportional, we should give *some* percentage, and ten percent is a good benchmark. For some people, 10% should really be the beginning of their giving and not the end of it.

vi. If our question is, "How little can I give and still please God?" then our heart isn't in the right place at all. We should have the attitude of some early Christians, who essentially said: "We're not under the tithe – we can give *more*!" Giving and financial management are *spiritual* issues not only financial issues (Luke 16:11).

d. **That there may be food in My house**: The purpose of the tithe was primarily to support the priests who ministered before the LORD. When the people did not bring their tithes, the priests were not properly supported and there was not enough **food** for them in the **house** of the LORD.

i. The tithe in Israel was also to be used to help the poor, and once every three years some of it was put aside for that purpose (Deuteronomy 14:28-29). Still, the main purpose of the tithe was to support the tribe of Levi and the priests (Deuteronomy 14:27).

ii. The same principle carries over in the New Testament. Some people claim that a paid ministry is an abomination before God, but Paul made it clear that not only do ministers deserve to be supported by those they minister to (1 Timothy 5:18, 1 Corinthians 9:4-14) but also that their support is even more worthy than the poor (1 Timothy 5:17). Nevertheless, Paul voluntarily yielded his right to be supported when he thought it was in the best interests of the gospel to do so (1 Corinthians 9:12, 9:15).

e. **And try Me now in this**: It's hard to find a comparable passage of Scripture – where the LORD *commanded* His people to test Him. Here, in regard to giving and His blessing of it, He told His people **try Me now in this**. It was as if God said, "See if you can give to Me and be the poorer for it. See if you can out-give Me."

i. "The context for God's words about tithes is the teaching that God is faithful. The matter of tithes is only an illustration of that teaching." (Boice)

f. **Open for you the windows of heaven and pour out for you such blessing that there will not be room enough to receive it**: This is the response God promised when His people give as He told them to. He would bless them both with provision and protection (**I will rebuke the devourer**).

i. The reference to the **windows of heaven** reminds us of the glorious account of provision in 2 Kings 7, when God provided in a completely unexpected way. God has resources that we know nothing about, and it is often of no help to try and predict – or worry about – how God will provide.

C. What good is it to serve God?

1. (13-15) God's people ask the question.

> "Your words have been harsh against Me,"
> Says the LORD,
> "Yet you say,
> 'What have we spoken against You?'
> You have said,
> 'It is useless to serve God;
> What profit *is it* that we have kept His ordinance,
> And that we have walked as mourners
> Before the LORD of hosts?
> So now we call the proud blessed,
> For those who do wickedness are raised up;
> They even tempt God and go free.'"

   a. **Your words have been harsh against Me**: Israel spoke against the LORD in a harsh and sinful way – and they apparently didn't even realize they did so.

   b. **It is useless to serve God**: These were the harsh words spoken by God's people against God. They saw the prosperity of the **proud** and those who did **wickedness**, and they felt that it was **useless to serve God** as long as those who didn't serve Him seemed to live comfortably.

   i. It cost something to keep God's **ordinance**, and they had to humble themselves to walk **as mourners before the LORD**. Yet it seemed to God's people that the cost wasn't worth the reward.

2. (16-18) The comfort of knowing that God remembers.

> Then those who feared the LORD spoke to one another,
> And the LORD listened and heard *them;*
> So a book of remembrance was written before Him
> For those who fear the LORD
> And who meditate on His name.
>
> "They shall be Mine," says the LORD of hosts,
> "On the day that I make them My jewels.
> And I will spare them
> As a man spares his own son who serves him."
> Then you shall again discern
> Between the righteous and the wicked,
> Between one who serves God
> And one who does not serve Him.

a. **Then those who feared the LORD spoke to one another**: Discouraged by the sense that it wasn't worth the trouble to serve God, the people of God came together – **spoke to one another** – and encouraged each other in the LORD.

i. When God's people speak to one another in this way, the LORD listens from heaven. He loves to see true fellowship and love among His people.

b. **A book of remembrance was written before Him for those who fear the LORD and who meditate on His name**: When they saw the wicked rewarded and the righteous suffer, it made them think that God forgot all their goodness. Here Malachi promises that not only will God remember, but He will write it down!

i. The thought that God has a **book of remembrance** is common but varied (Exodus 32:32-33; Psalm 69:28; 87:6; Daniel 12:1).

c. **They shall be Mine…My jewels**: In the midst of suffering, assaulted by doubt and discouragement, God's people didn't feel like God's **jewels**. Yet their feelings didn't change the fact, and they needed to let God's fact be greater than their feelings.

i. It was a spiritually low time for Israel – the priests and the people were steeped in corruption and mediocrity. At the same time, God always has His **jewels**. Even if everyone around you turns away from the LORD, you can still be one of His **jewels**.

ii. There are several ways that Christians are like **jewels**.

- They are hard and durable.
- They are prized for their luster.
- They are prized for their rarity.
- They are made by God alone.
- They are of all different sizes, yet they are all jewels.
- They are found all over the world.
- They are associated with royalty.
- They are protected.
- Some are hidden and undiscovered.
- Some are not yet polished.

d. **Then you shall again discern between the righteous and the wicked**: One day this dilemma will be cleared up. In the end, the distinction between the **righteous** and the **wicked** will be evident.

Malachi 4 – The Sun of Righteousness

A. The final resolution.

1. (1) Resolution of the wicked.

"For behold, the day is coming,
Burning like an oven,
And all the proud, yes, all who do wickedly will be stubble.
And the day which is coming shall burn them up,"
Says the LORD of hosts,
"That will leave them neither root nor branch.

> a. **The day is coming**: Discouraged by the apparent prosperity of the wicked and uselessness of serving the LORD, God's people needed to be reminded that **the day is coming**. God still has eternity to right all wrongs and reward all goodness.
>
> b. **Burning like an oven**: God promised a fire for His people (Malachi 3:2-3) and here He promised a fire for the wicked. But there is a big difference between the refining fire applied to God's people and the burning fire against the ungodly.
>
> c. **All who do wickedly will be stubble**: The wicked will not be able to stand against God's judgment. **Stubble** is the unusable part of the grain and lasts only moments if it is thrown into a fire.
>
> d. **Leave them neither root nor branch**: In that coming day, the wicked will have no hope of sprouting up again to life. As long as a root remains there is hope, but hope is gone for these because the judgment of eternity is final.

2. (2-3) Resolution of the righteous.

But to you who fear My name
The Sun of Righteousness shall arise
With healing in His wings;
And you shall go out

And grow fat like stall-fed calves.
You shall trample the wicked,
For they shall be ashes under the soles of your feet
On the day that I do *this*,"
Says the LORD of hosts.

> a. **But to you who fear My name**: In the previous verse God promised a judgment of fire for the *proud*, but God also said that those **who fear My name** will be saved.
>
> b. **The Sun of Righteousness shall arise**: From the time of early Christians like Justin Martyr to today, Christians have regarded the **Sun of Righteousness** as a reference to Jesus.
>
>> i. In many passages God is related to a planet or star (Psalm 84:11, Isaiah 60:19, Revelation 22:16, Numbers 24:17). Here, the Messiah is not only a **Sun** but also the **Sun of Righteousness** who brings **healing**.
>>
>> ii. "He went under a cloud in his passion, and brake forth again in his resurrection. From heaven he daily darts forth his beams of righteousness, and showers down all spiritual blessings in heavenly privileges." (Trapp)
>
> c. **With healing in His wings**: The **wings** of the sun are the rays or sunbeams it sends out. They bring healing, joy, and wholeness. When the **Sun of Righteousness** shines, we need no other light or warmth. Imagine trying to light a candle on a sunny day to help out the sun! That makes as much sense as trying to "improve" the work of Jesus for us with our own righteousness.
>
> d. **You shall trample the wicked**: When God's people see the final resolution of all things they will be so happy they will jump about like **stall-fed calves** set free from the pen. As they jump about with joy, the **wicked** are trampled beneath their feet.
>
>> i. "Understand the figure. The calf in the stall is shut up, tied up with a halter at night, but when the sun rises the calf goes forth to the pasture; the young bullock is set free. So the child of God may be in bondage. The recollection of past sins and present unbelief may halter him up and keep him in the stall, but when the Lord reveals himself he is set free." (Spurgeon)
>>
>> ii. We can see a glorious progression in those who look upon the risen **Sun of Righteousness** and receive the **healing in His wings**:
>>
>> - They **shall go out** – they will be free and enjoy their liberty.

- They shall **grow fat** – growing strong and prosperous in the LORD.
- They shall **trample the wicked** – enjoying the LORD's victory in their lives.

B. The concluding words of the Old Testament.

1. (4) Remember the Law of Moses.

"Remember the Law of Moses, My servant,
Which I commanded him in Horeb for all Israel,
***With the* statutes and judgments.**

> a. **Remember the Law of Moses**: In these last few prophetic words of the Old Testament, Malachi warns Israel to **remember** the **Law** because God's prophetic voice would be silent for some 400 years. We never need to despair when God seems silent, because what He has already said is rich enough – if we will only **remember**.
>
> b. **With the statutes and judgments**: The last few words of the Old Testament are a call back to the law, because under the old covenant man related with God on the basis of the law. Thank God for the new covenant – *for the law was given through Moses, but grace and truth came through Jesus Christ* (John 1:17).

2. (5-6) Elijah will come.

Behold, I will send you Elijah the prophet
Before the coming of the great and dreadful day of the LORD.
And he will turn the hearts of the fathers to the children,
And the hearts of the children to their fathers,
Lest I come and strike the earth with a curse."

> a. **I will send you Elijah the prophet**: In this unique promise, God assured His people that He would send **Elijah** to Israel again before **the great and dreadful day of the LORD**.
>
> > i. This was fulfilled in John the Baptist in a figurative sense (Matthew 11:14, Mark 9:11-13, Luke 1:17). Yet because this Elijah comes **before the coming of the great and dreadful day**, we know that the Elijah prophecy is only completely fulfilled before the second coming of Jesus. Matthew 17:11-12 and Revelation 11:3-12 speak of this future fulfillment, when God will either send Elijah back to the earth on this special errand or send someone uniquely empowered in the spirit and office of Elijah.

ii. In anticipation of this, Jewish homes set a place at the table for Elijah at Passover, just in case he might come on that night to announce the news that Messiah has come. The empty chair and the cup that is filled but is never drunk are a testimony to their anticipation of Elijah's coming.

b. **Elijah the prophet**: The promise regards **Elijah** because he ministered in a time of crisis in Israel, when the nation was far from God, and a time that immediately preceded a terrible judgment.

i. It is significant that in these closing words of the Old Testament, God refers to both Moses and Elijah. They both met God at Mount Sinai (also known as Horeb, Exodus 3:1 and 1 Kings 19:8-18). They also both met Jesus at the Mount of Transfiguration (Matthew 17:1-5). They are probably the two witnesses of Revelation 11.

c. **He will turn the hearts of the fathers to the children**: This promise speaks of more than the reconciliation of families. When God turns **the hearts of the children to their fathers**, it also has in mind turning to the God of their fathers; to the faith of the patriarchs.

d. **Lest I come and strike the earth with a curse**: The Old Testament ends with the threat of a curse, but also with the expectation of a new dawning of the Sun of Righteousness.

i. This ending of the book of Malachi bothered the ancient Jews. "The Masorites, who have given us most of the copies of the Hebrew Old Testament we have.... were so bothered by this that they repeated the next-to-the-last verse of Malachi after the last verse. Similarly, the Septuagint reverses the last two verses so the Old Testament ends, not with a curse, but with a blessing." (Boice)

ii. The end of the New Testament recognizes the rising of the Sun of Righteousness: *The grace of our Lord Jesus Christ be with you all!* (Revelation 22:21)

Bibliography

Hosea

Boice, James Montgomery *The Minor Prophets Volume 1: Hosea-Jonah (Grand Rapids, Michigan: Zondervan, 1983)*

Clarke, Adam *The New Testament with A Commentary and Critical Notes, Volume II (New York: Eaton & Mains, 1831)*

Hubbard, David Allan. *Joel and Amos, an Introduction and Commentary (Downer's Grove, Illinois: Inter-Varsity Press, 1989)*

Meyer, F.B. *Our Daily Homily (Westwood, New Jersey: Revell, 1966)*

Morgan, G. Campbell *An Exposition of the Whole Bible (Old Tappan, New Jersey: Revell, 1959)*

Morgan, G. Campbell *Searchlights From The Word (New York: Revell, 1926)*

Poole, Matthew *A Commentary on the Holy Bible, Volume III: Matthew-Revelation (London: Banner of Truth Trust, 1969, first published in 1685)*

Robinson, George L. *The Twelve Minor Prophets (Grand Rapids, Michigan: Baker Book House, 1953)*

Spurgeon, Charles Haddon *The New Park Street Pulpit, Volumes 1-6 and The Metropolitan Tabernacle Pulpit, Volumes 7-63 (Pasadena, Texas: Pilgrim Publications, 1990)*

Trapp, John *A Commentary on the Old and New Testaments, Volume*

Five (Eureka, California: Tanski Publications, 1997)

Wood, Leon J. "Hosea" *The Expositor's Bible Commentary, Volume 7: Daniel and the Minor Prophets* (Grand Rapids, Michigan: Zondervan, 1985)

Joel

Boice, James Montgomery *The Minor Prophets Volume 1: Hosea-Jonah* (Grand Rapids, Michigan: Zondervan, 1983)

Clarke, Adam *The New Testament with A Commentary and Critical Notes, Volume II* (New York: Eaton & Mains, 1831)

Hubbard, David Allan. *Joel and Amos, an Introduction and Commentary* (Downer's Grove, Illinois: Inter-Varsity Press, 1989)

Meyer, F.B. *Our Daily Homily* (Westwood, New Jersey: Revell, 1966)

Morgan, G. Campbell *An Exposition of the Whole Bible* (Old Tappan, New Jersey: Revell, 1959)

Morgan, G. Campbell *Searchlights From The Word* (New York: Revell, 1926)

Patterson, Richard D. "Joel" *The Expositor's Bible Commentary, Volume 7: Daniel and the Minor Prophets* (Grand Rapids, Michigan: Zondervan, 1985)

Poole, Matthew *A Commentary on the Holy Bible, Volume III: Matthew-Revelation* (London: Banner of Truth Trust, 1969, first published in 1685)

Robinson, George L. *The Twelve Minor Prophets* (Grand Rapids, Michigan: Baker Book House, 1953)

Spurgeon, Charles Haddon *The New Park Street Pulpit, Volumes 1-6 and The Metropolitan Tabernacle Pulpit, Volumes 7-63* (Pasadena, Texas: Pilgrim Publications, 1990)

Trapp, John *A Commentary on the Old and New Testaments, Volume Five* (Eureka, California: Tanski Publications, 1997)

Amos

Boice, James Montgomery *The Minor Prophets Volume 1: Hosea-Jonah* (Grand Rapids, Michigan: Zondervan, 1983)

Clarke, Adam *The New Testament with A Commentary and Critical Notes, Volume IV (New York: Eaton & Mains, 1831)*

Hubbard, David Allan. *Joel and Amos, an Introduction and Commentary (Downer's Grove, Illinois: Inter-Varsity Press, 1989)*

McComiskey, Thomas E. "Amos" *The Expositor's Bible Commentary, Volume 7: Daniel and the Minor Prophets* (Grand Rapids, Michigan: Zondervan, 1985)

Meyer, F.B. *Our Daily Homily (Westwood, New Jersey: Revell, 1966)*

Morgan, G. Campbell *An Exposition of the Whole Bible (Old Tappan, New Jersey: Revell, 1959)*

Morgan, G. Campbell *Searchlights From The Word (New York: Revell, 1926)*

Poole, Matthew *A Commentary on the Holy Bible, Volume III: Matthew-Revelation (London: Banner of Truth Trust, 1969, first published in 1685)*

Robinson, George L. *The Twelve Minor Prophets (Grand Rapids, Michigan: Baker Book House, 1953)*

Spurgeon, Charles Haddon *The New Park Street Pulpit, Volumes 1-6 and The Metropolitan Tabernacle Pulpit, Volumes 7-63 (Pasadena, Texas: Pilgrim Publications, 1990)*

Trapp, John *A Commentary on the Old and New Testaments, Volume Five (Eureka, California: Tanski Publications, 1997)*

Obadiah

Amerding, Carl E. "Obadiah" *The Expositor's Bible Commentary, Volume 7: Daniel and the Minor Prophets* (Grand Rapids, Michigan: Zondervan, 1985)

Baker, David W. "Obadiah" *Obadiah, Jonah, and Micah, an Introduction and Commentary (Downer's Grove, Illinois: Inter-Varsity Press, 1989)*
Boice, James Montgomery *The Minor Prophets Volume 1: Hosea-Jonah (Grand Rapids, Michigan: Zondervan, 1983)*

Clarke, Adam *The New Testament with A Commentary and Critical Notes, Volume II (New York: Eaton & Mains, 1831)*

Delitzsch, Franz and Keil, C.F. *Biblical Commentary on the Minor Prophets* (Grand Rapids, Michigan: Eerdmans, 1983)

Meyer, F.B. *Our Daily Homily* (Westwood, New Jersey: Revell, 1966)

Morgan, G. Campbell *An Exposition of the Whole Bible* (Old Tappan, New Jersey: Revell, 1959)

Morgan, G. Campbell *Searchlights From The Word* (New York: Revell, 1926)

Poole, Matthew *A Commentary on the Holy Bible, Volume III: Matthew-Revelation* (London: Banner of Truth Trust, 1969, first published in 1685)

Robinson, George L. *The Twelve Minor Prophets* (Grand Rapids, Michigan: Baker Book House, 1953)

Spurgeon, Charles Haddon *The New Park Street Pulpit, Volumes 1-6 and The Metropolitan Tabernacle Pulpit, Volumes 7-63* (Pasadena, Texas: Pilgrim Publications, 1990)

Trapp, John *A Commentary on the Old and New Testaments, Volume Five* (Eureka, California: Tanski Publications, 1997)

Jonah

Alexander, T. Desmond "Jonah" *Obadiah, Jonah, and Micah, an Introduction and Commentary* (Downer's Grove, Illinois: Inter-Varsity Press, 1989)

Boice, James Montgomery *The Minor Prophets Volume 1: Hosea-Jonah* (Grand Rapids, Michigan: Zondervan, 1983)

Clarke, Adam *The New Testament with A Commentary and Critical Notes, Volume II* (New York: Eaton & Mains, 1831)

Delitzsch, Franz and Keil, C.F. *Biblical Commentary on the Minor Prophets* (Grand Rapids, Michigan: Eerdmans, 1983)

Ellison, H.L. "Jonah" *The Expositor's Bible Commentary, Volume 7: Daniel and the Minor Prophets* (Grand Rapids, Michigan: Zondervan, 1985)

Meyer, F.B. *Our Daily Homily* (Westwood, New Jersey: Revell, 1966)

Morgan, G. Campbell *An Exposition of the Whole Bible* (Old Tappan, New Jersey: Revell, 1959)

Morgan, G. Campbell *Searchlights From The Word* (New York: Revell, 1926)

Poole, Matthew *A Commentary on the Holy Bible, Volume III: Matthew-Revelation* (London: Banner of Truth Trust, 1969, first published in 1685)

Robinson, George L. *The Twelve Minor Prophets* (Grand Rapids, Michigan: Baker Book House, 1953)

Spurgeon, Charles Haddon *The New Park Street Pulpit, Volumes 1-6 and The Metropolitan Tabernacle Pulpit, Volumes 7-63* (Pasadena, Texas: Pilgrim Publications, 1990)

Trapp, John *A Commentary on the Old and New Testaments, Volume Five* (Eureka, California: Tanski Publications, 1997)

Micah

Boice, James Montgomery *The Minor Prophets Volume 2: Micah-Malachi* (Grand Rapids, Michigan: Zondervan, 1983)

Clarke, Adam *The New Testament with A Commentary and Critical Notes, Volume II* (New York: Eaton & Mains, 1831)

Delitzsch, Franz and Keil, C.F. *Biblical Commentary on the Minor Prophets* (Grand Rapids, Michigan: Eerdmans, 1983)

Lewis, Clive Staples *The Problem of Pain* (New York: The MacMillan Company, 1943)

McComiskey, Thomas E. "Micah" *The Expositor's Bible Commentary, Volume 7: Daniel and the Minor Prophets* (Grand Rapids, Michigan: Zondervan, 1985)
McGee, J. Vernon *Thru the Bible, Volume 3: Proverbs through Malachi* (Nashville, Tennessee: Thomas Nelson, 1994)

Meyer, F.B. *Our Daily Homily* (Westwood, New Jersey: Revell, 1966)

Morgan, G. Campbell *An Exposition of the Whole Bible* (Old Tappan, New Jersey: Revell, 1959)

Morgan, G. Campbell *Searchlights From The Word (New York: Revell, 1926)*

Poole, Matthew *A Commentary on the Holy Bible, Volume III: Matthew-Revelation (London: Banner of Truth Trust, 1969, first published in 1685)*

Robinson, George L. *The Twelve Minor Prophets (Grand Rapids, Michigan: Baker Book House, 1953)*

Spurgeon, Charles Haddon *The New Park Street Pulpit, Volumes 1-6 and The Metropolitan Tabernacle Pulpit, Volumes 7-63 (Pasadena, Texas: Pilgrim Publications, 1990)*

Trapp, John *A Commentary on the Old and New Testaments, Volume Five (Eureka, California: Tanski Publications, 1997)*

Waltke, Bruce K "Micah" *Obadiah, Jonah, and Micah, an Introduction and Commentary (Downer's Grove, Illinois: Inter-Varsity Press, 1989)*

Nahum

Armerding, Carl E. "Nahum" *The Expositor's Bible Commentary, Volume 7: Daniel and the Minor Prophets* (Grand Rapids, Michigan: Zondervan, 1985)

Baker, David W. *Nahum, Habakkuk and Zephaniah, an Introduction and Commentary (Downer's Grove, Illinois: Inter-Varsity Press, 1988)*

Boice, James Montgomery *The Minor Prophets Volume 2: Micah-Malachi (Grand Rapids, Michigan: Zondervan, 1983)*

Clarke, Adam *The New Testament with A Commentary and Critical Notes, Volume II (New York: Eaton & Mains, 1831)*

Delitzsch, Franz and Keil, C.F. *Biblical Commentary on the Minor Prophets (Grand Rapids, Michigan: Eerdmans, 1983)*

Harrison, R.K. (Editor) "Nineveh" *Major Cities of the Biblical World* (Nashville, Tennessee: Thomas Nelson, 1985)

McGee, J. Vernon *Thru the Bible, Volume 3: Proverbs through Malachi* (Nashville, Tennessee: Thomas Nelson, 1994)

Meyer, F.B. *Our Daily Homily* (Westwood, New Jersey: Revell, 1966)

Morgan, G. Campbell *An Exposition of the Whole Bible* (Old Tappan, New Jersey: Revell, 1959)

Morgan, G. Campbell *Searchlights From The Word* (New York: Revell, 1926)

Poole, Matthew *A Commentary on the Holy Bible, Volume III: Matthew-Revelation* (London: Banner of Truth Trust, 1969, first published in 1685)

Redpath, Alan *Law and Liberty: The Ten Commandments for Today* (Grand Rapids, Michigan: Revell 1993)

Robinson, George L. *The Twelve Minor Prophets* (Grand Rapids, Michigan: Baker Book House, 1953)

Spurgeon, Charles Haddon *The New Park Street Pulpit, Volumes 1-6 and The Metropolitan Tabernacle Pulpit, Volumes 7-63* (Pasadena, Texas: Pilgrim Publications, 1990)

Trapp, John *A Commentary on the Old and New Testaments, Volume Five* (Eureka, California: Tanski Publications, 1997)

Habakkuk

Armerding, Carl E. "Nahum" *The Expositor's Bible Commentary, Volume 7: Daniel and the Minor Prophets* (Grand Rapids, Michigan: Zondervan, 1985)

Baker, David W. *Nahum, Habakkuk and Zephaniah, an Introduction and Commentary* (Downer's Grove, Illinois: Inter-Varsity Press, 1988)

Boice, James Montgomery *The Minor Prophets Volume 2: Micah-Malachi* (Grand Rapids, Michigan: Zondervan, 1983)

Clarke, Adam *The New Testament with A Commentary and Critical Notes, Volume II* (New York: Eaton & Mains, 1831)

Delitzsch, Franz and Keil, C.F. *Biblical Commentary on the Minor Prophets* (Grand Rapids, Michigan: Eerdmans, 1983)

McGee, J. Vernon *Thru the Bible, Volume 3: Proverbs through*

Malachi (Nashville, Tennessee: Thomas Nelson, 1994)

Meyer, F.B. *Our Daily Homily (Westwood, New Jersey: Revell, 1966)*

Morgan, G. Campbell *An Exposition of the Whole Bible (Old Tappan, New Jersey: Revell, 1959)*

Morgan, G. Campbell *Searchlights From The Word (New York: Revell, 1926)*

Poole, Matthew *A Commentary on the Holy Bible, Volume III: Matthew-Revelation (London: Banner of Truth Trust, 1969, first published in 1685)*

Robinson, George L. *The Twelve Minor Prophets (Grand Rapids, Michigan: Baker Book House, 1953)*

Spurgeon, Charles Haddon *The New Park Street Pulpit, Volumes 1-6 and The Metropolitan Tabernacle Pulpit, Volumes 7-63 (Pasadena, Texas: Pilgrim Publications, 1990)*

Trapp, John *A Commentary on the Old and New Testaments, Volume Five (Eureka, California: Tanski Publications, 1997)*

Zephaniah

Baker, David W. *Nahum, Habakkuk and Zephaniah, an Introduction and Commentary (Downer's Grove, Illinois: Inter-Varsity Press, 1988)*

Boice, James Montgomery *The Minor Prophets Volume 2: Micah-Malachi (Grand Rapids, Michigan: Zondervan, 1983)*

Clarke, Adam *The New Testament with A Commentary and Critical Notes, Volume II (New York: Eaton & Mains, 1831)*

Delitzsch, Franz and Keil, C.F. *Biblical Commentary on the Minor Prophets (Grand Rapids, Michigan: Eerdmans, 1983)*

McGee, J. Vernon *Thru the Bible, Volume 3: Proverbs through Malachi* (Nashville, Tennessee: Thomas Nelson, 1994)

Meyer, F.B. *Our Daily Homily (Westwood, New Jersey: Revell, 1966)*

Morgan, G. Campbell *An Exposition of the Whole Bible (Old Tappan, New Jersey: Revell, 1959)*

Morgan, G. Campbell *Searchlights From The Word (New York: Revell, 1926)*

Poole, Matthew *A Commentary on the Holy Bible, Volume III: Matthew-Revelation (London: Banner of Truth Trust, 1969, first published in 1685)*

Robinson, George L. *The Twelve Minor Prophets (Grand Rapids, Michigan: Baker Book House, 1953)*

Spurgeon, Charles Haddon *The New Park Street Pulpit, Volumes 1-6 and The Metropolitan Tabernacle Pulpit, Volumes 7-63 (Pasadena, Texas: Pilgrim Publications, 1990)*

Trapp, John *A Commentary on the Old and New Testaments, Volume Five (Eureka, California: Tanski Publications, 1997)*

Walker, Larry "Zephaniah" *The Expositor's Bible Commentary, Volume 7: Daniel and the Minor Prophets* (Grand Rapids, Michigan: Zondervan, 1985)

Haggai

Alden, Robert L. "Haggai" *The Expositor's Bible Commentary, Volume 7: Daniel and the Minor Prophets* (Grand Rapids, Michigan: Zondervan, 1985)

Baldwin, Joyce G. *Haggai, Zechariah and Malachi, an Introduction and Commentary (Downer's Grove, Illinois: Inter-Varsity Press, 1972)*

Boice, James Montgomery *The Minor Prophets Volume 2: Micah-Malachi (Grand Rapids, Michigan: Zondervan, 1983)*

Calvin, John *Commentaries on the Books Habakkuk through Malachi* (Grand Rapids, Michigan: Baker, 1979)

Clarke, Adam *The New Testament with A Commentary and Critical Notes, Volume II (New York: Eaton & Mains, 1831)*

Dean, W.J. "Haggai" *The Pulpit Commentary Volume 14: Amos-Malachi* (McLean, Virginia: MacDonald, ?)

Delitzsch, Franz and Keil, C.F. *Biblical Commentary on the Minor Prophets* (Grand Rapids, Michigan: Eerdmans, 1983)

Ginzberg, Louis *The Legends of the Jews, Volumes 1-7* (Philadelphia: The Jewish Publication Society of America, 1968)

McGee, J. Vernon *Thru the Bible, Volume 3: Proverbs through Malachi* (Nashville, Tennessee: Thomas Nelson, 1994)

Meyer, F.B. *Our Daily Homily* (Westwood, New Jersey: Revell, 1966)

Morgan, G. Campbell *An Exposition of the Whole Bible* (Old Tappan, New Jersey: Revell, 1959)

Morgan, G. Campbell *Searchlights From The Word* (New York: Revell, 1926)

Poole, Matthew *A Commentary on the Holy Bible, Volume III: Matthew-Revelation* (London: Banner of Truth Trust, 1969, first published in 1685)

Pusey, E.B. *Pusey on the Old Testament, Minor Prophets Volume II: Micah-Malachi* (Grand Rapids, Michigan: Baker Book House, 1982)

Robinson, George L. *The Twelve Minor Prophets* (Grand Rapids, Michigan: Baker Book House, 1953)

Spurgeon, Charles Haddon *The New Park Street Pulpit, Volumes 1-6 and The Metropolitan Tabernacle Pulpit, Volumes 7-63* (Pasadena, Texas: Pilgrim Publications, 1990)

Trapp, John *A Commentary on the Old and New Testaments, Volume Five* (Eureka, California: Tanski Publications, 1997)

Zechariah

Baldwin, Joyce G. *Haggai, Zechariah and Malachi, an Introduction and Commentary* (Downer's Grove, Illinois: Inter-Varsity Press, 1972)

Barker, Kenneth L. "Zechariah" *The Expositor's Bible Commentary, Volume 7: Daniel and the Minor Prophets* (Grand Rapids, Michigan: Zondervan, 1985)

Boice, James Montgomery *The Minor Prophets Volume 2: Micah-Malachi* (Grand Rapids, Michigan: Zondervan, 1983)

Calvin, John *Commentaries on the Books Habakkuk through Malachi* (Grand Rapids, Michigan: Baker, 1979)

Clarke, Adam *The New Testament with A Commentary and Critical Notes, Volume II* (New York: Eaton & Mains, 1831)

Dean, W.J. "Zechariah" *The Pulpit Commentary Volume 14: Amos-Malachi* (McLean, Virginia: MacDonald, ?)

Delitzsch, Franz and Keil, C.F. *Biblical Commentary on the Minor Prophets* (Grand Rapids, Michigan: Eerdmans, 1983)

Fry, William Francis *Notes and Outlines of the Books of the Bible* (Lubbock, Texas: Baptist Bible Chair, 1940)

Hunt, Dave *A Cup of Trembling – Jerusalem and Bible Prophecy* (Eugene, Oregon: Harvest House Publishers, 1995)

Luck, G. Coleman *Zechariah* (Chicago: Moody Press, 1969)

Maclaren, Alexander *Expositions of Holy Scripture, Volume Six* (Grand Rapids, Michigan: Baker, 1984)

McGee, J. Vernon *Thru the Bible, Volume 3: Proverbs through Malachi* (Nashville, Tennessee: Thomas Nelson, 1994)

Meyer, F.B. *Our Daily Homily* (Westwood, New Jersey: Revell, 1966)

Morgan, G. Campbell *An Exposition of the Whole Bible* (Old Tappan, New Jersey: Revell, 1959)
Morgan, G. Campbell *Searchlights From The Word* (New York: Revell, 1926)

Poole, Matthew *A Commentary on the Holy Bible, Volume III: Matthew-Revelation* (London: Banner of Truth Trust, 1969, first published in 1685)

Pusey, E.B. *Pusey on the Old Testament, Minor Prophets Volume II: Micah-Malachi* (Grand Rapids, Michigan: Baker Book House, 1982)

Richards, Lawrence O. *The Teacher's Commentary (Wheaton, Illinois: Victor Books, 1988)*

Robinson, George L. *The Twelve Minor Prophets (Grand Rapids, Michigan: Baker Book House, 1953)*

Spurgeon, Charles Haddon *The New Park Street Pulpit, Volumes 1-6 and The Metropolitan Tabernacle Pulpit, Volumes 7-63 (Pasadena, Texas: Pilgrim Publications, 1990)*

Taylor, John B. *The Minor Prophets (Grand Rapids, Michigan: Eerdmans, 1970)*

Trapp, John *A Commentary on the Old and New Testaments, Volume Five (Eureka, California: Tanski Publications, 1997)*

Malachi

Alden, Robert L. "Malachi" *The Expositor's Bible Commentary, Volume 7: Daniel and the Minor Prophets* (Grand Rapids, Michigan: Zondervan, 1985)

Baldwin, Joyce G. *Haggai, Zechariah and Malachi, an Introduction and Commentary (Downer's Grove, Illinois: Inter-Varsity Press, 1972)*

Boice, James Montgomery *The Minor Prophets Volume 2: Micah-Malachi (Grand Rapids, Michigan: Zondervan, 1983)*

Calvin, John *Commentaries on the Books Habakkuk through Malachi* (Grand Rapids, Michigan: Baker, 1979)

Clarke, Adam *The New Testament with A Commentary and Critical Notes, Volume II (New York: Eaton & Mains, 1831)*

Dean, W.J. "Malachi" *The Pulpit Commentary Volume 14: Amos-Malachi* (McLean, Virginia: MacDonald, ?)

Delitzsch, Franz and Keil, C.F. *Biblical Commentary on the Minor Prophets (Grand Rapids, Michigan: Eerdmans, 1983)*

Fry, William Francis *Notes and Outlines of the Books of the Bible (Lubbock, Texas:* Baptist Bible Chair, 1940)
Luck, G. Coleman *Zechariah (Chicago: Moody Press, 1969)*

McGee, J. Vernon *Thru the Bible, Volume 3: Proverbs through Malachi* (Nashville, Tennessee: Thomas Nelson, 1994)

Meyer, F.B. *Our Daily Homily (Westwood, New Jersey: Revell, 1966)*

Morgan, G. Campbell *An Exposition of the Whole Bible (Old Tappan, New Jersey: Revell, 1959)*

Morgan, G. Campbell *Searchlights From The Word (New York: Revell, 1926)*

Newell, William R. *Romans Verse by Verse (Chicago: Moody Press, 1979)*

Poole, Matthew *A Commentary on the Holy Bible, Volume III: Matthew-Revelation (London: Banner of Truth Trust, 1969, first published in 1685)*

Pusey, E.B. *Pusey on the Old Testament, Minor Prophets Volume II: Micah-Malachi* (Grand Rapids, Michigan: Baker Book House, 1982)

Robinson, George L. *The Twelve Minor Prophets* (Grand Rapids, Michigan: Baker Book House, 1953)

Spurgeon, Charles Haddon *The New Park Street Pulpit, Volumes 1-6 and The Metropolitan Tabernacle Pulpit, Volumes 7-63 (Pasadena, Texas: Pilgrim Publications, 1990)*

Taylor, John B. *The Minor Prophets (Grand Rapids, Michigan: Eerdmans, 1970)*

Trapp, John *A Commentary on the Old and New Testaments, Volume Five (Eureka, California: Tanski Publications, 1997)*

Author's Remarks

As the years pass I love the work of studying, learning, and teaching the Bible more than ever. I'm so grateful that God is faithful to meet me in His Word.

For the second time I am tremendously grateful to Alison Turner for her proofreading and editorial suggestions, especially with a challenging manuscript. Alison, thank you so much!

Thanks to Brian Procedo for the cover design and the graphics work.

Most especially, thanks to my wife Inga-Lill. She is my loved and valued partner in life and in service to God and His people.

David Guzik

David Guzik's Bible commentary is regularly used and trusted by many thousands who want to know the Bible better. Pastors, teachers, class leaders, and everyday Christians find his commentary helpful for their own understanding and explanation of the Bible. David and his wife Inga-Lill live in Santa Barbara, California.

You can email David at david@enduringword.com

For more resources by David Guzik, go to www.enduringword.com

www.ingramcontent.com/pod-product-compliance
Lightning Source LLC
Chambersburg PA
CBHW031130160426
43193CB00008B/95